MY SYSTEM

MY SYSTEM
A Chess Treatise

by

ARON NIMZOWITSCH

English Version by
PHILIP HEREFORD

LONDON
G. BELL AND SONS, LTD

First Published in 1929
Reprinted 1937, 1948, 1950, 1954, 1957, 1961,
1964, 1968, 1972, 1974

ISBN O 7135 0787 X

Printed in Great Britain by
Lowe and Brydone (Printers) Ltd, Thetford, Norfolk

TRANSLATOR'S PREFACE

FOR nearly twenty years Nimzowitsch has been the stormy petrel of the chess world. 'A law unto himself', 'Goes his own way, one, however, not to be recommended to the public', 'mysterious', such are typical examples of the kind of criticism which his revolutionary ideas had to meet. And yet this 'law', this 'way' has governed, has been followed by the whole modern school, call it hyper-modern, or neo-romantic, as you will; they are part and parcel of the game as it is played to-day. For a master, who is one of the four (I include Lasker) who are in common opinion held worthy to challenge the profound and brilliant player who now holds the world's championship, could not have arrived at such a position in the world of chess had his 'law' been based on a false philosophy; or his 'way' led to barren ground. His post-war record is sufficiently significant. In thirteen Master tournaments he has won outright six times, the most recent occasion being at the important Carlsbad tournament in August 1929. He has also been thrice bracketed 1st, has been 2nd three times, and 3rd once. It is, therefore, a privilege and a pleasure to be allowed to introduce his 'System' to the English-speaking public.

The literature of chess is enormous; but the number of books which may claim to reveal something of the spirit of the game, of its philosophy, may almost be told on the fingers of one hand. And while we must never forget what we owe to the writings of, for example, Dr. Lasker, Dr. Tarrasch, Capablanca (in his *Chess Fundamentals*), and indeed Mason, yet there is some justification for the claim which Nimzowitsch makes in his Preface to the German edition of this book, to have been 'the first to write a real treatise on the *game* of chess, not merely one on the openings', in that he is the first 'to reduce a welter of arbitrary ideas to a definite number of inter-related principles'; while he points with legitimate pride to his enunciation of the 'five special cases of the 7th and 8th ranks'. But no one who has studied his analysis of the principles governing the 'blockade', or the pawn-chain, or play in an open file, or his qualitative theory of pawn majorities, or his conception of the 'elastic centre', will deny the penetration of his thought or the influence which his teaching has had on the chess of to-day, as revolutionary perhaps as was that of Steinitz on his generation.

The difficulties in translating *Mein System* have been not inconsiderable, partly because the novelty of his presentation required a terminology peculiar to itself, for which a suitable English equivalent had to be sought, partly because—but a quotation from his preface will best serve here:—'It is the custom to write text books in a dry didactic style. It seems to be held that one would sacrifice his dignity did he let a humorous turn creep in, for whatever room is there for humour in a chess manual! This opinion I cannot possibly share; in fact I go further and hold it to be entirely wrong; for true humour often contains more inner truth than the most serious seriousness. As for me I am an avowed partisan of the humorously drawn parallel, and like to bring in allusions to events in daily life if I may thereby bring greater clarity into complicated situations on the chess board.' A literal translation has, therefore, sometimes been utterly impossible, since not seldom the author's humour (or pun!) would not bear transplanting to foreign soil.

In this English edition several additional games have been inserted, a few passages have, with the concurrence of the author, been omitted, and the arrangement has been slightly altered, e.g. for convenience of reference the illustrative games have been collected into one section instead of being scattered through the book. The reader is strongly urged to play through the several games at the appropriate places as indicated in the text. A full table of contents and lists of the games quoted in the text or included in the games section have been added. For convenience, too, one word has been left untranslated, namely *Zugzwang*, partly since it is become familiar in English chess circles, partly, in fact mainly, because the single word conveys an idea, or complex of ideas, which can only be expressed in English by a circumlocution. Those who are not familiar with the term will find it explained on page 25 in a footnote.

P. H.

29 *August*, 1929

BIOGRAPHICAL NOTE

ARON NIMZOWITSCH was born on 7th November, 1886, in Riga, the son of a wholesale merchant, who, besides being a poet, was a gifted amateur in other branches of art, and was, too, an excellent chess player. Nimzowitsch himself learned the game at the age of eight, and during the period when he first took chess seriously (1903-5) it was characteristic of him that he had no interest in any but combination play, that is to say he utterly neglected position play. Chastened by ill-success, he worked out an entirely original system for himself during the years 1906-13, and this, as it has developed, is that now described in this book. This system he used as a weapon against the ideas of the old school, and with such success that he gave the game a new direction which led to the hyper-modern or neo-romantic school. The last five games in the book, Nos. 46-50, may be said to belong in a special sense to his biography, since in them several of his new ideas first found public expression. The derivation of certain modern methods of treating the openings will not escape the notice of the student.

In addition to *Mein System*, Nimzowitsch was the author of many critical articles, notably his essay *Entspricht Dr. Tarrasch's 'Die Moderne Schachpartie' wirklich moderner Auffassung?* (1913), a brochure *Die Blockade* (1925), and *Die Praxis meines Systems* (1929).

Nimzowitsch had many successes in tournaments over a period of 30 years. In 1906 when still barely 20, he won first prize in a Munich tournament, ahead of Spielmann, Eric Cohn, etc. In 1910, he was placed third in the Hamburg tournament; Spielmann, Marshall, Alekhine were all below him. Fifteen years later at Marienbad, he was bracketed first with Rubinstein, ahead of Marshall, Réti and Tartakower. Next year at Dresden he was first with 8½ out of 9 points, with Alekhine 1½ points below him. At the Carlsbad tournament of 1929, he was again first, above Capablanca, Spielmann, Rubinstein, Tartakower, Bogoljubow, Vidmar, Marshall, etc.; this was almost certainly his greatest achievement.

Nimzowitsch's death in March 1935 at a comparatively early age and when still at the height of his powers was a very great loss to the world of chess.

CONTENTS

PART I

THE ELEMENTS

PART II

POSITION PLAY

xi

LIST OF ILLUSTRATIVE GAMES

LIST OF GAMES QUOTED

N.B. The References in the List of Games Quoted and throughout the text are to the Part, Chapter, and Section, e.g. I. i. 2. equals Part I, Chapter I, Section 2.

PART I
THE ELEMENTS

CHAPTER I

ON THE CENTRE AND DEVELOPMENT

Contains a short introduction and what the less advanced student must know about the centre and about development.

IN my opinion the following are to be regarded as the elements of chess-strategy:—1. The centre. 2. Play in open files. 3. Play in the 7th and 8th ranks. 4. The passed pawn. 5. The pin. 6. Discovered check. 7. Exchanging. 8. The pawn-chain.

Each one of these elements will in what follows be as thoroughly elucidated as possible. We shall begin with the centre, which we propose to treat in the first place with the less experienced player in mind. In the second part of the book, which is devoted to position play, we shall endeavour to investigate the centre from the point of view of the 'higher learning'. As you know, the centre was precisely the point round which in the years 1911-13 what amounted to a revolution in chess took place. I mean that the articles which I wrote, e.g., *Entspricht Dr. Tarrasch's 'Moderne Schachpartie' wirklich moderner Auffassung?* ran directly counter to the traditional conception, and sounded the call to a revolt which was in fact to give birth to the neo-romantic school. Hence the two-fold treatment of the centre, which we propose to undertake on didactic grounds, would seem to be justified.

And first a few definitions:

The line shown on Diagram 1 we call the frontier; 'line' is of course to be taken in its mathematical, not in its chess sense. The point marked on Diagram 2 is the mid-point of the board, again naturally in its mathematical sense. The mid-point is easy to find, it is the point of intersection of the long diagonals.

§1. *By development is to be understood the strategic advance of the troops to the frontier line.*

The process is analogous to the advance on the outbreak of a war. Both armies seek to reach the frontier as quickly as possible in order to penetrate into enemy territory.

Diagram 1

The Frontier Line

Diagram 2

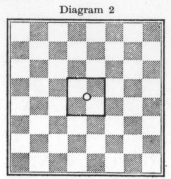

The Mid-Point. The Small Square is the centre

Development is a collective conception. To have developed one, two, or three pieces does not mean that we are developed. On the contrary, the situation demands that *all* pieces be developed. If I may so put it, the period of development should be inspired by a democratic spirit. How undemocratic for instance, it would be to let one of your officers go for a long walking tour, whilst the others kicked their heels together at home and bored themselves horribly. No, let each officer make one move only, and . . . dig himself in.

§2. *A pawn move must not in itself be regarded as a developing move, but merely as an aid to development.*

An important postulate for the beginner is the following:— If it were possible to develop the pieces without the aid of pawn moves, the pawn-less advance would be the correct one; for, as suggested, the pawn is not a fighting unit in the sense that his crossing of the frontier is to be feared by the enemy, since obviously the attacking force of the pawns is small compared with that of the pieces. However the pawn-less advance is in reality impossible of execution, since the enemy pawn-centre, thanks to its inherent aggressiveness, would drive back the pieces which we had developed. For this reason we should, in order to safeguard the development of our pieces, first build up a pawn-centre.

By centre is to be understood the four squares which enclose the mid-point, i.e., the squares K4, Q4 for both sides (Diag. 2).

The wrecking of a pawn-less advance is illustrated by the following:—

1. Kt—KB3, Kt—QB3; 2. P—K3. (Since the pawn has not been moved to the centre, we may still regard the advance as pawn-less in our sense.) 2.....P—K4; 3. Kt—QB3, Kt—KB3; 4. B—B4?, P—Q4. And now the faultiness of White's development

may be seen, the Black pawns have a demobilizing effect. 5. B—Kt3 (bad at the outset, a piece moved twice), 5.....P—Q5, and White is uncomfortably placed, at any rate from the point of view of the player with little fighting experience.

Another example is the following:—White without QR, A. Nimzowitsch, Black, an Amateur. White's QRP is at R3, 1. P—K4, P—K4; 2. Kt—KB3, Kt—QB3; 3. B—B4, B—B4; 4. P—QB3, Kt—KB3; 5. P—Q4, P×P; 6. P×P, B—Kt3. Black has now lost the centre, and, in addition, by neglecting to play 4.....P—Q3, he allows White's centre too much mobility; his development may therefore rightly be described as pawn-less, or, more strictly, one which has become pawn-less. 7. P—Q5, Kt—K2; 8. P—K5, Kt—K5; 9. P—Q6, P×P; 10. P×P, Kt×BP; 11. Q—Kt3, and Black who is completely wedged in by the PQ6 succumbs to the enemy assault in a few moves, in spite of the win of a Rook. 11.....Kt×R; 12. B×P ch, K—B1; 13. B—KKt5 resigns.

It follows from the rule given under §2, that pawn moves are only admissible in the development stage when they either help to occupy the centre, or stand in logical connexion with its occupation; that is to say a pawn move which protects its own or attacks the enemy's centre. For example, in the open game after 1. P—K4, P—K4, either P—Q3 or P—Q4—now or later—is always a correct move.

Diagram 3

Typical win of a tempo

If then only the pawn moves designated above are allowable, it follows that moves of the flank pawns must be regarded as loss of time; with this qualification, that in close games the rule applies to only a limited extent, since contact with the enemy is not complete, and development proceeds at a slower tempo.

To sum up: In the open game speed in development is the very first law. Every piece must be developed in one move. Every pawn move is to be regarded as loss of time, unless it helps to build or support the centre or attack the enemy's centre. Hence, as Lasker truly observes: In the opening one or two pawn moves, not more.

§3. *To be ahead in development is the ideal to be aimed at.*

If I were running a race with someone, it would be, to say the least, inopportune were I to throw away valuable time by rubbing, say, a smut off my nose, although I must not be considered as blaming that operation in itself. If, however, I can induce my

opponent to waste time by some similar action I should then get
an advantage in development over him. The repeated moving to and
fro of the same piece would be described as an action of this kind.
Accordingly we force our opponent to lose time if we make a developing move which at the same time attacks one of his pieces which he
has already moved (Diag. 3.) This very typical situation arises after
1. P—K4, P—Q4; 2. P×P, Q×P; 3. Kt—QB3.

§4. *Exchange with resulting gain of tempo.*

The moves just given show in the compactest form a manœuvre
which we may call a compound one. For why (Diag. 4) do we take
the QP? (2. P×P). The answer is to entice the piece which recaptures it on to a square exposed to attack. This was the first
part of the manœuvre. The second (3. Kt—QB3) consisted in the
utilization of the Queen's position which is in a certain sense compromised.

The compound manœuvre which we have just outlined is one of
the greatest value to the student, and we proceed to give a few more
examples. 1. P—Q4, P—Q4; 2. P—QB4, Kt—KB3; 3. P×P!.
And now two variations follow. If
3.....Q×P, then 4. Kt—QB3; and if
3.....Kt×P; 4. P—K4; so that in
either case White with his 4th move
will have made a developing move of
full value, which Black will be forced to
answer by wandering about. But perhaps the beginner may say in his heart:
Why should Black recapture? Many a
skilful business man displays in chess
an altogether unnatural delicacy of
feeling; he does not recapture. But
the master unfortunately knows that
he is under compulsion, there's no
remedy for it, he must recapture, else
the material balance in the centre would
be disturbed. It follows from the fact
that this is compulsory that the capture retards, for the moment at
any rate, the enemy's development, except in the case when the
recapture can be made with what is at the same time a developing
move. A further example:—1. P—K4, P—K4; 2. P—KB4,
Kt—KB3; 3. P×P!, Kt×P; forced, otherwise Black would be a
pawn down with no equivalent for it. 4. Kt—KB3! (to prevent
Q—R5), Kt—QB3; 5. P—Q3 (the logical complement of the
exchange P×P), 5.....Kt—B4; 6. P—Q4, Kt—K5; 7. P—Q5,

Diagram 4

White to move. The ex-
change is made in order to
entice the recapturing piece
on to a compromised square

and after 7.....Kt—Kt1 White will have the opportunity of gaining more tempi by 8. B—Q3 or 8. QKt—Q2. The latter contingency must be carefully weighed. The exchange of the time-devouring Kt at K5 for the new-born Kt at Q2 means loss of tempo for Black, since with the disappearance of the Knight there will vanish also the tempi consumed by him; that is to say there will be nothing on the board to show for them. (When a farmer loses a sucking pig through illness, he mourns not only the little pig but also the good food he has gambled on it, the bran, etc.)

An intermezzo is possible in the manœuvre: exchange with gain of tempo. After 1. P—K4, P—K4; 2. P—KB4, P—Q4; 3. P×QP, Q×P; 4. Kt—QB3!, Q—K3; the exchange manœuvre 5. P×P, Q×P ch, comes into consideration for White, since the square K4 must be looked on as an exposed place for the Black Queen. However after 5. P×P, there follows Q×P giving check, and White is apparently not able to make use of the position of the Black Queen. In reality, however, the check can only be regarded as an intermezzo; White simply plays 6. B—K2 (Q—K2 is still stronger), and after all gains tempi at the cost of the Black Queen by Kt—KB3 or P—Q4; e.g., 6. B—K2, B—KKt5; 7. P—Q4 (not Kt—KB3 because of B × Kt!, and no tempo is lost, since the Queen need not move), 7.....B×B; 8. KKt×B, Q—K3; .9. 0—0, and White has 5 tempi to the good (both Knights and a Rook are developed, the pawn occupies the centre, and the King is in safety), whereas Black can show but one visible tempo, namely the Queen on K3. This tempo, too, will later on be doubly or even trebly lost; since the Queen will have to shift her ground more than once (she will be chased away by Kt—B4, etc.), so that White's advantage is equivalent to at least five tempi. Exchange, intermezzo, gain of tempo: the exchange and the gain of a tempo are related, the intermezzo alters nothing.

§5. *Liquidation, with consequent development or disembarrassment.*

When a merchant sees that his business is not succeeding, he does well to liquidate it, so as to invest the proceeds in a more promising one. Translated into terms of chess, I mean by this that when one's development is threatened with being held up, one must adopt a radical cure, and on no account try to remedy matters by palliative measures. I will first illustrate this by an example. 1. P—K4, P—K4; 2. Kt—KB3, Kt—QB3; 3. P—Q4, P—Q4 (Black's last move is questionable, for the second player should not at once copy such an enterprising move as 3. P—Q4); 4. P×QP, Q×P; 5. Kt—QB3, B—QKt5. For the moment Black has been able to hold his ground, the Queen has not had to move away; but after

6. B—Q2, Black would still appear to be in some embarrassment (Diag. 5), for the retreat of the Queen, who is now again threatened, would cost a tempo. The right course, therefore, is to exchange 6.....B×Kt, 7. B×B (whole-hearted liquidation), and now with the same idea 7.....P×P (anything but a protecting move, such as,

Diagram 5

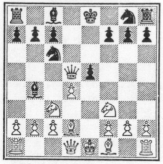

Black liquidates. How?

e.g., B—KKt5, or a flight move, such as P—K5; in the development stage there is no time for this); 8. Kt×P; Black can now proceed with his development with 8.....Kt—B3, and has relieved the tension in the centre and is in no way behind in development. This relief of tension in the centre, taken with the exchange, is a main characteristic of complete liquidation.

After 1. P—K4, P—K4; 2. Kt—KB3, Kt—QB3; 3. P—Q4, P—Q4?, White can also embarrass his opponent by 4. B—QKt5! (Diag. 6). Undeveloped as he is, the latter sees that he is seriously threatened by 5. Kt×P. What is he to do? The protecting move 4.....B—Q2 is here as inadequate as 4.....B—KKt5. Both these moves have the common failing that they do nothing towards relieving the tension in the centre. 4.....B—Q2 loses, after 5. P×QP, Kt×P; 6. B×B ch, Q×B; 7. Kt×Kt, P×Kt; 8. Q×P, a valuable pawn; while 4.....B—KKt5 could here be answered by 5. P—KR3 (in this case a forcing move). E.g., 4.....B—KKt5; 5. P—KR3!, B×Kt (best do it while he can! if 5.....B—R4?, then 6. P—KKt4 followed by Kt×P); 6. Q×B. From here the Queen exercises a decisive influence on the centre. 6.....Kt—KB3; 7. P×QP, P—K5 (or a pawn is lost); 8. Q—K3!, Q×P; 9. P—QB4, with decided advantage to White.

Relatively best for Black would have been (Diag. 6) immediately 4.....P×KP; and he liquidates thus since his means do not allow him the luxury of maintaining a position of instability in the centre. The continuation might be 5. Kt×P, B—Q2, and Black threatens to win a piece by Kt×Kt. 6. B×Kt, B×B; 7. 0—0, B—Q3; 8. Kt×B, P×Kt; 9. Kt—QB3, P—KB4, and Black has a satisfactory development and does not stand badly. Or again, 6. B×Kt, B×B; 7. Kt—QB3, B—Kt5; 8. 0—0, B×Kt; 9. P×B, and now perhaps 9.....Kt—K2. After 10. Q—Kt4, 0—0; 11. Kt×B, Kt×Kt; 12. Q×P, White, it is true, has a pawn more, but Black seizes the King's file by 12.....R—K1, and now after 13. Q—B3, Kt—R4 (the process of development is over and manœuvring begins); followed later by P—QB3 and the occupation of White's weak squares at his QB4 and Q5 by Kt—B5 and Q—Q4, Black stands rather the better. Thus timely liquidation has brought back into the right track the second player's questionable process of development.

Another example is furnished by the well-known variation in the Giuoco piano. 1. P—K4, P—K4; 2. Kt—KB3, Kt—QB3; 3. B—B4, B—B4; 4. P—QB3, Kt—B3; 5. P—Q4, P×P (forced surrender of the centre); 6. P×P, B—Kt5 ch; 7. B—Q2, and now the Black Bishop is under the slight threat of B×P ch followed by Q—Kt3 ch, etc. On the other hand the White centre pawns are very strong, and it is absolutely necessary to break them up. However if at once 7..... P—Q4; 8. P×P, Kt×P, then 9. B×B, either Kt×B; 10. Q—Kt3 and White stands rather the better. The correct play is therefore 7.....B×B ch (getting rid of the threat to his Bishop); 8. QKt ×B, and now the freeing move 8. ....

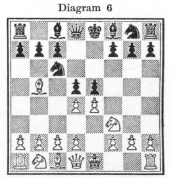

Diagram 6

Black to move. He ought to liquidate in order to relieve the tension in the centre. How is he to do it?

P—Q4. After 9. P×P, Kt×P; 10. Q—Kt3, Black makes himself secure by the strategic retreat 10.....QKt—K2 with about an equal game.

As we have seen the exchange properly used furnishes an excellent weapon, and forms the basis of the typical manœuvres which we analysed above: (1) exchange with consequent gain of a tempo, (2) liquidation followed by a developing or freeing move. We must, however, give a most emphatic warning against exchanging blindly and without motive, for to move a piece several times in order thus to exchange it for an enemy piece which has not moved, would be a thoroughly typical beginner's mistake. Therefore exchange only in the two cases outlined above.

An example of a wrong, unmotived exchange:—1. P—K4, P—K4; 2. P—Q4, P×P; 3. P—QB3 (White offers a gambit), 3.....B—B4?. Curious that this move, which must devour a tempo, should be a beginner's first or second thought. He may consider 3.....P×P, but having perhaps heard somewhere that one ought not to go pawn hunting in the opening, rejects it in favour of B—B4. The continuation, a sad one for Black, will be 4. P×P, B—Kt5 ch (moving the Bishop again!); 5. B—Q2, B×B ch (unfortunately forced), 6. QKt×B, with an advantage of three tempi. The mistake lay in B—B4, but (after 4. P×P) B—Kt3 would at any rate have been better than B—Kt5 ch, which led only to a disadvantageous exchange.

§6. *The centre and its demobilizing force. Some examples as to when and how the advance of the enemy centre is to be met. On the maintenance and the surrender of the centre.*

As we have already noticed, a free mobile centre is a deadly weapon of attack, since the advance of the centre pawns threatens to drive back the enemy pieces. In every case the question is, whether the hunted Knight, losing all control over himself, will have to flit aimlessly from pillar to post, or whether he will succeed in saving himself or the tempi for which he is responsible. An example:— 1. P—K4, P—K4; 2. P—Q4, P×P (the White King's pawn is ready to march and is only waiting for an enemy Knight to show himself on his KB3 to put him speedily to flight); 3. P—QB3, Kt—KB3!. Black lets what will happen, and this is what every beginner should do in order to gain experience of the consequences of an advance in the centre. 4. P—K5, Kt—K5!. The

Diagram 7

Black to move. Can he keep his tempi? Where is the Kt to move?

Knight can maintain himself here, for 5. B—Q3 will be answered by a developing move of full value, namely 5. .... P—Q4. Not of course a further wandering by 5. .... Kt—B4?; for this move, after 6. P×P, Kt×B ch; 7. Q×Kt, would yield an advantage of four tempi to White. On the other hand after 1. P—K4, P—K4; 2. P—Q4, P×P; 3. P—QB3, Kt—KB3!; 4. P—K5, it would not be advantageous to move the Knight to Q4, for the poor fellow would not find repose here. E.g., 4. .... Kt— Q4; 5. Q×P (not B—QB4 because of Kt—Kt3, and the Bishop in his turn will have to lose a tempo), 5..... P—QB3; 6. B—QB4, Kt—Kt3; 7. Kt—KB3. White has here six tempi as against two or one and a half, for the Knight is not better placed at QKt3 than at KB3, and the PQB3 is really not a whole tempo, since no move of a central pawn is here in question. (Diag. 7.)

Another example. 1. P—K4, P—K4; 2. P—KB4, P×P (loss of time); 3. Kt—KB3, Kt—KB3!; 4. P—K5, and now we have the same problem. 4. .... Kt—K5 would not here spell 'maintenance', on the contrary there would follow at once 5. P—Q3, Kt—B4?; 6. P—Q4 etc. But here is an exceptional case when the square KR4 is a satisfying one (as a rule border squares are not favourable for Knights), e.g., (after 4. P—K5), 4..... Kt—R4; 5. P—Q4, P—Q4 (or P—Q3 in order to force the exchange of the White KP for the QP which has only moved once), and Black does not stand badly (Diag. 8).

In general the Knight seeks to establish himself in the centre, as in our first example (Diag. 7), only exceptionally on the side. After 1. P—K4, P—K4; 2. Kt—KB3, Kt—QB3; 3. B—B4, B—B4; 4. P—QB3 (a discomforting move which plans an assault on Black's centre so as to disturb him in his mobilization), 4.....Kt—KB3; 5. P—Q4, P×P; 6. P—K5, 6.....Kt—K5 would be a mistake because of 7. B—Q5; but now the Knight can no longer maintain himself of his own strength, so he calls in the aid of the QP, thus: 6.....P—Q4, and if now 7. B—Kt3, then Kt—K5 and establishes himself there.

An example of how such establishment is maintained. In the position which we have already examined, after 1. P—K4, P—K4; 2. P—Q4, P×P!; 3. P—QB3, Kt—KB3; 4. P—K5!, Kt—K5!; 5. B—Q3, P—Q4!, there

Diagram 8

Where is the Kt to move?

follows 6. P×P, and Black cannot hug himself with the thought that he is out of the wood, for a tempo-gaining attack on the Knight is in the air (Kt—QB3). Black however develops and attacks at the same time, for instance by 6.....Kt—QB3; 7. Kt—KB3, B—KKt5 (threatening the QP), or again by 6..... P—QB4, but

Diagram 9

Which is on principle the right move for Black, P×P, or P—Q3? How is B—B3 met? Why is P—KB3 bad?

not by the illogical 6.....B—QKt5 ch?, for, e.g., 6..... B—QKt5 ch; 7. B—Q2, and Black will be forced to a tempo-losing exchange.

It is nevertheless more prudent to hold the centre intact. Even should we succeed in breaking the shock of the advancing mass of pawns (by a proper withdrawal of the Knight as outlined above), yet the line of play is difficult, and what is more the 'pawn-roller' need not advance at once, but may hold its advance as a continual threat over our heads. Hence, if it can be done without counter-balancing disadvantages, hold the centre (Diag. 9).

After 1. P—K4, P—K4; 2. Kt—KB3, Kt—QB3; 3. B—B4, B—K2 (quite playable, though B—B4 is certainly more aggressive); 4. P—Q4, Black will do best to support his centre by 4.....P—Q3 and thus hold it intact. After 5. P×P, P×P, White's centre is immobile. In order to maintain the centre, support by a pawn is indicated (of course not by P—KB3; that would be a horrible mistake, the open diagonal—White's QB4 to KKt8—would be decisive), since the pawn is the born defender. If a piece has to protect any attacked piece or pawn he feels himself under restraint, whereas in similar circumstances a pawn would find himself perfectly at ease. In the case under consideration, protection by a piece, i.e., by B—B3?, would only support the KP but not the centre considered in the abstract. For instance, 4.....B—B3?; 5. P×P, Kt×P; 6. Kt×Kt, B×Kt; 7. P—KB4, and the exchange has occurred in accordance with our rule: Exchange followed by a gain of tempo (by P—KB4).

§6a. *Surrender of the Centre.*

1. P—K4, P—K4; 2. Kt—KB3, Kt—QB3; 3. P—Q4, P×P! (P—Q3 would be uncomfortable for Black, e.g., 3.....P—Q3; 4. P×P, P×P; 5. Q×Q ch., K×Q, else the KP falls, and Black has lost the right of castling, and with it a convenient means of connecting his Rooks); 4. Kt×P. In the position now arrived at Black can, after mature consideration, play 4.....Kt—KB3, since, after 5. Kt×Kt, KtP×Kt, possible attempts to demobilize the Knight by say P—K5 can be parried by Kt—K5 (B—Q3, P—Q4). But with this Black will have solved only a part of his problem, namely the little problem of how to develop his KKt, but not the larger problem of the centre as such. To this end the following postulates are necessary. (1) If one has allowed the enemy to establish a free, mobile centre pawn, the latter must be regarded as a dangerous criminal. Against him all our chess fury must be directed: so that the second postulate follows at once: (2) Such a pawn must either be executed (i.e., P—Q4, P×P must be prepared for), or be put under restraint. Accordingly we condemn the criminal either to death or to imprisonment for life. Or we can pleasantly combine the two by, say, first condemning him to death, then commuting his sentence to life imprisonment; or, what is the commoner case, we keep him under restraint until he is quite impotent, and then show our manly courage by executing the death sentence (i.e., arriving at P—Q4 and P×P). Restraint would be begun by 4.....P—Q3, and perfected by Kt—KB3, B—K2, O—O, R—K1, B—KB1; by which procedure any ruffianly advance is kept under close observation. White on his side will do all in his power to make the (criminal) KP mobile, by, for example, P—KB4, R—K1 etc., as occasion offers. The game might run somewhat as follows: 1. P—K4, P—K4; 2. Kt—KB3, Kt—QB3; 3. P—Q4, P×P; 4. Kt×P, P—Q3; 5. B—K2, Kt—KB3; 6. Kt—QB3, B—K2; 7. O—O, O—O;

8. P—KB4!, R—K1! (not 8.....P—Q4 because of P—K5); 9. B—K3, B—B1; 10. B—B3, B—Q2.

Each side has completed its mobilization, White will try to force P—K5, Black to prevent this advance. This situation (Diag. 10) gives rise to most interesting struggles, and we recommend the student to practise himself in contests playing in turn for and against the centre, for he will thus strengthen his positional insight.

The restraining process is not easy, and to kill off the mobile centre pawn seems simpler, though cases when this is feasible do not very often occur. A few examples follow: 1. P—K4, P—K4; 2. Kt—KB3, Kt—QB3; 3. P—Q4, P×P; 4. Kt×P, Kt—KB3; 5. Kt—QB3, B—QKt5; 6. Kt×Kt (in order to be able to make the protecting move B—Q3); 6.....KtP×Kt!; 7. B—Q3, and now the second player need no longer lay siege to the KP by, say, P—Q3, 0—0, and R—K1, since he can at once resort to 7..... P—Q4, and after the further moves 8. P×P, P×P, the disturber of his peace has disappeared. A like fate overtook the centre pawn in the game Lee—Nimzowitsch in Ostend. 1. P—Q4, Kt—KB3; 2. Kt—KB3, P—Q3; 3. QKt—Q2, QKt—Q2; 4. P—K4, P—K4; 5. P—QB3, B—K2; 6. B—QB4, 0—0; 7. 0—0 (Diag. 11), P×P!; 8. P×P, P—Q4!, and at a blow the proud KP, despite his freedom and mobility, vanishes, is pulverized! After 9. B—Q3 (if P×P then 9.....Kt—Kt3 followed by Kt×P), 9.....P×P; 10. Kt×P, Kt×Kt; 11. B×Kt, Kt—B3 (here is our exchange with consequent gain of tempo); 12. B—Q3, Kt—Q4; 13. P—QR3, B—KB3, and now Black stands better because of White's rather weak QP. For the continuation see Game No. 4.

Diagram 10

The fight in support of and against the White P at K4

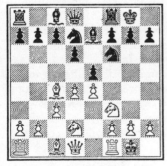

Diagram 11

Lee—Nimzowitsch
Black to play and destroy White's centre

As a third illustration take the opening moves of my game against Yates (White) at Baden-Baden. 1. P—K4, Kt—QB3; 2. Kt—KB3, Kt—KB3; 3. Kt—QB3 (or 3. P—K5, Kt—Q4; 4. P—QB4, Kt—Kt3; 5. P—Q4, P—Q3; and Black threatens to win back the three tempi he has sacrificed, though perhaps 6. P—K6, BP×P might be played with attacking chances for White), 3.....P—Q4; 4. P×P, Kt×P; 5. P—Q4, and White has established a free centre pawn. There followed 5.....B—KB4; 6. P—QR3, P—KKt3 (the alternative was to restrain the QP by P—K3, ultimately seizing the Q file and keeping the QP under observation); 7. B—QB4, Kt—Kt3; 8. B—R2, B—Kt2; 9. B—K3, P—K4!; Black has thus not played to restrain the QP but to kill it. There followed 10. Q—K2, 0—0; 11. P×P, B—Kt5; and Black recovered the pawn with a freer game.

§7. On pawn hunting in the opening. Usually a mistake. Exceptional case of centre pawns.

Since the mobilization of the forces is by far the most important operation in the opening stages, it strikes anyone who knows this as comic that the less experienced player should so eagerly plunge into an utterly unimportant side line, by which I mean pawn hunting. This eagerness may be more readily explicable on psychological grounds, for the young player wants to give rein to the energy which smoulders in him, which he can do by getting the scalps of perfectly harmless pawns, while the older player is—well, the older player is not loath to show how young he really is. In the event both come to grief. What, therefore, the inexperienced player, young or old, must take to heart is the commandment: *Never play to win a pawn while your development is yet unfinished!* and to this there is but one exception, which we shall discuss later.

Diagram 12

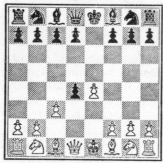

Black to move

We shall begin by showing the best manner of declining a gambit, which we can do very shortly, since we have already considered some analogous cases. In the Centre Gambit, after 1. P—K4, P—K4; 2. P—Q4, P×P!; 3. P—QB3, Black can play 3.....Kt—KB3, or any other developing move with the exception of course of 3.....B—B4??; thus for instance: 3.....Kt—QB3; 4. P×P, P—Q4; or 3.....P—Q4; or lastly even 3.....P—QB3; 4. P×P, P—Q4. (It will be noticed that the QBP stands now in logical connexion with the centre.) If 3.....P—QB3; 4. Q×P, Black still plays 4.....P—Q4; 5. P×P, P×P, to be followed by Kt—QB3. Again in the Evans Gambit: 1. P—K4, P—K4; 2. Kt—KB3, Kt—QB3; 3. B—B4, B—B4; 4. P—QKt4, we decline the gambit with B—Kt3 in order to avoid being driven about the place, which would happen if we played 4.....B×P; 5. P—QB3. Black by

playing 4.....B—Kt3 has by no means lost a tempo, since the move
P—Kt4, which White was able to throw in gratis without Black being
able in the meanwhile to develop a piece, was, in the sense of development, unproductive—unproductive as every pawn move must be in
the nature of things, if it does not bear a logical connexion with the
centre.   For suppose after 4.....B—Kt3;   5. P—Kt5 (to make a
virtue of necessity and attempt something of a demobilizing effect
with our ill-motived KtP move), 5.....Kt—Q5 and now if 6. Kt × P,
then 6.....Q—Kt4 with a strong attack.

The beginner should decline the King's Gambit with 2.....B—B4
(1. P—K4, P—K4; 2. P—KB4, B—B4), or by the simple
2.....P—Q3, which move is better than its reputation.   For
instance: 1. P—K4, P—K4; 2. P—KB4, P—Q3; 3. Kt—KB3,
Kt—QB3;   4. B—B4, B—K8!;   after
5. B × B,   P × B;   6. P × P,   P × P,

Black has with good development
two open files for his Rooks (the
KB and Q files), and in spite of his
doubled pawn, stands rather the better.
If after 4.....B—K8; 5. B—QKt5,
then perhaps 5.....B—Q2; for since
White has wandered about with his
Bishop, Black may do the like.   The
student should notice particularly that
after 1. P—K4, P—K4;   2. P—KB4,
P—Q3;   3. Kt—KB3, Kt—QB3;
4. Kt—QB3, Kt—KB3; 5. B—K2,
the manœuvre 5.....P × P is possible,
and if then 6. P—Q3, 6.....P—Q4;

Diagram 13

White   continues   Kt × P,
Kt × Kt, P—Q4, in the spirit
of §7a

that is timely surrender of the centre and a speedy recapture of the
same.

Acceptance of the gambit is allowable: 1. P—K4, P—K4;
2. P—KB4, P × P; 3. Kt—KB3, Kt—KB3!, not, however, with
the idea of keeping the gambit pawn, but rather to subject the
strength of White's centre to a severe test (4. P—K5, Kt—KR4),
or to arrive at the counter thrust P—Q4 (after 4. Kt—QB3).

§7a.   *A centre pawn should always be taken if this can be done without
too great danger.*

For example, 1. P—K4, P—K4;   2. Kt—KB3, Kt—QB3;
3. B—B4, Kt—KB3; 4. P—QB3?, Kt × P!, for the ideal win (of a
pawn) which the conquest of the centre implies, is not dear at the
cost of a tempo.   It is of less importance to keep the pawn; it is the
ideal not the material gain with which we are here concerned.   Put

otherwise: the win of a pawn anywhere on the side of the board brings
no happiness in its train; but if you gain a pawn in the middle, then
you really have something to talk about, for thus you will get the
possibility of expansion at the very spot round which in the opening
stages the fight ·usually sways, namely the centre; in other words
you will get elbow room (Diag. 13).

With this we close the first chapter, and would refer the reader to
Nos. 1 and 2 of the illustrative games at the end of the book.

CHAPTER II

ON OPEN FILES

§1. *Introductory. General considerations and some definitions.*

THE theory of open files, which was my discovery, must be regarded as one of the polishing stones of my system. I published the law of the establishment of outposts in open files about fourteen years ago in the *Wiener Schachzeitung*, but at that time I had not yet arrived at the perception that this manœuvre must logically be subordinate to the main objective of any operation in a file, namely the eventual occupation of the 7th or 8th rank. In other words, in order to break down the enemy's resistance in a file we must establish outposts in it, but without for a moment relaxing our aim at the 7th rank, whose occupation must be regarded as the ideal to be arrived at in such operation. The establishment of an outpost is therefore merely a subsidiary manœuvre.

A file is said to be open for the Rook when no pawn of his is in it, or, if there be one, it is masked as, for example, it is in the KR file in Diagram 14. This definition implies that in deciding whether a file is 'open' or 'closed', we are not concerned with the question whether that file gives an avenue of attack on unoccupied, peaceful points,

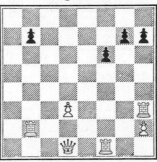

Diagram 14

White's QKt, KB, and KR files are open, the latter from the point KR3. The Q file is closed

or on living enemy pieces (as a rule pawns). There is in fact no fundamental difference between play against a piece or against a point. Let us, for example, imagine a White R on KR1, the Black K on his KKt1 and a Black P on his KR2. White is attacking the P at his KR7. Suppose that pawn removed, White is still attacking the point KR7, which he wishes to conquer. In either case he will attempt, with the further material which he has at command (this was taken for granted: I give only the most important elements of the position), to establish a preponderance at his KR7, i.e., bring up more pieces to the attack of this point than the defence can command. Having succeeded in doing this, he will ultimately play either R×P or R—KR7, as the case may be. That is to say our procedure is the same whether we are attacking the point KR7 or a Black P at that point; for the measure of the mobility of the pawn will tend to zero, since every object of attack must be made as nearly immobile as possible.

§2. *The genesis of open files: By peaceful means. By assault. The objective.*

From the definition of an open file it follows at once that a file will be opened by the disappearance of one of our own pawns. This disappearance will be brought about peacefully if the enemy feels it incumbent on him to exchange one of our well, because centrally, posted pieces, and the recapture is made by a pawn (Diag. 15).

Diagram 15

Black playing B × B opens
White's KB file for him

We must here stress the word 'central', for it will be but seldom, and never in the opening, that you will be able to force your opponent to open a file by the exchange of a piece which you have posted on a flank. You will gain your object much more quickly if it is centrally posted; for pieces thus established in the middle of the board, and exercising their influence in all directions, are those which will be exchanged.

A position from the game Thomas—Alekhine, Baden-Baden, 1925, provides a good example. White: K, KR1; Q, K1; R's, QR1, KB1; B's, QB1, Q1; Kts, K3, KB3; P's, QR2, QKt2, QB2, Q3, KB4, KKt2, KR2. Black: K, KKt1; Q, K8; R's, QR1, KB1; B's, QKt2, KKt2; Kts, Q4, Q5; P's, QR2, QKt3, QB4, K2, KB2, KKt3, KR2. Black's Knights are centrally posted, and White finds himself forced to exchange them; so, 1. Kt (B3) × Kt, P × Kt (=opening of the QB file), and after the further moves 2. Kt × Kt, Q × Kt; 3. B—B3, Q—Q2; 4. B × B, Q × B; the significance of this file is considerable. There followed, 5. P—QB4! (On QB2 the pawn would have been untenable), 5..... P × P e.p., opening the Q file also, since his own obstructing pawn at Q5 disappears (every pawn is an obstruction to his own Rooks); and after 6. P × P, Black followed with QR—QB1 and KR—Q1 with play in both the files (Game No. 11).

Hence post your pieces centrally, so long as you can do so safely, i.e., without inviting the advance of the 'pawn-roller'. Thus will your opponent be provoked into an exchange which will give you an open file.

Let us in Diagram 15 imagine the continuation, 1..... B—Kt3; 2. Q—Q2, 0—0; 3. 0—0—0, P—KR3? (Diag. 16), we shall then get a typical example of an effective opening of a file. Thanks to Black's PKR3 White can now bring about the speedy disappearance of his KKtP; Black's P—KR3 was therefore bad; bad, but hardly as a waste of time, for Black had already completed his development; and after all there is a difference between going to sleep after or over our work! The mode of advance against Black's KR3 (the objective or object of attack) is P—KR3, P—KKt4, P—KKt5; on P×P the P is then recaptured by a piece, whereupon R—KKt1 takes possession of the file which now is open. True, one of his own pieces is in the way, but this is of no consequence, for it is elastic; it is only a pawn which is obstinate, and we have our work cut out if we want to induce him to change his state.

As an example for practice let us suppose that in the position shown on Diagram 16, the Bishops at K3 and QKt3 do not exist, and that Black's KRP is at KR2, his KKtP at Kt3. The objective is now Black's KKt3, and the KR file (always the one next to the objective) should be opened. The plan is P—KR4—R5×P. But in this position, after P—KR4 we must, before going on, first give the Kt at KB3 a dig in the ribs, since he is in the way; perhaps by Kt—Q5, and this done the P can advance to KR5 in all comfort and without any sacrifice. As a last resort the attacked party may attempt to give the pawn the slip;

Diagram 16

The objective is here Black's PKR3

that is on P—R5 to play P—KKt4; which, however, here would hardly answer since the square KKt4 is unprotected.

§3. *The ideal (goal) of every operation in a file. On some accompanying phenomena. Marauding raids. Enveloping operations.*

The ideal which lies at the root of every operation in a file is the ultimate penetration by way of this file into the enemy's game, that is to say to our (White's) 7th or 8th rank. –

A very important postulate is the following. Supposing that by operating in the Q file we reach the 7th rank by a round-about way, by, say, the manœuvre R—Q1—Q4—QR4—QR7, this cannot be regarded as a direct exploitation of the Q file. A few elementary examples will now be given.

(Diag. 17.) Line of operation the KR file. This will be seized by 1. Q—KR1 ch, K—Kt1; and now according to rule either Q—R7 or Q—R8, the latter not being feasible, 2. Q—R7 ch, K—B1, and

c

now 3. Q—R8 ch followed by a marauding expedition (for so we designate every forking attack on two pieces), which is here not a chance raid, but rather a not untypical concomitant of an entry by force at the 7th or 8th rank. If in Diagram 17 the Black Q were at her Q2 instead of QKt1 our method would be 1. Q—KR1 ch, K—Kt1;

Diagram 17

Catastrophe in the KR file

2. Q—R7 ch, K—B1; 3. Q—R8 ch, K—K2; 4. Q×P ch, K—K3; 5. Q× Q ch, K×Q; 6. P—Kt7, and the result would be no less unpleasant. We may describe this triangular manœuvre of the Q (R7, R8, Kt7) as an enveloping attack. Putting it shortly, we may say: Given deficient resistance (that is no enemy pawn on his KR3 or KR5), the attacker, after safeguarding the lines of invasion, raids the 7th and 8th ranks, and, doing so, will not seldom be rewarded by the chance of a marauding expedition or of an enveloping attack.

So far the operation has been as readily intelligible as it is easily executed. Unfortunately in real life there are often great obstacles to overcome, as §4 will show.

§4. *The possible obstacles to be met with in the line of operations. The block of granite and how to mine it. The conception of protected and unprotected obstacles (pawns). The two methods of conducting the attack against obstructing enemy pawns. The 'evolutionary' and 'revolutionary' attack.*

We have seen how great may be the significance of a forced entry into the 7th and 8th ranks. This being the case, it is natural to presume that nature herself, so to speak, may have done something for the protection of this sensitive area, just as good wise mother nature has given the human heart a place magnificently protected behind the ribs. The characteristic and natural defensive position is shown in Diagram 18. Here the Black P at KKt3 prevents White from invading the 7th rank. The road to the 7th or 8th rank leads only over my dead body, the doughty peon seems to say.

If, however, this enemy KKtP be protected by another pawn, it would be futile to run one's head up against such a block of granite by, shall we say, tripling our forces in the file. Rather will it be the path of wisdom first to mine it by, for instance, P—KR4—R5, followed by P×P, after which the granite block will have shrivelled up to a defenceless pawnling. In Diagram 18 P—QKt5 and P×P would have the effect of such a mining operation.

The pawn, as we have before insisted, is to be regarded as a sure defender. Protection by pieces may almost be called a confusion of terms; the pawn alone will stand on guard solidly, patiently, without a grumble. Hence a 'protected pawn' means a pawn protected by one of his fellows. If our pawn has been enticed away from the confederation of pawns he will be subject to attack by many pieces.

The obvious idea is then to win the pawn by piling up our attacks on it, firstly for the sake of the gain in material, but secondly in order to break down the resistance in the file. This will be technically managed by first bringing up our pieces into attacking positions. A hot fight will then be waged round the pawn. As often as we attack, Black covers; so we now seek to obtain the upper hand by thinning the ranks of the defending forces, which can be done (a) by driving them away, (b) by exchange, (c) by shutting off one of the defending pieces. That is to say we transfer our attack

Diagram 18

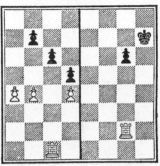

Black's QBP defended by his QKtP is a protected obstacle

The KKtP an unprotected obstacle

from our opponent to his defenders, a perfectly normal proceeding, often practised at school (in a rough-and-tumble, I mean).

The following end game, see Diagram 19, will illustrate the method,

Diagram 19

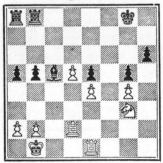

Converging attack on the Black KRP (evolutionary attack)

1. R—R2, K—R2; 2. R (K1)—R1. White can pile up the attack since the obstructing P at R6 is without pawn protection, 2..... B—B1, 3. Kt—B5, R—Kt3. Attack and defence balance one another, but by White's next move, 4. P—Q6, the defending Black R on his Kt3 will be shut out of the fight, and the KRP will fall, while simultaneously the entry into the 7th and 8th ranks via the KR file will be made possible. Had two Black rooks stood on their 3rd row, the sacrifice of the exchange by R × P would have been possible, but with the Rooks so placed, such a move as B × QP would have been very bad, for the consequence would have been, after 4. P—Q6, B × P; 5. R × P ch, K—Kt1; 6. R—Kt6 ch, K—B2; 7. R—Kt7 ch, K—K1; 8. Kt × B ch, R × Kt; 9. R—R8 mate.

Or take the skeleton position: White R's, KB1, KB2; Kt, Q4. Black having an obstructing P on KB3 protected by the KKKt2 and BQ1 with R at QB1. The play would be 1. Kt—K6 ch, K any move; 2. Kt×B, R×Kt; 3. R×P, i.e., the ranks of the defenders are thinned by exchange. The manœuvre against the obstructing pawn so far considered is contained in the conception 'evolutionary attack'. The whole manner of concentration against one point, in order eventually to get superior forces to bear upon it, implies this. The goal, too, was symptomatic; it was, in fact, partly material gain (the win of a pawn was welcome) which tempted us, partly the ideal hovering before us of conquering the 7th rank. This mixture of motives was significant.

Diagram 20

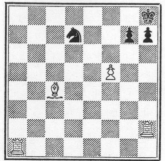

Break through at KR7—Revolutionary attack

Quite another picture is revealed in the process employed in Diagram 20 (only the most important actors are shown). Granted that play in the KR file by QR—KR1 would be idle because of Kt—B3 or P—KR3 (with a granite block in the file); how may White otherwise make use of the KR file? The answer is that he gives up all idea of material profit, and instead does everything, stops at no sacrifice, in order to get the offending pawn out of the way. Hence 1. R×P ch, K×R, 2. R—R1 mate. Simple as is this ending, it seems to me to be of the greatest importance as bringing clearly before us the difference between the 'evolutionary' and 'revolutionary' forms of attack.

We will therefore give yet another example (Diag. 21.) An evolutionary attack would, after 1. QR—KR1, Kt—B1; 2. B—K7 (thinning defenders' ranks by exchange), lead to the winning of the objective. The revolutionary attack on the other hand would dispense with the winning of the Black

Diagram 21

How would here proceed the 'evolutionary' and 'revolutionary' attacks?

KRP as follows: 1. R×P, K×R (there can be no talk of having won the pawn here for White has given up a Rook for it); 2. R—R1 ch, K—Kt1; 3. R—R8 mate. The idea of the revolutionary attacks lies, as is here clearly shown, in opening by sheer force an entry to the 7th or 8th rank which had been barred to us. One Rook sacrifices

himself for his colleague, that the latter may reach the objective,
the 8th rank. Yes, even on a chess board there is such a thing as
true comradeship!

In what chronological order are these two methods of attack
to be employed? The answer to this is:—First try the converging
attack, i.e., attack the obstructing pawn with several pieces; by so
doing opportunity may be found to force the defending pieces into
uncomfortable positions where they will get into one another's way:
for the defence will often be cramped for space. Afterwards see
whether among other things there is a possibility of a break through
by force, in other words of a revolutionary attack.

§5. *The restricted advance in one file with the idea of giving up that
file for another one, i.e., the indirect exploitation of a file. The file as a
jumping-off place.*

In the position shown in Diagram 22 the direct exploitation of the
KB file, with eventual R × BP (after, say, first driving off the protecting Rook), would be impossible with the scanty material available.

Diagram 22	Diagram 23
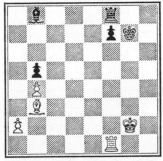	
The simplest example of the restricted advance in a file followed by the manœuvring of the R to another file 1. R—B5, 2. R × P, 3. R—Kt7	The file as 'jumping off' place: a positional example, cf. Game No. 11

The simple R—B5, however, clearly wins a pawn, and later R—QKt7
may follow. It is important that we examine this manœuvre to see
its logical meaning. Since R—B7 was impracticable, there could be
no question of a direct exploitation of the KB file in our sense. On
the other hand it would be pushing ingratitude to an extreme length
if we went on to assert that the KB file had no bearing whatever
on the capture of the QKtP, etc. Where then does the truth lie?
The answer is:—The file was here used not directly, nor to its fullest
extent, but indirectly, as a kind of jumping-off place. See Diagram
23, where another instance of the use of a file in this manner is given.

As a further example consider the skeleton position: White: R, KKt1; B, K3; P, KR2. Black: K, KR2; P, KR3. The manœuvre B—Q4, R—Kt7 would be a direct, and R—Kt3—R3 × RP would be an indirect exploitation of the KKt file.

§6. *The outpost. The radius of attack. With what piece should one occupy an advanced position on a centre file, and on a flank? Change of rôles and what this proves.*

Let us glance at Diagram 24. White has the centre and the Q file. Black has a pawn at his Q3 watching the centre, and also holds the K file. In other respects the positions are equal. White with the move will now attempt some operation in the Q file. This

Diagram 24

White establishes an out-post in the Q file

presents some difficulties since the protected Black pawn at his Q3 represents a 'granite block'. If White, in spite of the rules laid down in §4, proceeded to assail Black's QP by R—Q2 and R(K)—Q1, not only the esteemed reader but the Black QP himself would deride him; so we had better keep to the rules, and perhaps try to undermine the position by P—K5 (see §4); but this too proves to be impossible, for the enemy's possession of the K file is a quite sufficient bar to any projected P—K5. Accordingly let us give up the Q file as such, and content ourselves with an indirect exploitation of it by the restricted advance R—Q4, to be followed later by R—QR4, etc., as laid down in §5. But this manœuvre, too, is here somewhat weak, for Black's Q side is too compact. Note that if Black's QRP were isolated it would be wholly in place to bring up by a similar process the KR to the QR file via the Q file. Since all attempts have so far broken down we begin to look round for some other base of operations, and we should be wholly wrong in so doing, for the Q file can be exploited in this position.

The key move is 1. Kt—Q5, and the Knight here placed we call the outpost; by which we mean a piece, usually a Knight, established in an open file in enemy territory, and protected (of course by a pawn). This Knight, protected and supported as he is, will, in consequence of his radius of attack, exercise a disturbing influence, and will, therefore, cause the opponent to weaken his position in the Q file, in order to drive him away, by P—QB3. And hence we may say:—

a. An advanced post forms a base for new attacks.

b. An outpost provokes a weakening of the enemy's position in the file in question.

After 1. Kt—Q5, P—QB3 (R—QB1 would also serve, and in fact in the position given would be the defence adopted by a strong player, but it takes iron nerves to let a Knight so threateningly posted remain in his place for hour after hour! moreover there may come a time when Black will be forced to make the weakening move P—QB3), there follows: 2. Kt—B3, and now the Black QP, after White's R—Q2 and KR—Q1, will certainly not laugh derisively any longer.

It is important for the student to know that the strength of an outpost lies in its strategical connexion with its own hinterland. The outpost does not derive its strength from itself, but rather from this hinterland, namely from the open file and the protecting pawn; and if suddenly one or other of these points of contact failed, it would almost entirely lose its prestige and significance. For instance, in Diagram 24 let us suppose a White pawn at Q3, the Q file would in this case be closed, and then if 1.....P—QB3; 2. Kt—B3, the QP would not be weak; for how should a body be weak if it is not exposed to attack? Or again (Diag. 24), suppose the White P at K3 instead of K4. Contact with the pawn now fails, as is painfully evident after the moves 1.....P—QB3; 2. Kt—B3, P—Q4!, and White has achieved nothing; whereas with the White pawn at K4 the Black QP would remain paralysed (backward), at any rate for some considerable time. Hence the file to its rear and the protecting pawn are essential accompaniments to an advanced post.

In the position arising out of the Giuoco Piano, White: K, KKt1; R's, QR1, KB1; Kt, QB3; P's, QR2, QKt2, QB2, Q3, K4, KKt2, KR2. Black: K, KKt1; R's, QR1, KB1; B, K2; P's, QR2, QKt2, QB2, K4, KB3, KKt2, KR2 (we can imagine *x* other pieces on each side). White has the KB file with an advanced post at KB5, Black the Q file with one at Q5. Both files at the moment 'bite on granite' (on protected pawns). To sap this strength White will direct his Knight via K2 and KKt3 to KB5. Arrived there the Knight attacks the point KKt7, and this attack can be still further accentuated by, say, R—B3—KKt3. The obvious course for Black is to drive away the Knight by P—KKt3, but by inducing this the strategical mission of White's outpost will have been accomplished; for Black's KBP is now become a weakness. It is important to notice that Kt—KB5 was the starting point of a new attack, namely on Black's KKt2.

Very often the outpost will be exchanged at his station. If the attacking player has played correctly, the retaking piece or pawn will yield full compensation for the piece which has been taken. Here a conversion of advantages is the order of the day. For instance, if after Kt—KB5 a piece take the Knight, this will be recaptured by the KP, and White now gets the point K4 for a Rook or his other Knight, and in addition some possibility (after P—KKt4—Kt5) of opening the KKt file. Further the P now at KB5 will effectively render immobile the Black pawn at his KB3, which is the object of attack (Diag. 25; also Game No. 5, v. Haken—Giese).

In a flank file the advanced post should be occupied by a piece of heavy metal. Flank files are the QR, QKt, KKt, KR; centre files the QB, Q, K, KB files.

In Diagram 25 a flank file is in question, and the occupation of an advanced post in it by a Knight would have little effect, for the

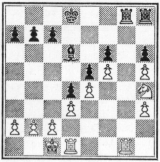

Diagram 25

In a flank file the outpost a R (R—Kt6) not a Kt

attacking range of a Knight at KKt6 would be small (still smaller of course on a R file). R—Kt6 is in fact indicated, since thus we go some way towards gaining control of the KKt file, which so far has been in dispute, or towards getting some other advantage. It should be noted that the file was disputed since neither side could move up or down it unchallenged; freedom to do this is the only sure sign that a file is controlled. It therefore remains for White to find a suitable point on which to double his Rooks. It can be found if we seek it. 1. R—Kt2?, R×R; 2. Kt×R, R—Kt1; and Black holds the file. Or, 1. R—Kt4?, R×R; 2. P×R, R—Kt1; 3. Kt—Kt6, and White will hardly be able to make anything of his backward extra pawn. But 1. R—Kt6! (outpost), R×R (else QR—Kt1 and the Rooks are doubled), 2. RP×R, with a giant of a passed pawn! and the possibility (after Kt—B3) of R—Kt1—Kt4—R4. So though because of RP×R White's open file is dead, there has arisen from its ashes a passed pawn, with possibilities of attack in the KR file. This is a good example of the conversion of advantages referred to above in the case of the exchange of an outpost.

Let us stop for a moment longer at Diagram 25, and we shall come, after 1. R—Kt6, R×R; 2. RP×R, R—Kt1; 3. R—Kt1, on the track of a characteristic exchange of rôles. Before 1.....R×R the White RP protected the RKt6; after the exchange a White R supports this same RP which now has advanced to Kt6. This action, in which gratitude and kindly feeling are beautifully displayed, shows, too, that there is a real strategical connexion between the KKt file as such and the pawn (here the KRP) which protects the advanced post in it.

We shall close this chapter with an example, chosen not for entertainment but for instruction, taken from a game between Nimzowitsch (White) and an amateur (Diag. 26). 1. Kt—B4. Development is a principle well worthy of attention right into the end-game, one, however, which is neglected by less experienced players even in the opening. 1.....QR—KKt1, 2. R—R7! For present purposes we would ask the reader to regard this move simply as the occupation of an advanced post; for of course it could also be regarded as an invasion of the 7th rank. 2.....

Diagram 26

B—K1; 3. QR—R1, R×R; 4. P×R (conversion of the 'file' into a 'passed pawn'; 4. R×R, K—B1; 5. Kt—R5, with, at an opportune moment, sacrifice of the Knight at B6, would also have been good), 4.....R—KR1; 5. Kt—Kt6 ch, B×Kt; 6. P×B, and the passed pawn is become a protected passed pawn. 6.....K—K3, 7. R—R5! This 'restricted' advance stops any attempt of Black to free himself by perhaps K—K4 or P—KB4, giving access to White's KKtP. 7.....P—QKt3; 8. P—QB4 (still more paralysing would be 8. P—QKt4, but White follows other plans), 8.....P—QB4; 9. P—QR4, P—QR4; 10. P—QKt3, P—QB3; 11. K—Q2, K—Q3; 12. K—K3, K—K3; 13. K—B4, K—Q3; 14. K—B5! Now White's plan for breaking through is revealed. By *Zugzwang,** i.e., by exhausting Black's available moves, so that finally his K is forced

* Note on *Zugzwang*. There are combinations in chess, for as such must be regarded any series of moves, however quiet, which stand in a logical relationship to one another, which are based on the fact that to move in his turn is obligatory on a player. This obligation, in general a welcome one, may weigh heavily on him if his pieces are disposed for attack and defence as favourably as the circumstances allow, and when any change in their configuration can only be detrimental. In such a position his condition will get worse step by step until he is forced, by the necessity of making a move, to relax his hold on, or weaken, some key point, and his game collapses. A combination directed to bring about such a catastrophe is called by the Germans *Zugzwang* (compulsion to move), and the player who succumbs under it is said to have got into *Zugzwang*. The ending just examined under Diagram 26 is an excellent example. With 7. R—R5 White announces *Zugzwang*. To prevent White succeeding in his object to break through in the KB file it is vital for Black that his K maintain contact with his K4. To do this he is confined to the squares K3 and Q3. At last compelled to make a move he is forced to give up this contact, and White breaks through. Since the player under *Zugzwang* cannot have the resource of marking time without sensibly altering his position, it will be clear that the opportunity to use the *Zugzwang* weapon will normally present itself only in the end game, and most often when only K's and P's remain on the board.

P. H.

to break contact with his K4, White is able to play P—K5, whereupon the Black KBP disappears, and the entry of the White Rook at KB7 will become possible. 14.....K—K2; 15. P—K5, P×P; 16. K×P, K—Q2; 17. R—B5. Now it will be clear that the move R—R5 had all the elements of the manœuvre which we have called a restricted advance in a file, since R—R5—B5—B7 must, willy nilly, despite the time intervening, be regarded as the manœuvring of the Rook from one file to a new one. Black resigned, since R—B7 and R×KKtP would have yielded two united passed pawns.

CHAPTER III

THE SEVENTH AND EIGHTH RANKS

§1. *Introductory and general. End-game or Middle-game. The choice of an objective. 'Thou shalt not shilly shally!'*

As we have seen in the second chapter the entry into enemy territory, in other words into the 7th and 8th ranks, forms the logical consequence of play in a file. I have sought to illustrate this entry by some particularly marked, because catastrophic, examples; but I must here, to off-set this, emphasize the fact that, in the normal course of events, it will only be late, when we pass into the end-game stage, that the 7th rank will be seized; for catastrophes of whatever nature are, after all, only the result of serious mistakes of our opponent, and consequently cannot be regarded as the normal. We are therefore disposed to regard the 7th and 8th ranks as end-game advantages, and this despite the fact that numberless games are decided by operations in these ranks in the middle game. The student should, however, try to break into the enemy's base as early as possible, and if he at first find that the invading Rook can accomplish nothing, or is even lost, he must not be discouraged on that account. It is part of our system to instruct the student at the earliest possible moment in the strategical elements of the end-game. Accordingly, after treating of the '7th and 8th ranks', 'Passed Pawns', and the technique of 'Exchange', we shall insert a chapter which, though properly coming under the heading 'Position Play', must, for instructional purposes, find a place thus early. And after assimilating this, the 7th and 8th ranks will be to the student not merely a mating instrument, but, much more, a keen-edged weapon for use in the end-game. As already remarked it is both, but its use as an end-game weapon predominates.

It is of the greatest importance to accustom ourselves to carry out operations in the 7th rank in such a manner that we have from the start some settled, definite objective. It is characteristic of the less practised player that he chooses an opposite course; in fact he shilly shallies, that is, he looks now to the right now to the left without any fixed plan. No, settle on your objective is the rule. Such an objective, as we have learnt, may be a pawn or a point; which, matters nothing. But aimlessly to drift from one to another, this will expose you to a strategical disgrace.

§2. *The convergent and the revolutionary attack in the 7th rank. The win of a point (or pawn) with acoustical echo (i.e. with simultaneous check).*

In the position shown in Diagram 27 White chooses the QBP as his objective. After Black's R—QB1, attack and defence balance one another; but by a procedure analogous to that used in a file, we now seek to disturb this equilibrium to our advantage. Accordingly let us suppose White to have a Bishop at K1 and Black a Knight at KKt3, we should then attain our end by B—Kt3; and if our Bishop had been at KB1 (instead of K1), by B—R6 driving away the defending Rook. Next let us suppose the forces in Diagram 27 increased by a White R at Q1, and a Black Knight at KKt3, and that the White KRP is wanting. The logical course would now be R—Q4—QB4, or else 1. R—Q8 ch, R×R; 2. R×R ch, Kt—B1, and White gets

Diagram 27

Diagram 28

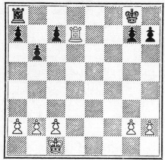
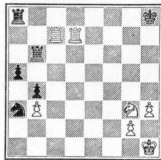

The 7th rank

Black   to   move. Fight   for
Black's KR2

back into the 7th row by 3. R—B8, P—QB4; 4. R—B7, etc. In Diagram 27 as it stands it should be noted that the march of the White K to his QB6 would be the course to be aimed at, since the point QB7 is our chosen objective.

The affair takes a similar course in the position in Diagram 28. White's objective is his KR7, since the win of this point would give the possibility of a deadly enveloping movement. 1.....R—KR3; 2. Kt—B5, R—R4; 3. P—KKt4, R×P ch; 4. K—Kt2, R×P; 5. R—R7 ch. He has got there; the defender, the Black Rook, had to flee; White wins the point KR7 and gives mate. 5.....K—Kt1; 6. R(B7)—Kt7 ch and 7. R—R8 mate. The nature of a convergent attack on a chosen objective would seem to have been sufficiently illustrated by this example. Before, however, passing to the 'revolutionary' form of attack, we would underline as important the following rule:—If the objective take to flight, the Rook must attack him from the rear. For example, a Rook in the 7th rank holds the Black pawn at QKt2 under attack. If now 1.....P—QKt4, then 2. R—QKt7, and not a flank attack in the 5th rank. This rule finds its explanation in the following considerations:—(a) The 7th rank is to be held as long as possible, since it is here that new objectives may present themselves. (b) The enveloping attack (and R—QKt7 was such) is the strongest form of attack (ranged in ascending scale: i, frontal, ii, flank, iii, enveloping), which (c) often forces the enemy to undertake cramping defensive measures. It should be noticed that in the case considered above a flank attack on the QKtP would be comfortably met by R—QKt1.

Diagram 29

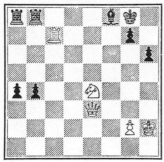

Win by force of, the objective, Black's KR2

Diagram 30

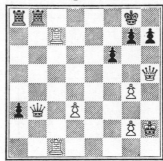

Win by force of, the objective, Black's KR2

In Diagram 29 let us 'choose' Black's KKt2. The fact that this point is well protected does not frighten us. We concentrate our attack by means of 1. Kt—Kt3, P—QR6 (the passed pawns are very threatening) 2. Kt—B5, P—R7; 3. Q—K5 (and now mate is threatened by R×P ch) 3.....P—R8=Q, the KKtP is now protected and White loses; so our objective, Black's KKt2, was ill chosen. The right one is Black's KR2, and its conquest follows from a 'revolutionary' attack. 1. Kt—B6 ch, P×Kt; 2. Q—K6 ch, K—R1; 3. Q—Q7. Or, 1. Kt—B6 ch, K—R1; (Black is stubborn) 2. Q×P ch (White still more so!) 2.....P×Q; 3. R—KR7 mate, and on the chosen spot. This example shows us the idea of a revolutionary attack applied to the 7th rank. One pawn is forcibly got out of the way in order that action in the 7th rank may be extended to that neighbouring point which we had thought of as our objective.

Another example is shown in Diagram 30. Here the point KKt7 would be hard to attack successfully, though if White's PKKt4 were absent this would be easier: for instance by 1. Q—Kt4, P—Kt3; 2. Q—KR4, P—R4; 3. Q×BP, etc. With the pawn there, however matters are not so easy, for if 1. R—Q7 (threatening R(B1)—B7)

1.....R—QB1;   or is 1. R(B1)—B4 (threatening Q—B7 ch)
1.....R—KB1.   The right play is 1. R × P ch (KR7 is our objective),
K × R, 2. R—B7 ch, K—R1; 3. Q × P mate. The capture at
KKt7 extended the range of action in the 7th row to KR7. If
2.....K—B1, 3. Q × P would also have won, since the 7th row could
not be held by Black in any manner. Still more precise, however,
would be the employment of the Queen with gain of tempo; thus:
3. Q—R6 ch, K—K1; 4. Q—K3 ch, K—B1; 5. Q—K7 ch (enters
the 7th row with 'acoustical echo'), 5.....K—Kt1; 6. Q—Kt7
mate. This last manœuvre deserves comment; it is typical, since by
its means any approach of the enemy reserves can be prevented.
Take another position. White: K, B1; Q, KR5; P's, Q4, K3,
KB5. Black: K, KKt1; R's, QR1, KB1; Kt, KR8; P's, KB2,
KB3. White wishes to take the Knight with a check; this he does by
1. Q—Kt4 ch, K—R2; 2. Q—R3 ch, K—Kt2, 3. Q—Kt2 ch,
K—R3, and now Q × Kt ch.   That is to say we drive the King to the
desired side of the board without losing
contact with the piece or point we wish
to win.

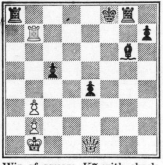

Diagram 31

Win of square K7 with check.
Mate in 4 moves

Now see Diagram 31. The point to
be won is K7. Either 1. Q—R4 or
1. Q—B2 ch would fail miserably
because of P—K6 ch and R—R8 mate;
e.g. 1. Q—B2 ch, K—K1; 2. Q × BP,
P—K6 ch, etc. The right move is
1. Q—B1 ch, K—K1; Q—Kt5 ch,
K—B1; 3. Q × P ch, K—K1; 4. Q—
K7 mate. We could also state the
problem as follows:—White to take
the point QKt5 with check. After
1. Q—B1 ch, K—K1, 2. Q—Kt5 ch,
White has contact with the point QB5, and, at the same time, does not
lose his driving effect on the enemy King, who is tied to his own square.

§3.   *The five special cases in the 7th Rank.*

1. '7th row absolute' with passed pawns. 2. Doubled Rooks
give perpetual check. 3. The drawing apparatus R + Kt 4. The
marauding raid in the 7th rank. 5. Combined play in the 7th and
8th ranks (enveloping manœuvre in the corner of the board).

By '7th rank absolute' we mean that our control is such that the
enemy King is shut in behind it. For example White: R, QR7.
Black: K, KB1; P, KB3. On the other hand were the pawn at
KB2 control would not be absolute.

(1) The first special case. 7th row absolute with well advanced passed pawns wins almost always. An example: White: K, KR1; R, K7; P, QKt6. Black: K, KR1; R, Q1. White plays P—Kt7 after which R—QB7, and R—QB8 ch cannot be prevented. If the Black King had been at KKt3 the game would have been drawn. In the position in Diagram 32 the following is decisive. 1. Q×B ch, R—R3; 2. Q×R ch, P×Q; 3. P—Kt6, since the 7th row is now 'absolute'. If it were not, if the Black KKtP still stood on his original square, the game would be drawn. In the following position (Tarrasch—Lasker. Berlin, 1918): White: K, KB2; R, Q7; P's, Q4, KKt3, KR5. Black: K, K5; R, QR4; P's, QR2, KB3, KKt2, KR3; Lasker in a note points out a win by 1.....R—R7 ch; 2. K—B1?, P—QR4; 3. R×P, P—R5; 4. R—Kt6, P—R6; 5. R×BP, R—QKt7. If White's KKtP were on its original square, K—R2 would still have given a drawing chance; as it is, however, the rank is 'absolute' and Black wins. Interesting on the other hand would have been, after 1.....R— R7 ch, the attempt to neutralize the 'absolute' 7th row by 2. K—K1!. Lasker gives the continuation 2.....P—QR4; 3. K—Q1, P—R5; 4. K—B1, P—R6; 5. K—Kt1 with a draw.

Diagram 32

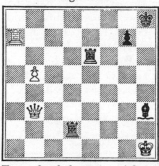

Example of the 1st special case

(2) The second special case. Draw by perpetual check, which has an interest from a psychological error which is common. White: K, KR2; R's, Q7, KB7; P, KR3. Black: K, K1; R, KB8; B, KB6; P's, K4, KB5. White, a player of little experience, sees the desperate position of his King and plays for a draw by R(B)—K7 ch, quite rightly recognizing that R(Q)—K7 would lead to the Black King's eventually reaching sanctuary. (1. R(Q)—K7 ch?, K—Q1; 2. R—Q7 ch, K—B1; 3. R—B7 ch, K—Kt1, and White has no checks left.) After 1. R(B)—K7 ch, K—B1; 2. R—B7 ch, K—Kt1; 3. R—Kt7 ch, K—R1; 4. R—R7 ch (if 4. R—Kt1??, R—B7 ch!) 4.....K—Kt1; 5. R(R)—Kt7 ch!, K—R1; 6. R—R7 ch, K—Kt1, he looks his opponent in the eye; does he really think he can escape? repeats the checks as above a few times, and then just for the variety's sake gives check with the other Rook, 7. R(Q)—Kt7 ch, after which his game is lost, since the King reaches sanctuary at his QKt1. From which follows a moral, that variety is not always profitable. The R at Q7 was a sturdy sentinel, and as such should not have been needlessly disturbed.

(3) The third special case. The drawing apparatus (for perpetual check) R+Kt. White: K, R2; R, QKt7; Kt, KB6. Black: K,

KB1; P's, QB7, Q7, K7.   Black has three embryo queens; so White seeks to draw by perpetual check. 1. Kt—R7 ch, K—K1; 2. Kt—B6 ch, fails because of K—Q1. The solution is found in 1. R—Q7, since now after, e.g., 1.....P—K8=Q the drawing apparatus works to perfection. Observe that the key move, 1. R—Q7, brings R and Kt into strategical contact.

Let us in the same position imagine a Black Rook at his QB1. In this case 1. R—Q7 would not suffice, but would also be unnecessary, for his own Rook at QB1 stops the Black King's flight and makes a sentinel at Q7 superfluous, so in this case 1. Kt—R7 ch, K—K1; 2. Kt—B6 ch, K—Q1??; 3. R—Q7 mate. The Black King was a clever fellow; he committed suicide in the middle of the board, when a less talented sovereign would have been satisfied with the corner for this purpose.

(4) The fourth special case is quite simple, but is indispensable in view of the very complicated 5th case. It consists in a driving manœuvre. The King will be forced out of his corner, and then will follow a marauding raid. An example.—White: K, KR2; R's, QR7, QKt7; P's, KKt2, KKt6, KR3. Black: K, KR1; R's, QB1, Q1; B, KB8. 1. R—R7 ch, K—Kt1; 2. R(QR)—Kt7 ch, K—B1; 3. R—B7 ch, and wins the Bishop. A necessary condition for success was the protected position of the R at KR7. Had it been otherwise 3.....K—Kt1 would have prevented the capture of the Bishop. In this 4th case the capacity of the combined Rooks to drive the King from his corner (to KB1 or QB1) must be noted.

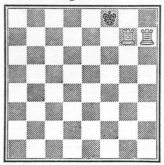

Diagram 33

The basis of the enveloping manœuvre

This capacity provides the basis of the 5th case.

(5) The fifth special case. In the position:—White: R's, QR7, Q7. Black: K, KR1, Q, QKt1, White who designs to seize the 8th rank, tries to do this by low cunning, since the direct road seems to be barred by the Black Queen. He seizes the corner, drives the enemy King out of it, and thus makes room for the enveloping attack of his Rook. 1. R—R7 ch, K—Kt1; 2. R(QR)—KKt7 ch, K—B1; and now 3. R—R8 ch, winning the Queen. The position arrived at after the two checks at KR7 and KKt7 is the typical starting point of all enveloping manœuvres in the 7th and 8th rows (Diag. 33).

The analysis of this position shows us two Rooks each ready for a turning movement, but also a resourceful King, whose contact with the R at Kt7 protects him from the worst (mate at R8). So

long as this contact is maintained mate cannot be given. The King's
case is somewhat like that of a pedestrian who is set upon by a foot-
pad; the latter raises his weapon to strike, but the former seizes his
arm and keeps fast hold of it, knowing that so long as contact is
kept up the robber cannot use his arm for the decisive blow. And so
the rule runs:—the King who is threatened by an enveloping attack
must maintain contact with the nearer Rook as long as possible.
The Rooks on their side must seek to shake loose from the contact.
The second rule follows directly:— the King who is threatened
must struggle towards the corner, the Rooks must and will drive him
from it.

Starting from the typical position White can try three manœuvres:
(a) for immediate material gain; (b) for a mating combination by
breaking off contact between K and R (c) for a tempo-winning
combination.

(a) has been already considered. If, say, an enemy Queen stand
anywhere in her 1st row there will result from the position R—R8 ch
with win of the Q for the R at KKt7.

(b) Contact can be broken either through the protection of the R
at KKt7 (by pawn or piece), or by driving away the K by a check from
another quarter. For example: White:

Diagram 34

R's, KKt7, KR7; B, K1. Black: K,
KB1; Q, QR1; R, QR7. There follows
1. B—Kt4 ch, K—K1, and now the R's
have a free hand to deal the death blow
2. R—R8 mate. Instead of a B at K1
we may imagine a P at K6, and the
continuation would be 1. P—K7 ch,
K—K1; 2. R—R8 ch; the enveloping
operation has been made possible, but
the Black King has now a flight square
which before was closed to him, i.e.,
2.....K—Q2; but this plays no rôle,
for the air we have allowed him was

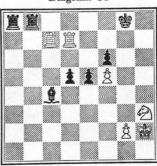

alas!—poisoned. 3. P—K8=Q double ch, and mate is not far
off. Now turn to Diagram 34. First White gets the typical position
as shown on Diagram 33. 1. R—Kt7 ch, K—B1; 2. R—R7,
threatening mate, 2.....K—Kt1, the flight towards the corner;
3. R(B)—Kt7 ch, K—B1; and now there follows 4. Kt—Kt5!
(Weaker would have been 4. Kt—B2, threatening Kt—Kt4 because of 4.....B—K7; 4.....P×Kt, P—B6, with mate at R8.
Or, 4. Kt—Kt5!, P—Q5!; 5. Kt—K6 ch, B×Kt (forced); 6. P×B
followed by the driving of the King from B1 by P—K7 ch, and
history repeats itself. This check at K7 which broke contact could
only have been parried by R—K1, leading to the loss of a Rook,

D

e.g., 6..... R—K1; 7. P—K7 ch, R×P; 8. R×R, and White wins
easily even if Black has one or two passed pawns to the good, for
there would have been brought into play that capacity which Rooks
possess, to which we have called especial attention, of attacking
fleeing pawns from their rear in the 7th rank.

(c) (Diag. 35.) With 1. R—R7 ch, K—Kt1; 2. R(B) —Kt7 ch,
K—B1, the typical position is reached, but how are we to proceed?
Neither (a) i.e., 3. R—R8 mate?, nor (b) i.e., forcing a break in the
contact, seem feasible. Of course, if the White K were already at
KKt5, then K—R6 would follow; but as matters stand it would seem
as if White must content himself with perpetual check. However,
appearances are deceitful. There follows:— 3. R×P, threatening
mate at R8, so 3..... K—Kt1. Now White repeats the little
manœuvre, 4. R(Q)—KKt7 ch, K—B1;   5. R×P, and again

Diagram 35   Diagram 36

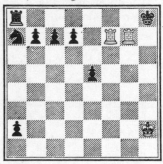

Win of a tempo. White wins

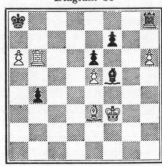

Nimzowitsch—Bernstein

Black is forced to play K—Kt1; he has no time for the P—R8=Q
of his dreams. (If our opponent has no time for something which
otherwise would be most advantageous to him because he is forced to
make some positional move irrelevant to his purpose, while we
advance our project, then we have gained a tempo.) White now
plays 6. R(B)—Kt7 ch, and the ending runs: 6..... K—B1;
7. R×P, K—Kt1; 8. R(Kt)—Kt7 ch (R×Kt would still be a gross
error because of P—R8=Q), 8..... K—B1;   9. R×Kt, R×R;
10. R×R, and wins the QRP and the game. We may sum this up
thus, that in (c) we have the case that White gathers new strength
by touching the typical starting position, or more simply, by bringing about this position he creates a new mating threat and so a free
tempo for gathering loot, i.e., gain of tempo.

We have now sufficiently illustrated the five special cases, and have
made it clear that the first thing to do is to bring about the 'starting
point position'. We will close with two more end games. Diagram
36 shows the position which White had obtained after 50 moves in the

tournament game at Wilna, 1912. My opponent here played 50.....R—KB1, in order, after P—KB3, to reduce the material on the board to such an extent that there would not be enough left to win with. I answered calmly 51. R×KtP, P—KB3; for now I manufacture out of its several components my 1st special case in the 7th rank (passed pawn and 7th row absolute), which was even at that date known to me. The continuation was 52. B—B5, R—QB1 (forced; 52.....R—B2 fails after 53. R—Kt7, R×R; '54. P×R ch, K×P; 55. P×P, and Black's Bishop has more work than he can do); 53. P×P, R×B; 54. P—B7 (the passed pawn), R—B1; 55. R—Kt7 (the 7th row absolute! The extra enemy piece is an illusion), 55.....B—Q6; 56. R—K7 (obviously), B—Kt4; 57. K—B4 (White avoided 57. R—K8, B×R; 58. P—B8=Q, though thereby he had treated himself to the pleasure of getting a new Queen, since after 58. B—B3 ch and R×Q, the Queen would have vanished and with her also....all joy!), 57.....R—KR1; 58. P—R7, B—QR5; 59. K—K5, B—Kt4; 60. K—B6, P—K4; 61. K—Kt7, resigns.

In the position on Diagram 37 there first occurred 1. P—R6, Q—QR1 (threatening R—R2 and R×P). In this difficult situation White saved himself by the following 'subtle trap', as the *Dünazeitung* called it, or by a combination based on a thorough knowledge of the terrain (7th row!), as we would call it. The game went on. 2. P—QKt3, R—QKt1 (better to be sure would be R—R2); and now followed the Q sacrifice: 3. B—R3!!, R×Q; 4. B×B, R—B1; 5. R×Kt ch, K×R;

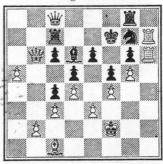

Diagram 37

Nimzowitsch—Eliasstamm
Riga 1910
White, without QKt

6. B—K5 ch, K any move, and the Rook gives on R8 and R7 perpetual check. It is worth noting that after the Q sacrifice, White has at least a draw in all variations, e.g., 4.....Q×P; 5. B—K5, K—K1; 6. R—R8 ch, K—Q2; 7. R(R6)—R7; Q—R7 ch (to leave the square R3 open); 8. K—Kt3, P—QB4; 9. R×Kt ch, K—B3; 10. R×R ch, K—Kt4; 11. R×P ch, K—R3; 12. R—R8 ch winning the Q; or 4.....Q—KKt1; 5. B×R, R×RP; 6. P×P, followed by B—K5; or, 4.....Q—KKt1; 5. B×R, P×P; 6. B×R, P—Kt7; 7. R×Kt ch!, Q or K×R; 8. R—R1 and White has much the better prospects because of his strong QRP.

CHAPTER IV

THE PASSED PAWN

§1. *To get our bearings. The neighbour who is somewhat disturbing and the* vis-à-vis *who is wholly unpleasant. The pawn majority. The 'candidate'. The birth of a passed pawn. Rules for 'candidates'.*

A PAWN is passed if he has nothing to fear from an enemy pawn in front of him, i.e., in the same file, or from one on a neighbouring file, and whose road to Queen is therefore open (Diag. 38). If a pawn is only checked in his advance (blockaded) by enemy pieces, the fact does not prejudice our conception.

An especial recognition is due to a pawn from the fact that enemy pieces must sacrifice a part of their effective strength in order to keep him under observation, and in fact under continual observation. If further, we bear in mind that the pawn enjoys another advantage over the pieces in that he is the born defender, we shall slowly discover that even on the 64 squares the pawn, our foot soldier, is worthy of all respect. Who checks an ambitious enemy pawn best? A pawn. Who protects one of his own pieces best? A pawn. And which of the chess men works for least wages? Again the pawn; for a steady job, such as protecting one of his own fellows or keeping in restraint one of the enemy's men, does not appeal to a piece at all; moreover, such occupation draws off troops from the active army. When a pawn is so employed this last applies in very much less measure.

Diagram 38

The White QR and K Pawns and the Black QP are passed. The White KP is passed but blocked

In the position on Diagram 38 neither the QKtP nor the KKtP is free; yet the former seems to be less hampered than the latter, for the QKtP has at any rate no direct antagonist. The *vis-à-vis* might be compared to an enemy, while the pawn in the next file reminds us rather of a kindly neighbour, who, as we know, can have his drawbacks. If, for instance, we are rushing downstairs to keep an important engagement, and a neighbour suddenly buttonholes us and involves us in a long talk, ranging from the weather and politics to the high cost of beer, he keeps us from our job, just as in Diagram 38

36

the Black QBP may be a vexation to White's QKtP. Nevertheless a somewhat gossipy chatterbox of a neighbour is far from being a bitter enemy, or to apply the simile to our case, an annoying pawn on a neighbouring file is far from being an antagonist. In our diagram the White KKtP's aspirations to greater things can never be satisfied, whereas the QKtP can always dream of an advance.

Let us now turn to the passed pawn's family. In this connexion we must first consider the question of the majority on one side or the other. At the beginning of the game after the first exchange of pawns in the centre (e.g., after 1. P—K4, P—K4; 2. P—Q4, P×P; 3. Q×P) pawn majorities loom up. White has now 4 to 3 on the K side, Black 4 to 3 on the Q side. Let us imagine the Black QP standing at Q3 for the purpose of curbing the ambitions of White's KP. The configuration on the K side will then be: White: P's, K4, KB2, KKt2, KR2; as against Black's P's at KB2, KKt2, KR2; and on the Q side White has P's at QR2, QKt2, QB2, as against Black's P's at QR2, QKt2, QB2, Q3. In the course of the game if Black can arrive at P—KB4, thus killing White's free centre pawn, the majority will be in yet clearer evidence, namely White's P's, KB2, KKt2, KR2, as against Black's P's, KKt2, KR2.

Diagram 39

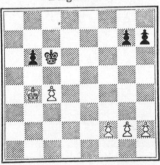

Majority on the K side

Rule:—Every healthy, uncompromised pawn majority must be able to yield a passed pawn. Of the 3 pawns on the K side in Diagram 39, the KBP is the only one to have no opponent, he is therefore the least trammelled, and accordingly has the greatest claim to become 'free' or passed. He is therefore the legitimate 'candidate'. Put more precisely the rule takes the following shape:—The spear-head of the advance is furnished by the candidate, the other pawns are only to be regarded as supports; so P—B4—B5, then P—Kt4—Kt5 and P—B6. If Black pawns are at his KKt3, KR4, then White must play P—KB4, P—Kt3 (not at once P—KR3 because of P—R5 and White's majority is crippled), P—R3, P—Kt4, and P—B5. How simple! and yet how often we see weaker players in this position advancing first with the KKtP, to which Black replies with P—KKt4, and White's majority is worthless. I have often racked my brain to discover why less experienced players begin with P—KKt4, yet the matter bears a simple explanation. The players in question are in two minds whether to begin on the right (P—R4) or on the left (P—B4), and in their perplexity decide, after good respectable custom, to choose the golden mean.

§2. *The blockade of passed pawns.* Proof *of the obligation to block-ade and why the said proof must be of the greatest importance to the practical player as well as to the theoretician* (*chess philosopher*). *The exceedingly complicated, because ever varying, relations between the passed pawn and the blockader. On strong and weak, elastic and inelastic blockaders.*

In the position shown on Diagram 40 Black has a passed pawn, which can however be blocked by Kt—Q4 or B—Q4. By blockade we mean the mechanical stopping of an enemy pawn's advance by a piece, which is brought about by placing our piece directly in front of the pawn to be blockaded. Here and in all similar cases the question comes up: Does not this blockade connote an unnecessary expenditure of energy? Would it not suffice to keep the pawn under observation (here by the Kt or B bearing upon Black's Q5)? Is keeping up a blockade work worthy of an officer? Will not his

Diagram 40

The problem of the blockade

mobility, so long as he takes his blockading problem seriously, be to a considerable extent diminished? Is he not thus degraded to the status of a stopped (immobile) pawn? In a nut-shell, Is the blockade economical? I am glad to be able to offer you, as I think, an exhaustive solution to this problem. The mediocre critic would settle the question by laying down quite shortly the general thesis that pawns must be stopped; but in my eyes this were a proof of poverty of understanding. The why and the wherefore are of extra-ordinary importance.

There are three reasons which logically make the blockade imperative. In what follows these will be analysed under §§2a, 2b, 2c; under §3 the effective strength of the blockader will be assessed in detail.

§2a. *First reason: The passed pawn is a criminal, who should be kept under lock and key. Mild measures, such as police surveillance, are not sufficient. The passed pawn's lust to expand. The awakening of the men in the rear.*

We return again to Diagram 40. The Black forces, B, R, and Kt, are as we should say, grouped round the passed pawn, that is to say they conform to a complex of which the QP is the nucleus. Kt and B guard the passed pawn; the R, however, supplies him with a certain

impetus, gives him a supporting impulse in fact. So powerful is the
pawn's desire to press on here, to expand (of which fact indeed visible
recognition is given in the way the 'officers', laying aside all pride of
caste, picturesquely group themselves round this simple 'foot soldier'),
that our QP often seems ready to advance on his own account, when
to do so will cost him his life. So, for instance, 1. P—Q5, Kt or
B×P; and now of a sudden the Black forces in the rear come to life.
The B from QKt2 commands a diagonal bearing on the enemy King,
the Rook has a clear file, while the Kt has a new square for himself in
the centre. Such an advance at the cost of self immolation, for
the purpose of opening a file, is, as a rule, only characteristic of
a 'pawn-roller', a compact advancing mass of pawns in the centre
(cf. the game at odds in I. i. §2, p. 3), and therefore furnishes a
brilliant proof of the lust to expand inherent in a passed pawn;
for the mobile centre (the pawn-roller) is endowed with an
almost incredible energy. Again, the
clearing of a square for one of his
own Kts is a very special characteristic of an advance of this kind.
Accordingly we say that the first consideration which logically compels the
blockade, is that the free passed pawn
is such a dangerous 'criminal', that it
is by no means sufficient to keep him
under police supervision (by the KtQKt3
and the BKB2 in the Diagram), the
fellow must be put in prison, so we take
away his freedom utterly by blockading
him with the Kt at Q4.

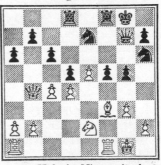

Diagram 41

te Kolsté—Nimzowitsch
Baden-Baden 1925

Black sacrifices a 'candidate',
and a piece to the rear comes
to life. How is this done?

The example just considered, we
mean the sacrifice of the pawn (for he
intended to die in the advance), is
thoroughly typical, although it is not in
the least necessary that a whole host of men to the rear should
be freed by the operation. It is often but a single piece standing behind it that profits (Diag. 41). Black, whose Q side and
centre seem to be threatened, seeks to turn his 'candidate' to
account. Since the candidate is 90 per cent. a passed pawn, the same
rules apply for him as do for a passed pawn. Accordingly 19.....
P—B5!; 20. P×BP, P—Kt5!; 21. B—Kt2, Kt(R)—B4; i.e., sacrifice
of a 'candidate' with the result that the square KB4 is cleared for the
Kt at R3. The continuation was 22. Q—Kt3, P×P; 23. Q×P ch,
K—R1; 24. Q—B3, P—KR4; 25. QR—Q1, P—R5; 26. R—Q3,
Kt—Q4; 27. Q—Q2, R—KKt1. Black supports his pawn majority
with vigour. 28. B×Kt, P×B; 29. K—R1, P—Kt6; and Black

gets the attack. In the game Alekhine—Treybal (Diag. 42) the following interesting manœuvre occurred:—27. P—K4. The mobile pawn centre sets itself in motion. 27.....P—B3 (for Kt—B2 would lose the QBP); 28. P×Kt, P×Kt. The passed pawn which has suddenly come into existence is clearly but as an ephemera, the fruit of some sudden inspiration, and seemingly destined to as speedy a death; but appearances are deceptive, even this creature of a moment knows how to subject itself to the iron laws of chess, and

Diagram 42

Alekhine—Treybal
Baden-Baden 1925

so there followed 29. P—Q6!!. The purpose of this pawn sacrifice was not to free the square from which it moved, and yet the advance wholly fulfils the spirit, if not the letter, of our rules. The pawn intends to lay down its life in advancing, and the main variation would be 29.....P—K5 ch! (So as to prevent P × P which could follow R × P); 30. K×P, R×P; 31. K—K5!!, QR—Q1; 32, B×P. Note that the entry of the King into Black's game was made possible only by the pawn sacrifice.

For a complete game which shows in its full setting the very important operation which we have been discussing, see Leonhardt—Nimzo-witsch, Game No. 12, which the reader is urged to study before proceeding further.

We now pass on to an analysis of our second reason.

§2b. *The second reason. Optimism in chess, and the immunity of the blockading piece against frontal attacks. The enemy pawn as our bulwark. The deeper-lying mission of the blockading piece. The blockading point a weak enemy point.*

In my book *Die Blockade* I wrote on this point as follows:— 'The second reason which we are now to analyse is of great importance from both the strategic and the instructional points of view. In chess in the last resort optimism is decisive. I mean by this that it is psychologically valuable to develop to the greatest length the faculty of being able to rejoice over small advantages. The beginner only "rejoices" when he can call checkmate to his opponent, or perhaps still more if he can win his Q (for in the eyes of the beginner this is if possible the greater triumph of the two). The master on the other hand is quite pleased, in fact royally content, if he succeed in espying the shadow of an enemy pawn weakness, in some corner or other of the left half of the board. The optimism here characterised is the indispensable psychological basis of position play. It is this optimism, too, which gives us strength, in face of every evil, however great, to discover the faintest hint of a bright side to the picture. In the case under consideration we can lay it down as established that an enemy passed pawn represents an unquestionably serious evil for us, yet even this evil has its tiny gleam of brightness. The situation is this, that in blockading this pawn we can by good fortune safely post the blockading piece under the shelter of the enemy pawn itself, so that it is immune from any frontal attack. Thus:— Consider a Black passed pawn at his K5, a White blockader at his K3 is not subject to an attack from an enemy Rook on the K file (K1 to K6), and hence stands there in a certain measure of security.'

So far *Die Blockade*. And to these remarks there is perhaps only this to add, that the relative security here outlined must in truth be at bottom symptomatic of that deeper mission which the blockader has to fulfil. If nature, yes, and even the enemy, too, are concerned about the safety of the blockader, he must have been set apart for great deeds. And in fact we are not out in our reckoning; for the blockading point often becomes a 'weak' enemy point.

Diagram 43

Tartakower—Lasker
Petrograd, 1909
Weak White points

I can well imagine that the road to a real conception of 'weak points' may have led across the blockading field. The enemy had a passed pawn; we stopped its progress, and now suddenly it appeared that the piece with which we effected this exerted a most unpleasant pressure, and the enemy pawn actually provided a natural defensive position which the blockader could use as an observation post. This conception once grasped was subsequently widened and dematerialized. Widened, because we now classed as weak every square in front of an enemy pawn, whether passed or not, if there were any possibility of our being able to establish ourselves on it without risk of being driven off. But the conception of a weak point was also dematerialized. When, for instance, Dr. Lasker talks of White's weak squares in the position in Diagram 43 (from the game Tartakower—Lasker, Petrograd, 1909) the presence of an enemy pawn as a bulwark for the piece occupying a weak square is certainly no longer a *conditio sine qua non*.

§2c. *The third reason. The crippling induced by a blockade is by
no means local in its nature. The transplanting of the crippling
phenomena to the ground in the rear. On the dual nature of the pawn.
On the pessimistic outlook, and how this can be transformed into the
blackest melancholy.*

In game No. 12, Leonhardt—Nimzowitsch, the White BQB4
blocked Black's PQB3, one of the consequences being that Black's
BQKt2 was held a prisoner in his own camp. This state of affairs
seems to be typical; only, very often, a whole complex of enemy pieces
is sympathetically affected. Large tracts of the board are made
impracticable for any manœuvring of the swifter kind. At times,
too, the whole enemy position takes on a strangely rigid character.
In other words, the crippling effect has shifted from the blockaded
pawn further back to its rear. In Diagram 44 the Black KP and
QP are completely blockaded, and the
whole of Black's position seems be-
numbed. B and R are prisoners in
their own camp, and White, in spite
of his inferiority in material, actually
has winning chances.

Diagram 44

Transplanting the effects of the
blockade to the region in the rear.

The state of affairs here sketched
need not surprise us in the least. We
have often pointed out that any pawn
may be an obstacle in the way of his
own pieces, and that to get rid of him
may often be our dearest wish, as for
instance, if we are planning to open a
file or to free a square for a Kt (see §2a,
p. 39). We see then that the blockade
is not only embarrassing to the pawn itself, but much more so really to
his comrades in arms, the R's and B's. In connexion, by the way,
with the pawn, it is important for the student to appreciate a certain
dual nature which he possesses. On the one hand the pawn, as we
have shown above, is quite willing to commit suicide, while on the
other he clings tenaciously to life, for the presence of pawns, as he
knows, is not only of great importance for the end game, but still
more helps to prevent the establishment of enemy pieces within his
own lines, which but for them might be possible; or to put it otherwise,
prevents the creation of weak points in their territory. The mobility
of a passed pawn, particularly of a centre one, is often the very life-
nerve of the whole position; its crippling must therefore naturally
find its echo throughout the whole of that position. We have seen,
then, that weighty reasons support the establishment of a blockade
at the earliest possible moment, whereas those which seem to tell

against it, namely the apparently uneconomical use made of an officer, seemingly degraded to being a mere sentry (=blockader), will be seen on closer examination to carry weight only in certain cases. To be able to recognize these we must now consider the blockader himself.

§3. *The blockader's primary and secondary functions. The conception of elasticity. Various forms of the same. The strong and the weak blockader. How the blockader meets the many demands made on him, partly on his own initiative; and why I see in this a proof of his vitality.*

The primary function of a blockader is obviously to blockade in a businesslike manner the pawn concerned. In exercising this he has himself a tendency towards immobility. And yet, admire his vitality! he very often displays pronounced activity: (1) by the threats which he can exercise from the place where he is posted (see Game 12, Leonhardt—Nimzowitsch, in which Black's KtK3 prepared the way for P—KKt4), (2) by a certain elasticity which finds expression in the fact that he does on occasion leave his post. He seems to be entitled to a furlough, (a) if the journey promise much in results, when the connexions must all be made by express, so to speak; (b) if he can be sure of returning quickly enough to take up the blockade again on another square, should the pawn have advanced in the interval; (c) if he be in a position to leave a deputy in his place to look after the blockade. It is obvious that such a deputy must be chosen from those pieces which are seconding (protecting) the blockader. This last consideration, for all its apparent insignificance, is of great importance; for it shows clearly the extent to which elasticity, at any rate in the form considered under (c), is directly dependent on the degree of weakness or strength of the blockade.

In connexion with (a) see the end-game Nimzowitsch—Nilsson (Diag. 61).

In connexion with (b) consider the position: White: K, Q1; R, KR4. Black: K, QR1; R, KR1; P's, QKt5, KR4. In this simplest of positions the blockading Rook takes a little holiday trip 1. R×KtP. It goes without saying that the passed pawn will seize the opportunity to advance 1.....P—R5; 2. R—Kt2, P—R6; 3. R—KR2. Master Rook appears in the office, bows to the boss, nods to his fellow employees, and, as if he were fresh as paint and thoroughly rested (though he had to do some bustling to get back in time), takes his seat at his (blockading) desk. He has, however, changed his seat, from R4 to R2. The manœuvre here shown may be found repeated in many an example.

In connexion with (c), see the rôle played by the White B at KB4 in game No. 15, Nimzowitsch—Freymann, White's 26th move.

From the above little discussion (under *a*, *b*, and *c*), we see that elasticity is slight if the pawn to be blockaded is far advanced. The maximum elasticity is on the other hand developed when a half passed pawn in the centre of the board is the object of the Blockader's attentions; in such a position as, for instance: White: Kt, Q4; P's, K3, KB2; Black: B, QKt2; P, Q4. The blockading Kt at Q4 is here very elastic; he can take long journeys from his post and in all directions, and yet not neglect his primary duty which is to prevent the advance of Black's QP. So much on the subject of elasticity. We will now analyse the actual effect of the blockade itself.

§3a. *Effect of the Blockade.*

The forces to maintain a blockade should be developed systematically and of set purpose, whereas elasticity often comes of itself without seeking. The blockading effect is intensified by bringing up supports, which, however, in their turn must be safely stationed. Compare the two Diagrams, 45a and 45b.

The bishop in Diagram 45a will for motives of personal safety

Diagram 45a

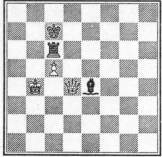

Black to move. Is the R at QB3 a strong blockader?

Diagram 45b

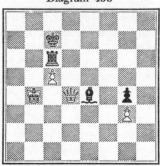

Black to move. Can the blockader hold his own?

migrate to KKt3, though to be sure the blockading Rook will thus lose a powerful support. Nevertheless for the B to play about on the long diagonal is a somewhat risky game, for the eye of the law (QQ4) is upon him. After 1.....B—Kt3 there follows, however, 2. K—Kt5, and now the attempt to restore the abandoned strategical connexion by 2.....B—K1 fails badly after 3. Q—K5 ch, K—Q2; 4. Q×B ch, K×Q; 5. K×R. On the other hand, in Diagram 45b, the B can go to KB6 where he stands safe and cannot be dislodged, and the R at QB3 thus gains so much in importance that a draw seems inevitable. We have shown a similar state of affairs to exist in our study of outposts. In like manner here the blockader derives

his strength, not so much from himself as from his strategical connexion with the country to his rear. A blockader who is insufficiently
or imperfectly protected will not be able to hold his own against the
enemy pieces which are hotly pressing him. He will be put to flight,
and either taken or put out of action; whereupon the pawn whose
road had before been blocked will resume his advance. In connexion
with the problem of the defence, the reader will find the rules which
will be treated in Part II of this book on the over protection of
strategical points extraordinarily valuable. The blockading point
is as a rule a strategically important square, and therefore it is a
part of wisdom to protect it even more than is absolutely necessary.
So do not wait for attacks to pile up, but rather lay up a reserve
of defensive force, just as before a dance one lays up a store of
sleep.

And so a remarkable fact appears, that whilst the effect of the
blockade can only be intensified or even maintained by laboriously
bringing up supports, the other secondary virtues of the blockader,
elasticity, and the threats he can exercise from his post, prove to be of
hard growth; that is to say they come to fulfilment without any
particular exertion on his part (like thistles on stony ground). This
is explicable, (1) by the state of affairs in which a protecting piece
takes the place of the blockader who has gone on his travels; (2)
by the fact that, as explained under 2b, the blockading square tends
to become a weak point for the enemy. Keeping contact with a
strategically important square must according to my system work
wonders. This will be considered in greater detail under position
play.

We can sum all this up in the following principle:—

Though in the choice of a blockader elasticity and the threats he
can exercise must be borne in mind, yet it is often sufficient merely to
strengthen the blockade; elasticity and the rest will then not seldom
come of themselves.

It must now be clear that an officer in no sense compromises his
dignity by answering the summons to act as a blockader, for the post
proves itself to be a most honourable one, safe, yet allowing full
initiative. The student should thoroughly test the truth of this
observation from master-games or games played by himself. He
should compare the blockaders with one another, their respective
merits, their ultimate fate, and how they came to fail or to succeed
in their duty, and he will get more benefit out of a thorough knowledge of one 'actor' than from a nodding acquaintance with the
whole 'troupe'. It is when working under limitations that the
master reveals himself. This true saying applies wholly also to
the aspirant to mastership, indeed to every student who is in
earnest.

§4.   *The fight against the blockader. His uprooting. 'Changez les blockeurs!'   How to get a stand-offish blockader replaced by one who is more affable.*

When we said that the blockader derived his effective strength from his connexion with the country to his rear, this was an indisputable truth; yet he can, and should, contribute something of himself to the protection of the blockading rampart. This he does in that, thanks to his attacking radius, he wards off the approach of enemy troops from himself. It is also a merit in him if his origin be humble, the humbler the better. By this we mean that a blockader should have a thick hide. The rather exaggerated sensitiveness displayed by the King or Queen would ill consort with the rôle of blockader. A minor piece (Kt or B) can stand up to an attack—in case of need he has only to call up aid; whereas the Queen reacts to the slightest attack to such an extent, that she at once, though with head proudly erect, leaves the field. In general the King would also be a poor blockader, but in the end-game his royal attribute of being able to change his colour stands him in good stead; so that if he be driven away from a black blockading square, he can try at the next halting place to establish a blockade on a white square. For instance:—White: K, KKt4; B, Q1; P, KKt5. Black: K, KKt3; Kt, QR2. The check B—B2 ch drives the Black King from Kt3, but now he takes up the blockade again at Kt2.

Since the blockaders as we have seen, may be of varying quality: strong or weak, elastic or inelastic, the obvious thing to do is to get one blockader replaced by another, if this would suit us better. If I take a blockader, the recapturing piece takes over his rôle, and by so doing the command 'changez les blockeurs' becomes a *fait accompli.* The following combination is typical:—In Diagram 46 the opening moves would be 1. R—Kt8 ch, R—B1, and now the attacking range of the B renders difficult the approach of the White K, which would else be decisive. There followed, however, 2. R×B, R×R; 3. K—Kt7. This new blockader, the R at QR1, now shows himself to be an accommodating fellow, and nothing is further from his thoughts than to stay an attempt at approach, so 3.....R—KB1; 4. P—R8=Q, R×Q; 5. K×R, and the pawn end-game is for Black untenable since (Diag. 48) the Black KP's flank will be turned. 5.....K—Kt2; 6. K—Kt7, K—Kt3; 7. K—B6, K—Kt4; 8. K—Q7!, K—B4; 9. K—Q6 and wins. On the other hand 1. R—Kt8 ch, R—B1; 2. K—Kt6? (instead of R×B), B—Q4; 3. K—B7, K—B2; 4. R×R, K×R; 5. K—Kt8 would fail because of 5.....K—B2; 6. P—R8=Q, B×Q; 7. K×B, K—Kt3; and Black wins. In the position shown on Diagram 47 Black would be perfectly safe if his K were not so far away. White makes the more

accommodating Black R take the place of the embarrassing B.   Thus
1. R×B, R×R;   2. K—Kt4, and the White P's become mobile and
the Black K arrives too late.   2.....R—B1;   3. P—Kt6, K—Kt4;
4. P—B5, K—B3;   5. P—Kt7, R—KKt1;   6. P—B6, K—Q3;
7. K—B5, frustrating K—K3, and wins.   The idea is this: The
attacking party is prepared to come to an understanding with the
blockading company, but wishes first to see its apparently rather
unsympathetic spokesman replaced by some one else.   This done,
negotiations may begin!

The 'negotiations', alias the uprooting.

How are these 'negotiations' to be pursued?   Well, we concentrate
as many attacks as possible on the blockader concerned.   The latter

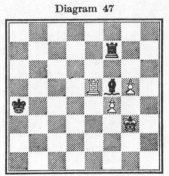

Diagram 46   Diagram 47

From one of my games; the block-   Changez les Blockeurs
ading Bishop at Black's QR1
will be replaced by the Rook

will naturally call up reserves in his support.   In the fight now raging
round the blockader we seek, following the best practice, to bring to
bear a superiority of forces, and this by trying to kill off the defenders
by exchanges, or to drive them away, or otherwise to divert them.
Finally the blockader will have to retire and our pawn can move
forward.   In the end game in the event of a blockade we usually
drive away the blockader's supports, in the middle game on the other
hand we seek to busy them.   A very instructive example of all this
is furnished by my game against von Gottschall, Breslau, 1925.   See
Game No. 13, which the student is advised to study at this point.

§5.   *Frontal attack by the King against an isolated pawn as a kingly
ideal.   The turning movement.   The rôle of leader.   The tripartite
manœuvre, made up of frontal attack, the enemy's forced withdrawal,
and the final turning movement.   The 'reserve' blockading point.   The
superseded 'opposition!'*

Many a stout fellow who has grown grey at chess will gasp at this:
What?   Is the 'opposition' also to be abolished now?   Yes, I am

sorry, but this blow must fall. And first, to get our bearings, let us remark that to conceive the centre arithmetically means counting the pawns standing there, and regarding a numerical majority as giving a guarantee of preponderance. A wholly untenable conception. In reality it is only the greater or lesser degree of mobility which can be counted decisive in passing judgment upon the position in the centre. Now if we look deep enough we find that the opposition certainly has a relationship with the centre 'arithmetically' conceived: and the inner significance of both the one and the other is assessed on purely outward characteristics. In what follows I shall give my entirely new theory, which in eliminating the 'opposition' analyses the inner meaning of what is happening.

In Diagram 48 (right) the creation of a passed pawn by means of P—R3, P—B3, P—Kt4, would not be sufficient to win, since the White K has lagged behind his passed pawn. The K must here play the rôle of leader, something like a pacemaker in a bicycle race, and not stay comfortably at home reading the news from the race track. The student, too, must be fully alive to one point, that the King in the middle game and the same King in the end game are two totally different persons. In the middle game the King is a timid soul, shuts himself up in his fortress (castled-position), and only when he feels himself in contact with his Rook, with his own Knights and Bishops attentively grouped around him, does the old fellow feel himself passing well. In the end game the King changes into a hero (not so difficult after all, as the board is swept almost clean of enemies!), and scarcely is it begun than he leaves his castled home and stalks slowly but imposingly to the centre—clearly to be in the middle of things; but of this more in Chapter VI. He shows, however, particular courage in a fight against an isolated pawn. Such a fight will be started with a frontal attack, as e.g., in White: K, KB4; Black: P, KB4. Such a frontal position is an ideal which the King aims at, and is one in fact well worth striving for, because, given the necessary material, it can be attained, and thus the capture of the beleaguered pawn facilitated, or, in a purely pawn ending, it may lead to the eventual turning of the position.

And so, if fighting forces be still available, the Black PKB4 will be exposed to multiple attacks, which may lead to the protecting

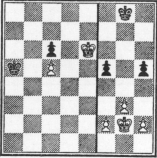

Diagram 48

Right: White wins one of the enemy pawns. Left: White, himself threatened with an enveloping movement, turns the enemy position and wins his objective, the P at QB3. How does he do it?

pieces having to take up less comfortable positions, while if it come to a plain duel between the two Kings with no pieces left on the board, the weapon of exhaustion, *Zugzwang*, will be at the disposal of the attacker. As an example suppose on Diagram 48 (right) a White B at KB1, and a Black B at KB2. After 1. K—B3, K—Kt2; 2. K—B4 (the ideal position), K—B3; there follows 3. B—Q3, B—K3, and the difference in value between the active White B at Q3 and the passive Black B at K3, who is chained to the PKB4, weighs by no means lightly in the scale (see Chapter VI, §2). The purely pawn end game on the other hand would run somewhat as follows:—See Diagram 48 (right) 1. K—B3, K—Kt2; 2. K—B4, K—B3; 3. P—KR4. This is the first stage of the manœuvre. Then comes 3. . . . . K—Kt3, and this is the second stage: the enemy King must willy-nilly go to one side, a direct consequence of the *Zugzwang*. And now follows the third and last stage, namely the White turning movement 4. K—K5 and wins. The frontal attack has developed into a turning movement, an advantage, for an enveloping movement is, as we know, the strongest form of attack (in ascending order: frontal, flank, and enveloping).

Diagram 49

Right: White turns the enemy position. Left: White wins the point QKt5 as a station for his K

That the enveloping attack is very strong in the end game is impressed on us by the examples shown on Diagrams 48 (left) and 49 (right). In the latter there follows 1. K—R6, K—B1; 2. K—Kt6, K—K2; 3. K—Kt7, K—K1; 4. K—B6, K—Q2; 5. K—B7. Notice the tortuous manner of approach of the White K, who works with *Zugswang* as his weapon. In Diagram 48 (left) the continuation is 1. K—Q7!, K—Kt4; 2. K—Q6; but not 1. K—Q6?, because of K—Kt4, and White has no good move left, and is in fact himself in *Zugzwang*, in a straight jacket, shall we say? Or finally take the position: White: K, KR5; P's, QR4, QR5, KB5. Black: K, Q4; P's, QKt2, KB3. 1. K—Kt6, K—K4; 2. P—R6!, P×P; 3. P—R5. Here White sacrificed a P in order to throw the unpleasant duty of moving on to his opponent.

Now that we have seen the significance of the enveloping movement, which, by the way, can only succeed against a stationary object (which in its turn limits the movements of its own King!), it will be intelligible to us why we should go to such trouble, in carrying out this tripartite manœuvre, to bring off this form of attack.

We will now consider this tripartite manœuvre in its three stages

E

in a position where there are no enemy pawns (Diag. 49, left). The
question at issue here is the win of the point QKt5 for the White K.
Why precisely the point QKt5? Because the position of the K at
QKt5 would ensure the advance of the passed pawn as far as QKt6;
for if the K occupies this point, he has only to move to one side, say
to QB5, and the P whom we imagine as having already reached Kt4
will without question reach Kt6. In the same diagram the QKt6
is the first unsafeguarded stage on the pawn's road to Queen; for the
points Kt4, Kt5 are already secured by the KQB4. We therefore
institute a frontal attack on the point QKt5. 1. K—Kt4 (this is the
first stage), 1.....K—R3 or B3 (the forced withdrawal of the K.
This is the second stage); 2. K—B5 or R5 (the third stage, the turning movement completed); and now, as he wished to do, the white K
reaches Kt5. For instance 2.....K—Kt2; 3. K—Kt5!. In the
position now reached (White: K, QKt5; P, QKt3. Black: K,
QKt2), the White King's last move may itself be regarded as a frontal
attack on the next halting place Kt6. The tripartite manœuvre
directed against QKt6 will run an entirely analogous course, namely,
3. K—Kt5, K—R2 or B2; 4. K—B6 or R6, with K—Kt6 to follow.

The application of this method of thought to the defence is still
simpler. In the position, White: K, QB4; P, QKt4; Black: K,
QB3, Black can draw because the White K has lagged behind.
All that Black has to do is to watch that the White K does not assume
the rôle of leader, and next to keep well in mind that after the blockading point, the 'reserve' blockading point is his safest position.
(With a White P on QKt4 Black's QKt4 is his blockading point,
QKt3 his 'reserve' blockading point.) In the position under consideration Black's reply to 1. P—Kt5 ch, is 1.....K—Kt3 (blockade); 2. K—Kt4, K—Kt2 (reserve-blockade); 3. K—B5, K—B2
(but not 3.....K—Kt1 or B1, for that would allow the White K to
gain ground). 4. P—Kt6 ch, K—Kt2 (blockade); 5. K—Kt5,
K—Kt1 (reserve blockade); 6. K—B6, K—B1; 7. P—Kt7 ch,
K—Kt1; 8. K—Kt6 Stalemate.

To avoid any possibility of misunderstanding let us repeat that
with a White P at his QKt6, Black's QKt1 is the reserve blockading
point; if he is at his QKt5 then Black's QKt2 is the reserve point.

In the position, White: K, QB5; P, QKt5; Black: K, QKt2,
1.....K—Kt1 would be a horrible move, for it would leave the whole
field open to the White K and give him the chance of assuming the
rôle of leader. Thus:—1.....K—Kt1??; 2. K—Kt6 with a decisive
frontal attack on the point QKt7 (our tripartite manœuvre).

The theory of the opposition is in its want of clarity only to be
described as obscurative; whereas the truth is so clear. The attacking King fights to get into the lead, his opponent strives to prevent
this with the aid of the 'reserve-blockade point'.

§6. *The privileged passed-pawn: (a) two united, (b) the protected, (c) the more remote. The King as hole-stopper. On preparations for the King's journey.*

As in life, so on the chessboard, the goods of the world are not altogether equally divided, so that there are some passed pawns who have far greater influence than other, ordinary passed pawns. Such 'privileged' passed pawns deserve to be highly regarded by the student, who should never miss an opportunity of creating one for himself. In what follows we shall attempt to explain the effect of these 'privileged' pawns by a consideration of their characteristics, from which rules will be deduced for our direction, the pros and cons in the fight with or against the stout fellows we are going to consider.

(a) The typical ideal position of two united passed pawns is shown on Diagram 50. The relationship between them is one of the truest comradeship, and therefore the position where the two pawns are on the same rank must be regarded as the most natural one.

The strength of passed pawns so placed lies in the impossibility of blockading them; for their position (on KR4, KKt4) seems to rule out any blockade on the squares R5 or Kt5. However the march of events will cause the two passed pawns to give up their ideal position; for though they are, maybe, doing noble work at Kt4 and R4, the innate ambition towards higher things, common to all passed pawns, will drive them forward. And the moment one of them moves, possi-

Diagram 50

The QBP is a protected passed pawn, the KKt and KRP's are two united passed pawns in the ideal position

bilities of blockading them will arise. For instance, after P—R5 Black pieces could blockade them at their Kt4 and R3. From this consideration, coupled with the fact that these united passed pawns can have no dearer wish than to advance together to Kt5 and R5, there follow these rules: The advance of a passed pawn from the ideal position must take place only at a moment when a strong blockade by enemy pieces is impossible of execution; and further: If the proper pawn has advanced at the right moment, any blockade which may be attempted will be weak and easily overcome, his companion must then advance as soon as possible, so as to recover the ideal position.

Accordingly (Diag. 50) at the right moment the proper pawn, say the KtP, will advance (P—KKt5), a move which affords the

enemy the chance of setting up a blockade at his KR4. The blockading piece, which by hypothesis was badly supported (hence the
term 'weak blockade'), will be driven off, and the move P—KR5
will bring about the ideal position again.

Very important service can here be rendered by the White King
stepping into the breach which was caused by the advance of the
first pawn. Thus, in Diagram 50, after say 1. P—KKt5, Kt—R4,
the K, whom we imagine to be at hand, with K—Kt4 will slip into
the breach and close it. The manœuvre here described we shall call
hole-stopping; and our King need never be afraid of being out of
work, for at worst he can get a job as a travelling dentist and stop
cavities!

Diagram 51 shows a position which occurred in a club match in
Stockholm in 1921. White played 1. P—Kt6 ch, and thus allowed
the Black King to establish an absolute blockade at his QKt2;

Diagram 51

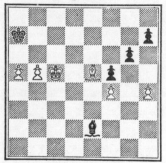

absolute, because from the nature of
things the King can never be driven
away. There followed 2. K—Q6 and
the K wandered to his KKt7 and
refreshed himself with the KRP; but
at that very moment Black played
B—R4, and there was nothing more
for the King to eat on the K side.
Dolefully his Majesty then wandered
back to the other wing, but here, too,
there was nothing for him, since Black's
Bishop, now freed from guarding the P,
made the board unhealthy. A fitting
punishment overtook White for breaking the rules by his advance.
Correct was 1. P—R6, B—Q6; 2. B—Q4, B—B8; 3. K—Kt4 ch!
(plans to stop the hole at R5), K—R1; 4. K—R5, B—K7; 5. P—Kt6.
Everything according to programme: the QRP advanced first, since
the hindrance which can now be put in White's way (blockade is here
almost too strong a term) can be easily brushed aside; the K stops the
hole caused by the advance; the QKtP moves on in his turn, and the
two pals are again united.

Thus like two trusty comrades on a battlefield, they will advance
together, step by step, and it will be but seldom, and then only if far
advanced, that it may happen that one of them will push on alone,
ruthlessly leaving his friend to be slaughtered. Such an exceptional
case is shown in Diagram 52.

(b) The difference in value between a protected and an ordinary
passed pawn is well shown in the following example (Diag. 53)
White opens fire on the enemy's pawn majority. 1. P—QR4,
K—K4; 2. P×P (2. P—QB4? would have been wrong because of

2.....P—Kt5, with a protected passed pawn. The two Kings would then have had the scarcely pleasant job of walking up and down keeping an eye on the pawns, hardly an inspiring occupation for a King!), 2.....P×P; 3. P—B4, P×P (forced, 3.....P—Kt5 would not help, for the White P's would go on to Queen); and now we have got a position which is characteristic of the difference in value between the pawns; for, as is clear, the White K can gobble up the Black passed pawns one after the other without any trouble, whereas the immunity of the protected KBP from any attack by the Black King is brilliantly in evidence. True we have in our day seen how a player of little experience, ignoring this immunity (in the position

Diagram 52

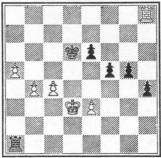

Perlis—Nimzowitsch
Carlsbad, 1911

Black moves. The KKtP shamefully leaves his comrade the KRP in the lurch. He got uppish and forgot the ties of friendship . . . so 1.....P—Kt5!; 2 R×P, P—Kt6 and wins

Diagram 53

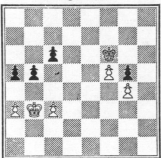

White wins through the difference in value between a protected and an ordinary passed pawn

White: K, QR1; P's, KB5, KKt4. Black: K, K4; P, KKt4), with a pleased grin on his face and flushed with the lust of battle, going after the KKtP. After 1.....K—B5; 2. P—B6, he sees his error and begins in all seriousness to chase the fleeting pawn. The last scene of the comedy runs then thus:—1.....K—B5; 2. P—B6, K—K4!!; 3. P—B7, K—K3!!; 4. P—B8=Q, Resigns. We may formulate the case thus: The strength of a protected passed pawn lies in his immunity from attack by the enemy King.

(c) In Diagram 54 the KRP is the 'remoter' passed pawn (that is more remote from the mid point of the board). After the indirect exchange of the two passed pawns, i.e., after 1. P—R5 ch, K—R3; 2. K—B5, K×P; 3. K×P, the Black King is out of play, the White King on the contrary is well, because centrally, developed. And this is decisive. The remoter passed pawn is therefore a trump card (with great power of causing a diversion), but like any other trump card must be hoarded, not played out too quickly; and this must be our rule. The exchange of pawns which drew off the enemy King, was only the preliminary to the White King's journey which followed (Diag. 54). This journey, however, should be fully prepared for before the pawn advance takes place. Compare the position: White: K, K4; P's, QR4, QB4, KR2. Black: K, Q3; P's, QR4, K4, KKt2. White in the QBP has the remoter passed pawn. His immediate advance would, however, be a mistake; for after 1. P—QB5 ch, K×P; 2. K×P, the King's journey to his Kt7

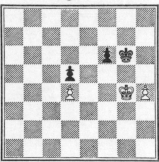

Diagram 54

The more remote passed pawn, whose capture entices the enemy King away from the middle of the board

would be a mere waste of time, for his travelling companion the KRP has been too dilatory. The right move is 1. P—KR4. The travelling companion reports himself! and this induces 1..... P—KKt3. For this obliging advance we have to thank the *Zugzwang* weapon, of which we should make diligent use, particularly in the case of the 'remoter' passed pawn. There now follows 2. P—B5 ch!, K×P; 3. K×P, K—Kt5; and Black arrives one move too late: e.g., 4. K—B6, K×P; 5. K×P, K—Kt6; 6. P—R5, P—R5; 7. P—R6, etc.

Rules to be observed: Prepare for the King's journey before the sacrifice (or exchange) which is to divert the enemy King is made. Make use of the *Zugzwang* weapon whenever possible. Let the travelling companion advance. The impediments to the journey (i.e., enemy pawns on the wing to which the King is to travel) must be enticed forward. All this before the move which is to divert the enemy King out of action is made (Third example, Diag. 58).

§7. *When a passed pawn should advance: (a) on his own account, (b) to win ground for his King who is following him (stopping the holes), (c) to offer himself as a sacrifice to divert the enemy. On the measure of the distance between the enemy King and the sacrifice which is to be offered him as bait.*

It is an old story that the less experienced amateur as a rule lets his passed pawn advance at the very moment least suitable for it. With two united passed pawns we saw him in Diagram 51 play 1. P—Kt6 ch?, and thus allow an iron blockade to be set up. It may therefore be of practical use to note the cases in which an advance is indicated.

We have to ask ourselves: when is a passed pawn ready to march? We shall differentiate three cases.

(a) When the advance brings the passed pawn nearer to its goal (which will only be when there is a weak blockade), or when the advanced passed pawn gains in value in that he will then help to protect important points. (See my game against v. Gottschall, No. 13, where 27. P—Q6 helped to protect the point K7, with the threat Kt or R—K7.) On the other hand it is wrong to push forward a pawn if he can be hopelessly blockaded, and in his new position will only be protecting unimportant points. It is easy to bring a passed pawn into the world, it is a much more difficult thing to provide for his future.

(b) When the advancing passed pawn leaves the ground clear for a following piece, and in particular gives his own King the chance of advancing against a new enemy pawn (Diag. 55, right). The game proceeds: 1. P—B5, K—B2; 2. K—K5, K—K2; 3. P—B6 ch, K—B2; 4. K—B5, K—B1! The KBP has no future to look forward to. 5. K—Kt6 and wins the RP. Here the advance was made simply and solely to drive away the Black King, so that his own King might get near the RP.

(c) When the advance takes place with the intention of sacrificing the pawn, so that the enemy King may be decisively drawn off from the field of battle (Diag. 54). Another example would be the following:—White: K, KKt3; P's, QR4, KR2. Black: K, KR4; P, QR4. Here White's KRP is to be offered as a sacrifice, is to die for King and country. It only remains to decide how and, especially, where. Since the effect of the sacrifice as a diversion varies directly as the distance between the bait to be sacrificed and the enemy King, it would not be advantageous to let the KRP advance, for this distance would become smaller. The right course is rather to play the King at once over to the other wing, thus 1. K—B4, K—R5; 2. K—K5, K—R6; 3. K—Q6, etc. Wholly bad on the other hand would be 1. P—KR4??. (Not content with sacrificing him, he actually serves him up on a platter! Which I should call exaggerated politeness.) After 1. P—R4??, there would follow 1.....K—Kt3; 2. K—B4, K—R4; 3. K—K5, K×P; 4. K—Q5, K—Kt4; 5. K—B4, K—B4; 6. K—Kt5, K—K3; 7. K×P, K—Q2; 8. K—Kt6 (threatening K—Kt7), K—B1; 9. K—R7, K—B2, shutting in the White King and drawing. After 1. K—B4!, K—R5; 2. K—K5, K—R6; his Black Majesty may console himself with the fact that his walk from R4 to R6 has given him an appetite, so that the KRP becomes a pleasant meal after the fatigues of the tour, but this is all the consolation he will get. The student must take this to heart, that though the sacrifice to divert the enemy K is willingly made, it must occur under circumstances which will cause the maximum loss of time to the enemy.

It is not always so easy to recognize the motives of a pawn advance (Diag. 55, left). Play proceeds: 1. P—B5, K—B2; 2. K—Q5, K—Q2; 3. P—B6 ch, K—B2; 4. K—B5, K—B1 (reserve-blockade); 5. K—Q6, K—Q1; 6. P—B7 ch, K—B1; 7. K—B6. The pawn advance seems to be quite unmotived, neither cases *a*, *b*, nor *c*, above, seem to apply; but there follows 7.....P—QR4, for Black is now drawn into a *Zugzwang*; he must send forward his pawn, and with this the curtain rises on an exciting drama.   The Black P goes a double stage, he storms ahead full of energy and youthful arrogance; but we choose rather the quiet 8. P—QR3 as an answer, in order to prove to our youthful opponent that repose is a very valuable trait.   After 8.....P—R5; 9. K—Q6 the game is decided. Suppose

Diagram 55

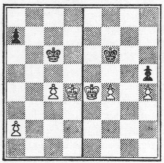

Right: advance of the KBP to gain ground for the following King. Left: an affair of tempi

that our young friend the Black QRP, recalled and soundly scolded for his impetuosity, now goes the modest stage 7. P—QR3. We then demonstrate to the luckless youth that energy is also a trump card, and we play 8. P—QR4. Again after 8.....P—R4; 9. K—Q6 Black is lost. The idea was the following: The stale-mating of the Black King forces an advance of his QRP, and then White's QRP will time his advance to meet him so that after the RP'S have run their course White has the move. The latter then plays K—Q6 or K—Kt6 and wins. This advance of the QBP may therefore be rubricked under (*a*).

He has advanced on his own account, for the affair of the tempi between the QRP's makes of him a winning pawn, who otherwise, remembering the backward position of the White King, could only have been considered as a drawing pawn.

We close this chapter on the passed pawn with some end game studies, reminding the reader that the chapter is to be regarded as an introduction to position play.

§8. *End Games illustrating the passed pawn.*

White (Diag. 56a) had the move and sacrificed the exchange. The whole idea of the combination, throughout its weary length (there's no other phrase to use), lay in the one thought, the King must strive to attain the 'ideal' position, namely frontal attack on an isolated pawn (see §5).   I succeeded in carrying out this hidden plan, although it could have been frustrated, because Rubinstein seemed to be handicapped by being not quite familiar with the postulates of my

system, which were of course well known to me. I know no other
ending in which this struggle of the King to reach the 'ideal' position
is more sharply brought out. The game proceeded:—1. R—K6 ch,
K—Q4; 2. R×B, P×R; 3. P×P (threatening 4. P—QB4 ch,
K×P; 5. P—Kt6, etc.), 3.....P—QB5, and now White took the
KRP, although for it he had to give up his KRP and QKtP. There
followed 4. B×P, R—KR1; 5. B—Kt7, R×P; 6. B×P, K—B4;
7. K—Q2!, the point; all that has happened so far has been simply
and solely to one end, to prepare the road for the K to his KB4
(Diag. 56b). 7.....K×P?, a mistake; Black could have here
prevented the White King's contemplated journey by 7.....R—R3;
8. B—Q4 ch, K×P; 9. K—K3, R—K8 ch; 10. K—B4?, R—K5 ch,
followed by R×B and wins. The student should observe that

<table>
<tr><td>Diagram 56a</td><td>Diagram 56b</td></tr>
</table>

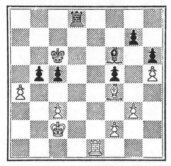 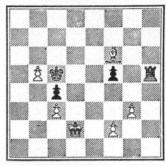

Nimzowitsch—Rubinstein, Breslau 1925

The White King's struggle for a frontal attack on an isolated pawn.
Black missed a win at his 7th move

10. K—B3 (instead of K—B4) would not have saved the game
for White either, since Black would then have played at his leisure
R—K5 and K×QKtP; after which the K would have marched to K8
followed by R—Q7, etc

In the game the continuation was 7.....K×P?; 8. K—K3,
K—B4; 9. K—B4! Now all's right with the world again.
9.....K—Q4; 10. P—KB3, with a draw in a few moves; since the
Black King and Rook cannot both be freed at the same time. If this
were possible a double attack on the QBP with consequent sacrifice
of the exchange would be feasible. An instructive end game. If
you ask why the White King struggled so obstinately for this frontal
attack, the answer is that such a struggle responds to an instinct which
is innate in him; moreover it must be remembered that in his action
he was also obeying the blockade law.

Our second example shows a simple case of a turning movement

(Diag. 57). Black played 1.....K—QB2 (he must do something to meet the threat P—QB3, which would yield a 'remoter' passed pawn), and the end game took the following very simple but effective course:—

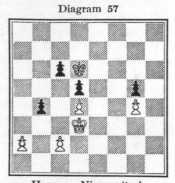

Diagram 57

Hansen—Nimzowitsch
From a simultaneous display
in Randers, Denmark

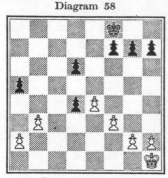

Diagram 58

Tarrasch—Berger

2. P—QB3 (if 2. P—QB4, K—Kt3; 3. P×P, P×P; 4. K—B2, K—R4!; gaining a tempo), 2.....K—Kt3!; 3. P×P, K—Kt4; 4. K—B3, K—R5; and the turning movement comes off to perfection despite the loss of a pawn, a result of the paralysis of White's forces.

The third example illustrates the diversion which can be effected by a remoter passed pawn (Diag. 58). The score of the game up to the exchange of Queens in the 36th move will be found in Game No. 6. There followed then, 37. K—Kt1, K—K2; 38. K—B2, P—Q4; 39. P—K5 (the simpler 39. P×P, K—Q3; 40. K—K2, K×P; 41. P—QR3, K—B4; 42. P—KB4 with eventually the diversion P—QKt4 ch, would also have won easily), 39.....K—K3; 40 K—K2 (40. P—KB4 would be weak because of 40..... P—KKt4; 41. P—KKt3, P×P; 42. P×P, K—B4), 40.....K×P; 41. K—Q3, P—KR4; 42. P—QR3 (P—KR4 first would be preferable), 42.....P—KR5! (creates a chance for himself later on); 43. P—QKt4, P×P; 44. P×P, K—Q3; 45. K×P, K—B3; 46. P—Kt5 ch. (White neglects the *Zugzwang* weapon which lies to his hand. 46. P—KB4 would, after other Black moves had been exhausted, have resulted in an obliging pawn move being made by Black, which would have furthered the subsequent excursion of the White King and the slaughtering of the Black pawns.) 46.....K×P; 47. K×P, K—Kt5!. Now this diversion has less significance than might have been the case, since after the win of the KKtP and KRP Black will only need a few tempi for his KRP to get home. The ending is interesting because of the mistakes which were made. The position was in the end won by White after Black had overlooked a drawing chance.

The fourth example is significant as illustrating the method of advancing united passed pawns. (See §6.) The game proceeded (Diag. 59) 1. P—B6! Here the choice of pawn to be first advanced rests not on the consideration of greater or lesser danger of a blockade, but on the reason that otherwise the QBP would be lost. 1..... Q—Kt3 (if 1..... R×P; 2. P×R, Q×R; 3. R×Q, Kt×Q; then 4. P—B7 with 'passed pawn and 7th rank absolute', see I. iii. §3; for instance 4..... Kt—Q2; 5. Kt—B6 and wins); 2. Q—K3, now the problem is to drive away the blockader·from QKt6 so that the QKtP who has lagged behind a little may catch up his friend. (See §6.) 2..... P—B5 (Kt×BP was threatened); 3. Q—K4, QR—Q1; 4. Kt—B3, R—Q3; 5. P—KR4!, holding the centre strongly (QK4), White intends now to prove that Black's defending pieces are somewhat in the air. 5..... Q—B4. The idea has worked, the blockader is getting more compliant. 6. Kt—K5 (good and pregnant of results would also have been 6. P—R5, Q×P; 7. P—Kt6 and the two comrades are happily united again); 6..... R—Q5 (the main variation would be 6..... R—Q7; 7. Kt—Q3, Q×QBP; 8. P—Kt6!, and heedless of the loss of a piece the pawns would have marched to Queen); 7. Q—K2, Kt×P; 8. P— Kt6 (all according to book!); 8..... R—QKt5; 9. R×R, P×R; 10. P—Kt7, Q—B6; 11. Q—K4, Kt—B4; 12. Kt—Q7, Resigns.

Diagram 59

Nimzowitsch—Alapin
Petrograd, 1913

The fifth example shows how impetuous a passed pawn can become. We do not as a rule regard him as being temperamental, yet knowing his ambitious nature this example will hardly surprise us (Diag. 60.) There followed: 1. P—KKt4, B×P; 2. P×P ch, K—B2. The King is here a bad, because a sensitive blockader. The danger of mate makes his blockading effect illusory. 3. B—Q5 ch! (in order to give the Rook an effective range, without loss of time; the latter will now support the passed pawn with all his might), 3..... P×B; 4. Q×R ch, K×Q; 5. P—B7 ch, K—B1. The last attempt at a blockade. But now one of our supports, the QB, comes to life (P—B7 had lengthened his diagonal), and calls attention to himself in most unpleasant fashion. 6. B—Kt7 ch!, K×B; 7. P—B8=Q mate. This end game illustrates most pointedly the ambition of a passed pawn.

The sixth example (Diag. 61) is characteristic of an elastic blockade. This end game was fully discussed in *Die Blockade*, so that we shall

here only consider the more important points. White intends
operations in the KB file, which he could start by K—Kt3, R—KB1.
The breaking-through point, KB6, he will open by P—KR4—R5—R6,
and for this reason the White King's presence on the K side is
required. In spite of the fact that the KB file controls the whole
game, White had the courage to withstand the impulse to exploit
it, and calmly played 1. R—R5!!, only taking up the fight in the KB
file later. The blockade by the RR5 is here possible, because the
blockader is elastic, that is to say he can at any moment be brought
over to the K side by forced marches.

The game proceeded as follows: 1.....K—B3; 2. K—Kt3,
K—Kt2; 3. R—KB1, K—B3; 4. R—B5, R—K2; 5. P—R4,
R(R)—R2; 6. P—R5, R—K3; 7. R—B8. The break through,

Diagram 60   Diagram 61

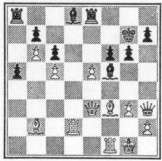 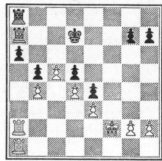

Nimzowitsch—Amateur
Nuremburg, 1904
White without QKt. The
triumph of the KP

Nimzowitsch—A. Nilsson
Northern Masters'
Tournament, 1924

and still the R stands at R5 keeping guard! faithful, motionless.
But the motionless watcher is prepared to intervene at any moment,
whether by R—R2—KB2 (proving his elasticity), or by R × RP,
if the Black Rook should move away. The possibility of R × RP,
it may be noted, should be classed under the threats exercisable from
the blockading point. There followed 7.....P—KKt3; 8. P—R6,
P—Kt4; 9. R—QKt8, K—B2; 10. R × QKtP, R × RP; 11. R—R4,
R—KB3; 12. R(Kt5)—R5, K—B1; 13. K—Kt4, P—R3; 14. R—R2,
R(QR)—KB2; 15. R × P, and won after a further 7 moves.

With this example we have suddenly found ourselves among the
blockaders. The reader is asked to loiter for a while in this mixed company and to turn to game Nos. 14 and 15. We know that a blockader
ought: (a) to blockade, (b) to threaten, (c) to be elastic, and we shall in
No. 14, be introduced to one who performs his manifold duties to perfection, while No. 15 provides an interesting counterpart to this game.

CHAPTER V

ON EXCHANGING

A short chapter whose purpose is to make clear the possible motives for exchanging.

In order to show the student the danger lurking in indiscriminate bartering, we propose to enumerate the cases in which an exchange seems to be indicated. If an exchange does not come under one or other of these it is bad. With the master the process of exchange is almost automatic. He holds files or safeguards his command of a strategically important point, and the opportunity of exchanging drops like a ripe fruit into his lap. Cf. Game No. 11. Note to the 35th move.

In Chapter I we analysed the 'exchange with consequent gain of tempo'. Again we often exchange in order not to be forced to retire, or to make time-losing defensive moves (liquidation with subsequent development). Both cases are in the last resort to be regarded as tempo-combinations, though in fact the question of tempo plays an essential part in every exchange. A salient instance is the exchange of a newly developed piece for one which has wasted several tempi. In the middle-game the tempo motif finds expression when:

(1) We exchange in order to seize (or open) a file without loss of time. A very simple example. In the skeleton position:—White: R, K1; B, K4. Black: K, KKt1; B, QKt6; Kt, QB3; P's, QKt2, KB2, KKt2, KR2. White wants to seize (or open) a file, in order to be able to give mate in the 8th rank. If to this end he play 1. B—B3 or R—QR1, Black would have time to take steps against the mate, e.g., K—B1 or P—KKt3. The right course is to exchange, 1. B × Kt. Black has no time to protect the mate, for he must retake; and this 'must' may also be taken in the psychological sense.

(2) We destroy a defender by exchanging. We destroy him, that is to say, because we look on him as a defender. In the previous chapters we have made the acquaintance of defending pieces whose functions varied: pieces which protect a pawn obstructing the road in an open file; pieces which stand by to aid a blockader, and pawns which help to protect an outpost, etc. The destruction of any one of these is in every single case worth striving for. But by a 'defender' we mean something much wider. A stretch of territory can also be defended, as for instance entry to the 7th rank, or a possible enemy approach can be warded off; as in game No. 14 (q.v.) where the

KtK3 'protects' the points KKt4, KB5 against a possible Q—KKt5 or R—KB4.   Further it is well known that a Kt at KB3 defends the whole castling wing (preventing, e.g., Q—KR5).   So, too, in the case of a centrally posted blockading piece, e.g., in the position: White: Kt, Q4; P's, K3, KB3, KKt3, KR3.   Black: B, K2; P's, Q4, KB2, KKt2, KR2, the attacking radius of the Kt protects and safeguards for White a wide terrain, so that this KtQ4 is also to be considered a 'defender' in our sense.   The rule therefore runs:—Every defender in the narrower or wider sense of the word must be regarded as an object of our destructive wrath.   In Diagram 62 where White wins by a series of exchanges, both kinds of motives are exemplified.   A glance at the position reveals a Black KtKR7 who has more or less gone astray, and his defender the BQKt1.   We play 1. P×P (opening a file without loss of tempo), 1.....P×P;   2. R—K8 ch (the R

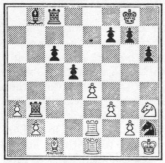

Diagram 62

Series of Exchanges illustrating cases 1 and 2

at QB1 is a defender of the 8th row and must therefore die), 2..... R×R; 3. R×R ch, K—R2;   4. R×B (the arch defender is now fallen), 4..... R×R;   5. K×Kt and wins.

(3) We exchange in order not to lose time by retreating.   We are here as a rule concerned with a piece which is attacked.   If we are faced with the choice whether to withdraw the piece with loss of tempo, or to exchange him for an enemy piece, we choose the latter alternative, especially if we can use to advantage the tempo we have saved ourselves by not withdrawing the piece. The question of tempo must therefore be an actual one in some form or other.   The simplest example would be: White: K, QKt1; R, QKt3; Kt, Q2; P, KB3.   Black: K, KR1; B, KB3; Kt, QKt3; P's, QR2, QR4.   1. Kt—K4, P—R5 (a counter attack);   2. R×Kt (to save a tempo) P×R;   3. Kt×B; and wins.   If a major piece on each side be attacked we have a special variety of this third case and we call it:—

3a. 'Selling one's life as dear as possible.'   In the position: White: K, KR2;   Q, QKt2;   P's, QR2, K5, KR3.   Black: K, QKt1;   Q, Q3;   Kt, QKt2;   P, QR5; the second player plays 1.....P—R6. White is prepared to exchange Q against Q; but if his Q is really condemned to death, the wish to sell her life as dearly as possible is surely very intelligible.   Like the soldier who is hemmed in on all sides, is ready to die, but carries on till his last cartridge is gone, wanting to account for as many enemies as possible, to sell his life dear, in fact; so White plays 2. Q×Kt ch!, in order to get at any rate something for the Queen.   For some extraordinary reason such a commercial investment of the Q is less intelligible to the beginner than a thorough-going heroic sacrifice. The latter is of common occurrence with him (though perhaps not the sacrifice of the Queen, since for her he has the most abject respect), whereas the former is quite foreign to him. Yet it is really no sacrifice, or at worst only a temporary one, and possibly it is in this amalgamation of sacrifice and sober conservation of material that lies the psychological difficulty, under which the beginner succumbs.

4. When and how exchanges usually take place.

Lack of space forbids a detailed discussion of this question, and we will only quite shortly point out that (a) Simplification is desirable if we have superiority in material. Whence it follows that exchanging can be used as a weapon to force the opponent from strong positions.

(b) When two parties desire the same thing a conflict arises. In chess this conflict takes the form of a battle of exchanges. For instance: White: Kt, K4; P's, KB3, KKt2, KR2; supported by BQB2, and RK1, and several other pieces. Black: P's, K4, KKt2, KR2; Kt, KB3; B, KKt3; RK1; etc. The key point is White's K4. White protects and over-protects the point with every means in his power. Black seeks to clear it, since a White piece on the latter's K4 is an annoyance to him on account of its attacking radius. And in the end it comes to a great slaughter at this point (White's K4).

(c) If we are strong in a file, a simple advance in that file is sufficient to bring about an exchange, for our opponent cannot suffer an invasion of his position, and at worst must seek to weaken it by exchanges.

(d) There is a tendency for weak points, or weak pawns to be exchanged, the one for the other (=exchange of prisoners). The following end game illustrates this (Diag. 63). The game proceeded:—31.....R—QR1; 32. R—QKt3, R × P; 33. R × P. The weak pawns at QR2 and QKt5 respectively have been reciprocally exchanged and have disappeared, and the same happens to the pawns Q5 and QKt2. 33..... R—R4; 34. R × QKtP, R × QP; 35. R— Kt8 ch! The simple exploitation of the

Diagram 63

Dr. Bernstein—Perlis, 1909

QKt file leads to the desired exchanges. 35.....Q × R; 36. Q × R ch, K→R1. As Dr. Lasker rightly pointed out, it would have been better to manœuvre the K to KB3. 37. P—QKt3, and Bernstein won by means of his QKtP, a brilliantly conducted end game.

We close this chapter with two end games. Diagram 64 shows the position in a game between Rosselli (White) and Rubinstein after

White's 21st move. There followed:—21.....R×R, else White had doubled his Rooks; moreover Black had really no other sensible move. 22. B×R, Kt—K1; 23. R—K2, Kt—Kt2; 24. B—Q2, Kt—B4!; 25. R—K1, P—QB4; 26. P×P, B×P. Now White's Q4 has become the centre of interest, and a battle will take place round it. 27. K—B1, P—KR5; 28. P×P, P—Kt5; 29. Kt—Q4!, B×Kt; 30. P×B. (See the last note.) 30.....R×P; 31. B—B3, R—R8 ch; 32. K—K2, R—R7; 33. R—KKt1, Kt—R5; 34. P—KKt3, Kt—B4; 35. P—QKt3, K—K3; 36. B—QKt2, P—QR3; 37. B—B3, Kt—Q3; 38. K—K3, Kt—K5; 39. B—K1. After some fruitless attempts by Rubinstein in the QB file the following position was reached after White's 55th move; White: K, Q3; R, KB1; B, QR5; P's, QR4, QKt3, Q4, KB2, KKt3. Black: K,

Diagram 64

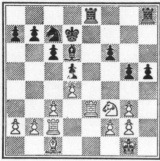

Rosselli—Rubinstein, 1925

Diagram 65

Nimzowitsch—Druwa
Riga, 1919

KKt3; R, K2; Kt, K5; P's, QR3, QKt4, Q4, KB4, KKt5; and the decisive break through took place with 55.....P—B5!; 56. P×P, R—KR2; 57. B—Q2, Kt×B! (kills the defender of White's KB2 and KB4); 58. K×Kt, R—R6; 59. P—B3, P×P; 60. R—B2, K—B4; 61 K—K3, K—Kt5; 62. P—QKt4. (If 62. P—B5, then 62.....K×P; 63. R×P ch, R×R; 64. K×R, P×P; 65. P×P, P—R4; and a successful turning movement against White's K will follow.) 62.....R—R8; 63. P—B5, R—K8 ch; 64. K—Q3, R—K5 and White resigned.

After this classic ending from a tournament game let us give one from a game at odds played in a coffee house, in which the exchange motif took an original shape (Diag. 65). White, who had given the trivial odds of Q for a Kt, 'risked' the break-through 1. P—Q5. There followed 1.....P×P (safer was Kt×QP), 2. P—K6, BP×P (he should have castled); 3. Kt—K5 (here we have the typical advance at the cost of self destruction; the Kt is the 'awakened rear-rank man'), 3.....Kt×P; 4. B—R5 ch, K—K2; 5. Kt×B ch!, a surprise, who would ever expect an exchange in the midst of a pursuit of the enemy?! 5.....P×Kt; 6. R—B7 ch, K—Q3; 7. Kt×Kt ch, P×Kt; 8. R—Q1 ch. Now the meaning is clear: the BB3 was a defender, because of the possibility of B—Q4 at this moment, 8.....K—K4; 9. B—B4 ch, K—K5; 10. B—B3 mate!

CHAPTER VI
THE ELEMENTS OF END GAME STRATEGY

Some General Introductory Remarks

IT is a well-known phenomenon that the same amateur who can conduct the middle game quite creditably is usually perfectly helpless in the end game. One of the principal requisites of good chess is the ability to treat both middle and end game equally well. True, it lies in the nature of things that the student should gather his first experience in the opening and middle game, but this evil, for such it is, must be rectified as early as possible. It should be pointed out to the beginner at the very start, that the end game does not merely serve up untasty fragments left over from the rich feast of the middle game. The end game is on the contrary that part of the game in which the advantages created in the middle game should be systematically realized. Now this realization of advantages, particularly those of an immaterial kind, is by no means a subordinate business. Very much the reverse, all the player's qualities as man and as artist are demanded for it. In order to know, and to be able to appreciate, what is happening in the end game, one must be acquainted with the elements out of which it is compounded, for the end game has its elements just as much as has the middle game. One of these elements, the passed pawn, we have already analysed thoroughly; there remain to be considered:—1. Centralization; with a sub-section on the management of the King, i.e., the 'shelter' and 'bridge-building'. 2. The aggressive Rook position and the active officer in general. 3. The rallying of all isolated detachments. 4. The combined advance, and finally 5. an element already touched upon, the materialization of files; to be understood in the sense that the file, which at first exercised an abstract influence, is narrowed down to a concrete point (protected by a pawn), or gains a concrete aspect. The end game would, in fact, be in itself most interesting, even had Rinck and Troitzky never lived.

§1. *Centralization.* (a) *Of the King,* (b) *of the minor pieces,* (c) *of the Queen. The journey to the King's castle.*

(a) The great mobility of the King forms one of the chief characteristics of all end game strategy. In the middle game the King is a mere 'super', in the end game on the other hand—one of the 'principals'. We must therefore develop him, bring him nearer to the fighting line. This is brought about by centralizing the King.

66

Accordingly the rule runs:—When the end game is entered let the King set himself in motion, and strive to reach the centre of the board, for from this point he can, according to need, make for the right or left, i.e., attack the enemy King or Queen's wing.

1st Example. White: K, KKt1; Black: R, K1 (only the most important actors are indicated) 1. K—B2, pushing towards the centre and at the same time protecting his base (the points K1, K2) against the entry of the enemy Rook by R—K7 or K8.

2nd Example. White: K, KKt1; R, Q2; P's, QKt2, KB4, KKt3, KR2. Black: K, KKt1; R, QKt6; P's, QKt2, KKt2, KR2. Here, too, the first moves are K—B2—K2, and in this position White chooses the Q side and plays K—Q1—QB2, thus protecting the QBP and releasing the R; who can now undertake something, say by R—Q7.

3rd Example. In Diagram 66 White played 33. Kt—B3, since the immediate centralization of the King would have miscarried because of B—Q4. For instance 33. K—B1, B—B5 ch; 34. K—K1, B—Q4, and forces the exchange of pieces or the win of a pawn. After 33.....B—B5; 34. P—B4, K—K2; 35. K—B2, K—Q3; 36. K—K3, K—B4; the proper moment for White to get in touch with the point Q4 was passed. If the K's had been at Q4, Q3, respectively, the win would have been much harder; the game, however, now plays itself. 37. P—KKt4, K—Kt5. This is the point; the central position QB4 is to be regarded as a stepping stone to an attack on the wing, and therein lies the significance of centralization. 38. K—Q4—too late. 38.....

Diagram 66

Rubinstein—Nimzowitsch
Carlsbad, 1907

The struggle of the Kings for
the centre square

B—QKt6; 39. P—Kt5, P—R5; 40. Kt—Kt1, B—K3; 41. P—Kt3, K—Kt6; 42. Kt—B3, P—R6; 43. K—Q3, P—Kt3; 44. K—Q4, K—B7!; 45. Resigns. In this Example we have been able to look at this advance to the centre from another side; and we have seen that it is meant not only to give our own King freedom to move about, but also to restrict the terrain accessible to the enemy King. For this reason the King will often fight for a point, as if a kingdom depended on it. The student should bear this carefully in mind, that he must leave no means untried to bring his King as near the centre as possible, partly for his own King's sake, but partly also in order to limit the scope of the enemy King, who must not be allowed a place in the sun.

(*b*) Centralization must not be regarded as a purely royal prerogative. The other pieces also develop a similar tendency. Take the position, White: K, K1; Kt, QKt3; P's, QR5, K2, KB2, KKt3, KR2. Black: K, KB1; B, KKt3; P's, QR3, Q3, KB2, KKt2, KR2. Here White has two choices: K—Q2—B3—Q4, and Kt—Q4 followed by P—K3. As in the previous example, the centralization of the Kt has here a double effect: (1) He keeps, from Q4, an eye on both wings. (2) He circumscribes the liberty of the enemy King, bars, for instance, his journey via K3 to Q4. If the enemy Rook be still on the board he will provide a rampart for his own King, who will take up a central position behind the Knight. Dr. Tartakower, the witty author of *Die hypermoderne Schachpartie* would call this an island of pieces; and a very simple example is one which would

Diagram 67

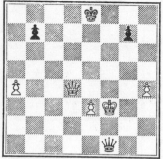

The centrally placed Q, protected and protecting, allows the White K to journey into enemy country. His goal will be QKt6 or KKt6 with a frontal attack on an isolated P

Diagram 68

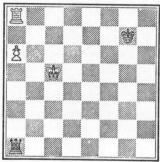

The shelter

result from the position, White: K, K2; Kt, QB2; P's, K3, KB2, KKt2, KR3. Black: K, KB1; R, Q1; P's, KB2, KKt2, KR2, namely by 1. Kt—Q4, followed by K—Q3 with the central island K, Kt, P.

(*c*) There is no more impressive proof of the importance of centralization than the fact that even the Q, who in truth exerts sufficient influence even if posted on the edge of the board, herself seeks to attain to a central position. The ideal one would be a centrally placed Q defended by a P, and in her turn defending other pawns. Under such a protectorate her King can undertake long journeys into enemy country. So for example the KKB3 in Diagram 67 will try to get to QKt6 or KKt6. After many and long wanderings he arrives at length on one of these squares, reaches safety, and wins (Diag. 79).

§1a. *How his Majesty manages to protect himself against storms. The shelter. Bridge building.*

In order to have protection from the various dangers which may threaten, let the King provide himself in good time with a serviceable shelter. Such a refuge will stand him in good stead should a storm come up. Consider the position in Diagram 68. Here 1. P—R7 would be an obvious mistake; for after 1.....R—R7; 2. K—Kt6 (to free the R), the White King would have no protection against the storm, here the series of checks by the R, to which he is exposed. The right course would be to consider the point QR7 as a shelter for the K, thus: 1. K—Kt6, R—Kt8 ch; 2. K—R7, R—Kt7; 3. R—QKt8, R—QR7; 4. R—Kt6, R—R8; 5. K—Kt7. The sun is shining again now, so the old King can venture out. 5.....R—R8; 6. P—R7 and wins.

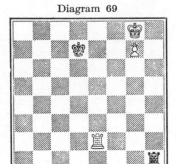

Diagram 69

Bridge building

Events would take a similar course in the position, White: K, K5; R; KKt1; P, Q5. Black: K, Q1; R, QR7. Here the point Q6 would be the shelter, so this must not be made impracticable by P—Q6. The right move is 1. K—K6, and if 1.....R—K7 ch; then 2. K—Q6 and Black has exhausted his checks, and is himself in danger since his K will be forced away from the queening square.

End game technique demands of us in addition that we should be able ourselves to build our own shelter, somewhat as the Boy Scout builds his tent. In this bridge-building is useful (Diag. 69). If White play K—B7, there will follow a series of checks, and in the end the White K will have to return whence he came, his purpose unaccomplished. The Key move is 1. R—K4!, one which at first sight is somewhat incomprehensible. There follows 1.....R—KKt8, and now the King may venture forth into the light of day again. 2. K—B7, R—B8 ch; 3. K—Kt6, R—Kt8 ch; 4. K—B6!, R—B8 ch; 5. K—Kt5!, R—Kt8 ch; 6. R—KKt4!. The bridge is built, the point KKt5 is become a perfect shelter. After 4. K—B6!, Black could also have marked time; thus: 4.....R—Kt7 (instead of R—KB8 ch), and then there follows a delicious operation, which every bridge-builder must envy. We transport in fact the whole bridge, with all that pertains to it, from one place to another; and move 5. R—K5!! and set up the bridge by means of R—KKt5; so that our shelter will now be at KKt6. This charming device belongs to the commonest of everyday manœuvres, a proof of the wonderful beauty of chess.

It will be interesting to see whether 1. R—K5 at once might not
serve. This as a matter of fact is the case, 1. R—K5 also wins;
though indeed less convincingly than the 'author's solution',
1. R—K4. After 1. R—K5 there would follow 1.....K—Q3;
2. K—B7, R—KB8 ch; 3. K—K8 (not K—Kt6 because of
3.....K×R; 4. P—Kt8=Q, R—KKt8 ch; etc.), 3.....R—KKt8;
4. R—K7, R—QR8; 5. R—Q7 ch, and wins; or 4.....R—KKt7
(instead of R—QR8); 5. K—B8, R—KKt8; 6. R—KB7, and wins.
Bridge-building for the provision of a shelter for the royal traveller is
a typical constituent in end game strategy, and is very closely connected with the manœuvre which will be treated in §3. For another
example of bridge-building see game No. 10, where 38. Kt—KB5
creates a shelter for the White King at KB3.

§2. *The aggressive Rook position as a characteristic advantage in
the end game. Examples and argument. The active officer in general.
Dr. Tarrasch's formula.*

The advantage of an aggressive Rook position in the end game is a.
most important one. See Diagram 70a (left). In this position,
assuming that both players still have pawns remaining on the King's
wing, the position of the White R can be made the basis of an advance on the K's side. Still more is this the case in the configuration
shown on Diagram 70b. White can by means of 1. P—KR4

Diagram 70a

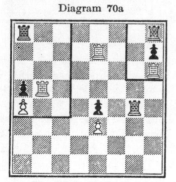

Diagram 70b

The White R has the aggressive, the Black R the passive position

followed when convenient by P—R5 and P×P lay bare Black's
KKtP to attacks. And whereas the White R is the very soul of this
new operation, the Black R cannot muster up sufficient elasticity to
get over to the K side to oppose a defence against the former's attack.
And so we formulate the matter thus:—The weakness of the defending
Rook lies in its deficient elasticity in the direction of the other wing,
and, further, in this too, that the enemy King wins greater manœuvring

freedom (as a rule he is afraid of Rooks, but when the cat's away, etc.!). In Diagram 70b, therefore, the threat of the White King's march to QKt6 (naturally by slow stages) is on no account to be underestimated.

It is of daily occurrence in games between masters that one of the parties will undertake extended manœuvres and go to immense trouble, simply in order, as a reward for all his pains, to get for himself the aggressive Rook position; that is to say to force a passive rôle on the enemy Rook.   On the other hand we must expect the passive Rook sometimes to go on strike; as happens in the following example. White: K, KKt1;   R, QB5;   P's, QR4, KKt2, KR2.   Black: K, KKt1;   R, QKt2;   P's, QR4, KKt2, KR2.   Black with the move begs to be excused from the passive rôle intended for his Rook (1.....R—QR2) and plays 1.....R—Kt7!;   2. R×P, R—QR7.

The Black Rook is now very mobile and the draw ought to be assured, whereas 1.....R—QR2 would probably have lost. We may then say, that if faced with the choice of protecting a pawn with a Rook and of thus condemning him to a passive, indeed meditative existence, or of sacrificing the pawn without further to-do, in order to employ the Rook in some active capacity, we should decide on the latter alternative.

When is a Rook's position, taken in regard to his own or an enemy passed pawn, to be considered as aggressive?

This question has already been answered by Dr. Tarrasch, whose ex-

Diagram 71

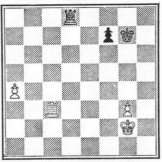

White to play should make the aggressive R move. Black with the move should find the most enterprising rook position

cellent formula runs:—The Rook's proper place is behind the passed pawn, whether it be his own or an enemy one (Diag. 71). White with the move plays 1. R—QR3 . . . taking up his position behind the passed pawn. The Rook's influence is enormous for he breathes into the passed pawn some of his own life. On the other hand, if it were Black's move, he must not post his Rook in front of the pawn, i.e., not 1.....R—QR1?; 2. R—QR3 and White wins, but on the contrary behind it, and this he can do by 1.....R—Q7 ch; 2. K—B3, R—QR7. The Rook position thus gained is aggressive (1) with regard to the White KKtP, who, if opportunity serve, may be gobbled up; (2) having regard to a possible journey of the White King. For instance, should the latter reach his QR6 Black can shut him in by R—QKt2, or should he venture to QKt8 or QB8, subject him to a series of checks from behind.

It is not only in the case of Rooks but also in that of minor pieces that the difference in value between an attacking or defending piece weighs heavily in the balance. The weakness of a defending Kt lies in the fact that he is uni-operative, he cannot move about and still keep up the defence of the point under his charge. This characteristic favours the *Zugzwang*. In Diagram 72 Black with the move will succumb under *Zugzwang*. White with the move, on the other hand, suffers only in appearance from a similar disease, for the agile White Kt can develop all manner of threats. White plays 1. Kt-K3 (or 1. K—Q5 with the threat Kt—K5) and the *Zugzwang* weapon is again at Black's throat. If the whole position were moved back one row, i.e., White: K, K4, etc., Black: K, K3, etc., White would still win.

In a defending Bishop, one characteristic stands out, that in the capacity to change front quickly he cannot compete with his attacking

Diagram 72

The weakness of the Kt as a defender often leads to *Zugzwang*

Diagram 73

colleague. This is brought out in the delightful winning attack in the position on Diagram 73.

The Black B is here defending, and the White B threatens to get to QKt8 via KR4, KB2, and QR7. It looks indeed as if this threat can be comfortably parried by a timely K—QR3. Thus: 1. B—R4, K—Kt4!; 2. B—B2, K—R3!; and if now B—R4 with the threat B—Q8—B7, the Black K can get back to B3 in plenty of time. White, however, plays 3. B—B5! (in order to cause the Black B to make a move, and at the same time to prevent B—Q3), 3.....B—Kt6. Now White's B goes back to get within range of QB7, thus 4. B—K7, K—Kt3!; 5. B—Q8 ch, K—B3; 6. B—R4!, and Black will no longer have time for the saving manœuvre K—Kt4—R3 which he used before, for White has managed to gain a move; so 6.....B—R7; 7. B—B2, and White wins by B—R7—Kt8, e.g., 7.....B—B5; 8. B—R7, B—R7; 9. B—Kt8, B—Kt8; 10. B—B4, B—R2; 11. B—K3. A lovely ending.

§3. *The rallying of isolated detachments and the general advance.*

Since these two manœuvres are very closely connected, so that the one often merges insensibly into the other, they will here be considered together. To bring single scattered detachments into contact with one another cannot be difficult; one has only to know the bearing one piece has on the other. We know several things; for instance that a Kt is able cunningly to construct a shelter for the King by building a bridge; we know, too, that this officer does not despise the hospitality of a private soldier (Kt protected by a P), and in gratitude is ready to draw his sword if it comes to defending his humble friend from one of his own class, or to an onslaught on an enemy pawn. See in this connexion the White Kt at KB5 in game No. 10 (38th move). We know further that a King stops the holes made by the advance of his own pawns. And we must not forget that a centrally posted Q can gather far off pawns into her net (Diag. 67). The contact between the White pieces in the position K, KB3; R, KB4; P's, KKt3, QR4 would be by no means bad.

Again the advance must be a collective one. For a passed pawn suddenly to run wild and rush away from his protectors and friends, as happened say in Diagram 52, is an absolute exception to the rule, which may be stated thus:—The advancing pawn must stay in close contact with his own people. The place vacated by the advance of a pawn must be as quickly as possible taken by a 'hole stopper'. Thus the square K4 left vacant by P—K5 should speedily be occupied by say Kt—K4 or K—K4. Instances could be multiplied.

It happens sometimes that an enemy Rook by annoying checks seeks to disturb a combined play, in which case he must be reduced to impotency or driven home. See game Post—Alekhine, Diagram 78.

Combined play forms 80 per cent. of the whole of end game technique; and the details which we have treated, such as centralization, bridge-building, the shelter, hole-stopping, are all subordinate to one end, combined play. Like a ratchet wheel in a piece of clock work, they see to it that the mechanism gets into motion, they intend to insure a slow but safe forward movement of the serried ranks of the army. A general advance is the order of the day.

The student should note that a 'centralization' is possible even on a remote flank. The pieces simply have to group themselves round a pawn as centre, and there can be no question but that 'centralization' is effectively carried out. See again the game Post—Alekhine, Diagram 78.

§4. *'Materialization' of the abstract conception of file or rank. An important difference between operations in a file in the middle and end game.*

A curious and by no means obvious difference must now be noted. In the middle game the exploitation of a file involves the expenditure of a great deal of energy, in other words is wholly active. We have only to remember the complicated apparatus used: for instance, in particular, the outpost Knight. In the end game, on the other hand, such operations run on simple lines, are in fact of the meditative order. Far and near not a trace of a Kt outpost. The lucky possessor of the file takes his time. At the most he sends forward a handful of men to clean up some position for his advancing Rook. And so we can say that operations in a file are in the middle game active, in the end game meditative, contemplative if you will. And the same applies to a rank. We will illustrate this by some examples (Diag. 74). White holds the clear 5th rank, and by the following simple series of moves manages to materialize the rather abstract effect of his possession of this rank, that is to say to condense it to a concrete point. The game proceeded: 42. R—B6 ch, K—Q2,

Diagram 74

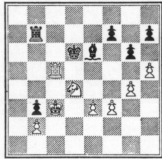

Nimzowitsch—Jacobsen, 1923
'Materialization' of the 5th rank

Diagram 75

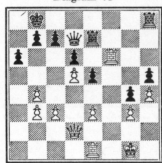

Capablanca—Martinez
Argentina, 1914

43. P×P!, RP×P; 44. Kt×B!, P×Kt; 45. R—B5 followed by R—KKt5 and P—KB4. The occupation of the point KKt5 is decisive, the more since the passive Black R will be forced by sympathy to the move R—KKt2.

Another example is furnished by my end game against Alan Nilsson (Diag. 61). Here scarcely a thing took place, at most the White KRP made a gesture of wishing to advance, and yet the White R succeeded in penetrating to the 8th rank.

The course of the game in the following position is also typical. White: K, KKt5; R, QB1; P's, QR2, QKt2, Q4, KB4. Black: K, KKt2; R, Q2; P's, QR2, QKt2, KB4, KKt3. White calmly goes for a 'walk'; P—QKt4, P—QR4, P—Kt5, P—R5, P—Kt6, and finally R—QB7. If this threat be parried by P—QKt3, then the move R—B6 is made possible. So, too, reverting to Diagram 70b, after the advance of KRP, etc., the 6th rank was condensed into the concrete point KKt6.

In the position shown on Diagram 75 in which White commands the KB file, and Black tries to defend his 1st and 2nd ranks, Capablanca won almost automatically by the mere deadweight of the file. 27. QR—KB1, KR—K1;   28. P—K4, Q—QKt4;   29. R—QR1! White takes his time, the KB file must in the end crush the opposition by its own weight.   29.....Q—Q2 (the threat was 30. P—QB4, Q—Kt3 ch;   31. P—B5, Q—Kt4; and the Q is quaintly trapped); 30. P—B4, R—KB2;   31. R×R, Q×R;   32. R—KB1, Q—KKt2; 33. R—B5, R—KB1;   34. Q—Kt5! winning a pawn. 34.....Q—R1; 35. Q×RP, Q×Q;   36. R×Q, R—B6;   37. K—Kt2, R×QKtP; 38. R—B5, and Black resigned since the KRP could not be stopped. E.g., R—Kt7 ch, R—B2, etc.

§5.   The moral application of this for the student may be thus formulated. If in the end game a file is in your permanent possession, do not worry about an eventual breaking through point, this will come of itself, almost without any assistance on your part.

We will now give a few end games exemplifying the four elements of end game strategy.

1st Example (Diag. 76).   With 20. B—B5!, Kt×Kt;   21. B×B, R×B;   22. P×Kt, O—O;   23. P×P, P×P;   24. Q×P ch, Q—B2; 25. Q×Q ch, R×Q;   26. B×P, White passed into the end game, for which he has to the good a temporary pawn majority, and more particularly a Bishop permanently posted in the centre. There followed 26. ....KR—B4; 27. P—KB4, R×P;   28. QR—QKt1, B—K2; Spielmann defends himself with his customary ingenuity.   29. K—B2 (progressive centralization), P—QKt3; 30. K—B3, R—R3;   31. KR—Q1, R— B5;   32. R—Q7, K—B2;   33. P—R5, P—Kt4;   34. R—K1, R(B5)—B3; 35. B—Q4, R(R3)—K3;   36. R—KR1, P—KR3;   37. R—Kt7, R(K3)—Q3;

Diagram 76

Nimzowitsch—Spielmann
San Sebastian, 1911

38. B—K5, R—K3;   39. K—K4. After the preparatory Rook manœuvres (notice that the RQKt7 is in close contact with the protected point QKt6, and that the 7th rank is to be materialized) the Black Rooks prove themselves to be 'passive' enough actually to invite a further advance of the White King.   B. K, and P now form a central island; the B is the bridge-builder, the point K4 is our shelter. 39.....R—B5 ch;   40. K—B5, R—B4;   41. R—Q1, P—Kt5, the game cannot be saved.   42. R—Q8, R×P;   43. R—KB8 ch!, K×R; 44. K×R, Resigns.

The 2nd Example again shows a centralization (Diag. 77). In his difficult situation Black tried 20.....K—B2; there followed 21. R—K1? (the right move was 21. P—KKt4), 21.....K—K2; 22. B—QB3, Kt—Q4, and after the further moves 23. R×R, K×R; 24. B—K5, the second player had overcome the worst of his difficulties. 24.....P—QKt4; 25. B—Kt3, Kt—B3; 26. K—B1, K—K2. And now Sir George could not resist any longer the temptation to win back the pawn and played 27. B×Kt, P×B; 28. R×P. Further since after 28.....P—K4 he exposed his R, by 29. R—KR4, Black got the upper hand, and by forceful centralization won as follows: 29.....B—B4; 30. K—K2, B—Kt3; 31. B—Q5, R—Kt1; 32. P—QB3, P—KB4; 33. B—Kt3, K—B3; observe the collective advance of Black's central forces. 34. B—B2, P—QR4!; played because White's majority on this side is really a minority, or if you will a majority forsaken by all its patron saints

Diagram 77

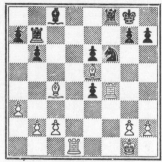

Thomas—Nimzowitsch
Marienbad, 1925

Diagram 78

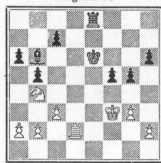

Post—Alekhine
Mannheim, 1914

(K and R). 35. R—R3, P—K5; 36. R—R4, P—Kt5; 37. RP×P, P×P; 38. R—B4, K—K4 (stops the hole); 39. R—B1, P—Kt6; 40. B—Q1, P—B5; 41. K—K1, B—B2; 42. P—Kt3, P—B6. White is all sewn up. There followed the sacrifice 43. B×P, P×B; 44. R×P, and after a stubborn fight Black won through his superiority in material.

The 3rd Example. An ending rich in combinations. The gifted, imaginative Franco-Russian seems in this game as if he wished to sweep away the rules of my system with the hurricane of his bubbling inspiration. This, however, is only apparently the case; in reality everything is done in the spirit of the system and of centralization (Diag. 78). 40.....P—KKt5 ch; the 'candidate' (PKB4) stops behind, but we are here concerned with a sacrificial combination. 41. K—Kt2 (41. K—B4?, K—B3; with mating threats), 41.....K—B2; 42. Kt × P, R—K8; 43. P—KR4, K—Kt3!; 44. Kt—Kt4,

P—KB5!; 45. P×P, R—KKt8 ch; 46. K—R2, P—Kt6 ch; 47. K—R3, B—B7. Now P, B, and R are united into one whole, but this whole has, at any rate for the moment, small possibility of expansion. 48. K—Kt4 (the threat was R—R8 ch, K—Kt4; R×P ch!, etc.), 48.....R—KR8; 49. P—B5 ch, K—B3; 50. Kt—Q5 ch, K—K4; 51. K—B3, K×P; 52. Kt×P, R×P; 53. Kt×P. Black has given up his whole Q side. With what justification? Well, because with the fall of White's KRP the capacity for expansion which was somewhat lacking before (see note to the 47th move) is now present in rich measure: the two united passed pawns, with the King there to stop the holes, demolish all resistance. 53.....R—B5 ch; 54. K—Kt2, P—R4!; 55. R—Q8, P—R5!; 56. R—KB8 ch (the R wants to stop the combined attack), 56.....K—Kt4; 57. R—KKt8 ch (R×R?, K×R; followed by K—Kt5, etc.), 57.....K—R4; 58. R—KR8 ch, K—Kt3; 59. R—K8 (in order after B—B4 to safeguard his base which would be threatened by R—B7 ch), 59.....B—B4; 60. R—K2, K—B4 (the hole-stopper draws near!); 61. P—Kt4, B—Kt3; 62. K—R3, R—B7; 63. Kt—Q6 ch, K—B5; 64. R—K4 ch, K—B6; 65. K×RP, B—Q1 ch!!; 66. K—R5, R—R7 ch; 67. K—Kt6. The White pieces are all 'away', the house stands deserted and desolate. 67.....P—Kt7; 68. Resigns.

As the 4th Example let us follow a King in his wanderings, which interests us inasmuch as they take place under the watchful eye of a centrally placed Queen (Diag. 79). The game proceeded:— 39. Q—K5, Q—Q8 ch; 40. K—B2, Q—Q4. The fight for the mid-point of the board. 41. Q—B4 ch, K—Kt3! Beginning of the wandering, Q—KB4 is now threatened. 42. K—K1, Q—B4!; 43. Q—Kt3 ch, K—R4; 44. Q—Kt7, Q—K5! The Black King is making

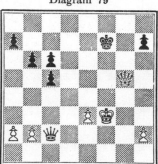

Diagram 79

E. Cohn—Nimzowitsch
Münich, 1906

preparation to go either to KR7 or K5 (Diag. 67). 45. Q—B7 ch, K—Kt5; 46. Q—Kt7 ch (or 46. Q—Q7 ch, K—R5!), 46..... Q—Kt3; 47. Q—Q7 ch, K—B6; 48. Q—R3 ch, K—K5! Our ideal frontal position. 49. K—K2, K—K4! After the K has gone to great pains and trouble to get to the point K5, he retires with the threat Q—B7 ch. This is the point of the manœuvre; namely to get time for the move P—B5, which forces the White Q perpetually to protect the point Q3. How the Black King, in order to be free of checks, now flees to his K2, and the Q side pawns carry out their irresistible advance, is as interesting as it is instructive.   50. K—Q2,   P—B5;   51. Q—B1,   Q—K5;   52. Q—K2, K—Q3;   53. Q—KB1, K—K2!;   54. Q—K2, P—Kt4;   55. Q—KB1, P—QR4;   56. Q—KKt1, Q—K4;   57. K—B2, P—Kt5;   58. Q—B2, Q—K5 ch;   59. K—B1, P—R5;   60. Q—Kt3, P—Kt6;   61. P×P, BP×P;   62. Q—B7 ch,   K—K3;   63. Q—B8 ch,   K—Q4; 64. Q- -Q7 ch, K—B5;   65. Q—KB7 ch, K—Q6;   66. Resigns.

CHAPTER VII
THE PIN

§1. *Introductory and General. Tactics or Strategy. On the possibility of reintroducing a pinning motif which has had to be abandoned.*

AFTER the difficult sixth chapter, difficult at any rate in the positional sense, the present one may appear very easy. And the question may perhaps be asked, whether the pinned piece can really be spoken of as an element in our sense, since a game may be laid out on the basis of an open file or a passed pawn, but surely never of a pin! This point of view we cannot share. True, pins as a rule occur in purely tactical moments as, for instance, in the pursuit of the fleeing enemy; on the other hand, however, a pin foreseen in the planning of a game may quite logically influence its whole course. In cónnexion with this possibility game No. 5 v. Haken—Giese (q.v.) is of especial interest. The move 25.....B—KKt3 signifies a resuscitation of the pin motif which had been dead since the 7th move, for now there is threatened an advance, when occasion serves, against the objective, White's PKR3, by P—KR4 and P—KKt5. The original White move P—KR3 was in its turn, however, conceived as a parry to the threatening pin, and hence stands in logical connexion with that motif. Consequently the attack on White's KRP should also be reckoned as a logical variation on the same theme, the pin motif; and this despite the fact that in the game as played Black did not pursue the adventure involved in or rather restarted by the move 25.....B—KKt3, but contritely returned to his K file, whereupon virtue found its reward. But this is quite immaterial, for it could easily have happened otherwise. What is of importance is that we should have learnt the great strategic range of the pin motif.

§2. *The conception of the wholly, and half pinned piece. The defence a pinned piece can give is but imaginary. Exchange combinations on the pinning square (=the square on which the pinned piece stands`, and the two distinct motives for such combinations.*

To a pin there belong three actors, (1) the pinning piece, (2) the pinned enemy piece, and (3) the piece standing behind the pinned piece. The first attacks the third across the second, that is to say the pinned piece stands in the way of the capture of the piece behind it by the pinning piece, and for shortness we shall call them the 'pinning', the 'pinned', and the 'screened' piece. The screened piece is usually of noble blood, that is King or Queen, for otherwise it would not be likely to hide itself behind another piece. All three actors stand either in the same file or the same diagonal (Diag. 80.) The pinned piece dare not move since if he did the piece behind him would be exposed to the attack from which it had previously been screened. If this immobility is absolute, that is, if the pinned piece dare make no move whatever, he is said to be wholly pinned. If on the other hand the pinned piece have any squares at his disposal in the line of the pin to which he can move, he is said to be only half pinned. In Diagram 80 the pin by the Rook is only a half pin since the move P—R4 is possible. A pinned Kt is always wholly pinned. Of other pieces we may say that a piece can only half pin one of its own kind. For instance, White; B, KR1, Black: B, QB3; K, QKt2. Here the Black BQB3 is only half pinned; he can move anywhere in the diagonal QB3 to KR8. A pawn can

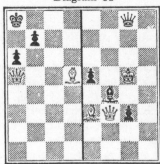

Diagram 80

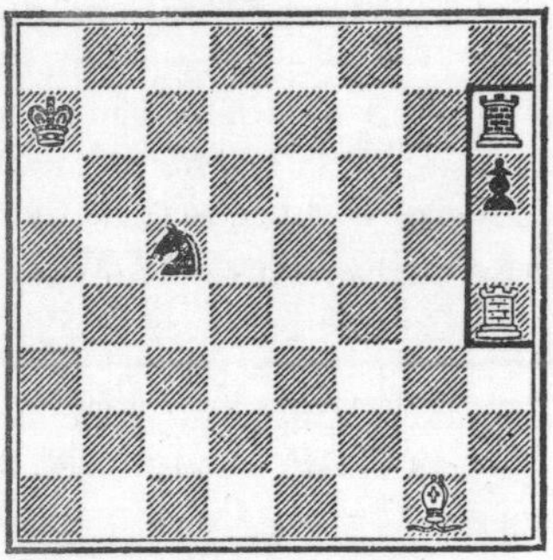

Diagram 81

White's RKR4 half pins Black's PR3; White's BKKt1 wholly pins Black's KtQB4. The screened pieces are the R and K respectively

Right: 1. Q × P ch, and wins KtQ.
Left: 1. Q × P ch and mates

only be wholly pinned by a diagonally moving piece; if the pin is in a column the pinning piece must block the pinned pawn (e.g., White: R, KKt6. Black: P, KKt2; K, KKt1), in order to enforce complete immobility. But such immobility has really no connexion with the pin: it could equally be the result of the blockade.

A pinned piece's defensive power is only imaginary. He only makes a gesture as if he would defend; in reality he is crippled and immobile. Hence we may confidently place our piece *en prise* to a pinned piece, for he dare not lay hands on it. An example will be found in Diagram 81. The winning moves 1. Q × KKtP ch or 1. Q × QRP ch are easy to find. All we have to be sure of is that the Black BB5 or PQKt2 is pinned, if this be the case the points (KKt3, QR6) which seem to be protected are really at our mercy. And so we may seek out such points which make a pretence of being protected, and at once rightly declare them to be free as air. How simple! And yet the less experienced amateur would rather put his head in the lion's jaws than put his Queen *en prise!*

It is very often profitable to play for the win of the pinned piece. To us, who know that every immobile, or even weakly restrained, piece tends to become a weakness, this fact will not appear surprising. But parallel with the problem of winning the pinned piece runs that of preventing its unpinning; for on this its mobility would be restored, and with that all its strength also.

Apart from the fact that the possibility of an unpinning must always be kept in view, the fight to win a pinned piece proceeds on the usual lines, namely by multiplying attacks, and in the case of adequate protection by thinning the ranks of the defenders. (See also I. ii. §4.) A clear profit may, however, sometimes be recorded, namely in the case when a pinned piece can be attacked by a pawn, for then this attack on it will be decisive. That this must be so follows from the consideration that a piece can only evade a pawn attack by flight. If, however, the piece is pinned, he is defenceless against an attacking pawn, since flight is denied him (Diag. 82.) On the right the course will be 1. R—KR1, P—KKt3; and then up will come the pawn 2. P—KKt4. On the left things are not made quite so easy for the pawns, there are one or two interferences to brush aside, and this is done by 1. R × B, P × R; 2. P—Kt6 and wins.

Diagram 82

Two elementary examples of the win of a pinned piece by a pawn attack

In general, the plan of attack against a pinned piece calls for a great effort to secure that preponderance in material which we have on various occasions particularized, that is to say a majority of attackers over the defenders of our objective, which in this case is the pinned piece; but the ideal to be aimed at is the pawn attack, which not infrequently will crown the whole enterprise. For example: In Diagram 83 (left) it is plainly visible that a close investment of the pinned Black PQKt3 has been instituted. We may remark that the ideal result of this siege may be registered in the passive state to which the Black defenders are reduced. But now the QRP moves forward, and this advance leads to a more tangible result.

In the same diagram (right) the Black KtKKt2 is in a pitiful state of pin. The screened piece is represented here by the mating

G

threat at White's KR7. By the advance of the KRP White has
prevented any unpinning of the Kt by K—R2—Kt3. The pressure
exerted on the pinned Kt by the pieces alone is here right grievous,
yet does not lead to any immediate result. But now the KBP
comes up with a dagger under his cloak, and decides matters. And
so while the officers may put on pressure (at times this suffices for the
win of the piece, and after all an officer is not one to joke with),

Diagram 83   Diagram 84

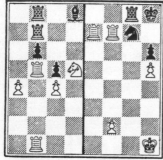

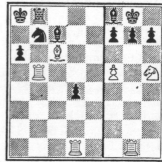

Pawn attack after an anterior investment carried out by pieces

The exchange combination.
Right: the 1st motive. Left:
the 2nd motive

the proper person to execute the death sentence will always be the
private soldier.

§3.   The exchange combination on the pinning square.

The first motive (Diag. 84, right).   In this position the capture of
the pinned Black PKKt2 may be our object. We pile up attacks
(the preponderance 3 : 2 has here already been achieved), and then
find to our disappointment that the pawn jauntily advances; the
beggar was not even pinned, or at best only half pinned, for though
a capture by the KKtP would not be feasible, P—KKt3 is. The
problem of how to win our objective, is, nevertheless, easy of solution,
and this by 1. Kt × P, B × Kt;   2. P—B6. The idea is that White
substitutes the wholly pinned B for the half-pinned PKKt2. A
substitution of this kind is our 1st motive.

There is, however, still a knotty question to answer, namely how
White, notwithstanding the surrender of one of his attacking pieces,
can yet maintain his preponderance against the point KKt7. The
answer of course lies in the fact that though Black still has two of his
original defenders (K and B) on the board, the B can no longer be
regarded as a defender of the threatened point, but is himself become
the pinned object of our attack at that point, whereas White still has

his R and the KBP which, close at hand, is ready to plunge into the fray; so that the operation 1. Kt×P, B×Kt puts out of action a piece on each side and the relative preponderance of White is unchanged.

The 2nd Motive. In the famous game, Morphy—Duke of Brunswick and Count Isouard, after the moves 1. P—K4, P—K4; 2. Kt—KB3, P—Q3; 3. P—Q4, B—KKt5?; 4. P×P, B×Kt; 5. Q×B, P×P; 6. B—QB4, Kt—KB3; 7. Q—QKt3, Q—K2; 8. Kt—QB3, P—QB3; 9. B—KKt5, P—QKt4; 10. Kt×P, P×Kt; 11. B×KtP ch, QKt—Q2; the position of the pinned Black KtQ2 was a very critical one. There followed 12. 0—0—0 (the quickest way to unite the Rooks for an attack in the Q file against the point Q7), 12.....R—Q1 (Diag. 85). In this position the simple doubling of the Rooks in the Q file would win the Kt; e.g., 13. R—Q2, Q—K3; 14. KR—Q1, B—K2; 15. B×KKt; but Morphy has a much stronger manœuvre at his command. There followed:

13. R×Kt, R×R; 14. R—Q1. This exchange combination on the pinning square deserves our notice. Did it take place in order to substitute a wholly pinned piece for one which is half pinned? No, for the KtQ2 as it was, was wholly pinned. Would it have taken place if the White R had already stood at Q2? No, for in that case doubling the Rooks would have sufficed. The exchange combination was evidently carried out in order, in the struggle for the point Q7, to gain a tempo.

Diagram 85

The 2nd motive

Let us dispassionately consider the state of affairs before and after R×Kt. Before this capture White had two attackers against two real defenders, for the KtKB3 is half dead, and the Q is too great a personage, and would cut a poor figure in a rough and tumble with minor pieces. After R×Kt White loses one attacker, whom he, however, at once replaces by a fresh R; whereas the defending R which previously stood at Q1 is irrevocably lost to Black. (Cf. our 'knotty question' above.) Accordingly White has profited to the extend of a fighting unit, and has thus a preponderance of forces in his fight for the pinned piece. The 2nd motive, therefore, is the gain of a tempo. After 14.....Q—K3; 15. B×Kt would have won easily; but Morphy preferred the prettier method 15. B×R ch, Kt×B; and now the Kt is in its turn pinned because of the mating threat at Q8. The Kt is, however, forced to move, whereupon mate follows: 16. Q—Kt8 ch!, Kt×Q; 17. R—Q8 mate.

In the position on Diagram 84 (left) the pinning R is attacked;

to withdraw him would mean giving the enemy the tempo he needs to get rid of the pin. For instance, 1. R—Kt2, K—R2; 2. R(Q)—QKt1, Kt—Q3. The correct play is 1. R × Kt, R × R; and now 2. R—QKt1 wins. Since the sacrifice at QKt7 was made only to avoid the loss of a tempo, our 2nd motive is obviously present.

The two motives can also appear together in one combination (Diag. 86). Here a general exchange is clearly indicated. However, after 1. B × B, R × B; 2. R × R, K × R; 3. P—Kt4, K—K4, the Black K would arrive on the scene just at the right moment. We must therefore bring about the exchanges more cleverly. This we can do by 1. R × B!, R × R; 2. P—Kt4; for now Black will have to lose a tempo with a K move. Thus 2. . . . . K—B2; 3. B × R, K × B; 4. P—Kt5 and now the P cannot be overtaken. A tempo-winning combination, you will say. Quite true, but the gain of a

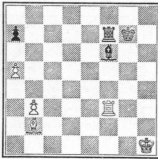

Diagram 86

The 1st and 2nd motives appear together

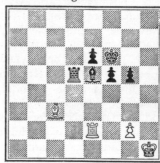

Diagram 87

From a game at odds by Dr. Tarrasch. The pin exploited by means of *Zugzwang*

tempo was only attained because we were able to replace the half-pinned B by the wholly pinned R. Taking one thing with another therefore we see that in this case we have an amalgamation of the two motives.

We will close this section with an example which will show us the utilization of the pin combined with the justly popular *Zugzwang* motif. That a pin may easily lead to a dearth of available moves is obvious, for often enough the elasticity of the defending pieces is very small; in fact, it not infrequently happens that the defence is uni-operative, i.e., cannot shift its ground and still maintain the protection of the threatened point. So in Diagram 87, after the initial sacrifice which we have so often discussed (1st motive), i.e., after the moves 1. R × B, R × R; there followed 2. P—KKt3!. But for P—KKt3 Black could have given his K air by means of P—B5; but now this move would fail after 3. P—Kt4, and Black succumbs

owing to the uni-operative quality of his defence of the RK4. After
3. P—Kt3, P—Kt5 Black is equally 'in the soup', and for the same
reason.

We have now, in essentials at any rate, exhausted the subject
of play against a pinned piece and will pass on to that of unpinning.

§4. *The problem of unpinning:* (a) *the 'question', its character and
the dangers involved.* (b) *Ignoring the pin.* (c) *Unpinning by bringing
up reserves.* (d) *Manœuvring and holding choice of policy in suspense.*
(e) *The 'corridor' and the defensive alliance of the beleaguered.*

After the moves 1. P—K4, P—K4; 2. Kt—KB3, Kt—QB3;
3. B—B4, B—B4; 4. Kt—QB3, Kt—KB3; 5. P—Q3, P—Q3,
White can set up a pin by 6. B—KKt5; and curiously enough this
simple little pin evokes a whole forest of possibilities (Diag. 88).

Diagram 88

The problem of unpinning

Should Black immediately put the
'question' to the bold Bishop by 6.....
P—KR3; 7. B—R4, P—KKt4; 8. B—
Kt3, or should he put the strictest
restraint upon himself and with an
unembarrassed smile play 6.....B—
K3. Or should he even risk a counter-
pin with B—KKt5? Again may he not
consider it reasonable to ignore the
threat involved in the pinning move
B—KKt5 (namely 7. Kt—Q5, with
consequent disorganization of his K
side pawn position, by B or Kt × Kt),
in order with 6.....Kt—Q5 quietly to
'centralize'? There is further 6.....Kt—QR4 to be considered, while
6.....0—0 must not be dismissed with a mere shrug of the shoulders.

(a) The 'Question'.

It will be clear without further remark that the premature advance
of the wing pawns must have a compromising effect. In the Scotch
game, to give an example, after 1. P—K4, P—K4; 2. Kt—KB3,
Kt—QB3; 3. P—Q4, P×P; 4. Kt×P, Kt—KB3; 5. Kt—QB3,
B—QKt5; 6. Kt × Kt, KtP × Kt; 7. B—Q3, P—Q4; 8. P × P,
P × P; 9. 0—0, 0—0; 10. B—KKt5, P—QB3; 11. Kt—K2,
there can follow 11.....P—KR3; 12. B—R4, P—KKt4? but now
after 13. B—Kt3 White has at command the attacking move
P—KB4, and also the possibility of occupying the squares KB5 and
KR5, which have been weakened by the advance of the KKtP, for
neither point can ever be attacked by P—KKt3. The 'question' was
therefore ill-timed.

On the other hand, there are occasions when the 'question' is very opportune. For instance, in the following opening of a tournament game, E. Cohn—Nimzowitsch: 1. P—K4, P—K4; 2. Kt—QB3, B—B4; 3. Kt—KB3, P—Q3; 4. P—Q4, P×P; 5. Kt×P, Kt—KB3; 6. B—K2, O—O; 7. O—O, R—K1 (Black has given up the centre, but has pressure on White's KP). 8. B—KKt5? (B—B3 was his right move), 8..... P—KR3!; 9. B—R4, P—KKt4!; 10. B—Kt3, Kt×P. It was to win this important pawn that Black puts up with the disorganization of his own position, in the spirit of Chap. I. §7a. The continuation was 11. Kt×Kt, R×Kt; 12. Kt—Kt3, B—Kt3; 13. B—Q3, B—KKt5!; 14. Q—Q2, R—K1; and after Kt—QB3 and Q—KB3, Black's position was consolidated; the PQ3 has in particular a stabilizing effect. Black won easily.

We have purposely taken two extreme cases in order to see what is at stake if the question be put; and we have found that the 'question' is disorganizing, and therefore should not be put unless there be compensation in another direction. Such compensation usually lies in the fact that the Bishop which has been driven off finds himself in a 'desert'. Such a desert will, however, at once be changed into a flowering garden if the centre can be opened. The following examples will make this point clear:

After the moves 1. P—K4, P—K4; 2. Kt—KB3, Kt—QB3; 3. Kt—QB3, Kt—KB3; 4. B—Kt5, B—Kt5; 5. O—O, O—O; 6. B×Kt, QP×B; 7. P—Q3, B—KKt5; 8. P—KR3, B—KR4; 9. B—KKt5 (9. P—KKt4 at once would be bad because of 9..... Kt×KtP; 10. P×Kt, B×P; followed by P—KB4), 9..... Q—Q3; 10. B×Kt, Q×B, it is perfectly correct to play 11. P—KKt4, for the Black B on arriving at KKt3 will find nothing to 'bite upon' but the unshakable mass of centre pawns. It should be noted that if Black still had his QP, i.e., a PQ3 instead of PQB3, this 'desert' could have been given life by P—Q4. True the Black B can eventually be brought to KB2 after P—KB3, but that costs time. White on the other hand has nothing to suffer, for with a compact centre a disorganized King's wing is easily defensible. And more than that, these disorganized K side pawns, will become a slowly but surely advancing instrument of attack (of the 'tank' order), especially with a Kt to help at KB5. (Cf. Game No. 16, Nimzowitsch—Leonhardt, of which the above are the opening moves.)

And now, having shown more or less definitely the logical connexion between a 'desert' and the 'centre', it will be profitable to analyse the position referred to at the beginning of this section. (Diag. 89.) After the moves: 1. P—K4, P—K4; 2. Kt—KB3, Kt—QB3; 3. B—B4, B—B4; 4. Kt—QB3, Kt—KB3; 5. P—Q3, P—Q3; 6. B—KKt5, P—KR3; 7. B—R4, P—KKt4; 8. B—KKt3, it will be interesting to see whether the desert into which the B has been forced can be made hospitable or not. To this end we must minutely examine White's possibilities of attack in the centre.

There are, as will be seen, two such possibilities, the one B—QKt5 followed by P—Q4, the other Kt—Q5 with P—QB3 and P—Q4 to follow. (In passing it may be remarked that the position of the KtQ5, as a diagonal outpost in the diagonal of the BQB4, is analogous to that of an outpost in a file.) After 8..... P—QR3 (to remove the first possibility), White could play 9. Kt—Q5; for example, 9..... B—K3; 10. P—QB3, B × Kt; 11. P × B, Kt—K2; 12. P—Q4, P × P; 13. Kt × P, and now Black can pocket a pawn, but after 13..... Kt × P; 14. 0—0, White's game is to be preferred, for the BKKt3, now come to life, will by no means have to kick his heels in idleness any longer.

After 8. B—KKt3 (Diag. 89) Black can also play 8..... B—KKt5, in order in some measure to curb White's aspirations in the centre. In a game (No. 17, Nimzowitsch—Fluss) the continuation was 9. P—KR4, Kt—R4 (R—KKt1 or even K—Q2 was possible here; Kt—R4 takes too many troops from the middle of the board); 10. P × P (Tempting as this move looks—for is it not the natural consequence of the pawn advance?—it is not good here; the right move was Kt—Q5. The argument is this: 9. P—KR4 has had 9..... Kt— R4 as a result, by which White has attained a preponderance in the centre which he can exploit by 10. Kt—Q5),

Diagram 89

The 'question' and its 'consequences'

10..... Kt—Q5. This transposition of moves loses, since White has a surprising combination in reserve. With 10..... Kt × B; 11. P × Kt, Kt—Q5, Black could have launched a lovely attack. Thus: 12. R × P, R × R; 13. P × R, B × Kt; 14. P × B, Q—Kt4. Or 12. Kt—Q5 (this attempt to exploit the centre comes too late); 12..... B × Kt; 13. P × B, Q × P; 14. P—KKt4, P—QB3; 15. R—R5, P × Kt!!, and wins, since the Q has as her travelling companions to the next world all White's pieces.

It is therefore of the utmost importance for the student to realize that the 'question', though seemingly only a matter concerning the wing, is fundamentally a problem affecting the centre. Later under (c) we shall demonstrate the reality of this connexion by another example.

(b) Ignoring the threat, or, in other words, permitting our pawn position to be broken up.

This method may be chosen if we can in return secure greater freedom of action in the centre, and by this we mean not merely a passive security such as was considered under (a) above; we must here have a guarantee that we shall get active security. For instance, after the same opening moves, 1. P—K4, P—K4; 2. Kt—KB3, Kt—QB3; 3. B—B4, B—B4; 4. Kt—QB3, Kt—KB3; 5. P—Q3, P—Q3; 6. B—KKt5 (Diag. 88), Kt—Q5 threatens unpleasantness. Nevertheless we can ignore the threat, thus 6..... 0—0; 7. Kt—Q5, B—K3. And now the break up of our K side pawns by 8. Kt×Kt, P×Kt; 9. B—KR6, R—K1; 10. Kt—R4, K—R1, would yield a game with chances and counter chances, yet White can by no means claim any striking advantage, for Black has the desired freedom of action in the centre (the possibility of P—Q4), and there is no more effective party to an operation on a flank than a counter-thrust in the centre. White has let his troops create a diversion, which has in fact made them lose contact with the centre. This diversion would only find real justification if it led to the permanent possession of the point KB5, and this seems questionable. After 8. B×Kt (instead of Kt×Kt), P×B; 9. Kt—R4, the outcome would also be uncertain.

Best for White, after 6..... 0—0; 7. Kt—Q5, B—K3, would be 8. Q—Q2, which keeps up the pressure. After the further moves 8.... B×Kt; 9. B×B, the unpinning by means of the 'question' is impracticable (9..... P—KR3; 10. B—R4, P—KKt4?; 11. B×QKt, P×B; 12. Kt×KtP), and White stands slightly better.

(c) Bringing up reserves in order to effect the unpinning by peaceful means.

For all who love the quiet life, this is a very commendable continuation. We have excellent examples of it in the Metger defence to the Four Knights Game, and in Tarrasch's match game (a Petroff) against Marshall.

The Metger defence is this:—1. P—K4, P—K4; 2. Kt—KB3, Kt—QB3; 3. Kt—QB3, Kt—KB3; 4. B—Kt5, B—Kt5; 5. 0—0, 0—0; 6. P—Q3, P—Q3; 7. B—KKt5, and now Metger plays 7..... B×Kt; 8. P×B, Q—K2, intending Kt—Q1—K3, and if the White B then goes to KR4, Black persistently follows him up by Kt—B5—Kt3 on which if B—Kt5 again, Black at last plays P—KR3. It is again evident that such a lengthy time-wasting manœuvre is only feasible if the position in the centre is solid. In reply to 8..... Q—K2 the usual continuation is 9. R—K1, Kt—Q1; 10. P—Q4, Kt—K3; 11. B—B1, P—QB4 (or B3) with about equal chances.

In the Petroff, Tarrasch, after the moves 1. P—K4, P—K4; 2. Kt—KB3, Kt—KB3; 3. Kt×P, P—Q3; 4. Kt—KB3, Kt×P; 5. P—Q4, B—K2; 6. B—Q3, Kt—KB3; 7. 0—0, B—KKt5, is wont to get out of the pin by the quiet manœuvre R—K1, QKt—Q2—B1—Kt3 and then P—KR3 (sometimes he plays P—KR3 first), and he has won some fine games thus. The logical framework, which seems to justify him in a manœuvre taking up so much time as this does, is based on the two following postulates: (1) the unpinning must be brought about as quickly as possible, (2) to the troops thus hurried up in support there is offered, as a kind of reward for the aid they bring, a favourable position with possibilities of getting contact with the enemy (e.g., by Kt—KB5). I should like to add the remark that, incidentally, the moderns are not disinclined to put up with the unpleasantness of a pin for some considerable time; we are no longer quite convinced that a pin must be shaken off without any delay. Our plan of action may be seen from (d).

(d) Manœuvring and holding the choice of (a), (b), or (c) in reserve.

Such a line of action is difficult, and makes great demands on our technical skill. As an example, in the position shown on Diagram 88, Capablanca played 6.....B—K3, and the continuation was 7. B—QKt5, P—KR3; 8. B—R4, B—QKt5!; 9. P—Q4, B—Q2. This advance of the QP which Capablanca provoked leaves White's KP lacking protection. 10. 0—0, B × Kt; 11. P × B (B × KKt could have been played first here), 11.....P—KKt4; 12. B—Kt3, Kt × KP (Black had postponed the unpinning until a suitable moment occurred); 13. B × Kt, B × B; 14. P × P, P × P; 15. B × P (Kt × P was possibly better), Q × Q; 16. QR × Q, P—KB3; 17. B—Q4, K—B2; 18. Kt—Q2, KR—K1 with a favourable end game for Black. His opponent, the author of this book, had to lay down his arms on the 64th move.

Diagram 90

(e) The corridor and the need for the defenders to maintain effective contact.

In an advanced stage of the game, particularly in tactical operations, the process of unpinning presents an entirely different aspect. In Diagram 90, for instance, Black plays Kt—Kt5 or Kt3. We call the space between pinning and pinned pieces and that between the pinned and the screened pieces the 'corridor'. By placing a protected piece in such a corridor the pin can be raised. Another possibility lies in the removal

Unpinning by occupying one of the points in the 'corridor'; here QKt7 to 5 and QKt3. Thus: Kt—Kt3 or Kt5

of the screened piece out of the line of the pin. Thus in Diagram 90 either K—B3 or K—B2 would put an end to the pin. If

the screened piece is not too valuable, we may achieve the same
end by giving it adequate protection; but in this case we must be
careful to maintain contact between the pieces concerned in the pin,
whether directly or, as defenders indirectly (Diag. 91). White
intends with R(R2)—Kt2, and B—Q3 to make the threat P—R4 an

Diagram 91   Diagram 92

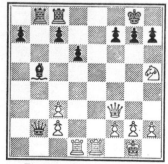

The beleaguered troops get in touch.   Black releases the pin

actuality.   How can Black anticipate this manœuvre?   By transferring his **R** from QKt3 to QKt2, and then safeguarding him by B—B3;
after which, for all he cares, P—R4 may be played at any time.
Notice, too, how the unpinning is effected in Diagram 92 by 1.....
R—Kt8 ch; 2. K any move, R—Kt7 ch, followed by B—Q5.   In
this position by establishing contact between B and R, the B, which
otherwise would have been lost, is saved.

Diagram 93

Another example of the pin (Diag.
93).   In the game White played 22. R—
QKt1, on which Black countered by
R—K1;   but as I afterwards showed,
22. R—K4 would have won.   The
main variation runs: 22. R—K4, B—
B3; 23. Kt—B6 ch, P × Kt. (If 23.....
K—R1;   24. R—KR4,   Q × P   (B2),
Kt × RP!), and now we come to a
direct pursuit of the Black K, who will
be driven to flight, but by no means to
an untroubled flight, rather one in
which some disagreeable pins lie in
wàit for him; for, as we observed at
the beginning of this chapter, the
pin is characteristic of a pursuit;
there follows 24. R—KKt4 ch, K—B1; 25. Q × KBP, B—Q2!;
26. R—Kt7, B—K3;   27. R × RP, K—K1; and now comes pin No.
1, namely 28. R—K1, threatening Q × BP ch!.   To escape this Black

Position from the game
Nimzowitsch—Vidmar
Carlsbad, 1911

must play 28.....K—Q2; but now the KBP is pinned (No. 2) and
29. Q×B ch wins easily. Let us, for the sake of practice, dwell a
moment on the position after 25. Q×BP, B—Q2. Here
26. R—KB4 would also win, for B—K3 will not do because of Q×B;
26.....B—K1 fails against 27. R—K1; and if 26.....K—Kt1,
then 27. Q×P ch, K—R1; 28. Q—B6 ch, K—Kt1; 29. R—B3
decides matters.

The reader is advised to study now Games Nos. 16, 17, and 18,
which illustrate the connexion between the pin and the centre.

CHAPTER VIII

DISCOVERED CHECK

A short chapter, but rich in dramatic complications.

§1. *The degree of relationship between the pin and the discovered check is more closely defined. Where should the piece which discovers the check move to?*

DIAGRAM 94 gives a clear picture of the degree of relationship between the pin and discovered check, and we see from it that the pinned piece, tired of eternal persecution, has changed his colour. This change has had the effect of transferring the once sickly youth into a doughty warrior; and so we can describe a discovered check as a pin in which the pinned piece has passed over with colours flying into the enemy camp. Further, in the discovered check, as in the pin, we have to do with three actors, namely: (1) the piece threatening a check which is now masked by one of his own fellows; (2) the masking piece; (3) the piece standing behind the masking piece; or more shortly (1) the threatening piece, (2) the masking piece, (3) the threatened piece. But whereas in the pin the immobility of the pinned (masking) piece is the source of all his troubles, in the discovered check the masking piece enjoys quite uncanny mobility; any and every square within his reach is open to him; he can even seize a point subject to multiple enemy attacks, for his opponent cannot touch him, since he is in check.

Diagram 94

In the discovered check on the right the Rook is the 'threatening', the Knight the 'masking', and the King the 'threatened' piece

If we examine the possible moves open to such a masking piece, we find that he can do three things:

(*a*) He can take anything within reach with impunity since the enemy cannot recapture him.

(*b*) He can attack any major enemy piece, not letting himself for one moment be disturbed by the thought that the square on which he so haughtily alights by right belongs to the enemy, that is to say one which is under heavy enemy fire.

(*c*) He can exchange his square for another one, if for any reason this appear more favourable to him than the one he has left.

Thus in Diagram 95 (*a*) could be carried out by R×QRP, or KRP ch. Notice that the R can make either capture quite fearlessly. If he choose to follow the course outlined in (*b*) he will play R—K5 ch or R—Q3 ch; while we find (*c*) followed, if we feel the reproach that his B is pinned, a fact which dulls his lordship's usually healthy appetite, and we have 1. R—Q1 ch, K any move; 2. B×Q, etc.

The (*c*) group has naturally a very wide range, but no purpose would be served by further elaboration, for the reasons why a piece is more effective placed 'here' than 'there' are manifold. We may refer, however, to yet another example under:—

Diagram 95

Diagram 96

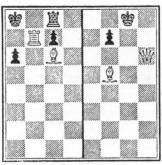

Two see-saws

Right: after 1. B—R7 ch, K—R1; 2. B—K4 ch, K—Kt1; and save that the B is on another, perhaps better, square, the position is un-altered, White still has the move

§2. *The see-saw. The long range masking piece can move to any square in his line of motion without spending a tempo, that is to say, wholly gratis.*

In Diagram 96 (right) White plays 1. B—R7 ch, whereupon the Black K has only one move, K—R1, and now the terrible weapon concealed in the discovered check is revealed. If White now play 2. B—Kt1 ch, Black with 2.....K—Kt1 escapes the discovered check, but with 3. B—R7 ch, White beckons him back again to the fatal square, since the Black King has but this move at his disposal, and only has this because the B by B—KR7 has masked the attack of the threatening piece. This stalemate position which we have described gives us thus a kind of see-saw, with the great advantage that the masking piece can occupy any square in the line of his withdrawal (here the diagonal KR7 to QKt1), without the manœuvre costing him a tempo, for White again has the move.

The see-saw can be the cause of frightful devastation. In

Diagram 97 the game would proceed, 1. B—R7 ch, K—R1; 2. B×P ch, K—Kt1; 3. B—R7 ch, K—R1; 4. B×P ch, K—Kt1; 5. B—R7 ch, K—R1; 6. B×Kt ch, K—Kt1; 7. B—R7 ch, K—R1; 8. B×Kt ch, K—Kt1; 9. B—R7 ch, K—R1; 10. B×R ch, K—Kt1; and now White gives back of his superfluity, somewhat like

Diagram 97

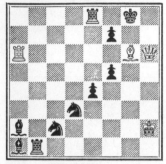

The See-saw
Great slaughter, the conciliatory sacrifice, and to crown all, mate

Diagram 98

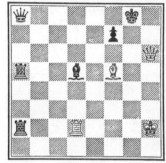

White wins

a usurer who has grown very rich and in his old age at small outlay turns benefactor. So 11. R—Kt6 ch, P×R; 12. B×B ch, and mate next move. The B has eaten his way to QKt1, in order, after the preparatory R sacrifice, to seize the diagonal QR2 to KKt8.

A similar but finer picture is shown in Diagram 98. Here the problem is to entice Black's BQ4 from the defence of his KBP, and this will be done by 1. B—R7 ch, K—R1; 2. B—B2 ch! (the 'better place' in the sense of (c) above), K—Kt1; 3. R—Kt2 ch!, B×R; and now again 4. B—R7 ch, K—R1; 5. B—Kt6 ch, K—Kt1; 6. Q—R7 ch, K—B1; 7. Q×P mate.

Diagram 99

Torre—Lasker, Moscow, 1925

Another example of the see-saw is seen in the game (Diag. 99) which Torre won against Lasker. In this threatening position (his RK1 is directly, and his BKt5 indirectly, attacked), Torre hit upon the move 21. P—QKt4!; there followed 21.....Q—KB4 (not Q×P, because of R—QKt1; better than the text move would however have been 21.....Q—Q4); 22. R—KKt3, P—KR3; 23. Kt—B4 (this intervention of the Kt would have been impossible had the Black Q been at Q4), 23.....Q—Q4; 24. Kt—K3 (Torre fights like a lion to break the pin, but without a point for his B to fall back upon, he could not have succeeded), 24.....Q—QKt4; 25. B—B6! (That this might have real effect it was necessary to entice the Q on to an unprotected square, which was the object of 24. Kt—K3), 25.....Q×Q; 26. R×P ch, K—R1 (and now we have a see-saw); 27. R×BP ch, K—Kt1; 28. R—Kt7 ch, K—R1; 29. R×B ch, K—Kt1; 30. R—Kt7 ch, K—R1; 31. R—Kt5 ch, K—R2; 32. R×Q, K—Kt3; 33. R—R3, K×B; 34. R×P ch, and wins.

§3. *Double check. Is brought about by the masking piece also giving check. The effectiveness of a double check lies in the fact that of the three possible parries to a check, two are nugatory, namely the capture of the piece giving check and the interposition of a piece. Flight is the one and only resource.*

(Diagram 100.) Here the choice lies between 1. Q—R7 ch, and and 1. Q—R8 ch. The former yields only an ordinary discovered check (1. Q—R7 ch, K×Q; 2. B—B6 ch) and allows the parry 2.....Q×R or Q—KR4. The second move, however, leads to a double check, and these parries are now automatically ruled out.

Diagram 100

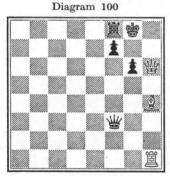

Double check

Diagram 101

Black with the move can force
a win

Therefore 1. Q—R8 ch!, K×Q; 2. B—R6 double ch, K—Kt1; 3. R—R8 mate. So again in the well-known position, White: Q, KB6; B, QKt2; Kt, K5. Black: K, Kt1; R's, K1, KB1; P's, KB2, KKt3, KR2. White mates in three, thus: 1. Q—R8 ch, K×Q; 2. Kt×BP double ch, K—Kt1; 3. Kt—R6 mate.

The double check is a weapon of a purely tactical nature, but of terrible driving effect. Even the laziest King flees wildly in the face of a double check.

We close this chapter with three apposite examples:

(1) In a game played some years ago between v. Bardeleben and Nisniewitsch there occurred the amusing position shown in Diagram 101. White's last move had been R(QKt7)—QB7 (obviously not R—Kt8 ch because of R—B1 ch and R×R). To R—QB7 Black replied with Q×R and the game was drawn. I subsequently pointed out the following win: 1.....R—B8 double ch; 2. K×R, Kt—Kt6 ch; 3. K—K1, Q—K6 ch; 4. K—Q1 (observe the driving effect; the King is already at Q1 and only a move or two ago he was sitting snugly at home!), 4.....Q—K7 ch!; 5. K—B1, Q—K8 ch!; 6. K—B2, Q×B ch; 7. K—B1, Kt—K7 ch!, and wins the Q and the game. Note that on the double check there was built a line of play, which is well known, and only strikes us as unusual because it takes place in a diagonal, and not as is usual in a file. This line of play (a tactical manœuvre) consists in breaking a link in the defence, by forcing a third piece between two mutually protecting pieces. In the position under consideration the K was enticed on to his QB2 between the QQKt1 and the BK4.

(2) The following well-known little game was played between Réti (White) and Dr. Tartakower (Black). 1. P—K4, P—QB3; 2. P—Q4, P—Q4; 3. Kt—QB3, P×P; 4. Kt×P, Kt—KB3; 5. Q—Q3 (a most unnatural move), 5.....P—K4? (the rather theatrical gesture of the first player, the move Q—Q3, has worked; Black has in mind a brilliant refutation of it, but his idea proves impossible of execution; for Q—Q3 was not as bad as all that! And so White gets the better game. The right move was 5.....Kt×Kt; 6. Q×Kt, Kt—Q2; followed by Kt—B3 with a solid position); 6. P×P, Q—R4 ch; 7. B—Q2, Q×KP; 8. 0—0—0, Kt×Kt (a mistake; he should have played B—K2); 9. Q—Q8 ch, K×Q; 10. B—Kt5 double ch, K—B2; 11. B—Q8 mate. If 10.....K—K1, then R—Q8 mate. The closing combination is really very pretty.

(3) In December, 1910, I gave a simultaneous display in Pernau (on the Baltic), on which occasion the following pretty little game was played. White: Nimzowitsch. Black: Ryckhoff. 1. P—K4; P—K4, 2. Kt—KB3, Kt—QB3; 3. B—Kt5, Kt—KB3; 4. 0—0, P—Q3; 5. P—Q4, Kt×KP?; 6. P—Q5, P—QR3; 7. B—Q3, Kt—B3 (7.....Kt—K2 would have saved the piece, but not the game. For instance: 8. B×Kt, P—KB4; 9. B—Q3, P—K5; 10. R—K1, P×B or Kt; 11. Q×P, with a strong attack); 8. P×Kt, P—K5; 9. R—K1, P—Q4; 10. B—K2!! (By forcing Black to protect his KP, White got time to remove his pieces from the fork unhurt; but instead he played his B to a square which allowed the capture of the Kt.), 10.....P×Kt (Black sees no danger and unconcernedly pockets the piece); 11. P×QKtP, B×P (if 11.....P×B; then simply P×R=Q for the KP is pinned); 12. B—QKt5 double check and mate.

CHAPTER IX

THE PAWN–CHAIN

§1. *General remarks and definitions. The base of the pawn-chain. The conception of the two distinct theatres of war.*

AFTER 1. P—K4, P—K3; 2. P—Q4, P—Q4; 3. P—K5, a Black and White pawn-chain has been formed. The P's at Q4, K5, and K3 and Q4 are the several links in the chain. The PQ4 is to be regarded as the base or foot of the White chain, while the PK3 plays a like rôle in Black's. Accordingly we call the bottom-most link of the chain, on which all the other links depend, the base.

Every Black and White pawn-chain, in other words, two consecutive series of pawns abutting on one another in consecutive diagonals, divides the board diagonally into two halves. For convenience we

Diagram 102a

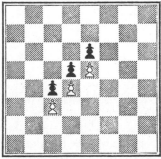

Diagram 102b

The Pawn-Chain

shall call such a Black and White pawn-chain simply the pawn chain (Diags. 102a, 102b).

Before the student tackles what now follows, he should make perfectly sure that he has grasped the principles of the open file and the blockade of the passed pawn; if he has not he should read through again Chapters II and IV, for they are indispensable to a proper understanding of what we have now to consider.

The question is this: After 1. P—K4, P—K3; 2. P—Q4, P—Q4; so long as White's P remains at K4, he can if he wish, open the K file with P×P, in order to start more or less permanent operations in the file, by planting say an outpost Kt at K5. By playing 3. P—K5 he renounces this chance, and in addition he relieves the tension in the centre, and this for no visible reason. Why then does

he do this?　Now I do not believe that the attacking energy latent in
White's position before the move P—K5 can suddenly disappear as
a consequence of P—K5; it must be present as before, though in a
modified form; for 3. P—K5 above all things checks the movement of
the Black pawns, and therefore implies a blockade.　But we know
that pawns, especially those in the centre, are consumed by an
enormous desire for expansion, i.e., to press forward, and we have
consequently inflicted on the enemy a not inconsiderable hurt.　Moreover, thanks to P—K5 there are now two theatres of war on the board,
of which the one is Black's K wing and the other the centre.

On the King's Wing.

(Diag. 103.)　The PK5 may here be described as a detachment
which has been pushed forward to form a wedge in enemy territory,
and to act as a demobilizing force.　The PK5 robs a Black Kt of the

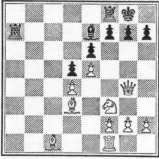

Diagram 103

The K's wing as theatre of war.
The troops engaged are Q, B and
Kt.　The R is held in reserve
ready for the possible enemy
counter P—KB4, P×P, B×P,
when he will attack in the K file

square KB3, and thus allows an easy
approach of the White storm troops
(QKt4).　Black's K wing which is
cramped by the same pawn is also a
target for bombardment by other pieces,
e.g., BQ3, KtKB3, and BQB1.　If
Black seeks to defend himself by opening communications in his 2nd rank,
by a timely advance P—KB4, and
eventually posting a Rook at his QR2,
our PK5 will approve himself an excellent wedge-driver; what we mean is that
when White attacks the point KKt7,
Black will play P—KB4 in order to
use his second rank for the defence of
the threatened point.　This otherwise
excellent defensive idea would, however,
fail because the PK5 would protest
violently.　The reply to P—KB4 would be P×P, e.p. and White,
after the recapture R×P, would use the K file, including the point
K5 in it, for bringing pressure on the backward enemy PK3.　In the
first case (i.e., King's wing as theatre of war) a White P at KB4 would
on the whole be a hindrance to White, since its negative effect (as
an obstruction to the QB and to any other of his pieces wishing to use
the square) would overshadow any positive advantage it might have.

In the centre.

Beside that of cramping the enemy King's wing White's PK5
pursues other and quite different ends.　White, in fact, intends by
P—K5 to fix the Black PK3 at his post, in order later to open fire on

him with P—KB4—B5; for KP×P would then imply the surrender of the base of Black's pawn-chain.   Should Black abstain from this move, White can either form a wedge by P—B6, or play P×P, P×P; R—B7—K7, which would mean the beginning of the end of Black's PK3.

In order the better to understand the association of ideas, it will be well to examine more closely the germ-cell of a flank, or an enveloping attack.   In Diagram 104 left we see the R in a frontal attack, in which the objective is bombarded at White's leisure.   To the right a frontal attack being out of the question, the manœuvre R—Kt6×P or R—Kt7—B7.×P is planned.   It is important for our purpose to emphasize the fact that the White PKB5 in this position is a necessary element of the problem, for if this were absent, a frontal attack against the Black KBP would not only be possible, but by far our easiest

Diagram 104   Diagram 105

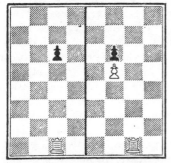 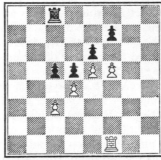

Left: frontal attack in simplest form. Right: Flank or enveloping attack in its simplest form

Skeleton representation of a central theatre of war. The two opponents attack the respective bases of the pawn-chain. The Rooks keep on the alert ready for the break through

course. Moreover, the attack, against the point KB6 if this had not been pinned down, would have no strategical sense, in conformity with the principle: the objective must first be reduced to immobility.   It follows that the position shown in Diagram 104 (right) represents the true germ-cell of the flank or enveloping attack.

This being established, the plan of action shown in Diagram 105 is seen to be logically justified, for its end is a preparation for such an attack as we have seen in germ in Diagram 104 right, and if this operation can be called an attack, as indeed it is, we can with a good conscience ascribe to the manœuvre P—K5 (chain building) followed by P—KB4—B5 a like significance. Accordingly the centre, in other words the Black PK3, is to be taken as a second theatre of war.

To recapitulate: P—K5, that is to say the formation of a pawn-chain, always creates two theatres of war, of which the enemy wing, cramped by the advance, forms one, and the base of the enemy pawn-chain the other. And further, P—K5 is inspired by the desire to attack. The attack on Black's PQ4 which was present before the advance of our KP has been transferred to Black's PK3, which has been reduced to immobility by our PK5, so as to be exposed to a flank attack by P—KB4—B5.

§2. *The attack against the pawn-chain. The pawn-chain as a blockade problem. ·The attack against the 'base'.*

There was a time, before 1913, when it was the firm conviction that a pawn-chain, with the disappearance of one of its links, must give up all pretension to a happy existence. To have shown this conviction to be based on pure prejudice is a service for which I may take credit, since as early as the year 1911 I have proved by some games (against Salwe, Carlsbad, 1911, Game No. 46, against Löwen-fisch, and against Dr. Tarrasch, in 1912, Game No. 20) that I was inclined to conceive of the pawn-chain as a purely cramping problem, and that the question was not whether the links of the chain were complete, but simply and solely whether the enemy pawns remained cramped. Whether we effect this by pawns or pieces, or indeed by Castles or Bishops at long range, is immaterial. The main thing is that they, the enemy pawns, should be cramped. This conception of mine, to which I had arrived through an intensive study of the blockade problem, did not fail, in those days, to arouse a storm of protest. To-day, however, everyone knows that all the things which I then said about the pawn-chain are incontestable truths.

It was disputed at that time (see in particular a violent article by Alapin in the *Wiener Schachzeitung*, 1913), that after 1. P—K4, P—K3; 2. P—Q4, P—Q4, any attack on Black's Q4 existed at all; but we, that is the friendly readers of my book, know well enough that such an attack does very much exist. Alapin did not know it, since he was not acquainted with the theory of the open file, which I originated. So, too, to take another disputed point, everyone recognizes to-day that in positions characterized by the advance P—K5 (at the 3rd or at a later move), the thrust P—KB4—B5 may well be, and often is, the logical sequence. We can learn a lot by a closer investigation of the question, why after 1. P—K4, P—K3; 2. P—Q4, P—Q4; 3. P—K5, the Black attack P—QB4 should hold the field rather than an immediate White attack by P—KB4—B5. As we have already insisted, the disposition of both the White and Black links in the chain is directed towards cramping the opponent. The White pawns wish to blockade the Black, and vice versa. Now after 1. P—K4, P—K3; 2. P—Q4, P—Q4; 3. P—K5, it is the Black pawns who are held up on their road to the centre, whereas the corresponding White pawns have already outstripped the middle of the board (compare the relative positions of the two KP's); hence we are justified in regarding the White as the cramping, the Black as the cramped pawns. And since the pawns' desire to expand is naturally greatest when directed towards the centre, we see that Black is more justified in the attack P—QB4 than White is in the corresponding thrust on the other wing (P—KB4—B5). The threat of the advance of the KBP exists, however, in spite of everything; and when Black's attack has burnt itself out, White's turn then comes for the thrust with his KBP.

That this threat fails in many games to be translated into action only goes to prove that White has plenty on his hands in meeting the attack P—QB4, or else that he has chosen the first of the two theatres of war (i.e., Black's cramped King's wing) for his operations.

As to what concerns the transference of our attack from Black's Q4 to his K3, the student will soon see how wide is the bearing of this proposition of mine. But let us proceed systematically.

§3. *Attack on the 'base' a strategical necessity. The clearing away of the links in the enemy chain is only undertaken with the idea of freeing our pawns which they had been cramping. Accordingly the problem of the chain is in essentials reduced to one of blockade.*

To recognize an enemy pawn-chain as an enemy and to go for it is one and the same thing; this may be formulated thus:— Freeing operations in the region of a pawn-chain can never be set on foot soon enough.

This war of liberation will, however, be conducted thus:— We first direct our operations against the base, which we attack with a pawn, and, by threats or otherwise, seek to cut off the base from its associates in the chain. This done, we turn our attention to the next opponent, namely the link which is now become the new base. For instance, after 1. P—K4, P—K3; 2. P—Q4, P—Q4; 3. P—K5, the Black pawns (K3, Q4) appear to be checked. The attack on the cramping White chain should, by our rule, be launched without any delay, and note, by 3.....P—QB4, not by 3.....P—KB3; for the link P—K5 corresponds to an architectural adornment to our building (the chain), whereas the PQ4 is the very foundation of the whole structure. If we wish to sap a building, we should not begin with its architectural ornaments, but we should blow up its foundations, for then the destruction of the ornaments with all the rest will automatically follow.

White has several replies to 3.....P—QB4. The plan of the

second player will stand out clearest if White plays ingenuously, as if he had no conception of the problem of the pawn-chain, therefore in some such way as this: 4. P×P, B×P; 5. Kt—QB3?, P—KB3!. Events have taken their logical course. The Hetman, the PQ4, was first put out of action, and then the PK5 got it in the neck. All things decently and in order, but we must always begin with the Hetman, the base of the pawn-chain. To continue our game: after 5.....P—KB3 there would follow 6. P×P (which is as artless as ever. Kt—KB3 was certainly better), 6.....Kt×P; 7. Kt—KB3, Kt—QB3; 8. B—Q3, P—K4! and thanks to White's faulty strategy, Black's freeing operations, which as a rule take up some 20–25 moves, may already be regarded as ended. Black first caused the links in White's chain voluntarily to disappear one after the other, beginning with the base (by the captures P×QBP, P×KBP) and thereupon let his own pawns advance in triumph, with P—K4. This advance, so eagerly sought after, affords the explanation of the energetic measures taken by Black with his 3rd and following moves, namely the recovery of their mobility for his cramped pawns. This was all that Black sought or desired. Accordingly it often happens that pawns thus advanced are filled with a particularly war-like spirit; we get the impression that they wish to take bitter vengeance for the humiliation they have suffered by being hemmed in.

Diagram 106

Here the right proceeding for Black is to attack the chain by P—QKt4-5 in order to provoke BP×P. P—KB3 would be wrong

Diagram 106 shows another example. Here White's PQB3 is the base of the White chain, not his PQKt2, be it well noted, for this pawn has not yet been attached to the association in the Black and White pawn-chain, since a Black colleague is wanting at White's QKt3; and against this base we send forward the QKtP to storm it; accordingly P—QKt4—Kt5. Having provoked BP×P, the PQ4 is now promoted to the base, but, unlike his predecessor, is not protected. The unprotected base (i.e., undefended by a pawn) is, however, a weakness, and hence gives occasion for a lasting siege, such as we propose to consider in §5. In the above example P—KB3 (instead of, correctly, P—QKt4—Kt5) would have to be labelled a mistake, for after the fall of the KP White's chain would still remain intact.

We are now on the road to a true understanding of the matter. The freeing operations in the domain of the pawn-chain are analogous to the fight against a troublesome blockader (Chap. IV) and accordingly our present problem is reduced to one of blockade.

§4. *The transference of the blockade rules from the 'passed pawn' to the 'chain'.   The exchange manœuvre (to bring about the substitution of a more amenable enemy blockader for a strong one) applied to the pawn-chain.*

It is clear to us, after studying Chapter IV, that every enemy piece which holds in check a pawn which would otherwise be mobile, must be conceived of as a blockader.   Nevertheless it must cause surprise that, after the moves 1. P—K4, P—K3; 2. P—Q4, P—Q4; 3. P—K5, we should agree to regard the PQ4 and PK5 as proper blockaders in our sense; and the surprise lies in seeing a pawn so described, for in general we think of pawns as being blockaded, and the rôle of a blockader we imagine to be reserved for an officer. This is in general true, but the pawns in a chain are pawns of a higher order, and in their functions differ from the common herd.   To conceive of the pawns in a chain as blockaders would then appear to be quite correct.

Recognizing this, let us now try to apply the 'exchange manœuvre on the blockading square', with which we became acquainted in Chapter IV, to the chain.   The exchange, as we there said, could only be justified if the new blockader proved himself to be weaker than his predecessor.   The same applies to the chain.

An Example: After 1. P—K4, P—K3; 2. P—Q4, P—Q4; 3. P—K5, P—QB4!; 4. Kt—QB3, Black can try to get the blockader (the PQ4) replaced by another (the QQ4).   In fact, after the further moves 4.....P×P; 5. Q×P, Kt—QB3, the Q turns out to be a blockader whom it will be difficult to maintain at her post, and hence the exchange is proved to be correct; and this in spite of a possible 6. B—QKt5, for after 6.....B—Q2, 7. B×Kt, P×B; Black has two Bishops and a mobile mass of pawns in the centre, and has the advantage.

On the other hand this exchange manœuvre would be weak after 1. P—K4, P—K3; 2. P—Q4, P—Q4; 3. P—K5, P—QB4; 4. P—QB3, Kt—QB3; 5. B—K3, for after 5.....P×P (Q—Kt3 is better); 6. B×P, the B would be a tough customer to deal with, and a further exchange, so as to be rid of him, i.e., say 6. Kt×B; 7. Q×Kt, Kt—K2; 8. Kt—KB3, Kt—QB3; 9. Q—KB4, would lead to the driving off of the blockading troops, but only at the cost of loss of time caused by the moves of the Black KKt.

In this position White stands quite well; his pieces are placed as they would be for a King's side attack, but have also a sufficient bearing on the centre.   For example: 9.....P—KB3 (to roll up White's chain); 10. B—Kt5, P—QR3; 11. B×Kt, P×B; 11. 0—0, and Black will never succeed in making his PK3 mobile, for if P×KP, then Kt×P, and the establishment of the Kt at this point, K5, would follow.

With this we have got further towards an understanding of the pawn-chain. All exchange operations in the region of a chain only take place with the object of replacing a strong enemy blockader by a weaker one, and the experience we have got from Chapter IV will be of great help to us here. We have, I mean, to decide in a given case whether the blockader in question is strong or weak, elastic or inelastic, and the faculty of discriminating rightly in such cases will be of enormous service to us. See, for example, Diagram 107. Here Q—B2 would be a weak move in spite of the sharp threat of B × Kt and B × P ch. The mistake lies in the fact that White had much better have done something towards the defence of his blockading wall, e.g., Kt—Q2, 0—0; Kt—B3. On the other hand if 1. Q—B2??, the continuation might be 1..... 0—0; 2. B × Kt, R × B; 3. B × P ch, K—R1; 4. B—Kt6 (or Q3), P—K4!. White, it is

Diagram 107

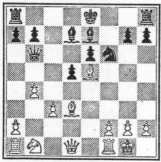

Permanently to occupy the points K5 and Q4 is White's immediate problem. Which move is the better to this end, Kt—Q2, or Q—B2?

Diagram 108

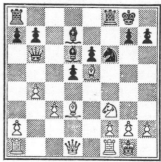

To attain a permanent blockade of Black's PK3 and PQ4, which is the better: 15. B—Q4, Q—B2; 16. Q—K2, or at once 15. Q—K2?

true, has won a pawn, but Black has overcome the blockade, and now stands ready to march in the centre. White should lose.

In Diagram 108, the manœuvre 15. B—Q4, Q—B2; 16. Q—K2 might be considered, with the intention of following with 17. Kt—K5. However, this plan to widen the blockading ring is impracticable, for, after 16. Q—K2, Kt—Kt5!!; 17. P—KR3, P—K4!, the Black pawns assert themselves whatever counter-measure be taken. The right move is rather 15. Q—K2; and there follows 15..... QR—QB1 (or 15..... B × B; 16. Kt × B, QR—QB1; 17. P—QB4!); 16. B—Q4!, Q—B2; 17. Kt—K5, and Black is seriously blockaded. We may say therefore that the line of play 15. B—Q4, Q—B2; 16. Q—K2 was bad because the reserve blockader who was keeping watch (the KtKB3) would have but slight blockading effect, that is to say would never succeed in reaching K5. In the notes to my game against Salwe

(No. 46, from which this example is taken) we shall prove our theory of exchanges by further examples.

§5. *The conception of a war of movement and that of siege-warfare applied to the region of the chain. The attacking party at the parting of the ways.*

If the attacking party has played in the spirit of the explanations given in this chapter (that is to say, attack on the 'base', and the correct application of the exchange operation on the blockading point), it will often happen that the full freedom of his hampered pawns will be his reward. There will be times, however, when the fight he has waged with the measures here indicated will reach a dead point, and in such cases the use of some new plan becomes necessary. As an example we will take the position given in Diagram 109. The opening moves of the game were:

Diagram 109

1. P—K4, P—K3; 2. P—Q4, P—Q4; 3. P—K5, P—QB4; 4. P—QB3, Kt—QB3; 5. Kt—KB3, Q—Kt3 (Black seeks by hook or by crook to induce White to give up his base, the PQ4. An attack with this purpose, one which aims at the rolling up of the chain, we class as a war of movement, of which the move Q—Kt3 must be regarded as a part. Q moves in the opening are as a rule out of place; here, however, the weal or woe of the pawn-chain dictates all our actions); 6. B—Q3 (Diag. 109), B—Q2. A very plausible move; and since White still hesitates to make the capture P×P, Black proposes to make his decision easier by 7.....R—QB1. The right move, however, was 6.....P×P; 7. P×P; and with it to adopt other methods,

Black with the move is at the parting of the ways between the war of movement and positional warfare. The former would take the course: B—Q2 in order finally to cause White to make the move P×P which Black desires; the latter takes the form P×P, P×P followed by a long siege of White's PQ4

namely siege or positional warfare. These were the opening moves of the game No. 46. Nimzowitsch—Salwe, played at Carlsbad in 1911. From first move to last it is highly instructive; moreover, I regard it as the first game to be played in the spirit of the new philosophy of the centre, which I originated. The student is advised to play through this game before proceeding further.

We have already said, and the course of the game shows, that at his sixth move (Diag. 109) Black could, and should, have sought a quieter channel by playing 6.....P×P; 7. P×P, B—Q2; with eventual Kt—K2—B4. He preferred, however, to play for the complete capitulation of his opponent (in the region of the chain, I mean). His plan was (1) to force White to play QP×QBP and KP×KBP, (2) to drive off any blockading pieces that might take their place, (3) triumphantly to advance his centre pawns, now freed. His plan failed because the substitute blockaders were not to be driven away, that is to say they had a strong blockading effect. The two following postulates are here of importance: (*a*) It makes no difference whatever to the strangled (i.e., hemmed in) pawns whether they are strangled by pawns or by officers; the operation is as painful in one case as in the other; whence it follows that (*b*) the destruction of the cramping pawns in the chain does not in itself imply a more or less complete liberating operation, for the substitute blockaders, the pieces, have still to be driven away. How and in what measure this last is possible is the question of really decisive importance.

The following, taken from my article, 'The surrender of the centre —a prejudice,' written in 1913, may serve to throw light on the relations between pawns and pieces:—'True, the pawns are best fitted for building up the centre, since they are the most stable; on the other hand pieces stationed in the centre can very well take the place of pawns.' Moreover, as we shall see later, the centre can often be effectively held at long range by Bishops and Rooks, so that the actual occupation of the centre by a pawn or pawns does not necessarily mean its control. The greater part of this article is reprinted in II. i. §7 (page 132); at the moment we would only remark that we are inclined to regard as most dangerous any liberating operation which is begun but not completed (as in Salwe's attempt in the game under consideration—No. 46), dangerous that is to say, to the one ostensibly freeing himself. And now to return to the position on Diagram 109.

§5a. *Positional warfare, in other words, the slow siege of the unprotected base. Repeated bombardment. The defending pieces get in one another's way. How can we maintain the pressure? The genesis of new weaknesses. The base as a weakness in the end game.*

Since in the position shown on Diagram 109 the move 6.....B—Q2 seems to give little promise of profit, Black, as we have several times insisted, had much better have played 6.....P×P. What does this move signify? The White base (PQ4) has thereby been made immobile, has been fixed at Q4. Before P×P took place White's QP could, whether for good or evil, at any rate leave his place (by QP×BP); but now this is no longer possible. We must be quite clear on one point, that by playing 6.....P×P Black has had to resign himself to renouncing his ambitious dreams of forcing his opponent into complete capitulation in the chain area, these are now gone to their grave. But Black does retain certain small yet real possibilities. For instance: White's PQ4 will be attacked by several pieces, not so much for the reason that the conquest of White's base is likely, but rather in order to force upon the defending enemy pieces a passive, because purely defensive, rôle. Black's aim is, in fact, an ideal one, the advantage of the aggressive position for his pieces discussed in I. vi. The continuation could be 6..... P × P; 7. P × P, B—Q2 (threatening Kt × QP, which, of course, could not be done before because of 7..... Kt × QP??, 8. Kt × Kt, Q × Kt; 9. B—Kt5 ch, winning the Q); 8. B—K2 (If 8. B—B2 Black with Kt—QKt5 could obtain the advantage of the two Bishops), 8..... KKt—K2!. Whether it be slow or quick, Black chooses the development which puts pressure on the base. And rightly, for in close games, i.e., those characterized by the presence of pawn-chains, the chain is the one true guide post. 9. P—QKt3, Kt—B4; 10. B—Kt2 (Diagram 110a), B—Kt5 ch!; this check shows up, and in the most glaring light, so to say, the dark side of an enforced defence by many pieces. The defending pieces are in one another's way. 11. K—B1 (for either 11. Kt—QB3 or QKt—Q2 would rob the base of a defender), 11..... B—K2. Tarrasch's idea, the student should ponder the argument on which this move is based. If he is to keep up the pressure on White's PQ4 Black must never allow the equilibrium of attack and defence

Diagram 110a

White's base, PQ4 under pressure. The typical siege of an 'unprotected' base

(now 3 : 3) to be disturbed to his disadvantage. The attacking pieces must strive to maintain their attacking positions. To effect this 11..... P—KR4 could be played (to prevent P—KKt4); the text move attains the same end by other means. If now 12. P—KKt4 the answer would be 12..... Kt—R5, an attacker and a defender would disappear together and the *status quo* would be maintained.

The typical strategy appropriate to the various cases which may arise is made clear by the following postulates:

(*a*) The enemy base being fixed to one spot, should be attacked by several pieces.

(*b*) By these means we shall at least obtain the ideal advantage of the aggressive position for our pieces. Worth mentioning in this connexion is the slight elasticity, i.e., capacity for manoeuvring, possessed by the defending pieces; for instance, in the case of a sudden attack on another wing, they will not be able to equal the attacking pieces in rapidity of motion, and will lag behind.

(c) We must seek to keep up the pressure on the base for as long as possible, at any rate until the appearance of new weaknesses in the enemy camp, which will follow as the logical consequence of his difficulties in development.

(d) When this occurs our plan of action will be modified; the original weakness, the base, will be left alone, the new one attacked with the greatest energy. And only much later, perhaps not until the end game, will the weak enemy base be again 'promoted' to the dignity of being our objective.

(e) The weak base is, when all is said and done, to be regarded as, in particular, an end-game weakness; since the specific attacking instrument, the open adjoining file (in this case the QB file) only comes completely into its rights in the end game (R—QB4 × PQ4, or R—QB7—Q7 × PQ4).

(f) The attacking party must never forget that he on his side has a base to defend. If his opponent succeed in making his part of the chain region healthy, i.e., in shaking off the pressure on his base (the PQ4 in our case), an entirely new and disagreeable turn may be given to the game by his playing P—KB4—B5, with attack on the base (PK3), or on the other hand launching an attack with his pieces on the King's position which is cramped by his PK5.

The application of (a) will hardly present any difficulties to the student. Take for instance the following position: White: K, Q2; R, QB1; Kt, QKt2; P's, QR2, QKt4, QB5, Q5, K4, KB5, KKt2, KR3. Black: K, QKt1; R, KB1; Kt, KR3; P's, QR2, QKt3, QB2, Q3, K4, KB3, KKt2, KR2. The chain we have to do with is formed of the K and QP's on both sides. Black's base is the PQ3. White now plays 1. P × QP, P × P; 2. R—B6, Kt—B2; 3. Kt—B4, R—Q1 (if R—QB1 then 4. P—Kt5, R × R; 5. QP × R with the superior end game); 4. P—QR4! (to maintain the attacking KtB4 on this square); White has now put the base PQ3, under pressure, and consequently has the advantage referred to of the more aggressive position for his pieces. The KtB4 is more aggressively placed than Black's KtB2, etc. This advantage could be exploited either by 5. P—Kt5 followed by, say, K—B3 and P—QR5, or by play on the King's wing, e.g., P—KR4, and then K—K3—B3—Kt4—R5 followed by P—KKt4—Kt5; when the parry P—KR3 would allow the King's entry at KKt6.

It is much more difficult for the student to assimilate the points made in (c) and (d). The direct exploitation of a pawn weakness is not, properly speaking, a matter for the middle game. (See point (e).) All that we may hope to attain is to cause our opponent to suffer for a considerable period under the disadvantage of the duties of defence which have been forced on him. If, as a result of these difficulties, a new weakness be induced in the enemy camp (as is by no means improbable), it is not merely permissible for the attacking party to release the base from pressure, in order to devote his attention to the new weakness, such a course is absolutely indicated. The further removed (geographically and logically) the two weaknesses are from one another, the better for us! This connexion of ideas was more or less unknown to the pseudo-classical school. Tarrasch, for instance, was wont with relentless persistence to keep under continual attack the base which he had once selected as his objective, or at least to remain true to the wing of his first choice. (See Game No. 19, Paulsen—Tarrasch.)

In opposition to this we lay stress on the principle that the weakness of the enemy base cannot be completely exploited until the end game (cf. *e*), or more accurately: in the end game our aim is the direct,

that is to say actual, conquest of the base which serves as our objective; in the middle game the bombardment of this base can and should only help to yield us indirect advantages. For example, suppose Black to be attacking the enemy base in the middle game; White's pieces will get in one another's way, difficulties of development will arise, and White will find himself forced to create a new weakness in his own camp, in order to remove those difficulties. On this Black now concentrates his attack, and only in the end game may he find it profitable to take up again the attack on his first objective, the enemy base.

Diagram 110b

Black to move. How is the pressure on White's Q4 to be kept up? The position of the K at KB1 is a disadvantage. How can this be exposed?

As an example of this indirect exploitation of a weakened enemy base we may take the position shown on Diagram 110b taken from Game No. 19, Paulsen—Tarrasch. After the moves 1. P—K4, P—K3; 2. P—Q4, P—Q4; 3. P—K5, P—QB4; 4. P—QB3, Kt—QB3; 5. Kt—KB3, Q—Kt3; 6. B—Q3, P×P; 7. P×P, B—Q2; 8. B—K2, KKt—K2; 9. P—QKt3, Kt—B4; 10. B—Kt2, B—Kt5 ch, White saw himself forced to forego castling by having to play K—B1; thus the pressure on his PQ4 has taken tangible shape. Black's problem, therefore, no longer consists in keeping up the pressure on the QP, which could be done by 11.....P—KR4 or 11.....B—K2 as we have already indicated (Diag. 110a); he should rather give up the attack on White's base, and do everything he can to expose and exploit the weakness of White's KKB1. This, indeed, is only possible by means of a hidden sacrifice of the exchange. In this position in reply to 11. K—B1 I play 11.....0—0. If then 12. B—Q3 to lessen the pressure on the QP, there would follow 12.....P—KB3; 13. B×Kt, P×B; with advantage to Black in his two Bishops. The main variation, after 11. K—B1, 0—0!!, lies in the continuation 12. P—KKt4, Kt—R3; 13. R—KKt1, P—KB3; 14. P×P, R×P!; 15. P—Kt5, R×Kt!; 16. B×R, (or P×Kt, R—B2), Kt—B4; 17. R—Kt4 (Diag. 110c). White's desolate King's wing and the weakly defended points in the KB file ought, in my opinion, to lead to a lost game. I give one possible continuation: 17.....B—K1 (R—KB1 is also good enough); 18. Q—K2, QKt×P; 19. R×Kt!, Kt×R; 20. Q—K5 (the last chance), B—Kt4 ch; 21. K—Kt2, Kt—B4; 22. B×QP (if 22. Kt—QB3 then 22.....B×Kt; 23. B×B, P—Q5 etc.).

Diagram 110c

The position after the exposure of White's disadvantage in the position of his KKB1. In spite of his material superiority White stands badly

22.....P×B; 23. Q×Kt, R—KB1; 24. Q×QP ch, R—B2! (a self pin for the purpose of safeguarding his KKt2 against a possible Q—Q4); 25. Q—Q4, B—B4, and White must resign. The decision took place, as was logical, on the King's wing; the second player was able to exploit to the full the new weakness without any regard to the old one. The student will do well to note most carefully the transfer of the attack from the centre (the base, PQ4) to the K wing which had been weakened by K—B1.

As an antithesis to the manœuvre we have just demonstrated we would emphasize the fact (Diag. 110b) that 11.....B—K2, after 12. P—KKt3 and K—Kt2, with the subsequent safeguarding and relieving of the PQ4 would give White good chances, for after his position had been consolidated White would be well able to turn the tables on his opponent as outlined in (f); i.e., by an attack on Black's King's Wing which is cramped by the PK5. (See Game No. 20, Nimzowitsch—Tarrasch.)

Before we proceed further, we would impress upon the student that he should practise so as to be able to take advantage of a weak enemy base in the end game. We recommend the study of game No. 15 and further the application of the following method. Set up a pawn-chain on the board, e.g., White: PQ4, PK5; Black: PQ4, PK3; give to each side some more pawns (White QR2, QKt2, KB2, KKt2, KR2. Black: QR2, QKt2, KB2 KKt2, KR2) and try to take advantage of the weakness of White's PQ4 in a purely pawn end game, there being either Rooks on the board or a Rook and a minor piece on each side.

§6. *The transfer of the attack.*

In the position on Diagram 109 Black had the choice, as we have often pointed out already, of two different lines of play, namely between 6.....B—Q2 with a war of movement, or 6.....P×P with positional or siege warfare directed against White's fixed base, the PQ4. It will be granted that a moment must come when Black will be forced to make his choice. It is not possible to keep open at will the choice between two lines of play, least of all when we are concerned with a pawn-chain, for the simple reason that the defending party, relying on the state of suspense in the position, and the possibilities arising out of it, can threaten an attack to free himself. Once this enemy threat becomes actual, we are forced to make an immediate decision. Another crisis which compels a decision occurs when our opponent threatens us on another wing, when we shall have to decide on as sharp a counter as possible, since any further flirting with two different plans would no longer be opportune.

Whereas we have up to now considered only the choice between two methods of attack, while the objective (White's PQ4 in the example we have taken) remained fixed, and was therefore not in doubt, it will be shown in what follows how painful even the choice of an objective can sometimes be. We are concerned with a pawn-chain which is to be attacked. 'What can there be doubtful in such a case?' the reader will ask. 'We must of course direct our attack against its base?' But what if the base is not to be shaken; would it not be better to direct our attack against a new base? How this is done will be seen from the stratagem of the transference of the attack which will now be sketched.

Let us consider the following chain resulting after 1. P—K4, P—K4; 2. Kt—KB3, Kt—QB3; 3. B—B4, B—K2; 4. P—Q4, P—Q3; 5. P—Q5, Kt—Kt1. White now chooses the centre as the theatre of war, and plays say B—Q3 and P—QB4, with the idea of eventually P—B5. (He could as an alternative have decided on an attack with his pieces—without playing P—QB4—on the enemy Q's wing which is cramped by the PQ5.) Black tries to make possible P—KB4, in order to shake White's base, the PK4. The pseudo-classical school held P—KB4 to be a refutation of White's P—Q5. This is, however, not the case, as I proved in my revolutionizing article on Dr. Tarrasch's *Moderne Sehachpartie*. P—KB4 is only a natural reaction to White's P—Q5, and as such every bit as endurable as P—QB4—B5. In essentials the position arrived at could be that shown on Diagram 111. Black's attack on the base PK4 does

not look as if it promised much; for if at any time BP × P, the answer
would be either P × P, and the base is well defended, or Kt (or B) × P
with a good 'substitute centre'. Hence Black plays P—KB5, thus
changing White's base from PK4 to PKB3. True the latter can be
sufficiently defended (against P—KKt4—Kt5 × BP which Black
plans), but White's King's position seems then to be threatened
and is certainly cramped. In other words White's King's position
marks out the PKB3 as a weaker base than the PK4.

And there are other circumstances which may make one base
appear weaker than another; hence the switching over of the attack
from one base to the next is not a mere matter of chance (as Alapin
and other masters seemed to think before the appearance of my essay
to which reference has just been made); it is in fact an additional
weapon in the fight against a pawn-chain. A judgment on the

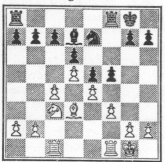

Diagram 111

strength of a pawn-chain as a whole
must run something like this: 'The
base K4 is difficult of attack, the base
KB3 (after P—KB5) is for such and
such reasons sensitive to attack, etc.,
hence it will pay to transfer our attack
to the new base, KB3.' This formulation of the case I may claim as my
discovery.

We must content ourselves with the
above concise suggestions else this
Chapter would stretch to too great
a length. This transference of attack
is typical, and we could give endless examples from games. We
will, however, only show the following opening here. 1. P—K4,
Kt—QB3; 2. P—Q4, P—Q4; 3. P—K5, B—B4; 4. P—KB4,
P—K3; 5. Kt—KB3, Kt—QKt5; 6. B—Kt5 ch, P—QB3;
7. B—R4, P—QKt4; 8. P—QR3!, Kt—R3; 9. B—Kt3, P—QB4;
10. P—QB3. Since White's base, the PQ4, seemed actually to be
over-defended, Black quite rightly played here 10.....P—B5,
transferring the attack from White's Q4 to his QB3. After the
further moves 11. B—B2, B × B; 12. Q × B, Kt—K2 (cf. II ii. on
Restraint), Black put under restraint White's King's Wing which
was ready to attack, i.e., by making the natural advance P—KB5
impossible, and then by means of P—QR4 and P—QKt5 finally
launched the attack on the new objective, White's base at QB3.

Before closing this chapter and with it the discussion of the
'elements' we should like to point out quite shortly how difficult it is
to conduct the game in the pawn chain correctly. Very soon after
the formation of the chain we have to choose whether a wing or the
base shall be our objective; then later, incidental to an attack on the

base we have to make the difficult decision between a war of movement and siege warfare; and, as if that is not enough, we have always to reckon with a possible transference of the attack to the next link of the chain. And in addition to all this we must never forget, in spite of all these possibilities of attack, that we, too, have a vulnerable base.

A difficult chapter, but one in which the inherent obscurity of its subject matter will, we hope, now have largely disappeared, thanks to our treatment of it.

It will have been seen that my laws governing pawn-chains have grown logically from those applying to 'open files' and 'play against the blockader'. The reader will find a further discussion of the subject in Part II, Chap. ii on the 'Centre' and 'Restraint'; he is urged at this point to play over the following games, Nos. 19 to 24 and No. 46, which illustrate the subject of the pawn-chain.

I

PART II

POSITION PLAY

CHAPTER I

THE CONCEPTION OF POSITION PLAY AND THE PROBLEM OF THE CENTRE

§1. *The mutual relations between the treatment of the elements and of position play.*

As the reader will soon see, my conception of position play is based for the greater part on the knowledge we have laboriously wrung from our consideration of the elements. Especially is this true of the devices of Centralization and of Restraint which we have outlined. The connexion which thus exists has the advantage, that it must give to this book a certain unity of structure, which can only be of benefit to the reader. It would, however, be an error on his part to indulge in the expectation that the exploration of the spirit of position play cannot now afford him any further difficulties worth mentioning. For firstly, position play contains other ideas than those we have met so far, as for instance the law of 'over-protection', which I discovered, or the very difficult strategy of the centre; while secondly, the actual transference of the ideas which we have learnt from the elements on to a new field, that of position play, is difficult enough. The degree of difficulty is much the same as that which faces a composer who wishes to adapt a violin sonata for a full orchestra. However unchanged the theme, the motives, may be, the whole must gain in depth and breadth. Let us explain this by a concrete case in chess, for instance 'restraint'. In the 'elements' this touches a comparatively small field; a passed pawn is to be checked, or an enemy pawnchain which is become free to move is to be prevented from advancing. In position play on the other hand the restraint theme makes a much more impressive appearance; now it is often a whole wing which must be held in check. In games in which the player who is putting restraint on his opponent is 'scoring' his theme very heavily (I have in mind for instance my game against Johner, No. 35), we have the whole board, both wings, every corner taking up the theme, and blaring it forth.

The second case is even worse for the student; for here the theme appears in epic breadth, with a series of seemingly purposeless moves, to and fro, mixed with it.   This kind of manœuvring corresponds in a way to the accompaniment in music.   Many people hold both this manœuvring and accompaniment as things which may be dispensed with; many lovers of chess go so far as to characterize this moving to and fro as a fruit of decadence.   In reality, however, this manœuvring often enough provides the only strategical—be it noted strategical, not merely psychological—way of throwing in the scale a slight advantage in terrain and the consequent capacity of moving our troops more quickly from one wing to the other.

§2.   *On certain noxious weeds which choke a proper understanding of position play, namely (a) the obsession to be for ever doing something which haunts so many amateurs, and (b) the overrating of the principle of the accumulation of small advantages which may inspire the Master.*

There are, it would seem, a number of amateurs to whom position play appears to mean nothing.   Twenty years' experience in teaching chess has, however, convinced me that this trouble can be easily removed, since it results from a faulty presentation of the subject. I maintain that there is nothing inherently mysterious in position play, and that every single amateur who has studied my 'elements', in the first nine chapters of this book, must find it an easy matter to penetrate into the spirit of this style of play; he has only (1) to destroy the weeds which perhaps choke his understanding, and (2) to carry out the precepts laid down in the rest of the book.

A typical and very wide-spread misconception is the assumption of many amateurs that each single move must accomplish something directly; so that such a player will only seek for moves which threaten something, or for a threat to be parried, and will disregard all other possible moves such as waiting moves, or moves calculated to put his house in order etc.   Positional moves as I conceive them, are in general neither threatening nor defensive ones, but rather moves designed to give to our position security in the wider sense, and to this end it is necessary for our pieces to establish contact with the enemy's strategically important points or our own.   This will be brought out later when we are considering 'over-protection', and the fight against enemy freeing-moves.

When a positional player, that is one who understands how to safeguard his position in the wider sense, engages one who is a purely combinational player, the latter who has only attack in his thoughts, is preoccupied with but two kinds of counter-moves, and looks only for a defensive move from his opponent, or calculates on the possibility of a counter-attack; and now the positional player dumbfounds him by choosing a move which will not fit into either of these categories. The move somehow or other brings his pieces into contact with some key point, and this contact has miraculous effects; his position is thereby imbued with strength, and the attack on it comes to naught. A similar disconcerting effect is also often produced by a move which protects a point which is under no sort of attack. The positional player protects a point not only for the sake of that point, but also because he knows that the piece which he uses for its defence must gain in strength by mere contact with the point in question. This will be considered further under 'over-protection'.

And now I will take a game which is an admirable illustration of very widespread misconception to which I have referred. I had the White pieces against a very well known and by no means weak amateur, who, however, was under the impression that a proper game must take some such course as this:—One side Castles K-side, the

other Q-side, a violent pawn attack is launched on both sides against the respective castled positions, and he who gets in first wins! We shall see how this amateurish conception was reduced ad absurdum. The game was played in Riga in 1910 and ran:— 1. P—K4, P—K4; 2. Kt—KB3, Kt— QB3; 3. P—Q4, P×P; 4. Kt×P, P—Q3 (this move is quite playable but only in conjunction with a strong defensive structure, attainable by say Kt—KB3, B—K2, 0—0, and R—K1 with pressure on White's KP); 5. Kt— QB3, Kt—KB3; 6. B—K2, B—K2; 7. B—K3, B—Q2; 8. Q—Q2, P—QR3?;

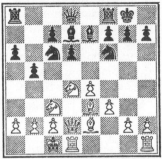

Diagram 112

The attempt of an attack by P—QKt4(?) is to be defeated by a positional move. What is this to be?

9. P—KB3, 0—0; 10. 0—0—0, P—QKt4. The attack seems hardly in place here, so that my opponent's expression, 'Now we're in for it,' charged as it was with the lust of battle, struck one as all the prettier. I understood him at once; he clearly expected the answer P—KKt4 with a consequent race between the pawns on both sides according to the motto 'who gets in first wins' (Diag. 112). What did happen however was 11. Kt—Q5. With this move, by which an outpost station in the Q file is occupied, White obeys another principle of position play, namely that premature flank attacks should be punished by play in the centre (=break through in, or occupation of the centre), there followed 11.....KKt×Kt; 12. P×Kt, Kt×Kt; 13. B×Kt, and White has very much the better game. He has a centralized position which cannot possibly be taken away from him by, say, 13.....B—KB3; 14. P—KB4, R—K1; 15. B—KB3

followed by KR—K1; and moreover Black has a disorganized Q wing which exposes bad weaknesses for the end game. And the moral of the story is: Do not be always thinking of attack! Safeguarding moves (in the higher sense), indicated by the demands made on us by the position, are often much more advisable.

Another erroneous conception may be found among Masters. Many of these and numbers of strong amateurs are under the impression that position play above all is concerned with the accumulation of small advantages, in order to exploit them in the end game. This mode of play is said to demand the finest intelligence and also to be aesthetically most satisfying.

In contradiction to this we would remark that the accumulation of small advantages is by no means the most important constituent of position play. We are inclined rather to assign to this plan of operation a very subordinate rôle. Moreover the difficulty of this method is very much overestimated, and lastly it is not quite easy to see how the petty storing up of values can be called beautiful. Does not this procedure remind one in some sense of the activities of some old pinch-penny; and who would think of calling them beautiful? And so we here note the fact that there are quite other matters to which the attention of the positional player must be directed, and which place this 'accumulation' wholly in the shade.

What are these things, and in what do I see the idea of true position play? The answer is short and to the point—in a 'prophylactic'.

§3. *My original conception of positional play as such: the well known idea of the accumulation of small advantages is only of second or third significance; of much greater importance is a prophylactic applied both externally and internally. My new principle of over-protection, its definition and meaning.*

As I have several times observed, neither attack nor defence is, in my opinion, a matter properly pertaining to position play, which is rather an energetic and systematic application of prophylactic measures. What it is concerned with above all else is to blunt the edge of certain possibilities which in a positional sense would be undesirable. Of such possibilities, apart from the mishaps to which the less experienced player is exposed, there are two kinds only. One of these is the possibility of the opponent making a 'freeing' pawn move. The positional player has accordingly so to arrange his pieces that enemy freeing moves may be prevented. In connexion with which it is to be noticed that we must examine every case that arises to see whether the freeing move in question really is freeing. For as I pointed out in my article on Dr. Tarrasch's *Die moderne Schachpartie*, the true saying, 'all is not gold that glitters,' applies to freeing moves. Many there are which only lead to an unfavourable premature opening up of the game, whereas other freeing moves should be considered as normal reactions, and as such must be calmly accepted; for it were a presumption to wish to fight against natural phenomena! In spite of the fact that freeing moves will be considered in detail in another place under 'restraint', it will not be amiss to give here two illustrations.

For an example of an incorrect freeing move, see Diagram 113. In similar positions the move P—K4 would properly be classed under freeing moves; for it opens up Black's otherwise cramped game, and in addition stands for the action in the centre, positionally indicated as a counter-measure to the encircling movement which White is striving for on the Q's wing. Nevertheless White rightly plays here P—QKt4! (instead of R—K1), as will be seen. 1. P—QKt4!,

Diagram 113

White by playing P—QKt4, allows his opponent to make the freeing advance P—K4. Was he right in so doing?

Diagram 114

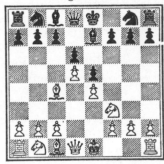

P—K4?; 2. P×P, Kt×KP; 3. B—KB4!, Kt×Kt ch; 4. Q×Kt, Q—Q1; 5. P—KR3 followed by QR—Q1 and the occupation of the square Q4 (blockading point) by B or Kt, with superior game for White: Black was, to start with, behind in tempi, hence the failure of his freeing manœuvre.

Our second example, Diagram 114, shows us that it is not possible permanently to hold up a freeing advance for which in the nature of the things the time is ripe; our object must therefore in similar cases be limited to making the freeing manœuvre as difficult of execution as possible, nor must we under any circumstances persist in the attempt, impossible of achievement from the start, to stop such an advance. The position in Diagram 114 was reached after the moves 1. P—K4, P—K4; 2. Kt—KB3, Kt—QB3; 3. B—B4, B—K2; 4. P—Q4, P—Q3; 5. P—Q5, Kt—Kt1. The pawn-chain made up of the K and QP's will make White strive for P—QB4—B5,

Black for P—KB4. Forcible measures, such as say 6. B—Q3, Kt—KB3; 7. P—KR3, 0—0; 8. P—KKt4? would not be in keeping with the position; on the other hand 6. B—Q3, Kt—KB3; 7. P—QB4, 0—0; 8. Kt—QB3, Kt—K1; 9. Q—K2 would seem to be indicated; in order in reply to 9..... P—KB4, to undertake the operation 10. P×P, B×P; 11. B×B, R×B; 12. Kt—K4 (cf. the remarks on Diag. 111).

We note then, that the prevention of freeing pawn moves (as far as this appears necessary and feasible) is of great importance in position play. Such prevention is what we wish to be understood as an exterior prophylactic. It is much more difficult to grasp the idea of an interior prophylactic, for here we have to do with an entirely new conception. We are in fact now concerned with the warding off of an evil, which has really never been understood as one, yet which can, and in general does, have a most disturbing effect on our game. The evil consists in this, that our pieces are out of, or in insufficient contact with their own strategically important points. Since I conceived of this condition as an evil, I was led to advance the strategical proposition that one must over-protect one's own strategically important points, that is, provide defence in excess of attack, i.e., lay up a store of defence. My formulation of this argument runs as follows:—Weak points, still more strong points, in short everything that we can include in the collective conception of strategically important points, ought to be over-protected. If the pieces are so engaged, they get their reward in the fact that they will then find themselves well posted in every respect.

There are two explanatory remarks to be made here; firstly, that as we have incidentally shown in our discussion of the passed pawn we have the enigmatical circumstance that blockading squares prove themselves as a rule to be in every respect good squares; and the pieces detailed for dull blockade duty find, unexpectedly, their reward in the possibility of a heightened activity from their blockading station, just as in a fairy-tale where good deeds are always rewarded. The idea of over-protection is in a certain sense no other than that above sketched though in an expanded form, as we may see from the following example (Diag. 115a). Here we over-protect the strong PK5 which has been pushed forward. The defence afforded by the QP is insufficient, since White plans to reply to P—QB4 by P×P (=surrender of the base of his chain and occupation of the point Q4 now become free.) We over-protect the KP by pieces thus 9. Kt—Q2, and the game (Nimzowitsch—Giese) continued 9..... Kt—K2; 10. Kt—KB3!, Kt—KKt3; 11. R—K1!, B—QKt5 (to get the B finally to QB2, and then, despite the over-protection of White's KP, to play P—KB3); 12. P—QB3, B—R4; 13. B—B4! (the third over-protection), 0—0; 14. B—Kt3, B—B2;

5. Kt—Kt5 (and now the inner strength of over-protection is manifested in a drastic manner; the seemingly lifeless over-protectors, the KtKB3, the BB4, and that old blade, the RK1, suddenly raise a considerable hub-hub), 15..... KR—K1; 16. Kt—B4, Kt—KR1;

Diagram 115a

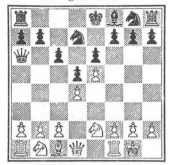

Nimzowitsch—Giese
White to move. What point must be over-protected?

Diagram 115b

The career of the 'over-protector'

17. Q—Kt4, Kt—B1; 18. R—K3 (the old soldier sniffs a fight and rejoices). 18..... P—QKt3 (rather better was B—Q1); 19. Kt—R5, Kt(R)—Kt3; 20. R—KB3, R—K2 (Diag. 115b); 21. Kt—B6 ch, K—R1; and now White could win right off by 22. Kt × RP, Kt × Kt; 23. Kt × BP ch, R × Kt; 24. R × R.

The idea was the following: It was a good deed to over-protect a strategically important point, the reward came in the form of a large radius of activity for the pieces engaged on that service.

Just one more example, for later on a whole chapter will be devoted to over-protection in all its bearings (Diag. 116). After 15. QR—Q1, QR—K1; there followed a manœuvre which seemed most unlikely, namely 16. R—Q2 and 17. KR—Q1: Why? Because the QQ3 (and perhaps too the PQ4) is the key stone of White's position, and hence over-protection is indicated. And in fact after a few moves the two rooks prove to be most serviceable combatants (they protect their own K excellently). After 16. R—Q2 the continuation was 16..... Q—Kt4; 17. KR—Q1, B—R2!!; 18. Kt—B4, Kt—B4; 19. Kt—Kt5, B—Kt1 and now R—K2 and R—K1 ought

Diagram 116

Nimzowitsch—Alekhine
Baden-Baden, 1925

Alekhine's last move was 14..... Q—B4! there followed 15. QR—Q1, QR—K1. Which point now calls for over-protection?

to have been played, when the over-protectors would have reaped
their merited reward.

Secondly, the rule for over-protection applies as is natural most
particularly to strong points, i.e., to important squares in the centre,
which are likely to come under heavy fire, to strong blockading
squares, or to strong passed pawns, etc. Ordinary weak points
should under no circumstances be over-protected, for this might
very well lead to the defenders getting into passive positions (cf.
I. vi. §2). However a weak P that forms the base of an important
pawn-chain may and should be well over-protected. To illustrate
this let us return to our old friend the pawn-chain made up of the
Q and KP's on each side. See Diagram 117a and compare it with
Diagram 117b. In the former the R's protect the weak base of the
pawn-chain (every such base is in a certain sense to be classed as

Diagram 117a	Diagram 117b
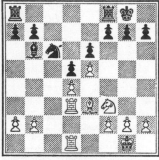	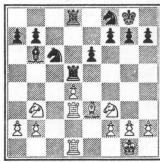
The safeguarded base Q4 increases the importance of the attacking (wedge) PK5. The heaping up of R's acts therefore as a deliberate over-protection	Here the piling up of the White R's does not have the effect of over-protection, but, absolutely, that of a passive defensive position which is classed as an evil

weak since the one sure defence, by a P, is wanting). Yet this
protection stands the strong PK5 also in good stead; for, as we know,
the strengthening of the base involves at the same time a strengthening throughout the whole chain. The reader is recommended to
play over again my game (No. 20) against Dr. Tarrasch, in which I,
after first laboriously over-protecting the point Q4, having achieved
my purpose, got a strong attack which led to victory. The soul of that
attack was however the PK5, who could so to speak trustfully lean up
against the PQ4, who by that time was thoroughly healthy. On the
other hand in the position shown on Diagram 117b the PK5 is wanting,
and hence the rôle which the RQ1 and RQ3 would otherwise have had
to play, is much restricted. In fact, of the once so responsible rôle
nothing really remains but the tedious obligation of preventing the PQ4
from going under. In other words, the disposition of the over-protection

in the case of Diagram 117b does not carry with it any sort of plan of attack for the future (in marked contrast to the case of Diagram 117a), and consequently we get nothing but that passive disposition of defending pieces, against which we had to register so emphatic a warning. To recapitulate:—The law of over-protection applies in general only to strong points. Weak points can only lay claim to over-protection in such cases where they help to support other and strong points.

§4. *Side by side with the idea of prophylactic, that of the collective mobility of a pawn-mass is a main postulate of my teaching on position play.*

In the last resort position play is nothing other than a fight between mobility (of the pawn-mass) on the one side and efforts to restrain this on the other. In this all-embracing struggle the intrinsically very important device of the prophylactic is merely a means to an end.

Diagram 118a

Diagram 118b

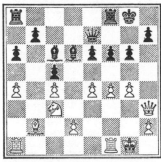

Nimzowitsch—Prof. Michel, Semmering 1926

White establishes a mobile pawn-mass and leaves one of them at home as nurse. How does he do it?

The Ps at K4, KB4, and KKt4, in conjunction with the diagonal QKt2 to KR8 lurking in the rear, form the storm troops. The backward QP after P—Q3, safeguards the QB and KPs

It is of the greatest importance to strive for the mobility of our pawn-mass; for a mobile mass can in its lust to expand exercise a crushing effect. This mobility is not always injured by the presence of a pawn that has possibly remained behind in the general advance i.e., by a backward pawn, who can perhaps be used as a nurse to tend his fellows at the front. In the case of a mobile pawn-mass we must therefore look for collective and not individual mobility, each pawn for itself. For instance in Diagram 118a we should expect sooner or later the levelling advance P—Q4, in order to be rid of the backward pawn. In the game, however, there was played more correctly 17. P—KB4, Q—K2; 18. P—K4!, B—B3; 19. P—KKt4 (Diag. 118b), and White won easily. See game No. 25.

Again in my game against Rubinstein (Black) in Dresden 1926 (No. 33) I was in no hurry to get rid of my backward pawn. Thus if after the opening moves 1. P—QB4, P—QB4; 2. Kt—KB3, Kt—KB3; 3. Kt—QB3, P—Q4; 4. P×P, Kt×P; 5. P—K4, Kt—Kt5; 6. B—B4, P—K3; 7. 0—0, Black had played 7.....P—QR3, I should not have been in any hurry to advance the backwards QP, for 8. P—Q4, P×P; 9. Q×P, Q×Q; 10. Kt×Q, B—QB4; 11. B—K3, B×Kt; 12. B×B, Kt—B7!; 13. QR—Q1, Kt×B; 14. R×Kt, Kt—B3; 15. R—Q2, P—QKt4, followed by B—Kt2 and K—K2 would have only lead to an equal game. I should rather, after 8. P—QR3, Kt(Kt5)—B3 have chosen 9. P—Q3 and after B—K3 and marshalling my major pieces I should have been well prepared to attack. In the game he played 7.....QKt—QB3 (instead of P—QR3) and after 8. P—Q3, Kt—Q5 (else 9. P—QR3); 9. Kt×Kt, P×Kt; 10. Kt—K2, White got, after P—KB4, a mobile pawn-mass, effectively supported by the BQB4.

We will now turn our attention to that terrible region in which the amateur (and on occasion also the Master) only too often trips up, namely the centre.

§5. *The centre. Insufficient watch kept on the central territory as a typical and ever-recurring error. The centre as the Balkans of the chess-board. On the popular, but strategically doubtful diversion of the attack from the centre to the wings. On the invasion of the centre. The occupation of central squares.*

It may be taken as common knowledge that in certain positions it is necessary to direct our pieces against the enemy centre; for instance in positions characterized by the presence of White P's at K4 and KB4 and of Black Ps at Q3 and KB2 (or White at Q4 and QB4; Black at QB2, and K3). On the other hand it is not so well known that it is a strategical necessity to keep the centre under observation even if it be fairly well barricaded. The centre is the Balkans of the chess-board; fighting may at any moment break out there. Take the position, already discussed under Diag. 89; which from the point of view of the centre seems harmless enough, yet after the moves 1. P—K4, P—K4; 2. Kt—KB3, Kt—QB3; 3. B—B4, B—B4; 4. Kt—QB3, Kt—KB3; 5. P—Q3, P—Q3; 6. B—KKt5, P—KR3; 7. B—R4, P—Kt4; 8. B—KKt3, Black's centre is threatened by two raids, (i) B—QKt5 and P—Q4, (ii) Kt—Q5 followed by P—QB3 and P—Q4. Another example is furnished by the opening of the game Capablanca—Martínez (1914). After 1. P—K4, P—K4; 2. B—B4, B—B4; 3. Kt—QB3, Kt—KB3; 4. P—Q3, Kt—QB3; 5. B—KKt5, P—KR3; 6. B—R4, P—KKt4; 7. B—KKt3, P—KR4; 8. P—KR4, P—Kt5; 9. Q—Q2, P—Q3;

10. KKt—K2, Q—K2; 11. 0—0, Black thought that he could treat himself to a move like 11.....P—QR3 (Diag. 119). The loss of time involved weighs the more heavily in the scale since the position is only in appearance a closed one, and in reality can be opened at any moment. (The same applies to 90% of all closed central positions.) There followed 12. Kt—Q5, Kt×Kt; 13. P×Kt, Kt—Q5; 14. Kt×Kt, B×Kt; 15. P—QB3, B—Kt3; 16. P—Q4, P—KB3!, and as I first pointed out White could get a decisive advantage by 17. KR—K1 (Capablanca played the weaker QR—K1), e.g., 17.....B—Q2 (if 17.....0—0, then 18. P×P, BP×P; 19. R×P, B×P ch; 20. Q×B, Q×R; 21. B×Q, R×Q; 22. K×R, P×B; 23. R—K1, and wins; but not 23. P—Q6 ch?, K—Kt2; 24. P×P, P—QKt4, followed by R—QR2); 18. P—QR4, 0—0—0; 19. P—R5, B—R2; 20. P—QKt4, followed by R(K1)—QKt1 and P—Kt5 with a winning attack. After the first six moves Black by a little more skilful strategy in the centre could have got the initiative, thus:—6.....P—Q3 (though 6.....B—K2 would be simplest), and if 7. Kt—Q5, P—KKt4; 8. B—Kt3, then 8.....B—K3; with the well known threat 9.....B×Kt; 10. P×B, Kt—K2; 11. B—Kt5 ch, P—B3; 12. P×P, P×P; and Black would dominate the centre. Another possibility was 6..... Kt—Q5 (instead of P—Q3). e.g., 7. Kt—Q5, P—KKt4; 8. B—Kt3, P—QB3!; 9. Kt × Kt ch, Q × Kt; 10. P—QB3, Kt—K3; 11. P—KR4, P—Q3, followed by B—Q2, 0—0—0, and when opportunity occurred, Kt—KB5.

Diagram 119

Capablanca—Martínez
White punishes the waste of time involved in Black's last move (P—QR3) by an invasion of the centre

All these examples teach us that the function of a Kt at QB3 does not solely consist in holding up a pawn advance to Q4. No, the Kt so posted is under obligation, the moment the enemy gives him the chance, of undertaking an invasion of the centre by Kt—Q5. Such a chance is often given by amateurs, who show a preference for starting a manœuvre on a wing before it is justified, without unfortunately giving much thought to the question whether they may perhaps be taking too many troops away from the centre: else how could such a line of play as the following persist for so many years, yes and even in Master tournaments! 1. P—K4, P—K4; 2. Kt—QB3, Kt—KB3; 3. B—B4, B—B4; 4. P—Q3, Kt—QB3; 5. P—KB4, P—Q3; 6. P—B5?? (Diag. 120: naturally 6. Kt—KB3 is the proper move), and now by 6.....Kt—Q5 followed by P—QB3, P—QKt4, P—QR4, Q—QKt3, and, when opportunity offers, P—Q4,

Black gets a strong game in the centre and on the left which yields him a pronounced advantage.

Another example, though this time a mild one, of the evils which follow an unwarranted change of front from centre to flank, against which the student cannot be sufficiently warned. 1. P—K4, P—K4; 2. Kt—KB3, P—Q3; 3. P—Q4, Kt—KB3; 4. P×P, Kt×P; 5. B—Q3, Kt—B4; 6. B—KB4, Kt×B (Black had the opportunity here, by Kt—K3 and P—Q4, to build up his position on scientific principles; the KtK3 would have been our strong, elastic blockader); 7. Q×Kt, Kt—QB3; 8. O—O (8. Kt—QB3 followed by O—O—O would please us better), 8.....B—K2; 9. P×P, B×P; 10. B×B, Q×B; 11. Q×Q, P×Q. See Diagram 121; there followed 12. R—K1 ch?, B—K3; 13. Kt—Kt5 (the change of front characteristic of non-positional players) 13.....K—Q2; 14. P—QB3,

Diagram 120

White's last move P—B5 does nothing in the sense of observation of the centre, but is rather a movement directed away from the centre. How is this faulty strategy to be punished?

Diagram 121

White, after R—K1 ch, B—K3, executed the popular change of front Kt—KKt5. What central strategy was indicated here (instead of R—K1 ch?, etc.)

and White does not stand particularly well. The right course was 12. Kt—QB3 (instead of R—K1 ch?), and, after 13. Kt—QKt5 and 14. Kt—Q4, he would be centralized and have the superior game.

It will be instructive to give here an example characteristic of the disregard so often shown even by strong players for central strategy; it is from a game played in 1920 in a Swedish tournament between K. Berndtsson (White) and S. J. Bjurulf (Black). 1. P—Q4, P—Q4; 2. Kt—KB3, Kt—KB3; 3. B—B4, P—K3; 4. P—K3, P—QB4; 5. P—QB3, P—QKt3 (the following line of play seems best here. 5.....Kt—QB3!; and if now 6. QKt—Q2, B—K2; 7. P—KR3, anticipating Kt—KR4, then 7.....B—Q3!; 8. Kt—K5, B×Kt; 9. P×B, Kt—Q2; 10. Kt—KB3, and now a fierce fight will be waged round the point K5. See Diagram 122a. We strongly recommend

the would-be positional player to exercise himself in such central
fights. In the present position a good plan would be 10.....P—QR3!;
11. B—Q3, P—KB3! [not 11.....Q—B2 because of 12. 0—0,
Kt×P?; 13. Kt×Kt, Kt×Kt; 14. Q—R5 and wins]; in order after
12. P×P, Q×P; to seize the hotly disputed point K4 by P—K4.
We recommend our readers to study this position.   The move
5.....P—QKt3 is a typical error in that it seems to disregard the fact
that there is such a thing as a central theatre of war.   6. QKt—Q2,
B—Q3;   7. Kt—K5 (this move pleases me well, although here
there is by chance a tactical possibility which is perhaps objectively
preferable, namely 7. B—Kt5 ch, B—Q2?;   8. B×KB, B×B;
9. P×P. But 7. Kt—K5 is the more logical move, since owing to the
loss of time involved in Black's P—QKt3, the centre was ripe for an
invasion.) 7.....B×Kt; 8. P×B, KKt—Q2; 9. Q—Kt4, R—KKt1;

Diagram 122a

Black to move. A typical
example of a fight for a central
point.   Here White's K5

Diagram 122b

White to move. The point K5
is in his undisputed possession.
But where should the attack be
directed, on the right, or the
left, or in the centre?

10. Kt—B3, Kt—QB3;   11. B—Q3, Kt—KB1 (Diag. 122b);
12. Kt—Kt5 (White commits the strategical error of underestimating
the importance of the point K5, the key point of his whole position.
Under no circumstances should the attack be so conducted as to
endanger its safety.   On the contrary, as we know, over-protection
of this point would here be indicated.   The right course to adopt was
to remain passive on the K's wing, to advance P—K4 in the centre
and on the Q's wing P—QKt4 and P—QR4, and in some such order
as this.   12. 0—0, B—Kt2;   13. P—QKt4!, P—B5 [not P×P;
P×P, Kt×P; because of B—KKt5 winning a piece or causing some
other similar unpleasantness.] 14. B—B2, Q—Q2;   15. P—QR4,
P—QR3! [if 15.....0—0—0, then 16. P—R5, P×P; 17. P—Kt5!,
with a winning attack.] 16. P—K4!, 0—0—0;   17. B—K3,
K—B2;   18. P—R5!, with a decisive attack.) 12.....Q—B2!;

13. B×RP, R—R1;   14. B—B2 (Diag. 122c). 14.....B—Kt2?
(Black must here seek to conquer the point K4, dangerous as this may
appear. So simply 14.....Kt×P!; and he would have got a satisfactory, in fact the better, game. For instance: 14.....Kt×P!;
15. Q—Kt3, P—KB3;   16. Kt—B3, Kt×Kt ch;   17. Q×Kt,
P—K4!; 18. Q×QP, B—Kt2; 19. B—R4 ch, K—K2, and Black
wins a piece. Or, 14.....Kt×P; 15. B—R4 ch, K—K2, with the
threat Kt—Q6 ch; on the other hand the reply 15.....B—Q2 would
have been bad, for White by means of 16. B×B ch, Kt(B1)×B;
17. Kt×KP!, P×Kt; 18. Q×KP ch, K—Q1; 19. Q×QP, would
get a strong attack, with three pawns for his sacrificed piece. But,
as suggested with 14.....Kt×KP; 15. B—R4 ch, K—K2, Black

Diagram 122c

Black to move. How shall
he best punish his opponent's
neglect to keep the centre (K5)
under observation in his last
moves

Diagram 122d

White can and must win back
the point K5. How?

could have got an excellent game. The strategical events in this
game present themselves as follows: 5.....P—QKt3 had no bearing
on the centre, and in consequence White waxed strong and mighty
there (Kt—K5); but at his 12th move he did not pay sufficient regard
to the key point (K5) and this, if Black had made the proper reply,
could have led to his losing all his advantage. We see then what
a dominating influence central strategy exercises.) 15. Kt—B3,
P—KKt3; 16. B—KKt5? (Scarcely had he by luck escaped the
dangers in the centre, than the leader of the White forces, always on
the look out for a combination, again sacrifices his chief possession
from a strategical point of view, the point K5. The over-protectors,
the KtB3 and the BB4 should have remained at their posts. His
proper course was indicated in the note to move 12:) 16.....Kt×P!
(now he shows courage!); 17. Kt×Kt, Q×Kt (Diag. '122d);
18. P—KR4. (It is absolutely essential for White to play to recover
the point K5. Accordingly, 18. B—B4! and if in reply 18.....Q—R4,

then 19. Q—Kt3, P—KB3; 20. B—Q6, and Black could hardly succeed in consolidating his position, which is threatened in every nook and corner. After the text move Black, on the contrary, could make himself fully secure.) 18.....P—QKt4? (not only spells loss of time but also weakens the PQB4 and allows P—QR4. The right move was 18.....Kt—Q2, and if 19. B—QR4, then 19.....P—KB3; 20. B—B4, Q—K5!; 21. B—QKt5, P—KKt4, or 21.....0—0—0, and Black stands well.) 19. 0—0, Kt—R2; 20. B—B4, Q—R4; 21. Q×Q, P×Q; 22. P—QR4 and White won the ending which he conducted very cleverly.

The moral of this game runs thus. (i) Watch the centre, cf. Black's 5th move, White's 12th and following moves, Black's 14th move. (ii) Over-protect the key point; cf. White's 12th and 16th moves. (iii) Do not divert your attack prematurely; cf. White's 12th and 16th moves. (iv) After the pawns are gone the key points must be occupied by pieces; cf. White's 18th move.

§6. *The leitmotif of correct strategy is the over-protection of the centre, with, further, a systematically carried out centralization of our forces. Wing attack met by play in the centre.*

In the very characteristic game which has just been quoted we saw how the diversion of the attack from the centre to a wing, and, what is in principle the equivalent, the disregard of the central key points, led to some curious situations. This 'diversion' sometimes appears also in games by Masters. We need only remind the reader of Game No. 22, Opocensky—Nimzowitsch, in which in the position shown on Diagram 123, there occurred the following moves: 13. Kt—K2?, Kt—R4; 14. Q—Q2, P—KKt3; 15. P—KKt4, Kt—Kt2; 16. Kt—Kt3, P—QB3!. The diversion of the Kt, now completed, has so altered the situation that Black, though much cramped on the Q's Wing, can venture to proceed to the attack!

Centralization is ever a characteristic of Master play—and the talented Czech Master Opocensky is of course no exception. Alekhine makes use of this

Diagram 123

White manœuvres the KtQB3 over to the K's side, though his true business was to look out for Black's P—QB3. Another example of an unseasonable diversion

strategy with special predilection, and this (with play against enemy squares of a particular colour) forms the leitmotif of all his games. Even when the knife seems actually to be at his

King's throat in a K side attack, he yet finds time to mass troops in the centre. A typical example is furnished by his game with me at Semmering in 1926 (No. 43), in which after the moves 1. P—K4, Kt—KB3 (Alekhine was Black); 2. Kt—QB3, P—Q4; 3. P—K5, Kt—Q2; 4. P—KB4, P—K3; 5. Kt—KB3, P—QB4; 6. P—KKt3, Kt—QB3; 7. B—Kt2, B—K2; 8. O—0, O—0; 9. P—Q3, Kt—Kt3, he got into some trouble through having omitted to play 9.....P—KB3. There followed 10. Kt—K2, P—Q5; 11. P—KKt4 (the beginning of a violent attack), P—KB3; 12. P×P, P×P (else would follow the centralization of the White Kt, by Kt—Kt3— K4); 13. Kt—Kt3, Kt—Q4!; 14. Q—K2, B—Q3!; 15. Kt—R4 (Diag. 124) Kt(B3)—K2!; 16. B—Q2, Q—B2; 17. Q—B2, and now the inner strength of the centralized structure of Black's

Diagram 124

Nimzowitsch—Alekhine
Semmering, 1926

White's PKKt4 and KtKR4 point to a diversion having been started. His KtKKt3 has a fairly clear conscience in the centralizing sense, but he has too his eye on KR5. Black as against this has in his PQ5 and KtQ4 the kernel of a beautifully centralized structure, which he completes in the sequel

position was made clear by the surprising continuation 17.....P—QB5!; 18. P× P, Kt—K6! and Alekhine had equalized the game.

I too, both theoretically and in practice, am absolutely on the side of centralization. Examine, say, my game against Yates (Semmering, 1926), in which I had the Black pieces. 1. P— K4, P—K3; 2. P—Q4, P—Q4; 3. Kt— QB3, B—Kt5; 4. P×P, P×P; 5. B—Q3, Kt—K2; 6. KKt—K2, O—0; 7. O—0, B—KKt5; 8. P—KB3, B—KR4; 9. Kt—B4, B—Kt3; 10. Kt(B3)—K2, B—Q3; 11. Q—K1. (Here B×B followed by Kt—Q3 would have comported with the spirit of centralization, and the points QB5 and K5 would then have been kept under perpetual observation.) 11.....P—QB4! 12. P×P, B×P ch; 13. K—R1, QKt—QB3; 14. B—Q2, R—K1; 15. Kt×B, RP× Kt! (creates a central point at KB4);

16. P—KB4 (the normal development of things would have been 16. Q—R4, Kt—B4; 17. Q×Q, QR×Q; and Black has a slight advantage for the end game), 16.....Kt—B4; 17. P—QB3, P—Q5!; 18. P—QB4, Q—Kt3; 19. R—B3, B—Kt5 (to clean up the central point K6); 20. P—QR3, B×B; 21. Q×B, P—QR4 (=restraint); 22. Kt—Kt1, R—K6; 23. Q—KB2, QR—K1; 24. QR—Q1, Q—Kt6!; 25. R—Q2, Kt—Q3; 26. P—QB5, Kt—B5!; 27. B×Kt, Q×B (White's QBP is weak, the blockading BQ3 has been got out of the way, and the central pressure is more

burdensome to White than ever.); 28. R—QB2, Q—Q4!; 29. R—QB1, Q—K5! (Diag. 125). With this move centralization is completed. White sacrificed a pawn, by 30. P—B5, in order to defend himself against the ever-increasing pressure in the K file, but lost the ending after 30.....R×R; 31. Kt×R, Q×P. Further striking examples of centralization will be found in great plenty in the games of the Masters; we will only mention Alekhine—Treybal, Baden-Baden, 1925, and Nimzowitsch—Spielmann, San Sebastian, 1912 (Game No. 49).

We now proceed to the analysis of play in the centre vs. play on a wing. The game Nimzowitsch—Alekhine, just given, furnishes an example of how such a struggle usually proceeds. The 'central player' always has the better prospects, and very especially in the frequently recurring positions which we are about to outline. One

Diagram 125

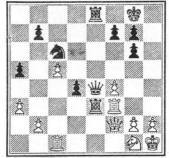

Yates—Nimzowitsch
Semmering, 1926

Possession of the open centre file, the PQ5, and in particular the position of the QK5 stamp Black's structure as being centralized in a high degree

Diagram 126

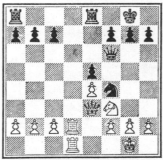

Plan to illustrate the theme 'centre file vs. flank attack'. The Black KtKB5 is the mainstay of the latter

party has undertaken a diversion against his opponent's King's wing which in itself promises a reward. All would be in the most perfect order, but that (there's always a 'but'!) his opponent holds an open centre file, and with astounding regularity the flank attack is shipwrecked on this rock.

We will first note (Diag. 126) the ground plan of such a situation. In the position shown Black's attack must always fail, because his Rooks are under the unpleasant obligation to guard their base (here their 1st and 2nd ranks) against an inroad of the White Rooks who are all ready for the adventure. In addition his K4 is insufficiently protected, and this again is not accidental, since the White KtKB3 is centralized in harmony with the rest of the White structure. As the whole matter is of extraordinary importance to an understanding of the spirit of the dogma of the centre, we will illustrate it by a complete game, Rubinstein—Nimzowitsch, San Sebastian, 1912.

1. P—Q4, Kt—KB3; 2. P—QB4, P—Q3; 3. Kt—KB3, QKt—Q2; 4. Kt—QB3, P—K4; 5. P—K4, B—K2 (probably there is nothing against the immediate fianchetto, P—KKt3, B—Kt2); 6. B—K2, 0—0; 7. 0—0, R—K1; 8. Q—B2, B—B1; 9. P—QKt3, P—QB3 (here, as Lasker very rightly pointed out, the sounder line of play was P—KKt3, B—Kt2, then P×QP and Kt—K4); 10. B—Kt2, Kt—KR4?; 11. P—KKt3, Kt—QKt1; 12. QR—Q1 (the centre file looms up!), 12.....Q—B3; 13. Kt—QKt1!, B—R6; 14. KR—K1, Kt—B5 (that I should be able to get the Kt to KB5 under any circumstances, I had foreseen when I played 10.....Kt—R4, a misfortune, for else I had withstood the temptation to undertake this diversion) (Diag 127);

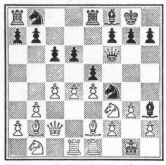

Diagram 127

White (Rubinstein) demonstrates by clever play the weakness of Black's diversion on the K-side

15. P×P, P×P; 16. Kt×P, R×Kt; 17. B—KB1 (after 17. B×R, Kt×B ch; 18. Q×Kt, Q×B; 19. R—Q8—the centre file! White would also have the advantage), 17. ....Kt—Q2; 18. Q—Q2 (now the Black pieces embarked on their diversion are in the air), 18.....B×B; 19. R×B, Kt—R6 ch; 20. K—Kt2, Kt—Kt4 (threatening mate in two); 21. P—KB4, Q—Kt3; 22. P×Kt, R×KP? (after 22.....Q× KP ch, 23. K—R3, R—K2; 24. R(Q1)—K1 would have won a piece. Relatively best was 22.....R—K2; the win then could only have been attained by 23. B—QR3!, P—QB4! [not 23..... Q×P ch; because of 24. K—Kt1, P—QB4; 25. R(B1)—K1]; 24. Kt—B3; for after 23.....P—QB4, which is forced, there is no possibility of Black playing Kt—QB4, while on the other hand White has his Q5 as a base for his operations); 23. Q×Kt, R—K7 ch; 24. R—KB2, and White won. See also Game No. 28, Kline—Capablanca for another variation on the same theme.

§7. *The Surrender of the Centre.*

As early as 1911 and 1912 I had published some notes on games, in which I put forward what was then an entirely new idea, that the centre need not necessarily be occupied by pawns; that centrally posted pieces or even lines bearing on the centre could, as I maintained, take the place of pawns, the main point being to place the enemy centre pawns under restraint. This idea I, in 1913, embodied in an article which, by the courtesy of G. Marco, Editor of the *Wiener Schachzeitung*, I am allowed to reproduce here, and do so, because in this the age of the 'neo-romantic school' it is in a high degree pertinent. The article ran as follows:—

When Black in the much disputed variation of the French Defence 1. P—K4, P—K3; 2. P—Q4, P—Q4; 3. Kt—QB3, plays 3.....P×P, he gives up, according to the current opinion, the centre. This view seems to me to rest upon an incomplete grasp, in fact a misconception, of what the centre is. In what follows the attempt will be made, (i) to show that this view is based on a prejudice, (ii) to set out its historical development.

And first the definition of the concept 'centre'. Here we have simply to abide by the meaning of the word. The 'centre' consists of the squares in the middle of the board, *squares*: not pawns. This is fundamental and must never under any circumstances be lost sight of.

The importance of the centre, that is to say the complex of squares in the middle of the board, as a base for further operations, is beyond question; and a note of Emmanuel Lasker's to a game is worth recalling. 'White,' he wrote, 'does not stand well enough in the centre, to undertake an operation on the wing.' This is finely conceived, and at the same time illustrates the close relationship between the centre and the wings, the centre being the dominating principle, the wings subordinate to it.

That control of the centre must be of great significance, is, other considerations apart, clear from one thing, that if we have built up our game in the centre, we have from thence the possibility of exercising influence on both wings at one and the same time, and of embarking on a diversion should opportunity offer. Without healthy conditions in the centre, a healthy position is definitely unthinkable.

We spoke of a control of the centre. What are we to understand by this? How is this conditioned?

Current opinion holds that the centre should be occupied by pawns; PK4 and PQ4 is the ideal, but in fact the presence of one of these two postulates occupation of the centre, provided the corresponding enemy pawn is wanting.

But is this really the case? Is the PQ4, after the moves 1. P—K4, P—K3; 2. P—Q4, P—Q4; 3. Kt—QB3, P×P; 4. Kt×P, justified in speaking of a conquest of the centre? If, in a battle, I seize a bit of debatable land with a handful of soldiers, without having done anything to prevent an enemy bombardment of the position, would it ever occur to me to speak of a conquest of the terrain in question? Obviously not. Then why should I do so in chess?

It dawns upon us then, that control of the centre depends not on a mere occupation, i.e., placing of pawns, but rather on our general effectiveness there, and this is determined by quite other factors.

This thought I have formulated thus:— With the disappearance of a pawn from the centre (e.g., P×P, Kt×P as above) the centre is a long way from being surrendered. The true conception of the centre is a far wider one. Certainly, pawns, as being the most stable, are best suited to building a centre; nevertheless centrally posted pieces can perfectly well take their place. And, too, pressure exerted on the enemy centre by the long range action of Rooks or Bishops directed on it can well be of corresponding importance.

We meet this last case in the variation 3.....P×P (v. supra). This move, so wrongly described as a surrender of the centre, as a matter of fact increases Black's effective influence in the centre very considerably; for with the removal by P×P of the PQ4, which is an obstruction, Black gets a free hand in the Q file, and the long diagonal

Diagram 128

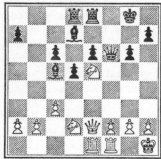

Diagram 129

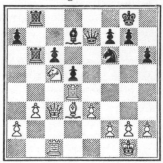

QKt2 to KR8, which he will open for himself by P—QKt3. Obstruction! that is the dark side of the occupation of the centre by pawns. A pawn is by nature, by his stability, his, so to speak, conservative spirit, a good centre builder, but, alas, he is also an obstruction.

That effective influence in the centre is independent of the number of pawns occupying it, appears from many examples, and of their abundance we will take one or two.

Pieces in the centre. (1) Black's PK3 and PQ4 held under restraint by the White KtK5 and PQB3 and Q4, e.g., Diagram 128 from the game Nimzowitsch-Löwenfisch, Carlsbad, 1911. (2) the isolated pawn couple (see II. iii, §6) at Q4 and QB3 rigidly blockaded by White pieces as in Diagram 129. The two cases quoted show us a blockade. But blockade is an elastic term and often a slight restraint induced by an annoying Rook whose primary function was to hold up the advance of the enemy centre may be the prelude to a complete crippling, which culminates in its mechanical stoppage.

The cases in which pressure is exerted on the enemy centre are without number. See, e.g., Diagram 130, where the course of events will lead either to a blockade with consequent destruction of the KP (for movement is life), or to uncomfortable positions for the defending pieces, which will lead to the downfall of the 'lucky possessor' of the centre.

All this teaches us that by counting the heads of the pawns in the centre, nothing, literally nothing, is gained. To make mere arithmetic the starting point of a philosophy of the centre can only be characterized as a mistaken proceeding. I am sure that in a very few years no one will regard 3.....QP×KP as a 'surrender' of the centre; and with the disappearance of such a prepossession, the way will be clear for a new and brilliant development in chess philosophy—and strategy.

Diagram 130

A word on the genesis of this prejudice, which is closely bound up with the history of position play. . . . First came Steinitz; but what he had to say was so unfamiliar, and he himself was so towering a figure, that his 'modern principles' could not immediately become popular. There followed Tarrasch who took hold of Steinitz's ideas and served them up diluted to the public taste. And now to consider the application to our case. Steinitz was, we repeat, deep and great, but deepest and greatest in his conception of the centre. When in his defence to the Ruy Lopez (P—Q3) he was able to transmute the enemy PK4, which was to all appearances so healthy, into one whose weakness was patent to every eye, this was an unsurpassable achievement. Nothing lay further from his thoughts than a formalistic, arithmetical conception of the centre. . . .

So far the article. For illustrations we would refer the reader to 1. iii, on the Pawn-Chain, and to game No. 26 (Tarrasch—Mieses). The reader is further urged to study before proceeding further Games Nos. 25—30 inclusive, which bear on this chapter.

CHAPTER II

THE DOUBLED PAWN AND RESTRAINT

§1.   The affinity between 'doubled pawn' and restraint; the former should favour the execution of enemy plans for restraint.   What does to labour under the disadvantage of a doubled pawn mean?   The conception of passive (=static) and active (=dynamic) weaknesses.   When does the dissolution of an enemy doubled pawn seem to be indicated?   The one real strength of a doubled pawn.

RESTRAINT is conceivable without the presence of enemy doubled pawns; but a really complete restraint, which extends over large tracts of the board and makes it difficult for the enemy to breathe, is only possible when the opponent labours under the disadvantage of a doubled pawn.   What do we mean exactly by labouring under this disadvantage?   Chiefly this, that in the event of an advance in close formation certain paralyzing phenomena may intervene.   See, for example, Diagram 131.   If a White P had been at QKt2 instead of QB2 the close advance P—Q4—Q5, followed by P—QB4, P—QKt4, and P—QB5 would have been possible.   But in the position on the diagram the QKtP is wanting, and hence any attempt at a transference of attack (see above I. ix on the Pawn-Chain) will be vain.   To P—Q4—Q5 and P—QB4 the answer will be P—QKt3, and the further advance P—QB5 we had planned is shown to be impossible of execution.   What we have just learnt about the chief weakness of compact (i.e., easily defendable) doubled pawns (which we would class as active, or dynamic, weaknesses) enables us to formulate this rule, that it pays to incite the possessor of a pawn-mass whose attacking value is lessened by the presence of doubled pawns to an advance.   Acting in this spirit Black in the case under consideration should, if White has played P—Q4, endeavour to move his opponent to continue his action in the centre.   So long as he can stop at Q4, the defect of the doubled pawn will be as little in evidence as is a limp in a sitting person.   It is only in the advance that the weakness will appear.

Diagram 131

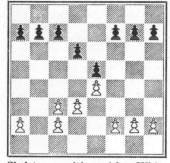

Skeleton position. After White has played P—Q4, any further advance by P—Q5, P—QB4—B5 is stopped by Black's P—QB3, which would not be the case if White's QKtP were present

We must differentiate an active and a passive, i.e., static weakness. The latter is, in contradistinction to that in our last example, revealed when we send forward our own pawns in a storming party against the doubled pawn. Let us imagine in Diagram 131 the White QP at Q5 instead of Q3, a White KKKt1 and RK2, and a Black KKB1 and RQB1. Here the static weakness of the doubled pawn is great; for after 1.....P—QB3; 2. P×P, R×P; or 1.....P—QB3; 2. P—QB4, P×P; 3. BP×P, R—B6, followed by R—QR6, Black will in either case get the advantage. The rule is therefore: Given a passive weakness in a doubled pawn an advance against this pawn is indicated, whereby the dissolution or undoubling of the enemy doubled pawn. need cause us no fear. The evil is in fact only half dissipated, a part of the weakness is got rid of, but for what remains behind the player has to suffer the heavier penance.

Let us turn now to Diagram 132. Black, the author of this book, let his opponent (E. Cohn) take the initiative in the hope that the resulting play would in the end lead to a simplification, after which in the end game it could not be very difficult to take advantage of the doubled pawn. The game proceeded: 16.....Q—Q2; 17. Q—K1, Kt—Kt3; 18. B—Q3, B—B3; 19. Q—KB2, B—K4 (Black relies on the solid strength of his K4); 20. R—QB2, R—KB1; 21. K—R1, P—QKt3; 22. Q—B3, QR—K1; 23. R(QB2)—KB2, Kt—R1; 24. Q—R5, P—QB3; 25. P—KKt4, P—KB3; and now Cohn let himself be carried away by the idea of an interesting attack, which, however, in the end only resulted in the simplification

Diagram 132

The indirect exchange of his PQ3 for White's PK4 seems to Black to be worth striving for. How should Black seek to bring this about?

of the game, and the exposure of the hopelessness of his pawn position, PK3 and PK4. He played 26. P—QB5, and after 26.....B×Kt; 27. R×B, QP×P; 28. B—B4 ch, Kt—B2; 29. P—Kt5, R—K4; 30. R—B5, R×R; 31. P×R, the win could be forced by 31.....K—R1; for the answer to 32. P—KKt6 would have been Kt—R3, and to 32. B×Kt it would be 32.....Q×B; 33. P—Kt6, Q—Q4 ch, followed by P—KR3. Black was therefore right in choosing a waiting strategy, for the wing attack must fail against the centre file, with Black's strong PK4, and the end game is hopeless for White. Although the waiting strategy was correct, yet the advance was also possible, for White's PK3, PK4, is here a static weakness. This advance could be executed somewhat as follows:— 16.....Kt—Q2 (instead of Q—Q2); 17. B—B3, Kt—B3;

18. Q—QB2, P—QB3! He 'sacrifices' the QP in order at once to get in its stead White's PK4.   After 19. QR—Q1, Q—K2, we get our 'exchange' and then White's PK3 can be bombarded in comfort.

The full rule, therefore, runs: To isolated doubled pawns, and to 'compact' doubled pawns, or those which are advancing the 'question' should be put (=be attacked by pawns).   An enemy doubled pawn complex which has not started its advance, should, before the 'question' is put to it, first be incited to action.

§1a.   *The one real strength of the doubled pawn.*

As we have seen, a pawn-mass which is afflicted with a doubled pawn has in it a certain latent weakness, which makes itself felt when the time comes to make use of that mass by advancing it.   We characterize this as we have said, as a dynamic weakness.   This mass if at rest, i.e., holding its configuration, may be very strong. Turn back to Diagram 131.   After White has played P—Q4, a position is reached out of which he can be driven only with the greatest trouble.   We mean by this that Black hardly possesses the positional means to be able to force his opponent to a decision to play P×KP or P—Q5.   On the other hand this would be much more possible if White's P were at QKt2 instead of QB2.   The doubled pawn in fact makes holding out easier.   Why this should be so it is difficult to explain; perhaps it is due to an equalizing act of justice, an attempt to compensate for dynamic weakness by static strength; it may be perhaps that the QKt file enters into the question; at any rate experience has shown that the doubled QBP does favour holding out.

In this tenacity we see the one real strength of the doubled pawn; cf. my game against Haakanson in the next section and further those against Rosselli and Johner (Nos. 34 and 35).

§2.   *The most familiar doubled pawn complexes (for short, double-complexes) are passed in review.   The double complex as an instrument of attack.*

See again Diagram 131.   The strongest formation for White is the one reached after he has played P—Q4; and this formation should be preserved for as long as possible.   However, after P—Q5 White's weakness will make itself felt; so that it is a strategical necessity for Black to force White to this move, and if possible without the aid of P—QB4.   For after ....P—QB4; P—Q5 the possibility of putting the question (by P—QB3) will have gone, as also the chance of occupying the point QB4 with a Kt.

In the same position (Diagram 131) many players, having Black.

make the mistake of letting loose at once with P—Q4, a course which runs counter to our rule, according to which an enemy double complex must first be incited to action.   Then and only then may the active (dynamic) weakness of the double complex be exploited.

We shall now give some examples which will illustrate the struggle between a defence which is trying to hold out in its position and an attacking force which is seeking to force a decision, and first one in which the defending party (in this case White) by one thoughtless move throws away all the trumps in his hand.

Haakanson—Nimzowitsch. Played in 1921. 1. P—Q4, Kt—KB3; 2. P—QB4, P—K3; 3. Kt—KB3, P—QKt3; 4. B—KKt5, P—KR3; 5. B × Kt, Q × B; 6. P—K4, B—Kt2; 7. Kt—QB3, B—Kt5; 8. Q—Q3, B × Kt ch; 9. P × B, P—Q3 (and now after P—K4, the double complex we have been discussing will have arisen); 10. Q—K3, Kt—Q2; 11. B—Q3, P—K4; 12. 0—0, 0—0; 13. P—QR4, P—QR4; 14. Kt—K1.   White stood well, for it is improbable that Black would have been able to force him to a decision (i.e., to P—Q5), but the rather ponderous text-move creates difficulties in his own camp.   His right course was 14. Kt—Q2 and P—KB3; his Q who is rather exposed at K3 would then have had a flight square at KB2, and nothing would have stood in the way of a further holding out in his formation. After 14. Kt—K1? there followed 14.....QR—K1; 15. P—KB3, Q—K3!, and now White ought to have eaten the bitter fruit, i.e., played P—Q5, but he moved instead 16. Kt—B2, and after 16..... P × P!; 17. P × P, P—KB4!; 18. P—Q5, Q—K4; 19. Q—Q4, Kt—B4; 20. KR—Q1, P × P; 21. P × P, Kt × B; 22. R × Kt, Q × KP, lost a pawn and the game.

Diagram 133

Janowsky—Nimzowitsch

Black with the move fights against White's persistence in holding to his pawn formation

The next example is of much heavier metal and is taken from the game Janowsky — Nimzowitsch, Petrograd, 1914. 1. P—Q4, Kt—KB3; 2. P—QB4, P—K3; 3. Kt—QB3, B—Kt5; 4. P—K3, P—QKt3; 5. B—Q3, B—Kt2; 6. Kt—KB3, B × Kt ch; 7. P × B, P—Q3; 8. Q—B2, QKt—Q2; 9. P—K4, P—K4; 10. 0—0, 0—0; 11. B—KKt5, P—KR3; 12. B—Q2, R—K1; 13. QR—K1 (Diag. 133). Black was now faced with the difficult problem of how to move his opponent to take action in the centre. He tried to solve it by the manœuvre Kt—R2—B1—K3. Another possibility was 13.....Kt—KB1, e.g., 14. P—KR3, Kt—Kt3; 15. Kt—R2, R—K2!; and if now 16. P—KB4, then P × BP;

17. B×P, Q—K1; and White has no way of comfortably defending his PK4. In the game, however, there was played, as already said, 13.....Kt—R2; and the continuation was 14. P—KR3, Kt(R2)—B1; 15. Kt—R2, Kt—K3!; 16. B—K3 (he holds on!), 16.....P—QB4 (because he sees no other way of breaking his opponent's obstinacy); 17. P—Q5, Kt—B5!; 18. B—K2, Kt—KB1, and the weakness of White's PQB4 and possession of the point KB5 offer Black chances of attack on both wings.

Since, as we have seen, it is often very difficult to induce an opponent who is hanging on to this 'crouching' position to take action in our sense, it is obvious that we ought only to bring about an enemy double complex if it seems likely that we shall succeed in forcing him out of it. In this connexion the following opening will be found extremely instructive.

Nimzowitsch—Rosselli, Baden-Baden, 1925. After the first 7

Diagram 134

Nimzowitsch—Rosselli

White with the move refrains from bringing about by B×Kt ch, P×B, a double complex in the enemy position since he recognizes the impossibility of inducing him to advance his QP to the 5th, for in reply to P—K4 he would merely stay where he was

moves. 1. Kt—KB3, P—Q4; 2. P—QKt3, P—QB4; 3. P—K3, Kt—QB3; 4. B—Kt2, B—Kt5?; 5. P—KR3!, B×Kt; 6. Q×B, P—K4; 7. B—QKt5, Q—Q3; White had the opportunity of giving his opponent a doubled pawn, e.g., 8. B×Kt ch, P×B; 9. P—K4. But what would he have gained by this? How was Black to be forced into playing P—Q5? So White played 8. P—K4 (Diag. 134), renouncing the idea for the time. 8.....P—Q5; but now with the advance P—Q5 already made the double complex would be a consummation devoutly to be wished; so to this end White played 9. Kt—R3 (threatening Kt—B4, Q—B2; B×Kt, P×B), and the game proceeded 9.....P—KB3!; 10. Kt—B4, Q—Q2; 11. Q—R5 ch, P—KKt3; 12. Q—B3, Q—QB2 (if 12.....0—0—0; then 13. Kt—R5,

KKt—K2; 14. Q×P); 13. Q—Kt4, and the diagonal KKt4 to Q7 very soon led to Black's resigning himself to the doubled pawn in order to be rid of other unpleasantnesses. For the whole game see No. 34.

If saddled with a double complex, the player has to take into account the fact that its mobility is very limited, and hence must suit his moves to the occasion, artfully contrived to bear on both sides. What is meant by this will appear from the next examples.

Nimzowitsch — Sämisch, Dresden, 1926. After the moves

1. P—QB4, P—K4; 2. Kt—QB3, Kt—KB3; 3. Kt—KB3, Kt—QB3; 4. P—K4, B—QKt5; 5. P—Q3, P—Q3; 6. P—KKt3, B—KKt5; 7. B—K2, P—KR3; 8. B—K3, B×Kt ch; 9. P×B, Q—Q2, White was fully conscious of the dynamic weakness of his double complex; and accordingly he made his plan to let the QP persist at Q3 or at most at Q4. Observe the artful little moves of the White pieces, which suit the conditions created by the pawn configuration in the centre; for with small working capital (and the slight mobility of White's pawns is analogous to this), the greatest economy is necessary. The continuation was 10. Q—B2!, 0—0; 11. Q—Q2! (if he had at once played 10. Q—Q2, the answer would have been 0—0—0, and the White Q would have been very awkwardly placed at Q2. After 10. Q—B2, 10.....0—0—0 would have been answered by 0—0 and KR—QKt1, and White would have had a fine ensemble, the QQB2 being not the least contributing factor), 11.....Kt—R2; 12. P—KR3!, B×P; 13. Kt—Kt1, B—Kt5; 14. P—KB3, B—K3; 15. P—Q4, and White won a piece and the game.

We have now submitted the doubled pawn complex to a very searching analysis. Seen in the light of this analysis many incidents of daily occurrence appear under a new aspect. In the position on Diagram 135, reached after the moves 1. P—K4, P—K4; 2. Kt—KB3, Kt—QB3; 3. Kt—QB3, Kt—KB3; 4. B—Kt5, B—Kt5; 5. 0—0, 0—0; 6. P—Q3, P—Q3; 7. B—Kt5, B×Kt; 8. P×B, Q—K2; 9. R—K1, Kt—Q1; 10. P—Q4, White is said, according to the current view, to have the attacking position in the

Diagram 135

White's attacking position in the centre has here, *inter alia*, to help conceal his own dynamic weakness (PQB2, PQB3); hence it must more rightly be regarded as a 'crouching' one

centre. This is not true, as I hold. It would be true if a White P were at QKt2 instead of QB2. But, as it is, the apparently attacking position of the PQ4 has but the deep purpose of hiding the weakness in his own camp, namely the PQB2, PQB3. Once P—Q5 has taken place this (dynamic) weakness would be evident. Hence the pawn configuration which we have in Diagram 135 will be regarded by one who has thought the matter out as a crouching position. The game proceeded 10.....Kt—K3; 11. B—QB1, P—QB3 (P—QB4 was the right move here; e.g., 11.....P—QB4; 12. P×KP, P×P; 13. Kt×P?, Kt—B2, etc.); 12. B—KB1, R—Q1; 13. P—KKt3, Q—B2; 14. Kt—R4, and White intends to play P—KB4. So had White after all the initiative in the centre?! No, the situation is

rather this:— Since Black at his 11th move did not take the opportunity to bother his opponent, White could, out of his crouching
position, build up an attack, but originally it was in fact but
such a position. The continuation was (we follow the excellent
game, Spielmann—Rubinstein, Carlsbad, 1911) 14.....P—Q4;
15. P—KB4!, P×BP; 16. P—K5, Kt—K5; 17. P×P, P—KB4!;
18. P×P e.p., Kt×P(B3); 19. P—B5, Kt—B1; 20. Q—B3,
and Spielmann won in brilliant style: 20.....Q—KB2; 21. B—Q3,
B—Q2; 22. B—KB4, R—K1; 23. B—K5, P—QB4; 24. K—R1,
P—B5; 25. B—K2, B—B3; 26. Q—B4, Kt(B1)—Q2; 27. B—B3,
R—K2; 28. R—K2, R—KB1; 29. R—KKt1, Q—K1;
30. R(K2)—Kt2, R(B1)—B2; 31. Q—R6!, K—B1; 32. Kt—Kt6 ch,
a brilliant breaking through combination, 32.....P×Kt;
33. Q—R8 ch, Kt—Kt1; 34. B—Q6. Black who is hemmed in
and pinned all round has nothing to oppose to an invasion at his
KKt1 via the KKt file. 34.....Q—Q1; 35. R×P, Kt(Q2)—B3;
36. R×Kt!, R×R; 37. R×KKtP! Resigns.

Diagram 136a

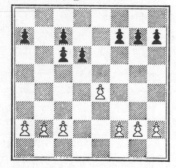

Diagram 136b

We now pass to a consideration of the next species of double
complex. See Diagram 136a and 136b; which as will be seen are
very similar, the White centre P being at K4 or Q4 according as
Black's double complex is on the Q or K side. The import of this
pawn configuration lies in this, that Black may regard his PQB3
(or PKB3) as compensation for his lost centre, since either pawn has
an action towards the centre. This action finds expression in the
fact that White, e.g., in the case of 136b, cannot use his K5 as an
outpost station; further in the threat of P—K4, and again in the
possibility of P—KB4, R—KKt1 (White: P—KKt3), P—KR4,
P—KB5, and P—KR5. In other words the mass PK3, PKB3,
PKB2, which in the first instance is defensive in its action, can deploy
and be thrown forward to the attack. Its weakness lies in the
isolated KRP. White will seek to neutralize the attack we have
outlined (R—Kt1, P—KB4, etc.) by posting his Ps at KB4, KKt3,

and KR2 with perhaps Kts at KB3 and KKt2. The game would then be equal. It is, however, extremely difficult for Black to decide the fitting moment when to emerge from the defensive with P—KB4. We give an example:—

Nimzowitsch—Dr. Perlis, Ostend, 1907. 1. P—K4, P—K3; 2. P—Q4, P—Q4; 3. Kt—QB3, Kt—KB3; 4. B—KKt5, P×P; 5. Kt×P, B—K2; 6. B×Kt, P×B; 7. Kt—KB3, Kt—Q2; 8. Q—Q2, R—KKt1 (this move might perhaps have been postponed); 9. 0—0—0, Kt—KB1 (protects the weakness, the isolated PKR2); 10. P—QB4, P—QB3; 11. P—KKt3, Q—B2; 12. B—Kt2, P—QKt3; 13. KR—K1, B—QKt2; 14. K—Kt1, 0—0—0 (Dr. Perlis has very skilfully turned the defensive strength of his 'complex' to good account, and will soon see the moment ripe to let his double complex appear as an attacking weapon); 15. Kt—QB3, K—Kt1 (Diag. 137); 16. Q—K3 (White feels the want of the outpost station K5 painfully), 16. . . . . Kt—Kt3 (already P—KB4—B5 is threatened, for the Kt now is looking after the point K4); 17. P—KR4, P—KB4; 18. Kt—K5 (at length!), P—B5!; 19. Q—B3, Kt×Kt; 20. P×Kt, P×P; 21. P×P, B—QKt5, with an equal game. 22. P—QR3, B× Kt; 23. Q×B, P—QB4; 24. B×B, Q×B; 25. R—Q6, R×R; 26. P×R, R—Q1; 27. R—Q1, Q—K5 ch; 28. K—R2, R—Q2, and the game was abandoned as a draw two moves later. In this game Dr. Perlis, who was an adept in such positions, took splendid advantage of his double complex, both defensively and in attack.

The treatment of the problem was

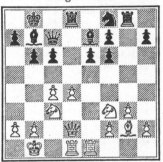

Diagram 137

Black has exploited his pawn complex defensively. White cannot use his K5 as an outpost station

less convincing in the game Yates—Dr. Olland, Scheveningen, 1913.

1. P—K4, P—K3; 2. P—Q4, P—Q4; 3. Kt—QB3, Kt—KB3; 4. B—KKt5, P×P; 5. B×Kt? (Kt×P first was better), P×B; 6. Kt×P, P—KB4? (the moment for the advance does not seem to me happily chosen. The construction of the characteristic position [=pawn skeleton] by means of P—QKt3, P—QB3, Kt—Q2, Q—B2, B—QKt2, and 0—0—0, as in the previous game, was more congruent with the position); 7. Kt—QB3, B—KKt2 (this B now undertakes the protection of the point K4, but the PKB3 was a more reliable watchman); 8. Kt—KB3, 0—0 (the answer to 8. . . . . Kt—QB3, which in 1913 I recommended as better in the *Wienerin*, could be 9. B—QKt5, 0—0; 10. B×Kt, P×B; 11. Q—Q3!, R—QKt1; 12. 0—0—0, and all Black's attempts to get an attack would probably

fail because of the possibility of a White invasion by Kt—K5, for instance 12..... Q—K2; 13. Kt—K5, Q—QKt5; 14. P—QKt3, etc.); 9. B—QB4? (9. Q—Q2 and O—O—O was here indicated), 9..... P—QKt3? (9..... Kt—QB3; 10. Kt—K2, P—K4!; 11. P×P, Kt×P; would have given the bishops space to move in, e.g., 12. Kt×Kt, B×Kt; 13. P—QB3, B—K3 and Black stands well. The important point for us to observe is that the possibility of playing P—K4 did after all arise; cf. our introductory remarks on the complex under consideration); 10. Q—Q3, B—Kt2; 11. O—O—O, Kt—Q2; 12. KR—K1, Q—B3; 13. K—Kt1, KR—Q1; 14. Q—K3, P—QB4? (P—QB3 seems better, in order on the one hand to nail White's QP down fast, and on the other to prepare for P—QKt4 and Kt—Kt3. The affair with the KBP (P—KB4) has not turned out well; the pawn mass did not become a weapon of attack, and the thrust P—KKt4 is already in the air); 15. P—Q5, P—K4; 16. P—KKt4 (the game now passes beyond the region of exact calculation. White ought to have been satisfied with getting a passed pawn, and against the pair of pawns (K and KB) a manœuvre of restraint would be in place, started say by Kt—Q2 and P—KB3. White would then not stand badly), 16..... P×P; 17. Kt—Kt5, B—KR3; 18. Kt(B3)—K4, Q—Kt3; 19. P—KB4, KP×P; 20. Q×KBP with tremendous complications. After some further mistakes on Black's part White won on the 44th move.

In the game just given Black's double complex did not make itself felt as an instrument of attack; quite otherwise in the following game, in which it is true we have to do with the complex PQB2, PQB3, PQ3 against PQB2, PK4, i.e., Diagram 136a and not 136b. We may regard the skeleton positions in these two diagrams as wholly identical in their main characteristics.

Teichmann—Bernstein, Petrograd, 1914. 1. P—K4, P—K4; 2. Kt—KB3, Kt—QB3; 3. Kt—QB3, Kt—KB3; 4. B—Kt5, P—Q3; 5. P—Q4, B—Q2; 6. O—O, B—K2; 7. R—K1, P×P; 8. Kt×P, O—O; 9. B×Kt, P×B; 10. P—QKt3, R—K1 (in addition to the problem of how to take proper advantage of his double complex, Black has another problem to solve, namely the restraint of the free enemy centre); 11. B—Kt2, B—KB1; 12. Q—Q3, P—KKt3; 13. QR—Q1, B—Kt2; 14. P—KB3 (he forgoes the chance of attaining, by P—KB4, to an aggressive development of his centre, and rather strives after a secure position), 14..... Q—QKt1 (the last measures are taken to make the effect of the intended P—QB4 a powerful one); 15. B—B1, Q—Kt3 (better according to Dr. Lasker was 15..... P—QR4, threatening P—R5!; Kt—QR4!, P—QB4; and if 16. P—QR4, then 16..... P—QB4; 17. Kt—Kt5, B—B3; followed by Kt—Q2 with a good game for Black); 16. Kt—R4, Q—Kt2; 17. Kt—Kt2!, P—QB4; 18. Kt—K2,

B—QKt4; 19. P—QB4, B—QB3; 20. Kt—QB3 (the configuration PQR4, PQKt3, PQB4 leaves in similar positions a sick child at QKt3, and thus robs White of all winning chances; that in the text aims at preventing the advance P—QR4—R5 without recourse to weakening pawn moves; Black would then also have on his hands his own weakness, the QRP), 20.....Kt—Q2; 21. B—K3, Kt—Kt3; 22. QR—QKt1, P—QR4; 23. B—KB2. And now 23.....Q—B1 should be played, see Diagram 138, for then P—QR5 would threaten. The reply to 24. Kt—Q5 would be Kt×Kt; 25. BP×Kt, B—Q2; followed by P—R5. Other trumps, except Kt—Q5, White hardly possesses. The impression we gain is this: P—QB4 frees the square for White's Kt—Q5, and is therefore to be regarded as somewhat two-edged. But if the primary condition be satisfied, namely if the KP is kept in a certain measure of restraint, and if an effective parry is in readiness

to meet a possible Kt—Q5, then the thrust P—QB4 may be held justified. The counter structure chosen in this game, namely White's PQB4, PQKt3, PQR2, with KtQB3 and KtQKt2, we regard as sound, but a win for White we consider impossible. Games played on these lines, cf. those of the match Lasker—Schlechter, lead in fact always to a draw.

On the other hand we hold the development P—Q4 to be bad, since it may easily provoke sinister restraints. In this connexion the game Billecard—Dr. Bernstein, Ostend, 1907, is very instructive. After the moves: 1. P—K4, P—K4; 2. Kt—KB3, Kt—QB3; 3. Kt—QB3, Kt—KB3; 4. B—Kt5, P—Q3; 5. P—Q4, P×P; 6. Kt×P,

Diagram 138

Aggressive utilization of the complex. White can after all get his outpost station at Q5. Observe the appropriate measures taken in support of and against P—QR5

B—Q2; 7. 0—0, B—K2; 8. B×Kt, P×B; 9. P—QKt3, 0—0; 10. B—Kt2, P—Q4; there followed: 11. P—K5, Kt—K1; 12. Q—Q2! (White rightly thinks that Black's doubled pawns will not get any stronger by advancing), 12.....P—QB4; 13. Kt(Q4)—K2, P—QB3; 14. QR—Q1, Q—B2; 15. Kt—B4, Q—Kt2 (Kt×P was threatened); 16. Kt—QR4 (this move ushers in a blockade by the occupation of the point QB5. It would be still worse for Black were his P's at QB2, QB3, Q4. The effect then of a Kt at QB5 would be simply crippling. This game is intended to help bring out the affinity between the doubled pawn and restraint to which allusion was made at the beginning of this chapter), 16.....P—B5; 17. B—Q4, P×P; 18. RP×P? (BP×P seems more logical), 18.....Kt—B2; 19. Kt—Q3, Kt—K3; 20. Kt(Q3)—B5, Q—B2;

21. Kt × B, Q × Kt;   22. Q—K3, Kt × B;   23. Q × Kt, QR—Kt1; 24. Kt—B5, Q—B4; . 25. Kt—Q3. White dominates the point QB5; but had he on his 18th move played QBP × P, the pressure in the open QB file would have been appreciably strengthened. With this 10..... P—Q4 seems to be refuted. The student who is interested in the deeper logical connexions will now say to himself: 'How easy the complex PQB2, PQB3, PQ4 must be to blockade! for Black succeeded in undoubling the pawns; in addition White made a serious mistake (18. RP × P instead of BP × P), and yet the mobility of Black's PQB3 and PQ3 remained as slight as it was before!' This calculation is in fact correct. The PQB2, PQB3, and PQ4 are very susceptible indeed to blockade infections; in other words the 'affinity' between the doubled pawn and restraint which we emphasized at the beginning of this chapter may already be accepted as probable. As we go on the probability is likely to be turned into a certainty (cf. game No. 12 Leonhardt—Nimzowitsch).

§3. *Restraint. The 'mysterious' Rook moves. On true and spurious freeing-moves, and how they are to be combated.*

In Diagram 139 (q.v.) White clearly intends to play P—Q4 at any moment when this move seems feasible. Black's R—K1 is intended to help make this freeing move difficult of execution for all time. We have here therefore to do with a preventive action.

Diagram 139

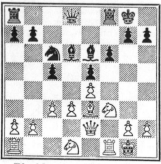

Blackburne—Nimzowitsch
1914
Black makes the 'mysterious' rook move R—K1. The rook's function is here to act as a preventative against P—Q4

Hence it is only the outer form of the move which is mysterious (a Rook to seize a file which is still closed), its strategical end is not. To demand of a piece only direct attacking activity is the stamp of the mere 'wood-shifter'. The keener chess mind quite rightly demands of the pieces that they also undertake preventive action. The following situation is typical: A freeing action (usually a pawn advance) planned by our opponent would in the result give us an open file. This potential file, to open which does not lie in our power, we nevertheless seize, and in advance, with the idea of giving our opponent a distaste for the freeing action. The 'mysterious' Rook move is an indisputable ingredient of a rational strategy. We will give some examples:

White: K, KKt1;   R's, QB1, KB1;   B, K2;   Kt, KB3;   P's,

QR2, QKt2, Q4, K3, KB2, KKt2, KR2. Black: K, KKt1; R's, Q2, KB1; B, QKt2; Kt, KB3; P's, QR4, QKt3, QB3, Q4, KB2, KKt2, KR2. The position is a constructed one, in the opening stage of a game, and White plays KR—Q1; that is to say he expects P—QB4 to be played at an opportune moment, and intends in this case, after P×P, P×P, to take advantage of the QB and Q files to bring pressure on the resulting hanging pawns (QB4 and Q4).

The 'mysterious' Rook move is generally an affair of the opening, though in the early stages of the middle game it also plays an important rôle. In Diagram 140 Black plays coolly 1.....R—R2. If White now plays 2. P—QR3 then 2.....KR—QR1. And now White can only realize his plan, to play P—QKt4 and P—QB5, at the cost of certain concessions to his opponent. The continuation

Diagram 140

Black tries by R—R2 and KR—QR1 to prevent White's plan of P—QR3, P—QKt4, and P—QB5; or at worst to lessen the effect of White's advance

Diagram 141

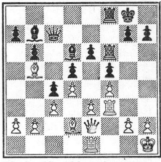

Black (Capablanca) starts a preventive action against White's P—KKt4, and carries it out with great virtuosity

might for instance be: 1.....R—R2; 2. P—QR3, KR—QR1; 3. Q—Kt2, Q—Q1; 4. P—QKt4, P×P; 5. P×P, Q—QKt1; 6. R×R?, Q×R, and Black keeps control of the QR file. Or 6. KR—QKt1, K—B1; 7. P—B5, KtP×P; 8. R×R, R×R; 9. P×P, Q×Q; 10. R×Q, R—R6; 11. R—QB2, B—B1!; 12. P—B6! (best; not however 12. P×QP, P×P; 13. Kt—Kt5, R—R8 ch; 14. K—B2, B—R3; and the game is about equal). 12.....Kt—K1 followed by P—KB4 with some counter play.

A further example (Diag. 141) is taken from an actual game, Kupchik—Capablanca, Lake Hopatcong, 1926. After White's 19th move the position shown in the diagram was reached. The pawn-chain calls for a Black attack on its base the White PQB3 by P—QR3, P—QKt4, P—QR4, and P—Kt5. But it is necessary for Black to safeguard himself against P—KKt4. With this idea Black played 19.....P—KR4!; 20. R(K1)—KB1, R—R3!! (the 'mysterious' Rook move, for Black sees White's P—KR3 and P—KKt4 coming, and wishes when this happens to be ready to attack in the KR file); 21. B—K1, P—KKt3; 22. B—R4, K—B2!; 23. Q—K1, P—QR3 (now timely!); 24. B—QR4, P—QKt4; 25. B—Q1, B—B3; 26. R—KR3 (a defensive move on the Q wing was here indicated), 26.....P—R4; 27. B—Kt5, R(R3)—R1; 28. Q—R4, P—Kt5; 29. Q—K1 (or B—B6; B—K2), R—QKt1; 30. R(R3)—B3, P—QR5, and Black pushed his attack home; 31. R(B3)—B2, P—R6; 32. P—QKt3, BP×P; 33. B×P, B—Kt4; 34. R—KKt1, Q×P, etc. The Rook manœuvre in this game R—KB3—KR3—KR1 stands out with plastic effect and must give pleasure to any-one who plays over the game.

In the position White: K, KB2; R, Q4; B, K3; P's, QR3, QKt2, QB5, KB4, KKt3, KR3. Black: K, KB2; R, QR1; B, QB3; P's, QR5, QKt2, K3, KB3, KKt2, KR4 from the game v. Gottschall—Nimzowitsch, Hanover, 1926, Black wanted to take advantage of his majority on the K side by the manœuvre K—Kt3—B4, followed by P—K4. However on K—Kt3 White would play P—KKt4; therefore I chose the 'mysterious' Rook move (even in an end game is such possible!), 28.....R—KR1!, and after the further moves 29. R—Q1, K—Kt3; 30. R—Q4, K—B4; 31. B—Q2, there again followed a 'mysterious' Rook move 31.....R—KB1, which we might more accurately call semi-mysterious, for whereas R—KR1 followed merely preventive ends, R—KB1 has this essential difference that its nature is purely active, there followed 32. B—K1, P—K4; 33. P×P, P×P; 34. R—KR4, P—KKt4; 35. R—QKt4, K—K3 ch; 36. K—K2, P—K5; 37. B—B2, R—B6. The passed pawn, the penetration of the R into the enemy position, and a certain weakness in White's QBP slowly wrought the destruction of White's game. See II. vi. §3, where the interesting ending of this game is given, interesting because of the tactics employed to break down White's resistance by manœuvring against both flanks.

The 'mysterious' Rook move, which places a Rook in a closed file, which can only be opened by the enemy himself, and if he does not do so our Rook is standing there with 'nothing doing', such a move must never be made, except consciously and with the intention of sacrificing something of the Rook's effective strength. This sacrifice is made in order to prevent an enemy freeing manœuvre, or at any rate to render it difficult. If we, however, recognize a freeing move planned by our opponent as illusory, i.e., as not really having a freeing effect, then it would be in the highest degree un-economic to make such a sacrifice. In the game which was quoted above, Blackburne—Nimzowitsch, the difference between a true and an illusory freeing move leaps to the eyes; and as it is also pertinent to our conception of prophylactic strategy we give it in full in the Games Section. (See No. 32.) The student is recommended to play it over before proceeding further.

The following postulate I regard as of the utmost importance: There is no such thing as an absolute freeing move. A freeing move in a position in which development has not been carried far always proves to be illusory, and, vice versa, a move, which does not come at all in the category of freeing moves, can, given a surplus of tempi to our credit, lead to a very free game.

Consider for instance the position on Diagram 142, White has obviously a substantial plus in tempi, and in these circumstances the Black freeing move P—KB4 only leads to a premature opening of Black's undeveloped game. For example 1.....P—KB4; 2. KP×P, KtP×P; 3. Kt—R5 followed by P—KB4 with a strong attack. This association of ideas was unknown to the pseudo-classical School, which knew only absolute freeing moves. Black's P—KB4 in a position with the central pawn configuration as in the diagram, was reckoned as such by it, and in 80 per cent. of cases was held worthy of commendation. We have reduced the proportion to about 60 per cent.; for even after the defensive White move P—KB3 (after 1.....P—KB4; 2. P× P, P×P) the strength of the pair of Black Ps at K4 and KB4 must not be rated too high. And now we suddenly

Diagram 142

Black's 'freeing-move' P—KB4 leads, owing to his backward development, to a premature opening up of his game which became in consequence compromised

find ourselves facing the germ-cell of restraint action, to which because of its importance a separate section will be devoted.

§4. *The germ cell of restraint action directed against a pawn majority is developed. The fight against a central majority. The qualitative majority.*

I find it impossible to present the germ cell of restraint by means of diagrams, so I will adopt another method. Black, shall we say, has a majority: PQR4 and PQKt4 against White's PQR3; or PK4 and PKB4 against PKB3. In both cases Black threatens to make a passed pawn, and in the second to attack White's castled position by the wedge P—KB5 in conjunction with R—KB4—KR4, etc. The idea of the restraint now lies in the plan of neutralizing the enemy's pawn plus by means of the open K file and two different blockade points. In the position under consideration, besides 'Knights, halberdiers, and archers', the possessor of the pawn majority has two threats at his disposal; the one consists in the advance P—K5, the other in the wedge P—B5, supplemented perhaps by the diversion R—KB4—KKt4 or KR4, or P—KR4, etc., and at the same time the establishment of a Black Kt at his K6 will be planned.

In what does the restraint idea now consist? In the case of P—K5 in P—KB4 with an eventual B—K3 to blockade Black's KP at that point, and on the other hand if Black should advance his KBP, P—KB5, to stop any further advance by Kt—K4. This Kt, thanks to his radius of action, will help to make Black's diversion difficult to carry out. It follows that we must look for the germ-cell of restraint action in an open file combined with a two-fold possibility of setting up a blockade.

A central majority must not be allowed to advance too far, otherwise the wedge threat would have a much too painful effect. For example in the position White: K, KKt1; P's, KB2, KKt2, KR2. Black: P's, K5, KB5, KKt2, KR2. (Imagine any number of pieces added.) Black with P—KB6 (the wedge) threatens to cut the White lines of communication between his KR and KKt P's and the rest of his 2nd rank (i.e., a White R on his QR2 could no longer protect either of these pawns), and Black's attack must, *ceteris paribus*, be reckoned as very strong. Hence it is necessary to fix an enemy central majority on its 4th rank, i.e., with the configuration Black: P's K4, KB4. White: PKB3.

The conception of the qualitative majority is an easy one to assimilate by anyone who has mastered the pawn-chain. In the position, White: P's, K5, Q4, QR2, QKt2, QB3, KB4, KKt4, KR3. Black: P's, K3, Q4, QB4, QR2, QKt2, KB2, KKt2, KR2. White has the qualitative majority on the King's Wing, Black on the Queen's. That is to say that majority which is the more advanced towards the enemy base is naturally regarded as qualitatively the superior one.

§5. *The different forms under which restraint is wont to appear are further elucidated. (a) The fight against mobile centre pawns. (b) The restraint of a qualitative majority. (c) Restraint of double-complexes. (d) My 'special variation' and its restraint motif.*

(a) The mobile centre pawn. White with a PK4 against Black's PQ3 and PKB2 (or PQ4 against PK3 and PQB3). Such a P can result from say 1. P—K4, P—K4; 2. Kt—KB3, Kt—QB3; 3. B—Kt5, P—Q3; 4. P—Q4, P×P; 5. Kt×P, B—Q2. Black's restraint operation will be begun by Kt—KB3, B—K2, O—O,

R—K1, B—KB1.   Another important aid towards the crippling of White's centre is the more passive pawn structure PQ3 and PKB3. The position White: P, K4.   Black: P's, Q3, KB3 is typical and I call it the 'sawing' position, since White's KP is to be sawn up between these pawns.

The sequence of events in a manœuvre directed against a mobile centre is usually: (i) the passive 'sawing position', then (ii) the more aggressive hindering action of a rook exerting pressure on it; (iii) making backward or isolated a once mobile centre pawn; (iv) mechanical stopping of the same by a blockading piece; (v) winning the pawn.

The aim of the restraining party in a game may be sufficiently summed up thus: First restrain, next blockade, lastly destroy!   To carry this out is difficult but remunerative, and the process is instructive for the student.   Hence the analysis, of the position reached after 1. P—K4, P—K4; 2. Kt—KB3, P—Q3; 3. P—Q4, P×P; 4. Kt×P is an excellent training, and as such cannot be too strongly recommended to the aspiring student.

The following illustrative game is apparently complicated, but it is this in its motives only; in reality it is the fight against White's PK4 which dominates. Shoosmith—Nimzowitsch, Ostend, 1907. 1. P—Q4, Kt—KB3; 2. P—QB4, P—Q3; 3. Kt—KB3, QKt—Q2; 4. Kt—QB3, P—K4; 5. P—K4, B—K2; 6. B—Q3, 0—0; 7. 0—0, P×P!   (If 7..... R—K1, then 8. P—Q5 and Black will be cramped for a long time. For instance, 8..... Kt—QB4; 9. B—K3, Kt×B; 10. Q×Kt, Kt—Q2; 11. P—QKt4, P—QR4; 12. P—QR3, etc.); 8. Kt×P, R—K1; 9. P—QKt3, Kt—K4; 10. B—QB2, P—QR3 (this advance of Black will soon be intelligible); 11. B—Kt2, B—Q2; 12. P—KR3, B—KB1; 13. P—KB4, Kt—Kt3; 14. Q—B3, P—QB3; 15. QR—K1, P—QKt4 (now the situation is clear: Black keeps an eye on White's KP and seeks at the same time to be rid of the disturbing QBP, since the latter makes his PQ3 backward); 16. Q—Q3, Q—B2; 17. K—R1, QR—Q1; 18. B—Kt1, P—Kt5!! (We have here to do with a chain formation, certainly rather an unusual one.   The links of the chain are White's PQKt3 and PQB4, Black's PQKt5 and KtQB4(!), for why as an exception should not an officer be allowed to play the rôle of a pawn in a chain?   The plan consists in the manœuvre B—QB1, Kt—Q2—B4 and P—QR4—R5 attacking the White enemy base the PQKt3.   Accordingly P—QKt5 involved the transference of the attack from White PQB4 to his PQKt3); 19. Kt—Q1, B—QB1; 20. Q—KB3, Kt—Q2; 21. Kt—B5, Kt—B4; 22. P—KKt4? (a mistake which leaves his PKB4 for a moment insufficiently defended; but this short moment is long enough to allow Black to break through brilliantly); 22..... Kt—K3! (exploiting White's mistake); 23. Q—Kt3, B—Kt2; 24. P—KR4.

P—Q4;   25. P—K5, P—QB4;   26. P×P, R×P;   27. K—Kt1
(B—K4?, R×Kt!), 27.....R—Q7; 28. Kt(B5)—K3, Q—B3; 29.
Resigns.

The reader may here be referred to my games against Teichmann
and Blackburne (Nos. 2 and 32).

(*b*) The fight against a qualitative majority. Let us imagine
that in Diagram 140 the Black Kt is at QB4 instead of KB3: we
should then have a typical case of the restraint of a qualitative
majority. If now Kt×Kt, then KtP×Kt and White's advance is
crippled. If however 1. P—QR3 intending to follow with P—QKt4,
then 1.....P—R5!; 2. P—QKt4, Kt—Kt6!; and this strongly
posted Kt is compensation for a possible White P—QB5. The
student should notice that the action of Black's flanking pawn is
made up of equal parts of passive and aggressive effect, for this

Diagram 143

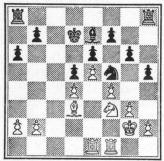

White's qualitative majority
appears to be held in restraint.
1. P—KR3 will be effectively
answered by P—KR5, and
2. P—KKt4 by Kt—KKt6

Diagram 144

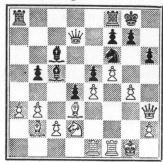

Van Vliet—Nimzowitsch

pawn, or the PKR4 in Diagram 143, is the true prop of our whole
restraint manœuvre. In both positions White's P—R3 will be
answered by P—R5.

Another typical example is shown in the following end game
(Diag. 144).   Here the advance in close formation planned by White,
namely Q—KKt3, P—KR4, P—KKt5, cannot be held up permanently. This advance (let us imagine for a moment that Black's
inevitable P—KB3 has taken place) would expose the base of Black's
pawn-chain (after P×BP, P×P). But the King's side attack
involved in White's advance would be much worse for Black. His
right plan will, therefore, be to hold up White's P—KR4 and
P—KKt5 long enough for the King to escape by flight. With this
idea Black played 21.....Kt—R2, and then followed 22. Kt—KB3,

Q—K2; 23. Q—Kt3, KR—K1; 24. P—KR4, P—KB3; 25. R—QR1
(White, too, has weaknesses), 25.....Q—QKt2; 26. R(B1)—K1,
K—B2!; 27. R—K2 (if 27. P—Kt5, then RP×P; 28. P×P,
K—K2! with a tenable game), 27.....R—KR1! (the 'mysterious'
Rook move!); 28. K—B2, Kt—B1; 29. P—KKt5, RP×P;
30. P×P, Kt—Q2. (White's K side attack may be said to have
spent itself, for after 31. P×KBP, P×P; 32. Q—Kt6 ch, K—K2;
33. Q—Kt7 ch, K—Q3, Black would have a splendid game.) The
game proceeded: 31. P×P, P×P; 32. Kt—R4, R(QR1)—KKt1;
33. Kt—Kt6, R—R4; 34. R—KKt1, R—Kt4; with advantage to
Black. The resource here demonstrated is worth the attention of the
student.

(c) Restraint of double complexes. Side by side with the dynamic
weakness of such a complex, which we have often emphasized, we
have to characterize the following
points as often decisive: (1) the im-
prisoned Bishop, (2) cramped terrain
and consequent difficulties in finding
a defence.

Bird's opening will give us an example
of (1) and in both forms of the opening.

I. 1. P—KB4, P—Q4; 2. Kt—
KB3, P—QB4; 3. P—Q3 (somewhat
unusual) Kt—QB3; 4. Kt—QB3, B—
KKt5!; 5. P—KKt3, B×Kt!!; 6. P×B,
P—K3; 7. B—Kt2, P—KB4!; 8. 0—0,
P—Q5 (a delightful play, the BKKt2
is now a prisoner in his own camp.
Black's weakness at his K3 is easily
protected (Diag. 145)); 9. Kt—Kt1,
P—QKt4; 10. P—QR4, P—Kt5;

Diagram 145

The 'dead' Bishop (KKt2) a
prisoner in his own camp.
The QB is in not much better
state

11. Kt—Q2, Kt—R4; 12. Q—K2, K—B2; 13. R—K1, Q—Q2;
14. Kt—B4, Kt×Kt; 15. P×Kt, Kt—B3; and Black (Dr. Erdman)
dictated the tempo.

II. 1. P—K3, P—K4; 2. P—QB4, Kt—KB3; 3. Kt—QB3;
Kt—QB3; 4. Kt—KB3, B—QKt5; 5. B—K2 (here was to be
considered 5. P—Q4, P×P; 6. P×P, P—Q4; 7. B—K2 with an
equal game), 5.....0—0; 6. 0—0, R—K1; 7. P—QR3, B×Kt;
8. KtP×B, P—Q3; and White laboured the whole game through
under the difficulty of making use of his QB. (From the game
Nimzowitsch—Réti, Breslau, 1925.)

Diagrams 146 and 147 are given to illustrate (2). The latter shows
us a blockading Kt whose effect on the double complex is simply
enormous: for not only is Black's majority in its collective value

illusory, but each single component of that majority seems individually to have its life threatened. Under these conditions White's majority will win, as it will. Even with Rooks present on both sides, e.g., White, RQR4; Black, RQ1 or RQKt3, the game would be untenable for the second player. This shows to what degree a restrained doubled pawn may cripple a position.

(d) My 'special variation' with its restraint motif. The line of play in question is 1. P—QB4, P—K4; 2. Kt—QB3, Kt—KB3; 3. Kt—KB3, Kt—QB3; and now 4. P—K4. As early as 1924 I had tried after the moves 1. P—KB4, P—QB4; 2. P—K4, Kt—QB3; 3. P—Q3 (originated by Dr. Krause); 3 . . . . . P—KKt3, the move 4. P—QB4, whose motif I visualized as a blockade spanning half the

Diagram 146   Diagram 147

   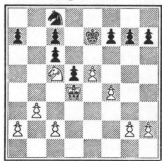

If his PQB2 were absent Black   The effect of a Kt who is
would have freedom to move   blockading an enemy doubled
about, as it is—bearing in   pawn is crushing
mind the threat B—Kt7—he is
almost stalemated

board, and in *Kagans Neueste Schachnachrichten* for 1925, p. 10, I made the following note to this move:—'Since this move is not inspired by the hope of preventing or even of making more difficult P—Q4, a special explanation is needed. Black wishes to build up the configuration PK3, PQ4. This done, he will consider the extension of his attack formation on the Q's wing, i.e., by Kt—Q5 when opportunity offers, in order after Kt × Kt, P × Kt; to bring pressure in the QB file on White's PQB2. The text move is made to forestall this possible extension of play on the Q wing. The hole at Q4 does not seem to be a serious matter.[2]

When I to-day ask myself whence I got the moral courage, for it takes moral courage to make a move (or form a plan) running counter to all tradition, I think I may say in answer, that it was only my intense preoccupation with the problem of the blockade which helped me to do so. To this problem I was ever seeking to bring out new sides, and so it came that, as Black in Dresden, 1926, after the moves

1. P—K4, P—QB4; 2. Kt—KB3, Kt—QB3; 3. Kt—QB3, I ventured the move P—K4, which at that time caused a huge sensation. My special variation given above, is to be considered merely a further step on a trail which had already been broken. Moreover the able Danish theorist Dr. O. H. Krause, has pursued an original inquiry into the possibility of a combination of P—K4 and P—QB4, in which, independently of my analysis, he has arrived at much the same conclusions as I did.

The student is advised now to study games Nos. 33 to 35, and in addition is referred to the investigation of the idea in my brochure, *Die Blockade*.

CHAPTER III

THE ISOLATED QUEEN'S PAWN AND HIS DESCENDANTS

§1. *Introductory.*

THE problem of the isolated QP is in my opinion one of the cardinal problems in the whole theory of positional play. We are concerned with the appraisal of a statically weak pawn, who, however, notwithstanding his weakness, is imbued with dynamic strength. 'Which preponderates, the static weakness or the dynamic strength?' So put, the problem gains in significance, in fact it strays in a sense beyond the circumscribed boundaries of chess.

It is indispensable that the student should face this problem himself, that is to say have personal experience of it. He should try as White to get the so-called normal position in the Queen's Gambit, i.e., 1. P—Q4, P—Q4; 2. Kt—KB3, Kt—KB3; 3. P—QB4, P—K3; 4. P—K3, P—QB4; 5. Kt—QB3, Kt—QB3, and then, alternately, in one game 6. B—Q3, P×QP; 7. KP×P, P×P; 8. B×BP and White has an 'isolani', in the other, 6. P×QP, KP×P; 7. P×P, B×P; and now White has to fight against the isolani. It will do him good to realize in his own person how dangerous an enemy isolani may be, and how difficult it is to save his own from an untimely end.

§2. *The dynamic strength of the isolated QP.*

The strength of an isolani (Diag. 149) lies in its lust to expand (=the tendency P—Q5), and in addition to the circumstance that this P protects, indeed creates the White outpost stations at K5 and QB5. As opposed to this, the Black outpost station at Q4 has not, at any rate in the middle game, the full equivalent value, for quite apart from any arithmetical preponderance (two outposts to one), White can point to the fact that a KtK5 (Diag. 148) must have a sharper effect than is ever possible to an opposing KtQ4; for it is clear that a KtK5 seconded by two powerful Bishop diagonals (Q3 to KR7 and KKt5 to KB6) must exert pressure on Black's King's wing, and what can be 'sharper' than an attack on the King? The lineal investigation yields therefore an undoubted plus to the first player.

On the other hand our pawn, as is well known, tends to become a weakness in the ending. How are we to understand this? Is the difficulty only this, that the PQ4 is hard to defend, or are there other calamities in store?

Diagram 148

Diagram 149

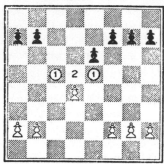

The isolated QP. Notice White's outpost station at his K5, Black's at his Q4

Skeleton diagram of the isolated QP. 1 = White outpost. 2 = Black outpost

§3. *The isolani as an end game weakness.*

Our judgment on the problem which we have sketched must be influenced by the circumstance that to the points K5 (White) and Q4 (Black) a different valuation must be assigned in the end game than was the case in the middle game; for in the ending attacks on the King are not in question, and so White's K5 loses much of its glory, while Black's Q4 gains in importance. And if White have not already got through to QB7, or have not other trump cards earned in the middle game to point to, his position will not be particularly enviable. White will suffer not only under the want of protection felt by his isolani, but also from the fact that the White squares such as Q5, QB4, K4 can easily become weak. Imagine in Diagram 149 a White KQB4 and BQ2, and a Black KQB3 and KtK2. Black by a check with the Kt drives the White K from QB4, plays then K—Q4, and pushes further forward with his K via QB5 or K5. In every pertinent case that may arise Q4 must be regarded as the key point of Black's position. With this point as base he will blockade, centralize, manœuvre. Black's Q4 will provide a gate of entry into the enemy position (cf. the above example) and also a point of junction in all possible troop movements, as for instance (imagine now Diagram 149 enlivened by the presence of Rooks and Knights) in the case of Black's R(Q1)—Q4—QR4, or Kt(KB3)—Q4—QKt5, or finally Kt—Q4—K2—KB4×QP. A Black Kt posted at Q4 exercises an impressive effect on both wings; a B at Q4 not seldom forces a decision even with Bishops of opposite colour (e.g., if there be Rooks remaining on each side). Obviously White may have counter-balancing, or even apparently preponderating, compensation for these trumps of Black's, for instance, should one of his Rooks have penetrated to his QB7; but such cases can only be considered as exceptions to the rule. To recapitulate: White's weakness in the end game rests on the fact that his PQ4 seems to be threatened, while Black's Q4 is extraordinarily strong, further, that the White squares, his QB4, Q5, K4, tend to become weak, whereas much of the one time importance of his K5 is spent. White's pawn position was in fact not 'compact', and other disadvantages to which we have called attention, such as a weakness pervading a complex of squares of a given colour, must necessarily attach themselves to a pawn position which is not compact, i.e., which is broken up. We earnestly recommend the student, as extremely profitable, that he sharpen his sense for compact positions and the reverse. He must also bear carefully in mind that it is not only the isolani itself that tends to become a weakness, but also the complex of squares surrounding it. In this the principal evil is to be found.

§4. *The isolani as a weapon of attack in the middle game.*

Solidity of construction and purpose should at the first sign of neglect on the part of the opponents (e.g., if he have withdrawn his pieces from the K wing) give place to a violent attack. Many players with an isolani proceed much too violently, but it seems to me that there is no objective motive for 'plunging' on a desperate attack. At first the utmost solidity is called for. The attack will come of itself in good time, for instance when

Diagram 150

Nimzowitsch—Taubenhaus

Black with the move played Kt—K1 (to get to Q3). This is the trumpet call for the attack for White. How will the attack be started, and what will be its course?

Black has withdrawn his KtKB3, which he will at some time naturally do, since the Kt wants to get to Q4. In the development stage (Diag. 148) we would therefore recommend the solid construction, BK3 (not KKt5), QK2, R's: QB1 and Q1 (not Q1 and K1), further BQ3 or QKt1 (not QKt3); and the first player cannot be too strongly warned against attempting surprise attacks in the early stages, started by perhaps Kt(K5)× KBP (a B being at QR2) or by a Rook sally (R—K1—K3—KR3). A solid position aimed at maintaining the security of the PQ4 is the one and only right course, and it must ever be remembered that the BK3 belongs to the PQ4 as does a nurse to a suckling child!

It is only when Black has withdrawn his pieces from the K's side that White may sound the attack, and this, if he will, he may carry out in sacrificial style (Diag. 150). White has developed his pieces in the spirit of this section, the text move (Kt—K1) gives him the chance which, as in all similar cases, he avidly seizes to launch a direct attack on the enemy King. The result in the present case is doubtful, but since the whole manner of conducting the attack is characteristic of 'isolani positions', we give a few variations 19.....Kt—K1; 20. Q—R5, P—KKt3 (if 20.....P—KB4, then 21. B—KKt5) 21. Q—R6, Kt—Kt2; (or 21. P—KB3; 22. Kt—Kt4) 22. B—KKt5! (the pieces now come out of their reserve), 22.....P—KB3; 23. B×KtP, P×B; 24. Kt×P, and now two variations arise according as the Q retreats to Q2 or Q3. If the former White has two courses open to him either 25. B—R4! or the more combinational 25. B×P, e.g., 24.....Q—Q2; 25. B×P, Kt×B; 26. Q—R8 ch, K—B2; 27. Kt—K5 ch, K—K1; 28. Kt×Q, R×Q; 29. Kt×Kt ch, with three pawns for the piece sacrificed. If Black play 24.....Q—Q3 (instead of Q—Q2) White can carry on with 25. Q—R8 ch, K—B2; 26. Q—R7, P×B; 27. Kt—K5 ch, and the continuation could be 27.....K—K1; 28. Q×Kt, Q—K2; 29. Q—Kt6 ch, K—Q1; 30. R—B6 with wild complications. So once more, build up a solid position, support the isolani (B—K3!) and only attack when opportunity really offers.

§5. *Which cases are favourable for White and which for Black?*

In general it may be said that the two following cases are worth striving for by White.

(i) When White has effected P—Q5, KP×P; a piece ×P, and thereby gets the better, because a centralized position (as in the game Rubinstein—Tartakower, Baden-Baden, 1925).

(ii) When White has built up a position in the QB file (cf. game No. 36, Nimzowitsch—Taubenhaus).

For Black the following are desirable.

(i) All cases (*ceteris paribus*) of a pronounced end game character.

(ii) Those where Black has played Kt(Q4)×Kt(QB3); KtP×Kt, with the idea of pinning down White's PQB3 from the start and of laying siege to it (cf. game No. 11, Thomas—Alekhine and see §7 below on the isolated pawn couple).

§6. *On the possible genesis of reflex weaknesses among the Q side pawns of the player with an isolani.*

An index of the weakness of the isolani appears in the possibility which is not seldom offered to the opponent, of transferring his attack from the QP to the Q's wing; such a case of 'reflex weakness' may be seen in game No. 23 (Rubinstein—Duras); a similar picture is presented in the following game (Rubinstein—Dr. Lasker, Moscow,

1925). After the moves 1. P—Q4, P—Q4; 2. P—QB4, P—QB3; 3. P—K3, Kt—KB3; 4. Kt—QB3, P—K3; 5. Kt—KB3, QKt—Q2; 6. B—Q3, P×P; 7. B×P, P—QKt4; 8. B—K2, P—QR3; 9. 0—0, B—Kt2; 10. P—QKt3, B—K2; 11. B—Kt2, 0—0; 12. Kt—K5, P—QB4; 13. B—B3, Q—B2; 14. Kt×Kt, Kt×Kt; 15. Kt—K4, QR—Q1; 16. R—QB1, Q—Kt1; 17. Q—K2, P×P; 18. P×P, R—QB1; 19. P—KKt3, Q—R1; 20. K—Kt2, KR—Q1; 21. R×R, R×R; 22. R—QB1, R×R; 23. B×R, P—KR3, Black took a strategically most interesting advantage of the weakness of White's PQ4. The continuation was: 24. B—Kt2, Kt—Kt3; 25. P—KR3 (since he wants to avoid the exchange of Q's, Q—QB2; Q—QB1 would be of no use) 25.....Q—QB1; 26. Q—Q3, Kt—Q4! (threatening KtKt5) 27. P—QR3, Kt—Kt3!! (Now White's PQKt3 is become weak); 28. K—R2, B—Q4; 29. K—Kt2, Q—B3; 30. Kt—Q2, P—QR4!; 31. Q—B3 (in his trouble he after all decides to submit to the exchange of Queens; but succumbs to the reflex weaknesses which have now arisen), 31.....B×B ch; 32. Kt×B (Q×B would fail on Q—B7; Q—QKt7, Kt—Q4!) 32.....Q×Q; 33. B×Q, P—QR5! (and now the weakness of White's Q side is evident); 34. P×P, P×P, and White lost since the attempt to save himself by 35. B—Kt4, failed against 35.....B×B; 36. P×B, P—R6; 37. Kt—Q2 and now 37.....Kt—Q4, whereby the approach of the White K via K2, Q3, and QB4 is prevented (the answer to K—K2 would always be Kt—QB6 ch). What is remarkable in this fine ending, in addition to the transference of the attack, is the masterly and varied use made of the point Q4.

On the manner of laying siege to an isolani I would make this additional remark, that we to-day no longer consider it necessary to render an enemy isolani absolutely immobile; on the contrary, we like to give him the illusion of freedom, rather than shut him up in a cage. (The principle of the large zoological garden applied to the small beast of prey.) How this is done is shown in the following game Lasker (whom we class under the moderns)—Tarrasch, Petrograd, 1914. 1. P—Q4, P—Q4; 2. Kt—KB3, P—QB4; 3. P—QB4, P—K3; 4. P×QP, KP×P; 5. P—KKt3, Kt—QB3; 6. B—Kt2, Kt—KB3; 7. 0—0, B—K2; 8. P×P, B×P; 9. QKt—Q2, and now the isolani has the choice whether he will become weak on Q4 or Q5. Tarrasch chose the latter and there followed 9.....P—Q5; 10. Kt—Kt3, B—Kt3; 11. Q—Q3, B—K3; 12. R—Q1, B×Kt; 13. Q×B, Q—K2; 14. B—Q2, 0—0; 15. P—QR4, Kt—K5; 16. B—K1, QR—Q1; 17. P—R5!!, B—B4; 18. P—R6, P×P (if P—QKt3, then Q—R4 threatening P—QKt4); 19. QR—QB1. And now all the pieces defending the PQ5 are in the air. There followed 19.....R—QB1; 20. Kt—R4, B—Kt3; 21. Kt—B5,

Q—K4; 22. B×Kt, Q×B; 23. Kt—Q6, winning the exchange. Taking everything into consideration the isolani is not an ineffective weapon in the middle game, but it can become very weak in the ending.

§7. *The isolated pawn couple.*

In the position on Diagram 151 Black can exchange at his QB6; if he then in the sequel succeed in holding back White's PQB3 and PQ4, and finally in blockading them absolutely, his otherwise rather doubtful strategy (Kt × Kt) will have been justified, for to have the pawns tied down in their own camp and close to the frontier will worry White not a little. The one trouble, namely the obligation to keep the PQB3 and PQ4 protected, will be aggravated by the other, a cramped terrain. The pawns blockaded on QB3 and Q4, and only these, are what I call the isolated pawn couple. A good example is met with in game No. 11 (Thomas—Alekhine).

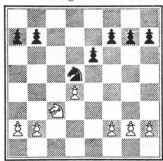

Diagram 151

The genesis of an isolated pawn couple, PQB3, PQ4, (1.....Kt × Kt; 2. P × Kt)

An essentially different picture is met with when the beleaguered player succeeds in advancing his QBP. We then have the PQB4 and PQ4. These pawns we no longer call an 'isolated pawn couple', but designate them as 'hanging' pawns.

It will not be difficult to decide where the preference lies between the isolated pawn couple, which has as a rule but slight mobility, and the two hanging pawns. It stands to reason that hanging pawns are much to be preferred, if only for the reason that they imply threats. And even if these should prove to be only apparent threats, which is after all what we might expect, nevertheless a doubtful initiative is always better than a passivity which is dead beyond all manner of doubt, as we have discovered in the case of a blockaded isolated pawn couple in Game No. 11. We have then the following postulate for our guidance: The possessor of an isolated pawn couple (Diag. 151, after the moves Kt × Kt, P × Kt) must do everything in his power to make P—QB4 possible; he must not at any cost allow a blockade. He must regard the awkward formation PQB3, PQ4 as a transition stage to the mobile structure PQB4, PQ4, with its eternal threat of P—B5 or P—Q5.

We will now give an example of the case where Black (who is saddled with an isolated pawn couple) struggles to make P—QB4 possible. Nimzowitsch—J. Giersing and S. Kinch, Copenhagen,

M

1924. 1. P—QB4, P—K4; 2. Kt—KB3, Kt—QB3; 3. P—Q4, P×P; 4. Kt×P, Kt—KB3; 5. Kt×Kt, KtP×Kt; 6. P—KKt3, P—Q4; 7. B—Kt2, B—QKt5 ch; 8. B—Q2, B×B; 9. Kt×B, 0—0; 10. 0—0, R—QKt1; 11. Q—B2 (White avoids P—QKt3, since he designs to manœuvre over QKt3, e.g., Kt—Kt3 or Q—R4) 11.....R—K1; 12. P—K3, B—K3; 13. P×P (13. Kt—Kt3, P×P; 14. Kt—Q4 was also to be considered), 13.....P×P (Black has now the isolated pawn couple in question: for the formation PQB2, Q4 deserves the designation 'isolated' even more than does PQB3, Q4: he therefore quite rightly tries to make P—QB4 possible); 14. Kt—Kt3, Q—Q3; 15. KR—QB1, KR—QB1; 16. Q—B5, Q×Q; 17. R×Q, Kt—Q2; 18. R—QR5 (in order on the next move, by R—QB1, to establish an enduring blockade), 18.....P—QB4!!; 19. R×RP, P—B5; 20. Kt—Q4, R×P!; 21. Kt×B, P×Kt; 22. R×Kt, P—B6 (Black has purchased the mobility of his QBP at the cost of a piece! White cannot force a win); 23. B—R3, P—B7; 24. B×P ch, K—B1; 25. R—B7 ch (B—B5 was also possible) K—K1; 26. B×R, R—Kt8 ch; 27. K—Kt2, R×R (or 27.....P—B8=Q; 28. R×R, Q×R; 29. R—B4); 28. R—QB7, P—B8=Q; 29. R×Q, R×R; and the game was drawn on the 42nd move.

§8. *Hanging pawns. Their pedigree and what we can learn from it. The advance in a blocked position.*

The evolution, or the story of the genesis of hanging pawns will be found illustrated in the trio of diagrams, 152a, 152b, 152c. A glance at this shows that we are minded to trace the descent of the hanging pawns from the isolani, and the 'family tree' shows very clearly the generations: Isolani, the founder of the family. Isolated pawn couple. Hanging pawns. This view, of which the soundness is demonstrable, will serve us in good stead, for it will enable us to compare the hanging pawns with their anything but distinct motives, with their grandpapa the Isolani whose motives are more plain. In short a study of their family history should help us to a better understanding of one particularly 'difficult' member of that family. From their grandpapa the hanging pawns have inherited one essential trait, namely that curious mixture of static weakness and dynamic strength. But whereas in the case of an isolani both strength and weakness stand out clearly, with hanging pawns both are masked. In these highly problematical creatures two things only may be held to be established: (i) that the two hanging pawns (as say in Diag. 152c) are 'unprotected', i.e., are not defended by any pawns, and that the bombardment to which, being in open files, they are subjected, will be all the more harassing on that account; (ii) that the possibility of attaining to a comparatively secure position, i.e., one in which one of the two hanging pawns protects the other (PQ4, PQB5, or PQB4, PQ5), often presents itself.

The problem however is this: If this possibility, to attain to relative security, is only to be bought at the cost of all initiative in the centre, if the pawns in getting this 'security' can be blockaded, is it not more advisable to forego this offered security and to remain 'hanging'?

The Isolani and his Descendants

A family tree from the game

Rubinstein—Nimzowitsch, Carlsbad, 1907

Diagram 152a

The Isolani

Diagram 152b

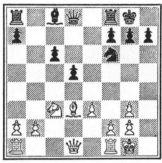

The isolated pawn-couple

Diagram 152c

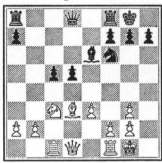

The two hanging pawns

The answer to this is not easy. It depends entirely on the particular circumstances; namely on the manner and the details of the resulting blockade. That to talk of the 'security' in which such a blockaded complex can rock itself is greatly to stretch the meaning of the word, this I concede in advance, for blockaded pawns all too easily tend to become weaknesses. Nevertheless, it would seem to be

entirely fitting, in certain cases, to let the hanging pawns advance in
a blocked position.   These cases are the following:—(i) When the
pawns in the enemy blockading ring are themselves attackable, as is
the White PQKt2 in Diagram 152c.   (ii) When the blockade would
cost the enemy too much, either because the blockading apparatus
is too great, or because the blockaders at his disposal prove to be for
some reason unfitted for their task whether for lack of elasticity or as
having insufficient threat effect from their positions (cf. I. iv. §3).
As an antithesis to this we may point to Diagrams 153 and 154.
Here the 'blockaded' security is shown to be deceptive; the advanced
pawns become weak.   And again the reason for this lies in the quality
of the blockading forces: in Diagrams 153 and 154 the KtQ3 and the
KQ3 are respectively excellent blockaders, which sufficiently accounts
for the miscarriage of the attempt to save the situation.

Diagram 153

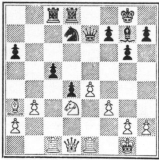

E. Cohn—Duras
Carlsbad, 1911

The 'security' achieved by the
hanging pawns was a very
relative one.   The PB4 is
weak, though it is true that the
PQ5 is passed

Diagram 154

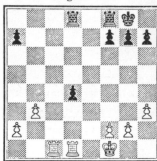

The PQ5 is the product of two
hanging pawns. Many moves
ago there occurred P—Q5,
KP×P, BP×P. The PQ5
will now be blockaded by
K—K2—Q3. White gets the
advantage

The truth seems, therefore, to lie in the following statement
of the case:—Just as our judgment on the isolani PQ4 depended on
the greater or lesser degree of initiative to which he could lay claim
(of course the outpost station which he supports must have some
import), so, too, we consider that we have the right to expect some
measure of initiative in hanging pawns which have attained to a
'blockaded' security.   Dead passivity has no prospects before it.

We will now give some examples:

In the position Rubinstein—Nimzowitsch, Diagram 152c, there
followed 15. Q—QR4, Q—Kt3 (Black holds tight); 16. Q—R3,
P—B5! (steps into 'blockaded' security, but here White's blockading
ring is attackable in the PQKt2.   Black's advance was therefore

justified); 17. B—K2, P—QR4; 18. KR—Q1, Q—Kt5; 19. R—Q4,
KR—Q1;   20. R(QB1)—Q1, R—Q2;   21. B—B3, R(R1)—Q1;
22. Kt—Kt1; (A waiting measure would be better here, e.g., R(Q4)—
Q2 etc.), 22.....R—QKt1;   23. R(Q1)—Q2, Q×Q!;   24. Kt×Q,
K—B1;   25. P—K4 (leads in the end to the loss of a pawn, but
White in any case stood unfavourably.   The equilibrium which still
existed at the 21st move—the weaknesses of the PQ4 and the PQKt2
balanced one another—has been clearly disturbed; the PQKt2 is
now become really weak, whereas the PQ4 seems to be actually over-
protected), 25.....P×P;   26. R×R, Kt×R;   27. B×P, Kt—B4;
28. R—Q4 (or 28. B—B6!, R—Kt5;   29. B—Q5, Kt—R5; with
advantage to Black), 28.....Kt×B;   29. R×Kt, R×P;   30. Kt×P,
R—Kt5;   31. Kt—Q6, R×R;   32. Kt×R, B×P; and Black won.
For the concluding moves see I. vi. §1, p. 67.

In master practice the move P—Q5 (from the hanging pawn

position PQB4, PQ4) occurs much more
frequently.   It leads quite prettily to
the closing of the somewhat original
circle from isolani through the hanging
pawns to isolani.   The whole point now
is whether the isolani which is newly
come into existence can maintain itself
or not.   An example taken from the
game   Nimzowitsch — Tartakower,
Copenhagen, 1923:—1. Kt—KB3, P—
Q4; 2. P—QKt3, P—QB4; 3. P—K3,
Kt—QB3;   4. B—Kt2, B—KKt5;
5. B—K2, Q—B2;   6. P—Q4, P×P;
7. P×P, P—K3;   8. 0—0, B—Q3 (we
have now a Queen's gambit declined with
colours reversed); 9. P—KR3, B×Kt;
10. B×B, Kt—KB3;   11. P—QB4!,

Diagram 155

Bernstein—Teichmann
Carlsbad, 1923
Some elegant pirouetting by
Black is seen

P×P; 12. P×P, 0—0; 13. Kt—QB3 (the construction Kt—Q2—Kt3,
Q—K2, QR—B1, KR—K1 would here have been in the spirit of
a holding tight policy, but I wished to 'realize' my stock-in-trade,
by P—Q5); 13..... KR—Q1;   14. Kt—Kt5, Q—K2;   15. Q—K2,
B—Kt1;   16. P—Q5, P×P;   17. Q×Q, Kt×Q;   18. B×Kt,
P×B; 19. P×P, B—K4!;   20. QR—QKt1, and the QP not only
managed to maintain himself, but also in the whole further course of
the game formed a counterweight to Black's majority on the Q-side
which was not to be under-estimated.   Tartakower did underestimate it, and lost.

The game from which Diagram 155 (q.v.) was taken did not run so
comfortable a course for the possessor of the hanging pawns.   The
game   proceeded   17. Q—R3, Kt—K5;   18. R—Q3, KR—Q1;

19. KR—Q1, Q—K3; 20. Kt—Q2, Q—QKt3; 21. Kt—B1, Kt—B3; 22. Kt—Kt3, QR—QB1;   23. P—KR3, P—KR3;   24. Kt—K2, R—Q2;   25. Kt—B3, Q—K3;   26. Q—R5, P—Q5! (he is tired of the eternal threats and seeks to substitute for the 'hanging position' the 'blockaded security' of which we have so often spoken, but it nearly cost him dear); 27. P×P, P×P; 28. Kt—Kt5 (how is the newly arisen isolani now to be saved?), 28.....Q—B4! (there followed some dexterous parries);   29. Q—R4!, R—B8!;   30. R×R, Q×R; 31. R—B8 ch, K—R2;   32. Q—B2, Q×Q;   33. R×Q, P—Q6!; 34. R—Q2 (the QP still seems to be in danger), 34.....Kt—K5!; 35. R—Q1, R—Kt2 (final liquidation!);   36. Kt—B3, Kt×Kt; 37. P×Kt, R—Kt7;   38. R×P, R×RP. Draw. The student should observe the way in which the QP was indirectly protected. This strategem furnishes the defending party with one chance the more to emerge from the distress of his hanging pawn position to more settled circumstances.

The 'hanging condition' must be regarded as a passing one and what we have to do is to find the proper moment for liquidating it. In general the defending party proceeds to this a move or two too soon, he does not hold tight long enough, perhaps because the consciousness of being 'in the air' is not greatly to the taste of the human psyche.   But if you have it in mind to realize your hanging pawns, do not do it unless you can sense behind the 'blockaded security' which you crave, a glimmer of an initiative.   Never let yourself be drawn into a dead blockaded position; rather remain 'in the air'.

Other games illustrating this chapter are Nos. 36 and 37.

CHAPTER IV

THE TWO BISHOPS

§1. *Introductory. Relative strength of Bishop and Knight.*

THE two Bishops are, in the hands of a skilful fighter, a terrible weapon, yet I confess that for a moment I dallied with the blasphemous thought of omitting them from any detailed examination in my book. My system, so I said to myself, only recognizes two things worthy of thorough investigation: the elements, and strategical devices. For instance, we regarded the isolani, which seemed to us in some way to have grown out of the problem of restraint, as a strategical device. Under what heading however were the proud Prelates to be placed?

This question which we have thrown out must not be dismissed without further to-do as an idle or a trifling one, rather does it appear to me to be one of decided theoretical interest. It would lead us too far to develop here the grounds on which my views on this are based, so I will content myself with giving the result. I have arrived at the conclusion that the advantage of the two Bishops can be called neither an element nor a strategem. To me the two Bishops are, and can be, nothing else than a kind of weapon. The examination of the various kinds of weapons and the determination of their applicability to given cases lies wholly outside the plan of my book. Moreover, Berger has made this the leitmotif of his book on the End Game. Nevertheless, the reader has naturally the right to expect that I should enlighten him, as far as I can, on the dangers in which a pair of enemy Bishops may involve him. And this I will proceed to do.

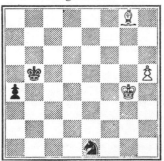

Diagram 156

Superiority of the long-striding B over the short-winded Kt. Black's game could not be saved even if his Kt were at QB6 or Q5 or KB1

The superiority of the B over the Kt is strikingly shown in one of the two positions given below.   Each player has one or more passed pawns (Diag. 156) which are supported by their own K.   The B wins because he is wonderfully good at holding up the advance of passed pawns, or at slowing it down.

On the other hand the game in Diagram 157 shows up the principal weakness of the B, namely that if his wish is to defend a terrain, he is usually helpless, for how shall a black Bishop protect white squares! Black's advance in Diagram 157 which puts the B to shame would develop somewhat as follows: 1..... Kt—R4 ch; 2. K—B3, K—R5; 3. B—B2, Kt—QB3; 4. B—K3, Kt—R2; 5. B—B2, Kt—Kt4 ch; 6. K—Q3, K—Kt6; and there will presently follow a Kt check at QKt7 or QKt5 whereby the Black K will win the point QB5, etc.

We ask the reader to regard the cases in the positions on Diagrams 156 and 157 as the two poles between which all other cases move.

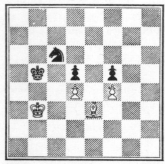

Diagram 157

White succumbs under the weakness of his white squares

That he can take long strides is the advantage which a Bishop has; his serious disadvantage lies in the weakness of the squares of an opposite colour to his.

Another point. In the position, White: BKKt2, PQB5. Black: KtQKt1, PQB3 (with other pawns and pieces *ad lib*), the advantage of the Bishop is as little demonstrable, as is its apparent inferiority in the position White; BQKt4; PQB5; Black: KtK3, PQB3. In both cases it is the strategical preponderance (i.e., the advantage of an active over a passive position of the pieces, which we analysed in its place) which makes itself felt, not any possibly inherent superiority of the class of weapon in question.

We repeat, the principal weakness of the Bishop consists in the defencelessness of the squares of opposite colour, its main strength in the fact that it is long-striding. And now it suddenly becomes plausible why two Bishops are held to be so strong. The reason is clear, their strength appears doubled, the weakness which we underlined is neutralized by the presence of the 'other' Bishop. It is scarcely possible to set down on paper all the many and varied situations in which two Bishops may make themselves unpleasant; we will, however, attempt to note the most important.

§2. *The Horwitz Bishops.*

Two Bishops when they rake two neighbouring diagonals (e.g., BQKt2, BQ3), and thus united bombard the enemy King's position, are sometimes called the Horwitz Bishops. Their effect. is often devastating: One B forces an enemy P move, which smooths the road for the second B. For instance, in Diagram 158 1. Q—K4 forces the move P—KKt3 which loosens up Black's position, on which the

BB2 intervenes with decisive effect. Events took a similar course in the following game. 1. P—K4, P—K4; 2. P—Q4, P×P; 3. P—QB3, P×P; 4. B—QB4, P×P; 5. B×P, B—Kt5 ch; 6. Kt—QB3, Kt—KB3; 7. Kt—K2, Kt×P; 8. 0—0, Kt×Kt; 9. Kt×Kt, B×Kt; 10. B×B, 0—0. He has castled and feels himself safe against Q—Kt4 (P—KKt3) as also against Q—Q4 (Q—Kt4), but overlooks the combined play which is characteristic of the Horwitz Bishops. 11. Q—Kt4!, P—KKt3, and only now 12. Q—Q4 and mate cannot be averted. The co-operation of the BB4 lies obviously in the pinning of Black's PKB2.

The Bishops in Diagram 159 (q.v.), I should regard as a variety of Horwitz Bishops, one indeed of the nobler sort. Of an attack on the King there is here no talk. Yet the attack on Black's PQR2 (I have only included the most important pieces) though, it is true, not

Diagram 158	Diagram 159
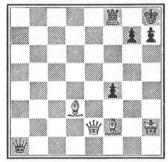	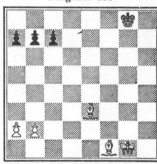
Q—K4 forces Black's KKtP to move and thus smooths the road for the BB2	Two B's attack a pawn-mass with the intention of winning stations for themselves

very intensive, is at all events unpleasant, and will, in the end, force the enemy to take up the position PQR2, PQKt3, PQB4, whereupon the road will have been smoothed for the other Bishop; for there then follows White's P—QR4 and P—QKt3, and the stations QR6, QKt5, and particularly QB4 are made available for the white Bishop. And now Black's majority appears crippled. A stratagem of this kind is not seldom to be found in Maróczy's games.

§3. *The effective support afforded by the two Bishops to an advancing pawn mass. The hemming in of the enemy Knights.*

A pawn mass, which need not by any means be a 'majority', guided by a pair of Bishops can roll forward fairly far, and thus lead to the imprisoning of the enemy knights. The well-known game Richter—Tarrasch may serve as an example (Diag. 160a). The game went on: 19.....P—QB4; 20. Kt—KKt3, P—KR4; 21. P—KB3 (he does not show great expertness in the defence; if the Kts are not to go under altogether, they must fight for stations for themselves. Hence 21.....P—QR4 followed by Kt—QB4 would seem to be indicated), 21.....B—Q2; 22. R—K2?, P—QKt4; 23. QR—K1, B—KB1!; 24. Kt(Kt3)—K4, R—KKt1 (in order to play P—KB4); 25. Kt—QKt3, R—QB1; 26. Kt(K4)—Q2, B—Q3; 27. Kt—K4, B—KB1; 28. Kt(K4)—Q2, P—KB4; 29. R—K5, B—Q3; 30. R(K5)—K2 (or R—Q5?; R—KKt3), 30.....R—QR1 (now the QRP is to advance); 31. Kt—R5, QR—QKt1 (else after Kt—Kt7 his hemming labour would have been in vain); 32. Kt(R5)—Kt3, P—KR5; 33. K—R1, R—KKt3; 34. K—Kt1, B—K3 (the barricading of the K file effected by the BQ2 and BQ3 has been up to this excellent move more of an 'ideal' nature. With 34.....B—K3

Diagram 160a

Tarrasch (as Black) hems in the White Kts

this is changed into a 'material' one, corresponding to the process we have before noted, where the 'ideal' restraint of a passed pawn gave place to a mechanical stopping (=blockade). So much on the strategic-theoretical meaning of the manœuvre chosen. The practical significance of the move lies, however, as Dr. Tarrasch himself very rightly notes, in the fact that fresh possibilities are opened up. (i) K—K2—Q2, (ii) P—QR3, R—QB1, then B—QKt1—QR2, and finally P—QB5. I may add this remark that P—QB5 must be regarded as without question the strategical plan indicated in the position. Why it is will appear in the note to White's 38th move.); 35. R—KB2, R—QR1? (He is untrue to his main plan, P—QB5, and again tries to make P—QR4 possible; and he succeeds, but only because his opponent neglects a subtle resource. Of course it is a fine thing to put into execution P—QR4 and completely to drive back the enemy forces; but one should not go so far as to subordinate a plan indicated by the position to the idea of a broader decorative effect. But then the pseudo-classical School had an incredible weakness for such embroideries!); 36. R(KB2)—K2? (A bad mistake. How could anyone allow P—QR4 to be played without a fight! In answer to 36. Kt—R5 Dr. Tarrasch gives the line 36.....B—B2; 37. Kt—Kt7, B—KB5, winning time for R—QB1 and P—QB5 by the threat B—K6. He overlooks, however, a hidden resource: 37.....B—KB5; 38. Kt×P!, B—K6; 39. P—QB4! and Black cannot win, as the White's Q wing is strong and the black squares, e.g., QB5 for the Kt, not less so. A plausible variation would be **39.....KtP×P; 40. P×P, R—QB1; 41. P—QKt4!, R—B2; 42. K—B1, B×R; 43. K×B** and White stands well); **36.....P—QR4; 37. Kt—Kt1, P—R5; 38. Kt(Kt3)—Q2** (Diag. 160b). (And now the break through follows, and there is nothing logically surprising in this, for, as we know, Black has a decided 'qualitative majority', as would show up even more obviously if we imagined added to the position a White and Black KP at their 4th. Here the possibility of a break through is still further enhanced by the miserable position of the White Kts, and by the large surface of friction, by which I mean the four pawn front.) **38.....P—QB5; 39. Kt—KB1, R—QB1; 40. K—R1, P—QB6; 41. P×P, P×P; 42. Kt—K3, P—QKt5**, etc. (The game plays itself. White resigned on his 47th move.)

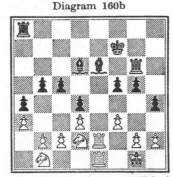

Diagram 160b

The hemming in accomplished

§4. *Fight against a pawn majority with simultaneous hemming in of the enemy knights.*

The hemming in of the Knights with simultaneous fight against a pawn majority is a very different problem, one would say, to the solving of which outstanding technical ability will be needed. But this is not so. Anyone who is moderately versed in the art of restraining and blockading pawn-complexes, will soon find to his satisfaction that in the class of positions in question the hemming in of the Kts is more easily compassed than in the case considered under §3. We can say with some justice that the restraint of the pawn-majority once in operation carries with it automatically the hemming in of the Kts; that is to say the blockading pawns may easily develop into obstructions to their own Kts. An example is found in the following game.

Harmonist—Tarrasch, 1889. **1. P—K4, P—K4; 2. Kt—KB3, Kt—QB3; 3. B—Kt5, Kt—KB3; 4. 0—0, Kt×P; 5. P—Q4, Kt—Q3; 6. B×Kt, QP×B; 7. P×P, Kt—B4; 8. Q×Q ch, K×Q; 9. B—Kt5 ch?, K—K1; 10. Kt—QB3, P—KR3; 11. B—B4, B—K3** (White's majority has but slight mobility); **12. QR—Q1, R—Q1; 13. Kt—K4, P—QB4; 14. R×R ch, K×R; 15. R—Q1 ch, K—B1; 16. P—KR3, P—QKt3; 17. K—B1, B—K2; 18. P—QR3, R—Q1; 19. R×R ch, K×R** (the exchange of Rs has sensibly increased the radius of action of Black's K); **20. P—QB3, B—Q4;**

21. Kt(B3)—Q2, K—Q2;   22. K—K2, P—KKt4;   23. B—R2,
Kt — R5;   24. P — KKt3,   Kt — Kt3;   25. P — KB4,   K — K3;
26. K—K3, P—QB5;   27. Kt—KB3, P×P ch;   28. P×P, P—QB4
(Diag. 161).   (In the position now reached White's pieces are fairly
well shut in.   This gratifying state of affairs has followed almost
automatically from Black's successfully executed blockade of White's
PK5 and in particular his PKB4.   This cannot surprise us; for have
we not often experienced how the whole situation may be favourably
affected, as if by a miracle, by a successful blockade?   The game
proceeded): 29. Kt—Kt3, Kt—R5; 30. Kt×Kt, B×Kt; 31. Kt—K4,
B—K2;   32. B—Kt1, B—QB3 (the intention is K—Q4 followed by
B—Q2—B4, driving the Kt yet further back); 33. B—B2, B—Q2;

Diagram 161

Harmonist—Tarrasch
1889

Diagram 162

Tartakower (as Black) realizes
one after the other various
chances given him by his B's

34. B—Kt3 (Kt—Q6 offered the possibility of a draw, by playing for
B's of opposite colour), 34.....K—Q4;   35. Kt—B2, P—KR4;
36. K—B3, B—B4 (Blockade!); 37. K—K3, P—QKt4; 38. K—B3,
P—QR4; 39. K—K3 (White is 'stalemated'), P—QKt5; 40. K—B3,
K—B3;   41. RP×P (White is lost), BP×P;   42. P×P, P×P;
43. Kt—K4, K—Q4;   44. Kt—Q6, B×Kt;   45. P×B, P—B6;
46. P×P, P—Kt6; 47. Resigns.

§5.   *The two Bishops in the end game.*

We regard as the ideal the transmutation of an advantage founded
only in the class of weapon employed to one which is clearly and
perceptibly strategical; for instance, that of the aggressive position
of our pieces as opposed to the passive one of our opponent's.   (See
I. vi. §2.)   Combined play with two B's, leading to such a transmutation as we have mentioned, comes out in the following example
(Diag. 162, Michel—Tartakower, 1925).   White's position is well
consolidated, the weakness of the black squares QB3, Q4, does not

appear important. The continuation was:— 40. K—Kt1, K—Kt2; 41. K—B1, B—QB3; 42. Kt—Kt1, P—KKt4; 43. Kt—B3, P—R4. (The two pawns advance, since they feel themselves to be a qualitative majority owing to the exalted protection which they enjoy, supported as they are by two Bishops.) 44. B—K2, R—K5!; 45. B—Q3, R—KB5; 46. K—K2, P—KKt5; 47. P×P, P×P; 48. Kt—R2, P—Kt6!; 49. Kt—B3 (Black has quite rightly not pursued any further the advantage to be got from hemming in the Kt; what he now has got is more valuable: White's PKKt2 is become a mark for attack, and the White pieces, particularly the KtKB3, are from now on forced to keep perpetual watch over him. This strategical advantage very soon brings a decision), 49.....P—Q5; 50. R—KB1, P—Kt5; 51. Kt—Q2, R—R5; 52. Kt—KB3, R—R1 (from here he threatens at once the point KR7 and the K file); 53. K—Q2 (for—with apologies to Goethe and his translator—where of good moves there's a failing, a botch

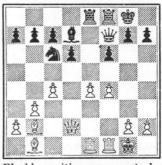

Diagram 163

steps promptly in as deputy!), 53..... R—R7!; 54. Kt×R, P×Kt; 55. R—KR1, B—K4; 56. B—B1, B—K5 (a charming situation!); 57. K—Q1, K—B3; 58. K—Q2, K—Kt4; 59. K—Q1, K—Kt5; 60 Resigns.

Black's position appears to be defensible

We have now done enough for the glorification of the Bishops, and a few words may be added on situations in which they do not cut such a good figure. These are wholly, or half closed positions, see for example games Nos. 15 and 38; while they are astonishingly weak against an unassailable, centrally posted Kt. Even in the position on Diagram 163 it would seem to me that Black can maintain himself against the Horwitz Bishops. In the next chapter we shall pass to 'over-protection'.

An excellent example of play with two Bishops will be found in Game No. 41, Lasker—Burn. See also No. 47, Gregory—Nimzowitsch.

CHAPTER V

OVER-PROTECTION

§1. Why we should systematically over-protect our own strong points.

A SHORT chapter, which in particular may serve to illustrate the various forms under which 'over-protection' may appear. In II. i. §3 we have already attempted to explain the spirit and inner significance of over-protection. We will therefore only repeat here that the contact established between the strong point and the 'over-protector' can only be of advantage to both parties; to the strong point because the prophylactic induced by such a process affords it the greatest imaginable security against possible attack; to the over-protector, since the point serves him as a source of energy, from which he may continually draw fresh strength.

Over-protection clearly represents a manœuvre, which from its very essence must have developed in close connexion with position play. Nevertheless even in the 'Elements' we came across traces of over-protection; for example in the open file. White: R, Q1; Kt, QB3; P, K4. Black: P's, QB2, Q3. The outpost Kt (after Kt(QB3)—Q5) must, as was emphasized in I. ii. §6, be protected not only by a pawn but also by a Rook. What can this compulsion signify other than the necessity of over-protecting the strategically important outpost!

Again, in the domain of the pawn-chain over-protection is a strategem which deserves every preference. Turn to the game Nimzowitsch—Giese (II. i. §3. Diag. 115), and notice in particular how the over-protection was not even intended for the base of the pawn-chain, however awesome the respect this inspired in us, but rather for a more humble candidate for that position; for we over-protected the PK5 since we had always to reckon with an eventual and inevitable QP×P, when the PK5 would be promoted to be the base.

The wonderful vitality of the over-protector may here be demonstrated by two further examples:

Nimzowitsch—Rubinstein, Carlsbad, 1911.

1. P—K4, P—K3; 2. P—Q4, P—Q4; 3. P—K5, P—QB4; 4. P—QB3, Kt—QB3; 5. Kt—KB3, Q—Kt3; 6. B—Q3, P×P; 7. P×P, B—Q2; 8. B—K2, KKt—K2; 9. P—QKt3, Kt—B4; 10. B—Kt2 (at the moment the PQ4 is barely protected, not more), 10.....B—Kt5 ch; 11. K—B1, P—KR4; 12. P—KKt3, R—QB1; 13. K—Kt2, P—KKt3; 14. P—KR3, B—K2 (intending to answer a possible P—KKt4 by Kt—R5 ch); 15. Q—Q2!, P—QR4;

16. KR—QB1, B—KB1; 17. Q—Q1!, B—R3; 18. R—B3, 0—0;
19. P—KKt4, Kt(B4)—K2; 20. Kt—QR3! (only now will it be
clear why White delayed with the development of this Kt. An
honourable post had been contemplated for him, namely as over-
protector of the PQ4), 20.....Kt—Kt5; 21. Kt—B2 (there now
follows a surprising and effortless unravelling of the skein of White
pieces on the Q's Wing), 21.....R×R; 22. B×R, Kt×Kt;
23. Q×Kt, R—QB1; 24. Q—QKt2! (whatever happens, PQ4 shall
stay over protected), 24.....B—QKt4; 25. B×B, Q×B; 26. B—Q2!
(the over-protector shows his teeth!), 26.....B—B1; 27. R—QB1,
P×P; 28. P×P, R—B3; 29. Q—R3 (over-protector No. 2 won't
take a back place to No. 1—see the last note), 29.....R×R. (A
pity! for on 29.....Kt—B4, White intended to offer a Q sacrifice,
e.g., 30. R×R, B×Q; 31. R—B8 ch, K—Kt2; 32. P×Kt with a
strong attack. An excellent index to the inherent elasticity of an
over-protector.) 30. Q×R, with the superior game.

Nimzowitsch—Spielmann, Stockholm, 1920.

1. P—K4, P—K3; 2. P—Q4, P—Q4; 3. P—K5, P—QB4;
4. Kt—KB3, Kt—QB3; 5. P—QB3, Q—Kt3; 6. B—K2, P×P;
7. P×P, Kt—R3; 8. Kt—QB3 (P—
QKt3, as in the last example, is more
prudent), 8.....Kt—B4; 9. Kt—QR4,
Q—R4 ch; 10. B—Q2, B—Kt5;
11. B—QB3, B—Q2 (preferable would
have been 11.....B×B; 12. Kt×B,
Q—Kt5—if Q—Kt3 then Kt—QR4!—
13. B—QKt5, 0—0; 14. B×Kt, Q×
KtP; 15. Kt—QR4, Q—Kt5 ch;
16. Q—Q2. White would then have
had the point QB5, Black a backward
pawn plus); 12. P—QR3, B×B;
13. Kt×B, P—KR4; 14. 0—0, R—
QB1 (Diag. 164); 15. Q—Q2, Q—Q1

Diagram 164

White develops his pieces in
the sense of a systematic
over-protection of the PQ4

(threatening P—KKt4); 16. P—KR3
(in order to parry P—KKt4 by the
riposte P—KKt4, e.g., 16.....P—KKt4; 17. P—KKt4, P×P;
18. P×P, Kt—R5; 19. Kt×Kt, R×Kt; 20. K—Kt2 followed
by R—KR1 with advantage to White), 16.....Kt—QR4;
17. QR—Q1, Q—Kt3; 18. KR—K1 (PQ4 and to a certain degree
PK5 are now systematically over-protected, and this strategy makes
it possible later to be automatically, so to speak, master of the
situation, whatever complications may arise), 18 ....Kt—B5;
19. B×Kt, R×B; 20. Kt—K2, B—R5; 21. R—QB1 (notice
how available an over-protector is for service in all directions, e.g.,

the RQ1 at QB1 and the KtK2 at KKt3), 21.....B—Kt6;
22. R × R, B × R; 23. Kt—Kt3, Kt—K2; and White stands rather
the better. (He won the game on the 61st move. See *Die Blockade*,
p. 69.)

So much on the over-protection of the base; the over-protection of
the following points is also of importance.

(*a*) Over-protection of the central points. We have already on a
previous opportunity emphasized the fact that the very common
neglect of the central theatre of war is reprehensible. But we have
here to do rather with a detail, or more accurately, with the examination of a quite definite, and, for the hyper-modern style of play,
typical situation. As is generally known, the hyper-modern knows
admirably how to resist the temptation to occupy the centre with
pawns, at any rate not until a really favourable opportunity presents
itself. If such offer, he casts aside all shyness, and the Pawns,
supported by the fianchettoed Bishops,
rush wildly forward, seize the centre,
and strive to crush the enemy. Against
this threatened evil the over-protection
of certain central points provides a
thoroughly proven remedy, which
cannot be too strongly recommended.
Let us glance at the following opening
of the game Réti—Yates, New York,
1924:

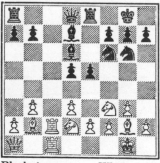

Diagram 165

Black to move. What point
is worthy of over-protection?

1. Kt—KB3, P—Q4; 2. P—QB4,
P—K3; 3. P—KKt3, Kt—KB3;
4. B—Kt2, B—Q3; 5. P—QKt3,
0—0 (Why this hurry? To put the
centre in order was much more pressing:
therefore P—QB3, QKt—Q2, and P—K4 was his proper line); 6. 0—0,
R—K1; 7. B—QKt2, QKt—Q2; 8. P—Q3?, P—QB3; 9. QKt—Q2,
P—K4 (the position now reached is undoubtedly more favourable for
Black; White ought to have played 8. P—Q4); 10. P × P, P × P;
11. R—QB1, Kt—KB1; 12. R—B2, B—Q2; 13. Q—R1, Kt—Kt3;
14. KR—QB1 (Diag. 165). White's Q manœuvre is significant; he
intends to undermine the enemy centre by P—Q4 when opportunity
offers and if Black reply P—K5, then Kt—K5. Hence Black's duty
is to over-protect his PK4, to excess even. His best course was first
14.....P—QKt4 aiming at White's Q-Wing which is compromised
by the position of his Q; if then 15. Kt—B1, there would follow
15.....Q—QKt1! (=over-protection of K4); 16. Kt—K3, P—QR4
and Black has the better game. This line of play which I pointed out
in *Kagan's Neuste Schachnachrichten*, 1924, met at the time with little
approbation. Nowadays things are different.

For a game which took a most instructive course, and in which I employed the same Q manœuvre (Q—QKt1) with the same idea as that indicated above, see No. 38.

(b) The over-protection of the centre as a measure of defence for our own King's wing.

The case which is about to be discussed in detail differs from that considered above under (a) in its general tendency, and is therefore treated here as an independent manœuvre, not as a subdivision of that case. In II. i. §6, under Diagram 124, a position was discussed which comes under the classification of the case now to be considered. Game No. 15 is also instructive in the same sense. In this game after the 13th move a position was reached which is shown in Diagram 166. Black's last move was 13.....P—KKt5! To the reply 14. P×P, P×P; 15. Q×P, he had planned R×B followed by

Diagram 166

White parries every attempt at an attack on his K by over-protection of a central point. How does he do it?

Diagram 167

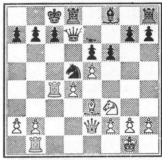

Consultation game. Three Amateurs—Nimzowitsch

B×P ch and B×QKtP. White, however, played 14. R—K1, and in doing something for his centre he at the same time strengthens the power of resistance of his position against flank attacks as well. There followed 14.....K—B1; 15. Kt—QB3! (the prelude to a blockading manœuvre) 15.....Q—K2; 16. B×Kt, P×B; 17. Q—K3, R—R3; 18. Kt—K2, P—QB4; 19. Kt—B4, and White has the better game, for the two B's have little to say in view of the strength of the unassailable Kt, moreover, the collective mobility of Black is right small, for though PQB4 and PQ4 have a certain measure of mobility, the rest are blockaded.

Of quite special interest in the same sense is the position shown in Diagram 167 which is taken from game No. 39. It was Black's move. That the KtQ4 was the pride of Black's position is beyond all doubt. It was, however, not easy to devise a suitable plan. White was preparing one; though it is true it presented no great danger, namely

Q—Q2 followed by Kt—K1—Q3—B5.   The train of thought which I
followed in the game brought me on the track of a hidden manœuvre,
which to this day I consider a good one.   The separate links in this
chain of ideas are these: (i) the KtQ4 is strong, therefore (ii) the over-
protectors, the QQ2 and RQ1 are also strong, but (iii) the RQ1 has
a duty in connexion with the K's position, which has a bearing on his
strength in the centre, therefore (iv) the KR must come to QB1!
Accordingly there followed 14.....K—Kt1;   15. Q—Q2, R—QB1!;
16. Kt—K1, B—K2;   17. Kt—Q3, KR—Q1.   The deed is done!
The RQ1 now feels that he can devote his whole attention to the
centre.   Since his colleague at QB1 is looking after the K.   The
further adventures of the RQ1 will be found in game No. 39.

We could name many more 'points' that are worthy of over-
protection, but will limit ourselves to the few examples we have here
given.   Before, however, passing on to the next strategical device,
we must once more stress the fact that only strategically valuable
points should be over-protected, not a sickly pawn, nor a K's wing
which rests on a weak foundation.   Over-protection must in no sense
be regarded as an act of Christian meekness and loving-kindness!
The pieces over-protect a point because they promise themselves
strategical advantages to be gained from contact with it.   We must
therefore seek to establish connexion with strong points.   A weak
pawn is only in a single exceptional case justified in claiming over-
protection, and that is when he is engaged in looking after a potential
giant of his species.   For instance: White: P's, Q4, K5.   Black: P's,
Q4, K3.   The PQ4 as the base of White's pawn chain is nurse to the
strategically important PK5; so that the over-protection of the PQ4
seems indicated.

§2.   How to get rid of weak pawns.

We are not concerned here with the actual way by which we may
get rid of weak pawns, but rather with the question what pawns
deserve to have this hardly kind treatment meted out to them.

The situation is always the same: an otherwise sound pawn
complex which, however, has to acknowledge a weakling in its body.
We distinguish two cases:

(a) the weakness of the pawn is patent.

(b) the weakness would only appear after a pawn advance, whether
of our own or of the enemy.

We shall give an example of each of these two cases.

(a) White (Nimzowitsch): K, QKt1;   R, QB1;   Kt, Q4;   P's,
QKt2, K3, KB3, KKt4, KR4.   Black (Jacobsen): K, KKt1;   R,
QKt2;   B, QKt4;   P's, QKt5, Q4, KB2, KKt3, KR2.   The game
proceeded 36. R—B5, B—Q2 (or 36.....B—Q6 ch;   37. K—B1,

R—Q2; 38. R—B8 ch and R—QKt8); 37. R×P. White is therefore now a pawn to the good. 37.....K—B1; 38. K—B2, P—Kt6 ch; 39. K—B3, K—K2 (White is in a position to bring his own flock of pawns, K, KB, KKt, under one shelter, and to do this he has only to play P—K4. Everything will then be beautifully protected, and the shepherd, the RQ5, can, with a clear conscience, turn his attention to other matters. Not quite! for that stupid little sheep, the PKR4, would scamper away from the shepherd—for at some time there would be threatened, for instance in a R ending, the manœuvre R—QR8—KR8×P, therefore he shall be cast out of the company of the righteous! There followed.) 40. P—R5!, B—K3; 41. R—QB5, K—Q3; 42. R—B6 ch, K—Q2; 43. P×P, RP×P (That's done!); 44. Kt×B!, P×Kt; 45. R—B5 followed by R—KKt5 and P—B4 with an easily won Rook end game. (The position reached after Black's 41st move has already been considered under another aspect in I. vi. §4 under Diagram 74.)

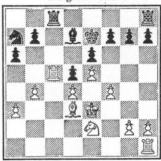

Diagram 168

Tarrasch—Barthmann

(b) Tarrasch—Barthmann, played when Dr. Tarrasch was still a youth (Diag. 168). Black played here 21..... R—B3; and there followed 22. KR— QB1, KR—QB1; 23. P—KKt4, P—KKt3; 24. P—KB5, KtP×P; 25. P×P, R—KKt1? (He ought not to have allowed P—B6 ch at any price, hence 25.....P×P was essential, e.g., 26. Kt—B4, B—K3; 27. R—KKt1, with a hard fight ahead); 26. P—B6 ch, K—B1; 27. R—KKt1, R×R; 28. Kt×R, K—Kt1; and Black's KRP forms a formidable weakness in Black's game. This drawback could have been avoided had Black on his 21st move played P—KR4 with the idea of only allowing P—B6 (as in the game) on the stipulation that both the KKt and KRP's should disappear in the exchange. The continuation might have been: 21.....P—KR4; 22. P—KR3, P—KKt3; (not 22.....P—R5?, because of 23. Kt— Kt1 followed by Kt—B3); and Black, after a few moves, would have obtained a more favourable position than he did in this game.

Whereas case (a) does not make very great demands on the player, the right handling of the strategical weapon discussed under (b) is extremely difficult. It demands, above everything, a pretty thorough knowledge of the various forms under which an advance of a compact pawn-mass, and particularly on a wing, may run its course. Many pages, however, of this book have been devoted to this advance with all its consequences, and to deal with it we may therefore leave the kind reader to his own, as we hope, not less kind fate. Only let him keep well in view that the strategical necessity of ridding himself of a troublesome pawn of his own may arise in the case of an advance of his pawns, just as much as in that of an enemy advance.　When the black sheep of the family should be cast out, whether before the operation begins, or during it, i.e., when the advance of the pawn-mass is under way, this question can only be decided on the merits of each case.

For a very instructive game illustrating over-protection see No. 39.

CHAPTER VI

MANŒUVRING AGAINST WEAKNESSES

Manœuvring against an enemy weakness. The combined attack on both wings

§1. *The logical components which go to make up a manœuvring action against a weakness.*

As an introduction to the following analysis I should like to try to present a scheme for the operation which is to be considered. I picture the course of a manœuvring action to myself somewhat as follows: An enemy weakness can be attacked in at least two ways: each of these attempts at attack would be met by an adequate defence. In order that in spite of this we may in the end conquer the enemy weakness, we take advantage of the greater freedom of movement which is ours, due to certain conditions of the terrain, so as to attack it in turn by different ways (manœuvring action), and thus oblige the enemy pieces to take up uncomfortable positions for its defence, whence an obstruction to the defence or something of the kind will intervene, and the 'weakness' will be proved untenable.

As we can see from this scheme, it would be quite a mistake to label this type of manœuvring as mere purposeless moving to and fro. On the contrary every move has set before it a clearly prescribed end, has the conquest of a quite definite weakness in view. The ways which lead to this conquest are, it is true, of a complicated nature.

§2. *The terrain. The conception of the pivot round which the manœuvring turns.*

The terrain over which any manœuvring action takes place must, if our plan is to succeed, be strongly built up. A characteristic of such action is this that the different troop movements always cross a quite definite square (or line of demarcation). An example is seen in Diagram 169. Here it is the point Q5 which the White pieces will wish to occupy, making it a base for further manœuvring. Accordingly the point Q5 might be described as a fortified post in the lines of communication; and it is therefore right and proper to regard it as the pivot round which the whole manœuvring action turns. It is in virtue of this fortified post Q5 that the whole operation is accomplished: every piece, even the RQ1, strives to get there at some time or other. The law governing this manœuvring action moreover demands that Q5 shall be occupied by different pieces in turn, for this will always create new threats and thus help to embarrass the enemy. The relationship between the White pieces and the pivot Q5 exactly corresponds, too, to the 'contact' between over-protectors and a strategically important point, which was discussed in the previous chapter. That in this case the pieces strive to establish contact with Q5 speaks plainly for the strength of that point. Notice, too, the device by which pieces exchange stations in, e.g., the sequence of White moves Kt—K3, Q—Q5, Kt—QB4, an operation which may serve the purpose of the general plan of the manœuvring action right well.

We will now give some typical examples of this type of manœuvring.

(a) A pawn weakness which is to be brought under bombardment from the 7th rank.

Rubinstein—Selesnieff (Diag. 170). There occurred 1 . . . . . P—QKt3

Diagram 169

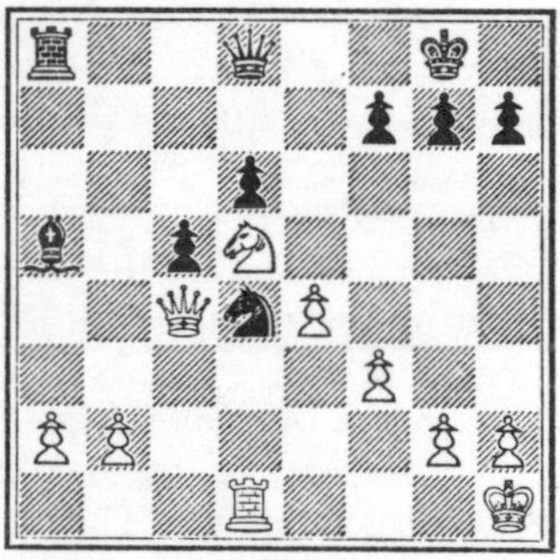

Diagram 170

White manœuvres against the PQ3 using the point Q5 as the pivot round which the operation turns

Rubinstein—Selesnieff

(1 . . . . . P—Q5 deserved the preference. For instance, 2. P × P, Kt × P; 3. B—Kt5, Kt—K7 ch; 4. K—B2! [else 4. R—KB2], 4 . . . . . R—B1 ch; 5. R—B6, R × R ch; 6. B × R, R—K3); the continuation was, 2. B—B2, R—KB1; 3. R—K1, R(K2)—B2; 4. R(R6) × Kt, R × B; 5. R—K8 ch, K—Kt2; 6. R × R, R × R; 7. R—K7, (and now begins some magnificent manœuvring against Black's PKR2), 7 . . . . . R—R1; 8. K—B2, K—B3; 9. P—KKt4, K—Q3; 10. R—KB7, P—QR4; 11. P—Kt5, P—R5; 12. P—KR4, P—Kt4; 13. K—Kt3, P—QB4 (Black now threatens to make for himself a passed pawn by P—Kt5, so Rubinstein attacks the weakness, PKR2, from the other side); 14. R—B6 ch!, K—B2; 15. R—KR6, P—Kt5; 16. BP × P, BP × P; 17. P × P, R—QR1; 18. R × P ch! (the 'weakness' has fallen), K—Kt3; 19. R—KB7, P—R6; 20. R—B1, P—R7; 21. R—QR1, K—Kt4; 22. P—Kt6,

K×P; 23. P—R5, Resigns. The pivot is here to be thought of as in the lines K7 to KR7 and KR6 to KR8. The student should seek to determine why the change of front of the 14th move could not take place earlier.

The following case is much more complicated.

(b) Two pawn weaknesses (Diag. 171), here White's PQB3 and PKR3. The pivotal point, round which action against PKR3 turns, i.e., Black's KB5, seems to be threatened, but is rescued, and actually by a timely attention paid to the weak PQB3 on the other side of the board; so that we here see the two separated theatres of war logically connected the one with the other. The game follows:

Kalaschnikow—Nimzowitsch: Black played 36.....K—K2. If White would only do nothing Black would get the advantage by a direct attack, by K—B2—Kt3 followed by P—KB4. White would then have to defend with P—KB3, and would thereby give his opponent the handle, to clutch which he has long wanted, namely (after of course moving the KtB5 out of the way) the posting of his B at KKt6, when the threat to the whole of White's line of defence could not be parried. . But White did not sit still; instead he did his best to hinder his opponent in the execution of his plan, and played 37. Kt—Kt2!; with this he hopes to bring off a general exchange which would lead to a clear draw, thus:—38. B×Kt, and if 38.....

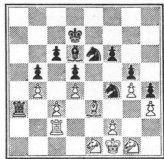

Diagram 171

Dr. W. Kalaschnikow—
Nimzowitsch, 1914

Kt×B, then 39. Kt×Kt, B×Kt; and there is nothing left. The threatened pivotal point KB5 thus threatened could not now be held but for the manœuvring chance on the other side of the board, so there followed 37.....R—R8 ch; 38. R—B1, R—R7!; 39. Kt—K1! (the relief expedition carried out by Black with his 37th and 38th moves has succeeded, for now with the R at QR7 White's intended exchange would lead to his own disadvantage; e.g., 39. B×Kt, B×B!; 40. R—Q1, B—Q7; 41. Kt—K2, Kt—B5! and after the further moves 42. Kt×Kt, P×Kt; 43. K—Kt2, R—B7, Black develops a remarkable appetite) 39.....K—B2. So Black has gained a tempo! But now the same game starts anew. 40. R—B2, R—R6!; 41. Kt—Kt2, R—R8 ch; 42. R—B1, R—R7!; 43. Kt—K1, K—Kt3; 44. R—B2, R—R6; 45. P—KB3 (this weakening move could not have been permanently avoided, otherwise P—KB4 would follow, and if P×P then K×P and P—Kt5 yielding a passed RP), 45.....P—KB4. It is accomplished! The end was peaceful. 46. K—B2, K—B3 (to make room for the Kt); 47. B—B1, R—R8;

48. K—K3, Kt—Kt3; 49. Kt—Q3, B—Kt6 (cf. the note to Black's 36th move) 50. Kt—K2, Kt(K3)—B5; 51. Kt—Kt1, Kt×Kt; 52. K×Kt, B—B5!; 53. Kt—K2, B×B; 54. Kt×B, Kt—B5 ch; 55. K—K3, Kt×P. After a heroic defence the fortress (PKR3) falls. There followed only 56. Kt—K2, P—B5 ch; and White resigned since R—KB8 wins another pawn.

(c) The King as a 'weakness' (Diag. 172). For the terrain there here function two possibilities of a driving action; as pivot we have a line of demarcation.

Nimzowitsch—Kalinsky, 1914. In this very piquant position there occurred first 1. B—Kt3 (the reply to 1. B—B2, P—B7; 2. R—Q1 would be K—K3, and White cannot win); 1.....P—Q5; 2. B—Q5, R—Kt5 (not at once P—B7 because of B×KP etc.); 3. R(R1)—R5, P—B7; and now White doubles his R's in the KB file with a gain of tempo. 4. R—B6 ch, K—K2; 5. R(R5)—B5,

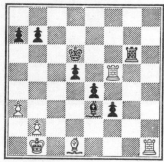

Diagram 172

Nimzowitsch—Kalinsky
1914

R—Kt8 ch; 6. K—R2, P—Q6. We shall use the position now reached as a touchstone of the correctness of our thesis. We explained in its place that a manœuvring action is only possible if certain conditions are fulfilled. These were: (a) the presence of a pivot, (b) a diversity of threats which might be directed against the weakness. The test turns out in our favour. Although this time the weakness is an ideal one, and no concrete pawn weakness, yet the circumstances (favouring a manœuvring action) are identical with those which we have laid down as typical; here, too, the variety of threats leaves nothing to be desired, for Black plans by their means not only to force the King to the edge of the board, but purposes also to arrange, when opportunity serves, a pretty hunt, which shall drive him into the middle of the board. Nor is the requisite pivot wanting, for the KB file (=line of demarcation across which the K cannot pass) serves this purpose. Thus visualized the following movements back and forth will be intelligible, indeed will gain in animation and in colour. The game proceeded (after 6.....P—Q6) 7. R—K6 ch, K—Q2; 8. R—B7 ch, K—Q1; 9. R(K6)—KB6, P—Q7; (the border position now reached cannot yet be taken advantage of, for 10. R—KR7 would fail against P—B8=Q, and 10. R—KR6 obviously won't do, so he manœuvres further); 10. R—B8 ch, K—K2; 11. R(B6)—B7 ch, K—Q3; 12. B—Kt3, B—Kt3? (Perhaps P—QR3 giving a loophole for the King to creep through was preferable); 13. R—B6 ch!! Now the King has to face the choice;

either he may return to the side of the board, where his position
will now be untenable, or he must go out into the open, where fate
in another form will overtake him.   There followed 13.....K—K4
(if 13.....K—K2;   then 14. R(B8)—B7 ch, K—Q1;   15. R—R6
and wins) 14. R—K6 ch!, K—Q5;   15. R×BP!, P—Q8=Q;
16. B×Q, R×B;   17. R—K2! and won the pawn and the game.

§3.   *Combined play on both wings, with weaknesses which though
for the moment wanting are yet hidden.*

Von Gottschall—Nimzowitsch, Hanover, 1926 (Diag. 173).   A
logical analysis of the position reveals the following data.   White's
PQB5 is, in view of the insecure position of the BKB2, to be regarded
as a pawn weakness.   On the other hand I cannot agree under any
circumstances in branding the pawn-mass PKKt3, PKR3 as a
'weakness', and this for the reason that
here, on the K's wing 'terrain' is lacking.

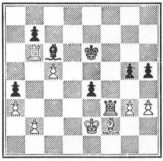

Diagram 173

Black chose the following manœuvre
which at first sight looks a most unin-
telligible one. 39.....K—K4; 40. R—
Kt4, K—Q4.   The explanation of this
combination which sacrifices a tempo
lies in the following: With these moves
a position is reached where White is in
a *Zugzwang*, for if the R goes back to
Kt6 (and he has no other plausible move,
for 41. R—Q4 ch fails against K×P;
42. R×KP dis ch?, R×B ch etc., while
as we shall see 41. P—KR4 would provide just that 'terrain' which before
was so sadly missed)—if the R goes
back to Kt6, there will follow after
the break through 41.....P—KR5;

v. Gottschall—Nimzowitsch
Hanover, 1926

Combined attack on both
wings.   The White weaknesses
are the PQB5 and as becomes
evident later the PKR3

42. P×P, P×P;   43. B×P, the inter-
mezzo 43.....K×P threatening the R; so White decided after all on
41. P—KR4, there followed 41.....P×P;   42. P×P, R—KR6!;
43. R—Q4 ch, K—K3;   44. R—Q8, B—Q4; and now Black began
systematically to manœuvre against the PKR4, with the point KKt5
as his pivot, and in fact by way of this point succeeded in breaking in
to his opponent's game.

The meaning of the strategy employed here appears out of the
following scheme which is applicable to all analogous cases.   We
manœuvred first against the obvious weakness, the PQB5.   By
means of the *Zugzwang* (with a slight mixture of threats) we succeeded
in inducing our opponent to make a deployment (P—KR4).   This,

however, but led to a weakness, which before P—R4 was merely latent, becoming patent and moreover easily assailable. To recapitulate: Play on two wings is usually based on the following idea. We engage one wing, or the obvious weaknesses in it, and thus draw the other enemy wing out of its reserve, when new weakness will be created on that reserve wing, and so the signal is given for systematic manœuvring against two weaknesses, as in the game Kalaschnikow —Nimzowitsch which we gave above.

This is the rule. As an interesting exception to the rule, I may call attention to the case where we may so act as if the exposure of the weakness on the other wing had already taken place.

The following is an example of such an exposure. Von Holzhausen—Nimzowitsch, Hanover, 1926.

(Diag. 174.) Black here hastened to bring about the exposure and moved 32..... R—R3. True, the real fight was to take place on

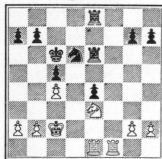

Diagram 174

the Q-wing (e.g., P—QKt4) but I knew that after I had succeeded in opening up the game (by P—QKt4 etc.) the advanced position of White's K side pawns could only serve my ends. There followed 33. P—KR3, R—KKt3; 34. R—K2, P—QR3; 35. R—B4, P—QKt4; 36. P—QKt3, R—Kt4; 37. P—KKt4, RKt4—K4; 38. K—B3, P—QR4! (The weakness PKR3 in conjunction with the possible chance of getting the PK5 unblocked made Black peremptory in his demand for 'terrain' with the pivot to go with it; it is for this that Black was fighting with his last moves.) 39. R(K2)—KB2, P—QR5 (now RP × P is threatened, followed by P × QBP allowing an invasion by the Rooks via the QR and QKt files); 40. P × RP, P × BP!; 41. R—B8, R(K4)—K2; 42. R × R, R × R; 43. Kt × P, Kt × Kt; 44. K × Kt, R—QR1 (the desired terrain is now won, it consists of the QR, QKt, and Q files. I should call Q5 the pivot.) 45. R—B7 (or K—Kt3?, K—Q4!) R × P ch; 46. K—Kt3 (K—B3 was rather better) 46..... R—Kt5 ch!; 47. K—B3, R—Kt2; 48. R—B5, R—R2; 49. K—B4, R—R5 ch; 50. K—Kt3, R—Q5 (the pivot!); 51. R—K5, K—Q3; 52. R—K8, R—Q6 ch; 53. K—B4, R × P (the proper use made of the 'terrain' has not failed to yield fruit; the weakness is fallen); 54. R × P, R—QR 6; 55. R—K2, R—R5 ch; 56. K—Kt5, R × KtP; 57. P—R4, R—QKt5 ch and won on the 71st move.

In Diagram 175 an elegant mating threat is used merely as an instrument to carry out with gain of tempo a weakening attack on the enemy's Q's wing. 31..... Kt—K3 (threatening R × Kt ch; Kt × R,

R × Kt ch; K × R, Q—B7 ch; K—R3, B—B5 and wins) 32. R—K2
(parries the threat, but now there follows with gain of tempo)
32.....Kt—Q5. The game went on: 33. R(K2)—K1 (if 33. R—KB2
then B—K6!); 33.....Q—Kt2!; (R—B1 cannot now be warded
off except by a sacrifice); 34. R × Kt (or 34. P—QB3?, P × P;

Diagram 175

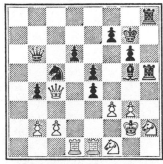

Teichmann—Nimzowitsch
San Sebastian, 1911

Diagram 176

Vestergaard—Nimzowitsch
from a simultaneous display
against 25 opponents

35. P × P, Q—Kt7 ch and wins) 34.....P × R and Black won after a
hard struggle. (See game No. 40.)

We will now give two end games which illustrate in miniature the
combined attack on two wings. As the position on Diagram 176
shows, Black (Nimzowitsch) has first
made a gesture as if he were going to
attack the Q's-Wing, but then has
chosen the K's-Wing for his field of
operation. White has taken up a tough
defensive position. It was my move,
and after a little reflection I played
1.....P—QKt4!! Great astonishment
among the spectators! On the Q's-Wing
Black has surely no troops for the attack.
However the sequel was 2. P × P, R—
R7; 3. Kt × R, R × Kt; 4. B—B1,
B × KtP! Now we have daylight. The
advance on the Q's Wing was conceived

Diagram 177

Seifert—Nimzowitsch

as a diversion against the K-wing. 5. B × B, Kt—R6 ch; 6. K—B1,
Q × R; 7. Q—K1, Q—Kt8 ch; 8. K—K2, Q × P ch; and mate in two
moves.

The next example also, Diagram 177, is characteristic of a surprising co-operation of two separate 'diversions'. It is taken from a game
played in a tournament of the lighter genre in Leipzig, 1926. The

game proceeded. 1.....P—KR5; 2. Kt×R, RP×Kt; 3. R—Q2, and now there followed a thrust on the other wing. 3.....P—QR4. My opponent parried with 4. P—Kt5, but after 4.....B×KRP; 5. P×B, Q×P ch; 6. K—Kt1, P—Q4!! (the point) he resigned since the effect of the check at QB4 is catastrophic. His right move was 4. B—B1, e.g., 4.....P×P; 5. R—QKt2, P—QB4, with a drawish position.

For further games illustrating this Chapter, see Nos. 40-45.

§4. *Manœuvring under difficult conditions, our own centre lacking protection.*

In conclusion we will give a game inspired with the true spirit of this form of manœuvring (Diag. 178). Black's cramped King's position is here a glaring weakness, and as such must Black's PQ3 be regarded. But his own weakness at K4 forces a certain reserve on White. The terrain bearing on the weak PQ3 has little elasticity. the PQ3 can only be attacked by the RQ1 and from the diagonal. Somewhat more varied seem the possibilities of an advance on the K's Wing, for Q and R can at any time change places on the KKt and KR files. To make these not precisely impressive possibilities the basis of an effective operation demands the highest skill of a Master. Lasker displayed it as follows in his game against Salwe. In the Diagram position the game continued 27.....Q—K1; 28. Q—B2! (if Kt—B4, the parry Kt—R3 would be possible); 28.....R—B1; 29. Q—Q2 (watches the PQ3 and hence makes the parry just alluded to impossible); 29.....Q—Kt1; 30. K—R1, R(B1)—K1; 31. R—Kt4!, R—Kt1 (if 31.....Kt—R3, then 32. Kt×BP with advantage to White); 32. R—Q1! (because the pressure was taken off the PK4): 32.....Q—Kt5 (with this the Q eventually gets into wrong paths. 32.....Q—K1· was decidedly preferable; but it was at this moment difficult to foresee that the circle of influence of the Q entering thus the enemy game would be so convincingly localized); 33. Q—KB2, Q—B6; 34. Q—R4 (now this old position taken up anew is stronger than ever), 34.....Kt—R3; 35. R—B4,·Kt—B2; 36. K—R2, R(Kt1)—K1; 37. Q—Kt3, R—KKt1; 38. R—R4 (in the Book of the Congress Lasker gives the following note here: 'If 38. R—Kt4, Kt—R3; 39. R—R4, the continuation could be 39.....P—Q4; 40. BP×P, P×P; 41. R×P, B—QB3. But now

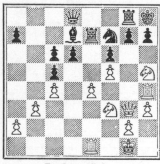

Diagram 178

Lasker—Salwe
1909

the manœuvre P—Q4 would fail after 39. BP×P, P×P; 40. Kt—B4.' So the attack on the PK4 is still in the air. Notice the preventive effect of White's manœuvre) 38.....P—KKt4 (the threat was Kt—B4, Kt—R3; R×QP) 39. P×P e.p., R×P; 40. Q—B2, P—KB4 (to be rid of the weakness at KB3); 41. Kt—B4, R—-B3; 42. Kt—K2, Q—Kt7; 43. R—Q2, Q—R8; 44. Kt—KKt3, K—Kt1; (White threatened 45. P×P, B×P; 46. Kt×B, R×Kt; 47. R×P ch) 45. P×P. B×P; 46. Kt—Q4!, P×Kt; 47. Kt×B, K—B1; 48. Q×P, Q×Q; 49. Kt×Q, Kt—K4; 50. R—R5, R(K2)—KB2; 51. P—B5, P×P; 52. R×Kt, P×Kt; 53. R×P, R—B7; 54. R—Q8 ch, K—Kt2; 55. R—QR5 and won.

The way in which Lasker conducts the game is impressive. How he manages, in spite of the small variety of threats at his disposal, to dominate the whole board, and almost wholly to eliminate his own weakness, is worthy of all admiration. The student may learn from this game that the presence of a variety of objects for attack, i.e., enemy weaknesses, can up to a certain point compensate for a lack of variety in threat-bearing lines of play.

With this magnificent example of master play we take leave of our readers.

ILLUSTRATIVE GAMES

1

Illustrating the consequences of pawn-snatching in the opening.

Carlsbad, 1911

White	Black
NIMZOWITSCH	ALAPIN
1. P—K4	P—K3
2. P—Q4	P—Q4
3. QKt—B3	KKt—B3
4. P×P	Kt×P

Surrender of the centre

| 5. KKt—B3 | P—QB4 |

To 'kill' the pawn (see I. i. §§6, 6a, on the surrender of the centre). 'Restraint' might have been effected by, say, B—K2, 0—0, P—QKt3, B—Kt2.

| 6. Kt×Kt | Q×Kt |
| 7. B—K3 | ...... |

It was to be able to make this move, which combines development and attack (the threat is P×P winning a pawn), that White exchanged Knights. (See I. i. §4.)

| 7. ...... | P×P |

Disappearance of tempo spells loss of time.

| 8. Kt×P | P—QR3 |
| 9. B—K2 | Q×KKtP |

Stealing a pawn. The consequences are grievous.

| 10. B—B3 | Q—KKt3 |
| 11. Q—Q2 | P—K4 |

The crisis. Black means to be rid of the unpleasant Knight, so that he may in some measure catch up in development.

| 12. 0—0—0! | P×Kt |
| 13. B×QP | ...... |

White's advantage in development is now too great.

| 13. ...... | QKt—B3 |
| 14. B—B6 | ...... |

Travels by express. Any other Bishop move could have been answered by a developing move, whereas now there is no time for this; Black must take.

| 14. ...... | Q×B |
| 15. KR—K1 ch | ...... |

Play in the K and Q files at the same time. The danger of a break through is great.

| 15. ...... | B—K2 |

or 15.....B—K3; 16. Q—Q7 mate!

| 16. B×Kt ch | K—B1 |

or 16. P×B; 17 Q—Q8 mate

| 17. Q—Q8 ch! | B×Q |
| 18. R—K8 mate | ...... |

2

White obtains a free, mobile centre pawn in his KP; Black keeps it in restraint by means of the resources which he has in the K file, succeeds quite properly in killing the 'criminal' (See I. i. §6a, p. 10), but then comes to grief. The end game is instructive as an example of the problems of restraint in the wider sense.

Carlsbad, 1911

White	Black
TEICHMANN	NIMZOWITSCH
1. P—K4	P—K4
2. KKt—B3	P—Q3
3. P—Q4	KKt—B3
4. Kt—QB3	QKt—Q2

The Hanham variation; makes development more difficult, but holds the centre. To call the move 'ugly' would be a question of—aberration of taste. Cf. Game No. 40 between the same opponents.

5. B—QB4	B—K2
6. 0—0	0—0
7. Q—K2	P—QB3

By which at least Black establishes a sort of pawn majority in the centre, though it is true White for the time calls the tune.

8. P—QR4

The close character of the game allows of pawn moves in the opening.

| 8. ...... | Q—B2 |
| 9. B—Kt3 | P—QR3 |

In order to be able eventually to advance the QBP.

10. P—KR3   P×P

Giving up the centre must not here be regarded as illogical; was happiness no happiness, because it endured for but a short time?—One cannot always be happy.

11. Kt×P   R—K1

Restraint strategy, directed against the KP. (Cf. Diagram 10 p. 11.)

| 12. B—KB4 | B—KB1 |
| 13. P—KB3 | Kt—B4 |

The attentive student will here have expected Black to take possession of an advanced post at K4; but he wishes first to exchange; a commendable stratagem in cramped positions.

14. B—QR2	Kt—K3!
15. B×Kt	B×B
16. Q—Q2	QR—Q1
17. KR—K1	B—B1
18. QR—Q1	Kt—Q2!

And now having harmoniously completed his development (though for harmony there was in truth not much room to spare in his cramped quarters), Black occupies the advanced post.

19. Kt—B5   Kt—K4

Commands the field. Large radius of attack. Any attempt to drive him away by P—KB4 would weaken the KP.

20. Kt—Q4   P—KB3

Observe the gradual paralysing of the KP.

21. K—R1	Q—KB2
22. Q—KB2	Q—Kt3
23. P—QKt3	Kt—B2

Now—P—KB4 is prepared for. The student will perhaps ask, What has the Kt at K4 accomplished? Quite enough, since White could undertake nothing.

| 24. K—R2 | R—K2 |
| 25. Kt(Q4)—K2 | P—KB4! |

'Killing the paralysed pawn.'

26. Kt—Kt3   P×P?

Overhasty; QR—K1 should have been played. e.g., 26. ....QR—K1; 27. P×P, B×P; 28. Kt×B, Q× Kt; 29. B—Kt3, R×R; 30. R× R, R×R; 31. Q×R, Q×QBP;

27. Kt(B3)×P.

After P×P the isolated KP would have been a bad weakness.

27.	P—Q4
28. Kt—QB5	QR—K1
29. Kt—Q3	R×R

Black has now got an equal game. 29. ....Kt—Q3 would surrender his K4 square (30. B—K5).

30. R×R	R×R
31. Q×R	Q—K3
32. Q×Q	B×Q

33. B—K3

This good move puts Black's pawn majority on the Q side under restraint. Black should now have contented himself with. a draw; he wished to get more and lost the game as follows:—33. ....B—Q3; 34. P—KB4, K—B1; 35. K—Kt1, P—KKt3; 36. K—B2, P—KR4;

37. Kt—QB5, B—QB1; 38. P—
QR5, Kt—R3; 39. P—QKt4, K—
B2; 40. P—B3, Kt—Kt1 (Kt—
B4 would have drawn); 41. K—B3,
Kt—B3; 42. B—Q4, B ×Kt; 43.
B ×B, B—K3; 44. B—Q4, Kt—
K5; 45. Kt—K2! (Not 45. Kt ×
Kt, P ×Kt ch. 46. K ×P because
of B—Q4 ch followed by B ×P),
45. ... .B—B4 (It is no use, Black
is in effect a pawn down; his major-
ity is paralysed, White's is mobile.)
46. P—Kt4, P ×P ch; 47. P ×P
Kt—Q7 ch (It would have been
much better to keep the Bishop at
home, thus: B—Q2); 48. K—Kt3,
B—B7; 49. Kt—Kt1, K—K3; 50.
K—R4, B—Q8; 51. Kt—R3, Kt—
K5; 52. P—B5 ch! (ingeniously
turns his majority to account!)
P ×P (If 52. ... .K—B2 then
53. P ×P ch, K ×P; 54. Kt—B4
ch would have been unpleasant);
53. Kt—B4 ch, K—B2; 54. P—
Kt5!, B—Kt5; 55. P—Kt6 ch,
K—K2; 56. P—Kt7, K—B2; 57.
Kt—Kt6. Resigns.

3

An excellent example of play in
the open file. Black by this alone
builds up a superior position and
without the establishment of any
outpost forces his way to the
enemy's base.

Ostend, 1907

White	Black
Van Vliet	Znosko-Borovsky

1. P—Q4   P—Q4
2. P—K3   P—QB4
3. P—QB3   P—K3
4. B—Q3   Kt—QB3
5. P—KB4   ......

The Stone Wall, a very close
opening.

5. ......   Kt—KB3
6. Kt—Q2   Q—B2
7. KKt—KB3   ......

o

Overlooks the threat involved in
Q—B2; 7. Kt—R3 followed by
Q—B3 would have been the better
course.

7. ......   P ×P!

Position after Black's 7th move

8. BP ×P   ......

Positionally the right move here
would usually be KP ×P (e.g.,
8. KP ×P and White has the K
file with an outpost station at K5,
while the P at QB3 closes the opponent's QB file, see I. ii. §4, p. 18,
but here this move would lose a
pawn, e.g., 8. KP ×P, Q ×KBP.
Nevertheless it was preferable to
the text move; for 8. KP ×P,
Q ×P; 9. Kt—B4, Q—B2, (Q—
Kt5, Kt—K3!); 10. Kt(B4)—K5,
B—Q3; 11. Q—K2, and White has
a fairly well protected outpost in the
K file, which Black cannot disturb
even by 11. ... .B ×Kt; 12. QP ×
B, Kt—Q2; 13. B—KB4, P—
KB3?; for then 14. P ×P, Q ×B;
15. P ×P, R—Kt1; 16. Q ×P ch
would win for white. So long as the
K file with the outpost KtK5, or its
full equivalent a PK5 (after P
recaptures), remains in White's
possession he would stand excellently, despite the pawn minus.

8. ......   Kt—QKt5
9. B—QKt1   B—Q2
10. P—QR3   R—QB1!

It is only by this subtle R move
that the somewhat beginner-like
Kt manœuvre gets a meaning.

11. O—O	B—QKt4!
12. R—K1	Kt—B7
13. B×Kt	Q×B
14. Q×Q	R×Q

The 7th Rank, seconded by the Bishops diagonal QKt4 to KB8 and the point K5 for the Kt.

15. P—KR3	B—Q3
16. Kt—QKt1	Kt—K5

No outpost in our sense (the open file behind is wanting), but yet a good substitute.

17. Kt(B3)—Q2	B—Q6
18. Kt×Kt	B×Kt

18. ....P×Kt with the B established at Q6 would also have been good.

19. Kt—Q2	K—Q2
20. Kt×B	P×Kt
21. R—QKt1	KR—QB1
22. P—QKt4	R(B1)—B6
23. K—B1	K—B3!
24. B—Kt2	R—Kt6
25. R—K2	R×R
26. K×R	K—Kt4
27. K—Q2	K—R5
28. K—K2	P—QR4

The decisive break through. The position of Black's R, holding the White KP under a continual threat, was also too strong to be withstood. The rest is readily understandable. 29. K—B2, P×P; 30. P×P, K×P; 31. K—K2, K—Kt4; 32. K—Q2, B—R6; 33. K—B2, R×B ch; 34. R×R, B×R; 35. K×B, K—B5; 36. P—KKt4, K—Q6; 37. P—Kt5, K×KP; 38. Resigns.

4

File—Outpost—7th Row

Ostend, 1907

White	Black
Lee	Nimzowitsch

The opening moves have already been discussed (I. i. §6a); they were:

1. P—Q4, Kt—KB3; 2. Kt—KB3, P—Q3; 3. QKt—Q2, QKt—Q2; 4. P—K4, P—K4; 5. P—QB3, B—K2; 6. B—QB4, O—O; 7. O—O, P×P; 8. P×P, P—Q4; 9. B—Q3, P×P; 10. Kt×P, Kt×Kt; 11. B×Kt, Kt—B3; 12. B—Q3, Kt—Q4; 13. P—QR3, B—B3;

14. Q—B2	P—KR3
15. B—Q2	B—K3
16. QR—K1	P—QB3
17. B—K3	Q—QKt3
18. P—KR3	QR—Q1
19. R—QB1	R—Q2

Quietly building up the position, the QP cannot move, so why get excited.

20. KR—K1	KR—Q1
21. Q—K2	Q—QB2
22. B—Kt1	Kt—K2

His work done (for the Knight has been working) a change of air is good. The Knight aims to get to KB4.

23. Kt—K5	B×Kt
24. P×B	Q×P
25. B×QRP	Q×Q
26. R×Q	R—Q8 ch

Black now invades the enemy position via the Q file.

27. R—K1	R×R(B1)
28. R×R	R—Q7

Now play in the 7th rank begins.

29. P—QKt4	Kt—Q4
30. B—K4	Kt—B3
31. B—B2	Kt—Q4
32. B—K4	R—QR7!

Allowing Bishops of opposite colour.

33. B×Kt	B×B
34. R—B3	P—KB4!

All according to my system. Black seeks an object of attack in the 7th rank; against the QRP nothing further can be done, so the second player intends to lay bare White's KKtP. This will be brought about by a close advance of the King's wing.

35. K—R2	K—B2
36. B—B5	P—KKt4
37. R—Q3	P—QKt4
38. B—Q4	B—K5
39. R—QB3	B—Q4
40. B—B5	K—Kt3
41. R—Q3	P—KR4
42. B—Kt6	P—KB5
43. B—Q4	K—B4
44. P—KB3	......

White stood very badly, the threat was P—Kt5 followed by P—Kt6 ch, P×P, R×P ch.

44.	P—Kt5
45. RP×P	P×P
46. K—Kt1	R—K7

The 8th rank (White's 1st rank) is also weak (P—Kt6 is threatened when opportunity arises) and White has not a plethora of moves at his command either.

47. P×P ch	K—K5!
48. R—Q1	B—Kt6
49. R—KB1	K×B

And won in a few moves.

In the two games which follow the Knight as outpost is the chief actor. In the first he is exchanged, but finds full compensation in the retaking pawn. In the second his capacity to manœuvre is exemplified.

5

Riga, 1913

White	Black
DR. V. HAKEN	GIESE
1. P—K4	P—K3
2. P—Q4	P—Q4
3. P×P	P×P
4. Kt—KB3	B—Q3
5. B—Q3	Kt—KB3
6. P—KR3	0—0
7. 0—0	P—KR3

In the exchange variation of the French defence with both KKts developed at their KB3 the pinning move B—KKt5 furnishes for both sides one of the leading motives. Here, however, this motif is ruled out by the moves of the KRP's, and, except for a moment, we see, and hear of, nothing but the K file.

8. Kt—QB3	P—QB3
9. Kt—K2	R—K1
10. Kt—Kt3	Kt—K5

The outpost.

11. Kt—R5	Kt—Q2
12. P—QB3	Kt(Q)—B3
13. Kt—R2	Q—B2
14. Kt×Kt ch	Kt×Kt
15. Kt—B3	Kt—K5
16. B—B2	B—KB4!

All pieces are directed towards the strategical point; this is also called emphasizing one's strength (here the Kt at K5).

17. Kt—R4	B—R2
18. B—K3	P—KKt4
19. Kt—B3	P—KB4
20. R—K1	R—K2

The pressure in the file grows acuter move by move.

21. Kt—Q2	P—B5
22. Kt×Kt	P×Kt

The place of the outpost Knight is now worthily taken by a 'half-passed' pawn.

23. B—Q2	QR—K1
24. P—QB4	P—QB4
25. B—B3	B—Kt3!

In order to be able to play K—R2 and P—K6; a timely advance against the P at KR3 is also threatened, e.g., by P—KR4, P—KKt5, an echo of the pin motif! v. I, vii. §1.

26. Q—Kt4	P×P
27. B×QP	B—K4
28. B×B	R×B
29. Q—Q1	......

If 29. QR—Q1 then 29. .....P—K6; 30. B×B, P×P ch; 31. K×P, Q—B4 ch; 32. K—B1, Q×P ch; 33. K—B2, Q—B4 ch; 34. K—B1, Q—Kt4 ch; 35. K—B2, Q×P

Position after Black's 28th move

ch; 36. K—B1, Q—Kt4 ch; 37.
K—B2, Q—Kt3 ch; 38. K—B1,
Q—R3 ch; 39. K—B2, Q×P ch;
40. K—B1, Q—R3 ch; 41. K—
B2, Q—Kt3 ch; 42. K—B1,
followed by the double exchange at
K8 and Q×B. A fine illustration
to the theme; the win of a pawn with
a check (see also I. iii. §3, Diagram
31). The game continued 29. . . . .
R—Q1; 30. Q—Kt1, R—Q7; 31.
B×P, Q—B4!; 32. B—Q5 ch,
K—Kt2; 33. Q—B1, Q×P ch;
34. K—R1, R(K4)×B. Resigns.

The above game provides a trans-
parent, therefore, a good, illustration to the outpost theme.

6

A game from the early days of
chess science.

Breslau, 1889

White   Black
Dr. Tarrasch   J. Berger

After the opening moves:—1.
P—K4, P—K4; 2. Kt—KB3, Kt—
QB3; 3. B—Kt5, P—QR3; 4.
B—R4, Kt—KB3; 5. Kt—QB3,
B—Kt5; 6. Kt—Q5, B—K2; 7.
P—Q3, P—Q3; Tarrasch with 8.
Kt—Kt4, B—Q2; 9. Kt×Kt, B×
Kt; 10. B×B, P×B, gave Black
a doubled pawn, whose weakness,
however, must be considered for the
present as problematic.

The game proceeded:—

11. 0—0	0—0
12. Q—K2	P—QB4?

This move would to-day be considered bad. The weakness of the
doubled pawn appears when Black
advances; while an advance by
White (in the centre) would not
reveal it; on the contrary, after
P—Q4, P×P, Black's P at QB3
would attack White's outpost station in the Q file! (One can see how
much easier thinking is made by
the system.) Right was, therefore,
R—K1 and B—B1 and await
events.

13. P—QB3

To be able at any cost to play
P—Q4 as quickly as possible. We
know to-day that the central attack
is by no means the only one to
bring happiness. The right course
was Kt—Q2—B4, followed after
due preparation by P—QKt4 or
P—KB4, leaving the centre passive.

13.	Kt—Q2
14. P—Q4	KP×P
15. P×P	B—B3
16. B—K3	P×P
17. B×P	R—K1
18. Q—B2	B×B
19. Kt×B	Kt—B4

On this position of the Knight
the whole fate of the game now
hangs. If this Knight be driven
away, Black's QBP may become
weak.

20. P—KB3	Q—B3
21. KR—Q1	KR—QKt1

White has the Q file with a point
at Q5. The K file is of no value to
Black, partly because of White's
protected KP, partly, however,
because his Rooks have been told
off to stop P—QKt4.

22. QR—QKt1	P—QR4
23. K—R1(!)	. . . . . .

The idea of this subtle move is
to use the centre as a weapon of
attack. The threat now (after K—
R1) is P—K5, Q×P; Kt—B6,
which before would have failed

because of Q—K6 ch. Of positive
value, however, there is little in
this K move, for in any case Black
would have to play R—Kt2, if
only to double the Rooks. (We
see that Black operates in the QKt
file against the thrust PQKt4.)

23. ......   R—Kt3

Not good, for White suddenly
becomes strong in the Q file (the
outpost station at Q5 will now be
occupied with attack on the R at
Kt3). More in place would be
R—Kt2 (given by Steinitz) or some
passive move (say 23..... P—KR3).
For instance: 23..... P—KR3; 24.
P—K5, P×P; 25. Q×Kt, P×Kt;
26. R×P, P—R5 (Black's QKt
file is telling); 27. R—QKt4, Q—
Q3, equalising comfortably. Or
23..... R—Kt2; 24. Kt—K2, QR—
Kt1; 25. Kt—QB3; and now 25.
....P—R5, and the QKt file
makes itself felt.

24. Kt—K2   Kt—K3
25. Kt—QB3   R—QB3

It is intelligible that Berger
should regard Kt—Q5 as not con-
ducive to his comfort, nevertheless,
it would have been better to retreat
in good order with 25..... Q—Q1;
26. Kt—Q5, R—Kt2; followed by
QR—Kt1.

26. Q—R4   R—B4
27. Kt—Q5   Q—Q1
28. R(Kt)—QB1   ......

White's manœuvre (Q—R4, R—
QB1) is clear as daylight. White
wishes to control the QB file, which
is still in dispute, in order at the
proper moment to play his trump
Q—QB6.

28, ...   R×R
29. R×R   P—QB4

Puts his QB2 out of danger, but
now his P at Q3 is become a delicate
child. Black, however, already
stood unfavourably; he had in
fact neglected the QKt file.

30. R—Q1   Kt—Q5
31. Q—B4   ......

White wishes to exchange the Kt
say by Kt—B3—K2, in order then
to be able to attack the Q pawn to
his heart's content. This attack
must succeed, for the protecting
pieces can easily get into uncomfortable positions (e.g., Black: R,
Q2; Q, K2; White: R, Q5; Q, Q3),
on which the K pawn will attack for
the 3rd time and the Black QP will
be won. From our point of view it
is of interest to notice how the
White pieces have their eyes fixed
on the point Q5 (Q—QB4!). What
happens is that if one is in possession
of such a point as Q5 here is, one
embarks on protracted manœuvring
with the point in question as base.
That is to say one's own pieces come
and go over the point Q5, the poor
Black QP is attacked now in one
way, now in another, and at last
Black loses his wind, that is, he
cannot keep pace with this tacking
to and fro, which is intelligible
enough since he not only has no
base on which to pivot, but is in
addition cramped for space (see II,
vi, on manœuvring against an enemy
weakness). True, in this game it
does not come to the sort of struggle
we have sketched, for Black makes a
mistake, which takes the game out
of the path of its logical development.

31. ......   R—QKt1
32. P—QKt3   R—QB1?
33. R×Kt   P×R
34. Kt—K7 ch   ......

Not 34. Q×R?, Q×Q; 35. Kt—
K7 ch, because then the QP would
queen.

34. ......   Q×Kt
35. Q×R ch   Q—B1
36. Q×Q ch   K×Q

And White won the pawn ending
by means of the 'remoter' passed
pawn. The ending is used as an
illustration to I, iv, §6 on privileged
passed pawns. See Diagram 58.

7

Baden-Baden, 1925

White	Black
RABINOWITSCH	NIMZOWITSCH

1.	P—Q4	Kt—KB3
2.	P—QB4	P—K3
3.	Kt—KB3	P—QKt3
4.	Kt—QB3	B—Kt2
5.	B—Kt5	P—KR3
6.	B—R4	B—K2
7.	P—K3	P—Q3
8.	B—Q3	QKt—Q2

Black has a solid but cramped game; such a game can as a rule only be slowly opened up.

9.	0—0	0—0
10.	Q—K2	P—K4

Slower, therefore more true to type, would be Kt—R4.

11.	P×P	B×Kt!

Not 11. Kt×P, Kt×Kt; 12. P×Kt, R—Q1; with pressure in the Q file.

12.	P×B	Kt×P
13.	B×Kt	B×B
14.	B—K4	R—Kt1

White with his Q file and a Knight outpost at Q5 will be able to force P—QB3, that is already clear. True the Black QP will not be difficult to defend, for it stands on a square of the same colour as his Bishop; but what is going to happen in the KKt file? This we shall soon see.

15.	QR—Q1	Kt—Q2!
16.	Kt—Q5	Kt—B4
17.	B—Kt1	P—QR4

No outpost, yet strong. The student should learn by careful practice how to establish Knights so that they cannot be driven away.

18.	K—R1	P—KKt3

This would in any event be forced by Q—QB2.

19.	R—KKt1	B—Kt2
20.	R—Kt3	P—QB3!
21.	Kt—B4	R—QKt2!

The situation in the KKt file may now be regarded as so far cleared up, that it is evident that the threat consists in a sacrifice at Kt6 (i.e., the 'revolutionary' attack). The slow undermining operations by P—KR4—R5 would be, on the other hand, difficult to carry through.

22.	Q—QB2	Q—B3
23.	P—QKt3	......

He might have gone in for the combination 23. Kt—R5, Q× QKtP; 24. R×KKtP, P×R; 25. Q×P; but the attack would hardly have succeeded.

23.	......	R—K1
24.	Kt—K2	......

In order to bring the Knight to Q4. White's dilemma consists in having two files, the Q and KKt; he cannot quite make up his mind which to use, and on this indecision his game goes to pieces.

24.	......	R(QKt2)—Q2
25.	R—Q2	R(K)—Q1
26.	Kt—B4	K—B1
27.	Q—Q1	P—KR4!!

Not merely to make B—R3 possible, but also because the KRP has a great role to play.

28.	Q—KKt1	B—R3
29.	Kt—K2	P—Q4

Gets rid of the weakness at Q3 and soon commands the Q file.

30.	P×P	R×P
31.	R×R	R×R
32.	P—B4	......

If 32. Kt—Q4, then 32.....
B—B5. For instance: 32. Kt—Q4, B—B5; 33. P×B, Q×Kt; 34. P—B5, P—KR5!; 35. R—Kt4, Q—B6; and the P at KB3 is hard to defend.

32.	......	B—Kt2

The decision to abandon the diagonal KR3 to KB5, a difficult one to have to make, is made comparatively easy to one who knows

that there will be impediments
(here very likely a Knight at Q5)
to be bombarded. I did not like
R—Q7 at once (instead of B—Kt2)
because of the reply 33. Kt—Q4,
B × P; 34. R—B3.

33. Q—QB1   ......
I had expected here (at last!)
the sacrifice at KKt6 and had in
anticipation prepared a real prob-
lem in reply; namely 33. B × KtP,
P—KR5!; 34. R—Kt4, P × B; 35.
R × P, Q—B4; 36. R × B, Q—
K5 ch; 37. Q—Kt2 (forced), R—
Q8 ch; 38. Kt—Kt1, and now the
point 38. . . . . P—R6; 39. Q ×
Q, Kt × Q; threatening mate at
B7.

33. ......   Q—Q3
The exploitation of the Q file
which now follows is all according
to book (I mean my book), but is
here embellished by a pretty feature.

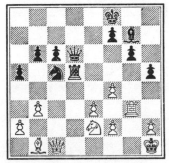

Position after Black's 33rd move

34. B—B2   Kt—K5
35. R—Kt2   P—R5
36. Kt—Kt1   ......
I was glad to be rid of the Knight
and played

36. ......   Kt—B6
This Knight manœuvre makes
possible the invasion of the enemy's
base (here his 1st and 2nd ranks).

37. P—QR4   ......
If P—QR3 then Kt—R7 winning
the QRP.

37. ......   Kt—R7
38. Q—KB1   Kt—Kt5
Here I had the unpleasant feeling
that I had let the Bishop escape,
had allowed him elbow-room.

39. B—K4   R—Q8
My first thought was: What a
pity! now the Queen will also find
her way into the open; but then I
saw the mating spectre loom up,
the same one which I had known
well ever since the 33rd move.

40. Q—B4   P—KB4
41. B—B3   P—R6
42. R—Kt3   Kt—Q6
43. Q—B2   R—QB8
and here I rejoiced over the Queen's
involuntary return home.

44. Q—K2   R—QKt8
45. Resigns, for the turning move
R—Kt7 will be deadly in effect.
The impression we get from this
game is that the system supports
combinative play most effectively.

And now a short game which is
especially interesting since the outpost appears only as a threat, as a
mere ghost, and yet its effect is
enormous.

8

Copenhagen, 1923

White	Black
SÄMISCH	NIMZOWITSCH

1. P—Q4   Kt—KB3
2. P—QB4   P—K3
3. Kt—KB3   P—QKt3
4. P—KKt3   B—Kt2
5. B—Kt2   B—K2
6. Kt—QB3   0—0
7. 0—0   P—Q4
8. Kt—K5   P—QB3
Safeguards the position.

9. P × P   BP × P
10. B—KB4   P—QR3!
Protects the outpost station QB5,
i.e., by P—QR3 and P—QKt4.

11. R—QB1   P—QKt4
12. Q—Kt3   Kt—QB3
The ghost! With noiseless steps
he presses on towards QB5.

13. Kt × Kt   ......
Sämisch sacrifices two tempi
(exchange of the tempo-eating Kt
at K5 for the Kt which is almost
undeveloped) merely to be rid of
the ghost.

13. ......   B × Kt
14. P—KR3   Q—Q2
15. K—R2   Kt—R4
I could have supplied him with
yet a second ghost by Q—Kt2, and
Kt—Q2—Kt3—B5, but I wished to
turn my attention to the King's side.

16. B—Q2   P—KB4!
17. Q—Q1   P—Kt5!
18. Kt—Kt1   B—QKt4
19. R—Kt1   B—Q3
20. P—K4   BP × P!
This sacrifice, which has a quite
surprising effect, is based upon the
following sober calculation: two
pawns and the 7th rank and an enemy
Queen's wing which cannot be disen-
tangled—all this for only one piece!

21. Q × Kt   R × P
22. Q—Kt5   QR—KB1
23. K—R1   R(B1)—B4
24. Q—K3   B—Q6
25. QR—K1   P—KR3!!
A brilliant move which announces
the *Zugzwang*. White has not a move
left. If, e.g., K—R2 or P—KKt4,
then R—B6. Black can now make
waiting moves with his King, and
White must, willy-nilly, eventually
throw himself upon the sword. So
26. Resigns.

9

Copenhagen, 1922

White	Black
NIMZOWITSCH	PRITZEL
1. P—Q4	P—KKt3
2. P—K4	B—Kt2

3. Kt—QB3   P—Q3
4. B—K3   Kt—KB3
5. B—K2   0—0
6. Q—Q2   ......
In order by B—KR6 to exchange
Black's B at KKt2.

6. ......   P—K4
7. P × P   P × P
8. 0—0—0   ......
The plan chosen by White is
seductive in the simplicity of the
means to be employed. He intends
after allowing the exchange of
Queens, to get some advantage in
the Q file.

8. ......   Q × Q
9. R × Q   ......

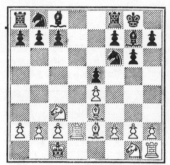

Position after White's 9th move

9. ......   P—QB3
Moves which weaken such important points (as Q3) should be
avoided if in any way possible; and
in fact a piece soon settles itself on
this square. The important point to
be observed by the student is that
before Black's P—QB3 the Q file
was only under pressure, whereas
after this move it is clearly weakened. It would, therefore, have
been better to forgo P—QB3 and to
play instead 9.....Kt—QB3; for
instance, the continuation might
be: 10. P—KR3 (in order to be able
to play Kt—KB3 without the fear
of the reply Kt—KKt5), 10.....
Kt—Q5!?; 11. Kt—KB3! (but not
11. B × Kt, P × B; 12. R × P, Kt—
Kt5!), 11.....Kt × B or Kt; 12. R
or B × Kt, and White stands better.

Nevertheless, 9. .... Kt—QB3 was the correct move, only after 10. P—KR3 Black must continue with B—K3. For example: 10. P—KR3, B—K3; 11. Kt—KB3, P—KR3; 12. KR—Q1, P—QR3. In the position here reached White has unquestionably full possession of the Q file; since, however, neither an invasion of the 7th rank by R—Q7 nor the establishment of an outpost by Kt—Q5 lies within the realms of possibility, the value of the file would seem to be problematical. White's KP is, in fact, in need of protection and this circumstance has a not inconsiderable crippling effect. Black has two courses open for consideration: (a) to play at once KR—Q1, with the idea R ×R ch, R ×R; R ×R ch, Kt ×R; Kt × KP, Kt ×KP; though this variation must be prepared for by K—R2 or P—KKt4, so as to safeguard the KRP against B—K3; else after the double exchange of Rooks and Kt ×KP, Kt ×KP, there would follow Kt ×Kt, B ×Kt, B ×RP. (b) the slow manœuvre KR—QB1, followed by K—B1—K1, and finally the challenge of the R's by R—Q1.

The fact that this last line of play is possible is significant proof of the small activity of White in the Q file.

10. P—QR4   ......
Apparently compromising, in reality well thought out; for firstly P—QKt4, which would be an indirect and therefore unwelcome attack on the PK4, must be prevented, and secondly Black's Queen's wing is to be besieged. We feel ourselves justified in pursuing this ambitious plan since now that 9. .... P—QB3 has been played our positional advantage in the centre is unquestionable, and should have a real effect even on the wings; a proposition which may be thus formulated: a superior position in the centre justifies a thrust on an extreme flank.

10. ......   Kt—Kt5
11. B × Kt   B × B
12. KKt—K2   Kt—Q2
In unusual situations ordinary moves are, it would seem, seldom suitable. The proper system of development here was Kt—R3, KR—K1, and B—KB1. The weakness at Q3 would then have been covered and the position would have been perfectly tenable.

13. KR—Q1   Kt—Kt3
14. P—QKt3   B—B3
15. P—KB3   B—K3
16. P—R5   Kt—B1
17. Kt—R4   ......
It is now clear that the suggested development by 12. .... Kt—R3, etc., would have wasted less time than that in the text (Kt—Q2—Kt3—B1). White has now a strong position on the extreme left and threatens to get a grip on the enemy with Kt—B5. We now see that 10. P—QR4! was not so very valueless as an attacking move.

17. ......   P—QKt3
An excellent parry. If 18. P ×P, P ×P; 19. B ×P, then naturally B—KKt4.

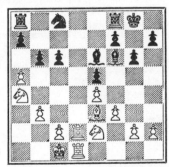

Position after Black's 17th move

The 'restricted' advance in a file, which here is revealed in a singularly plastic form, in that the Rook is brought from the Q to the QB file and thence to the QR file.

18. R—Q3   ......

18. ......   P×P

Bad. The right move was R—QKt1 and Black's position still had life in it.

19. R—QB3   Kt—K2
20. R—B5   KR—QKt1
21. Kt(K)—B3   ......

The QRP won't run away.

21. ......   P—QR3
22. R×RP   K—Kt2
23. Kt—Kt6   R—R2
24. Kt(B)—R4   ......

The one Kt made room for the other.

24. ......   R(R)—QKt2
25. R×RP   Kt—B1
26. Kt×Kt   R×Kt
27. Kt—B5   R(Kt)—QB2
28. R—Q6   ......

Now at last is the point seized which Black weakened by his 9th move; but its occupation had always been in the air.

28. ......   R—Q1
29. R×B   Resigns

In the notes to this game we have become acquainted with the resources at the disposal of the defender of a file. Since a knowledge of these is of the greatest practical value in the conduct of a game, we give another game which will be found instructive in the same sense.

10

Breslau, 1925

White	Black
NIMZOWITSCH	DR. TARRASCH
1. Kt—KB3	Kt—KB3
2. P—QB4	P—QB4
3. Kt—QB3	P—Q4

Playable; but 3. .... P—K3 seems better (3. .... P—K3; 4. P—Q4, P×P; 5. Kt×P, B—QKt5) or even 3. .... Kt—QB3. For example 3. .... Kt—QB3; 4. P—Q4, P×P; 5. Kt×P, P—KKt3, and now White could, it is true, try by

means of 6. P—K4 slowly to tie up his opponent, but this attempt could be adequately parried by 6. .... B—Kt2; 7. B—K3, Kt—KKt5! (Breyer's move); 8. Q×Kt, Kt× Kt; 9. Q—Q1!, Kt—K3! (suggested by me). The position reached after 9. .... Kt—K3 is fairly rich in resources for Black, e.g., (i) Q—R4, (ii) 0—0 followed by P—KB4, (iii) P—QKt3 and B—QKt2. The student should examine for himself these lines of play.

4. P×P   Kt×P
5. P—Q4   P×P

Best for Black would appear to be 5. .... Kt×Kt; 6. P×Kt, P× P; 7. P×P, P—K3.

6. Q×P   P—K3
7. P—K3   ......

A very cautious move, on which I determined because I recognized the more enterprising continuations 7. P—K4 and 7. Kt×Kt, P×Kt; 8. P—K4, as leading to little. For instance 7. P—K4, Kt×Kt!; 8. Q×Kt (after Q×Q ch and P×Kt he would have had a sick QBP in an open file to tend), 8. .... Kt—QB3; 9. P—QR3, Q—R4!; or 9. B—QKt5, B—Q2; with an equal game. Or, 7. Kt×Kt, P×Kt; 8. P—K4, P×P!; 9. Q×Q ch, K×Q; 10. Kt—Kt5, B—QKt5 ch; 11. B—Q2, B×B ch; 12. K×B, K—K2; with an equal game. The student who is interested in problems of development should test the following variation: 7. Kt×Kt, P× Kt; 8. P—K4, Kt—QB3 (instead of P×P! as given by us). After 9. Q×P, Q×Q; 10. P×Q, Kt—Kt5; there would follow B—QKt5 ch; and Black would have difficulty in finding a good continuation.

7. ......   Kt—QB3
8. B—QKt5   B—Q2
9. B×Kt   B×B
10. Kt—K5   Kt×Kt
11. Kt×B   Q×Q
12. Kt×Q   Kt—Q4
13. B—Q2   ......

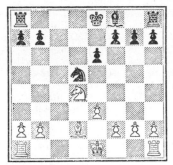

Position after White's 13th move

The position here shown is for all its harmless appearance full of poison. White threatens to take possession of the QB file, moreover he has at his disposal a convenient square for his K (K2), whereas Black enjoys this last advantage in only a restricted fashion. (See note to move 17.) In such positions the defence must be very carefully played.

13. ......   B—B4
In order to drive the Kt away from the centre; but as the Kt moves to Kt3 in order to promote his QB5 into an outpost station, B—B4 proves to be pleasant for White. Best appears to be 13. .... B—K2, intending B—B3. For example, 13. ....B—K2; 14. P—K4, Kt—Kt3; 15. R—QB1, 0—0; 16. K—K2; and now White is full of pride in his developed King, whereas his Black Majesty can in this case give up all thought of development since the BK2 is a crafty minister, who likes to keep the reins of government in his own hands. For instance: 16. K—K2, B—B3!; 17. B—K3, KR—QB1; 18. P—QKt3, B ×Kt; 19. B ×B; and now Kt—Q2, or else 19. .... R ×R (instead of Kt—Q2); 20. R ×R, R—QB1; 21. R ×R ch, Kt ×R; 22. K—Q3, and though it is true that the White King is now able to make his influence felt, it is questionable whether Black will not overtake his opponent, e.g., 22. ....

P—KB3; 23. K—B4, K—B2; 24. K—Kt5, P—QR3 ch! (else the Bishop sacrifice); 25. K—B5, K—K2; followed by K—Q2 with a draw. It follows that 13. ....B—K2 was the right defence.

14. Kt—Kt3   B—Kt5
Either B—Kt3 or B—K2 would have been decidedly better. B—Kt3 would have safeguarded QB2 against invasion, and this in the defence is an imperative duty.
After 14. ....B—Kt3; 15. P—K4, Kt—K2; White's advantage would have been infinitesimal.

15. R—QB1   R—Q1
16. B ×B   Kt ×B
17. K—K2   K—K2
Black has cleared a square for himself, but at what a cost of valuable time (B—B4—Kt5)!

18. R—B4   Kt—R3
An unpleasant retreat. If 18. ....Kt—B3; then not 19. Kt—B5 because of the answer Kt—R4 and P—QKt3, but rather a doubling of the Rooks, and Black's position would not be favourable.

19. KR—QB1   R—Q2
Black's position still makes an impression which inspires confidence in it, and this at a moment when it carries the seeds of death in itself. The next two moves of White reduce Black's Q file to passivity, that is to say take away from it any potential attacking value.

20. P—KB4!   KR—Q1
21. Kt—Q4   P—KB3
22. P—QR4!   ......

Even a full advance of a pawn can imply a waiting policy. White does not fear P—K4 in the least, for after 22. ....P—K4; 23. P ×P, P ×P; Black's KP would be weak. The more energetic 22. P—QKt4 was, however, also to be considered,

but would have been less ad-
vantageous because of the reply
P—QKt4. Now, however, this move
(P—QKt4) threatens to confine
Black within still narrower limits.

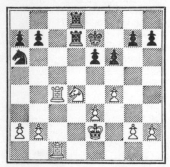

Position after Black's 21st move

Black intends P—K4. Is this a threat?
If not, find a sensible waiting move
for White.

22......   P—K4
In a cramped position the
attempt to hit out is explicable on
psychological grounds, even if it
be not always equally justified if
viewed dispassionately. So, too,
here. It is true that in any case
Black stands badly.

23.	P ×P	P ×P
24.	Kt—B3	K—K3
25.	P—QKt4	P—QKt3
26.	R(B1)—B2!	......

One of those unpretentious moves
which are more disagreeable to a
cramped opponent who is threatened on all sides than the worst
direct attack. The move is a defending and a waiting move, and moreover involves a threat; though this
from the nature of things is but a
small one, and is in fact of but
secondary importance. The (slight)
threat is Kt—Kt5 ch and Kt—K4,
and then P—QKt5, driving the
Kt back to Kt1.

26.	......	P—KR3
27.	P—KR4!	R—Q3
28.	P—KR5	......

As a result of 26. R—B2 entirely
new attacking possibilities have
arisen. Black's PKKt2 is become
backward. The manœuvre R—
KKt4 would, however, not only
help to expose the weakness of the
KtP, but, what is more important,
put the Black King in an extremely
disagreeable situation. All this fell
like ripe fruit into White's lap,
simply and solely as the logical (or
psychological) result of the waiting
move 26. R—QB2. The finest moves
are after all waiting moves!

28.	......	R—Q4
29.	R—KKt4	R(Q4)—Q2
30.	R—QB6 ch	R—Q3

If 30....K—B4? then 31.
R(B6)—KKt6 followed by mate.
After 30....K—Q4; 31. R(B6)—
KKt6, P—K5!; there would follow
32. Kt—Q2, Kt ×P; 33. Kt ×P,
with advantage to White.

31. R—Kt6 ch   ......
The possession of the points QB6
and KKt6 insures the complete
investment of the enemy King.
Observe how the QB file has been
used as a jumping off place to get
into the KKt file.

31. ......   K—K2
On 31....K—Q4 there would
have followed a pretty little catastrophe, i.e., 32. R(QB) ×R ch,
R ×R; 33. P—K4 ch!, K—B3; 34.
P—Kt5 ch, and the Kt, who had
felt so thoroughly safe at R3, to
his intense surprise meets his doom!

32.	R ×P ch	K—B1
33.	R ×R	R ×R
34.	R ×P	Kt ×P
35.	Kt ×P	R—K3

White wins. To make effective
use of a superiority in material is
one of the most important things
which a student has to learn. He
cannot practice himself enough in it.
White has now won two pawns. A
glance at the position shows (1) that
White commands the 7th Row; (2)

that White's KP is isolated and his
KKtP backward. The policy, therefore, is, taking full advantage of the
7th Row, to assemble (unite) our
isolated or badly placed detachments. To this end the Kt will be
brought, with gain of tempo, to
KB5.

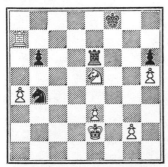

Position after Black's 35th move

36. Kt—Kt6 ch	K—Kt1!
37. Kt—K7 ch	K—B1
38. Kt—B5	Kt—Q4
39. P—KKt4	......

The Kt at KB5 has the effect
planned for him, he protects the KP,
attacks the KRP and makes K—
KB3 possible.

39. ...:...	Kt—B5 ch
40. K—B3	Kt—Q6

In order if R—R7 to protect the
RP by Kt—K4 ch and Kt—B2.

41. R—R8 ch!	K—B2
42. R—KR8	Kt—B4
43. R—R7 ch	......

On revient toujours à sa première
amour!

43.	K—Kt1

For if K—B1 then 44. Kt ×P,
and White gets a mating attack,
or else the advance of his KtP
cannot be stopped.

44. R ×P	R ×R
45. Kt ×R ch	K—B1
46. Kt—B5	Kt ×P
47. P—R6	K—Kt1
48. P—Kt5	K—R2

49. K—Kt4	Kt—B4
50. K—R5	......

According to the motto, the line
will advance! See I. vi. §3.

50.	Kt—K3
51. P—Kt6 ch	K—Kt1
52. P—R7 ch	K—R1
53. K—R6	Resigns

In the following game we come to
the 'restricted advance' (of a Rook)
in an open file, in which the file does
not show up sporadically like
summer lightning, but throughout
dominates the field. The student
may learn from this game how
closely the 'elements' are allied to
the higher technique of the game.
A thorough knowledge of the
elements takes us more than half
the road to mastership.

11

Baden-Baden, 1925

White	Black
Sir George Thomas	Dr. Alekhine

1. P—K4	Kt—KB3
2. P—Q3	P—QB4
3. P—KB4	Kt—QB3
4. Kt—KB3	P—KKt3
5. B—K2	B—Kt2
6. QKt—Q2	P—Q4
7. 0—0	0—0
8. K—R1	P—QKt3
9. P ×P	Q ×P
10. Q—K1	B—Kt2
11. Kt—B4	......

The position of this Kt is all the
(poor) consolation White has for the
want of harmony in his position
(BK2). Black stands much the
better. White at his 5th move or
even earlier ought to have played
P—QB4.

11.	Kt—Q5

Outpost in the Q file.

12. Kt—K3	Q—K3
13. B—Q1	Kt—Q4

(See the remarks on this position in I. ii. §2.)

14. Kt×Kt(Q5)	P×Kt
15. Kt×Kt	Q×Kt
16. B—B3	Q—Q2
17. B×B	Q×B

White has eased his position by the exchanges, but the open QB file forces the next disorganising move. (See again I. ii. §2.)

18. P—QB4	P×P e.p.
19. P×P	QR—QB1
20. B—Kt2	KR—Q1
21. R—B3	B—B3
22. P—Q4	......

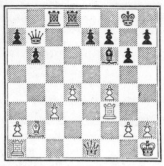

Position after White's 22nd move

We have now arrived at a well-known position in the QP opening only with the colours reversed. Compare the following, the opening of a consultation game, Nimzowitsch v. Professor Kudrjawzew and Dr. Landau, Dorpat, 1910. 1. P—Q4, P—Q4; 2. Kt—KB3, Kt—KB3; 3. P—QB4, P—K3; 4. Kt—QB3, P—QB4; 5. P×QP, KP×P; 6. B—KKt5, P×QP; 7. Kt×P, B—K2; 8. P—K3, 0—0; 9. B—K2, Kt—QB3; 10. Kt×Kt, KtP×Kt; and now with colours reversed we have the same pawn configuration as in the game Thomas—Alekhine. The game went on: 11. 0—0, B—K3; 12. R—QB1, R—QKt1; 13. Q—B2, B—Q2; 14. KR—Q1. The well-known theme of the isolated passed pawn now comes up for discussion. 14. ..... Kt—K1; 15. B×B, Q×B; 16. Kt—R4, Kt—B3 17. Kt—B5, R—Kt3; 18. R—Q4!, R(B)—QKt1; 19. P—QKt3, B—K1; 20. B—Q3, P—KR3; 21. Q—B3, B—Q2; 22. R—QR4, with marked advantage in position

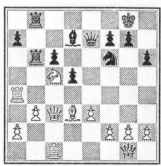

Position after White's 23rd move in the game Nimzowitsch—the Allies

We will now revert to the Thomas—Alekhine game

22.	Q—Q4
23. Q—K3	Q—QKt4
24. Q—Q2	R—Q4
25. P—KR3	P—K3
26. R—K1	Q—R5
27. R—R1	P—QKt4
28. Q—Q1	R—B5

The restricted advance, or else the QB file used as a jumping off place for the QR file. See I. ii. §5. Observe the similarity of the manœuvre in this game and the consultation game quoted above.

29. Q—Kt3	R—Q3
30. K—R2	R—R3

The Q file is also used as a jumping off place!

31. R(B)—B1	B—K2
32. K—R1	R(B)—B3

Very fine! The regrouping Q—QB5, R—QR5 and R—QR3 is planned.

33. R(B)—K1	B—R5
34. R—KB1	......

White dare not weaken his own base by say R—K5; e.g., 34. R—K5?, Q×Q; 35. P×Q, R×R; 36. B×R, R—R3; 37. B—Kt2, R—R7 and wins.

34. ......   Q—B5!
35. Q×Q   R×Q

The exchange is grist to Black's mill, for now White's QRP is become very weak. The student should notice that the exchange is the direct, almost automatic consequence of the quiet seizing of strategically important points. The beginner seeks to bring about an exchange in other ways; he pursues the piece, which tempts him, with offers to elope (aliter exchange), only to have them refused. The master occupies the strong points and the exchange which seems desirable to him falls like ripe fruit into his lap. See I. v.

36. P—QR3   B—K2
37. R(B)—QKt1   B—Q3
38. P—KKt3   K—B1
39. K—Kt2   K—K2

Bringing the K to the centre, see I. vi. §1.

40. K—B2   K—Q2
41. K—K2   K—B3
42. R—R2   R(B)—QR5
43. R(Kt)—QR1   K—Q4

Centralization is now complete.
44. K—Q3   R(R3)—R4
45. B—B1   P—QR3
46. B—Kt2   P—KR4

A new attack and yet the logical consequence of the play on the extreme Queen's wing; for the White R's are chained to this QRP, and even if we assumed the Black R's to suffer from a like immobility, which is not the case since they can be brought into play via their QB5 against the QBP, yet there remains to Black an indubitable advantage in the more enterprising position of his K. And that this advantage should weigh in the balance at all, we have once more

only to thank the fact that as a consequence of Black's diversion the White R's have lost their wind; for if they were mobile, White's advantage derived from his K's position would be illusory. Thus the attack on the extreme flank has not immaterially increased the importance of the mobility of Black's King. The strategic contact between the two seemingly separated theatres of war is now made clear. And now on the King's wing Black's P—KR4 is intended to provoke P—KR4, so that, with White's PKKt3 exposed P—K4 may exercise its full effect.

A very instructive case which the student is recommended to study.

47. P—KR4   P—KB3
48. B—B1   P—K4

The break through which sets the seal on White's downfall.

49. BP×P   P×P
50. B—Kt2   P×P
51. P×P   P—QKt5!

Obvious though this move be, it must yet delight every connoisseur, that the sole purpose of the break through was to get the disturbing White QBP out of the way.

52. P×P   R×R
53. P×R   R×B
54. Resigns

The 'restricted advance' has in this game been carried out with great virtuosity.

12

San Sebastian, 1912

White	Black
P. S. LEONHARDT	NIMZOWITSCH

1. P—K4   P—K4
2. Kt—KB3   P—Q3
3. P—Q4   Kt—KB3
4. Kt—QB3   P×P

Surrender of the centre. Black will seek to keep White's KP under restraint. (Cf. game No. 2.)

5. Kt×P	B—K2
6. B—K2	O—O
7. O—O	Kt—QB3
8. Kt×Kt	P×Kt

This exchange creates advantages for both sides. Black gets a more compact pawn formation in the centre, safeguards for instance his Q4 against its possible occupation as an advanced post by a White Kt; but the QRP is isolated, and, moreover, as in the game, his QB4 may become a weak point.

9. P—QKt3	P—Q4

Very playable here would also have been R—K1 and B—B1, directed against White's KP to keep it in restraint.

10. P—K5	Kt—K1
11. P—KB4	P—KB4

Otherwise P—KB5 with a strong attack.

12. B—K3	P—KKt3

White's KP is to be blocked; it is, however, by no means indifferent whether this blockade is effected by Kt or B. The latter would be inelastic, and its range of action small, at best as far as KKt5 (should White play P—KKt4 to attack the opposing pawn minority), while it would also be more attackable, e.g., by a Kt at QB5; which could not be driven off. On the other hand a Kt at K3 would be not only an excellent, because unassailable, blockader, but also a very aggressive one, among other things preparing the way for P—KKt4. It is often of the greatest importance to find the right blockading piece.

13. Kt—QR4!	Kt—Kt2
14. Q—Q2	Q—Q2

In order to follow with R—Q1 as soon as possible.

15. Q—R5	......

Combines continued pressure on Black's QB4 (cf. note to Black's 8th move) with play against the weak, isolated QRP.

15.	Kt—K3
16. QR—Q1	R—Q1
17. Kt—B5?	......

A positional mistake. White should seek to keep the Kt as a potential blockader, or at any rate only exchange him for a Kt. The situation is this: the two Kt's are here the chief actors (because the most effective in blockade) and whoever gives up his proud horseman for a prelate gets in this case the worst of the bargain. 17. B—B5 was the right move.

17.	B×Kt
18. B×B	B—Kt2
19. R—B3	K—B2
20. R—R3	K—Kt2
21. R—KB1	R—K1
22. R(R3)—KB3	QR—Q1

Since Q×RP is forbidden on account of R—QR1, Q×B, R(K)—QKt1. There is little that White can undertake.

23. R—Q1	P—QR3
24. P—QKt4	K—R1
25. Q—R3	R—KKt1
26. Q—QB3	R—Kt2
27. K—R1	R(Q)—KKt1

Black plans P—KKt4, and in this the blockading Kt at K3 would render priceless service. A comparison between the two blockading pieces, the Black Kt at his K3 and the White B at QB5, is here all in favour of the Kt. The B, it is true, does his work as a blockader pure and simple well enough, but otherwise his effective range of action is very small.

28. B—K3	P—QB4!

The advance which we have so often discussed! The B's diagonal is opened by the pawn sacrifice. But it may be objected that the QBP is here neither a passed pawn nor a 'candidate'. True, and yet logically he must be filled with that ambition to expand, for otherwise White would not have kept him under a blockade for so long. But now he takes vengeance for the restraint he has had to suffer.

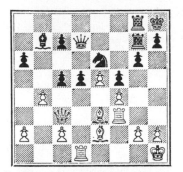

Position after Black's 28th move

The pawn's ambition to expand comes to fruition

29. R—KKt3 ......

Best, as given by Schlechter, would be 29. P×P, P—Q5; 30. R×P, Kt×R; 31. B×Kt, B×R; 32. B×B, with 2 B's and 2 P's for 2 R's.

29. ...... P—Q5
30. Q—R3 P—KKt4
31. B—QB4 P×BP

B—Q4 would have been good, if only to preserve the Kt.

32. B×Kt ......

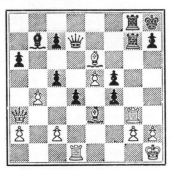

Position after White's 32nd move

How is Black to pursue his plan of breaking through?

32. ...... B×P ch!

P

Now the B runs amok! the death of the Kt makes him utterly reckless.

33. K—Kt1 ......

But behold he still lives! the saucy fellow; and indeed after 33. K×B (R×B? Q—B3), Q—B3 ch; 34. K—B1, P×R; 35. B×R, P×P; he would have been bloodily avenged.

33. ...... Q×B

He who would regard B×P as a bolt from a clear sky, shows thereby that he has not fully grasped the logic which lay in this sudden irruption of the B, who had been kept under restraint for such ages.

34. B×BP B—Kt2
35. P×P Q—Q4

and won. 36. P—B6, B×P; 37. K—B2, R×R; 38. P×R, Q—Kt7 ch, 39. K—K1, B—B6; 40. Q×P, Q—Kt8 ch. 41. Resigns.

13

An instructive example of the method of dealing with the supports of a blockader. In the end game they are usually driven away, in the middle game on the other hand —kept busy. See I. iv. §4.

Breslau, 1925

White   Black
NIMZOWITSCH VON GOTTSCHALL

1. Kt—KB3   P—K3
2. P—Q4   P—Q4
3. P—K3   Kt—KB3
4. P—QKt3   QKt—Q2

He should have played P—QB4 and Kt—QB3.

5. B—Q3   P—QB3
6. 0—0   B—Q3
7. B—Kt2   Q—B2

In order to play P—K4 and thus open up the game. To prevent this, White undertakes a counter attack.

8. P—QB4   P—QKt3

If now 8....P—K4, the continuation would be 9. P—B5, B—K2 (9....P—K5, 10. P×B, Q×P; 11. B—QR3, etc.); 10. P×KP, Kt—Kt5; 11. P—QKt4, QKt×KP; 12. Kt×Kt, Kt×Kt; 13. P—KB4, Kt×B; 14. Q×Kt, and White commands the diagonal QKt2 to KKt7.

9. Kt—QB3   B—QKt2
10. R—QB1   R—QB1
11. P×QP   KP×P
12. P—K4   ......

White opens all the lines.

12. ......   P×P
13. Kt×P   Kt×Kt
14. B×Kt   0—0
15. P—Q5   P—QB4

The two B's have now a clear line of fire to the enemy King's wing. Impressed by this the second player is inclined to underestimate the fact that the QP is now a passed one, in fact to overlook it altogether. And indeed what possible rôle could this most carefully blockaded passed pawn play? Why a reserve blockader is already stationed at Q2! But things turn out quite otherwise.

16. R—K1   Q—Q1
17. B—QKt1   ......

This attack leads to the instructive results that the blockading pieces, the BQ3 and KtQ2 are either cut off or killed off.

17. ......   R—K1
18. Q—Q3   ......

First R×R ch would have been more precise.

18. ......   Kt—B1

R×R ch would have been better.

19. R×R   Q×R
20. Kt—R4!   P—KB3
21. Kt—B5   R—Q1

Black is about to try to show up the weakness of White's QP, when

he is woken from his dream by the flash of a sacrifice.

22. B×P!   B×P ch!

In order not to lose a pawn Black must submit to this indirect exchange of his B. If 22....P×B then 23. Kt×B, R×B; 24. Q—KKt3 ch.

23. K×B   P×B

What a change! the BQ3 has disappeared and the reserve blockader, the KtQ2, will soon be landed at KKt3; the QP is therefore free!

24. Q—KKt3 ch   Kt—Kt3
25. P—KB4   ......

To allow R—K1; the passed pawn is indirectly protected.

25. ......   K—R1

Not B or R×P because of R—K1, and Kt—K7 ch, etc.

26. R—K1   ......

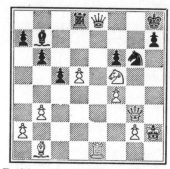

Position after White's 26th move

26. ......   Q—B1!

If 26....Q—Kt1, the passed pawn would have come into his own in a most interesting manner; namely as follows: 27. Kt—K7, Kt×Kt; 28. R×Kt (7th rank), Q×Q ch; 29. K×Q, R—KKt1 ch; 30. K—B2, R—Kt2. Apparently the 7th rank is now neutralized, but the passed pawn has something to say to that. 31. P—Q6, R×R; 32. P×R, B—B3; 33. B—K4, B—K1; 34. P—B5!, K—Kt2; 35.

B—Q5, and now the PK7 is un-assailable. 35. . . . . K—R3; 36. K—B3, K—Kt4; 37. K—K4, and Black is powerless against the threat B—Kt7, K—Q5, and B—B6, and the blockader must die.

27. P—Q6! **R—Q2**
Why not B—B1? Would not this have led to the winning of the passed pawn? The answer is no, for the continuation would be 28. Kt—K7 (By his P—Q6 White has provided him an outpost station at K7.), 28. . . . .Q—R3 ch (best); 29. K—Kt1, Kt ×P; and now 30. Kt ×B, R ×Kt; 31. P—Q7 and wins.

28. Q—QB3 . . . . . .
Threatening R—K8!, Q ×R, Q × P ch, K—Kt1; Kt—R6 mate.

Accordingly the 8th rank must be safeguarded by the retreat R—Q1. But in this case the 7th rank will be left without protection and White wins by R—K7. Note that the winning moves R—K7 or Kt—K7 (as in the last note), must be regarded as a direct consequence of the passed pawn's advance.

28. . . . . . . **R ×P**
A desperate expedient. If 28. . . . .R—KB2, then 29. P—Q7, R × P; 30. R—K8! would have been immediately decisive.

29. Kt ×R **Q ×Kt**
30. B ×Kt **P ×B**
31. R—K8 ch **K—Kt2**
32. Q—KKt3 **and White won**

32. . . . .B—B3; 33. R—K3, B—Q2; 34. P—B5!, Q ×Q ch; 35. K ×Q, B ×P; 36. R—K7 ch, K—R3; 37. R ×P, B—Kt8; 38. R—R6, P—QKt4; 39. P—R4, P × P; 40. P ×P, K—Kt4; 41. R—Kt6, B—K5; 42. P—R5, P—B4; 43. P—R6, P—QR5; 44. P—R7, P—B6; 45. R—Kt3, P—B5 ch; 46. K—B2, P—B7; 47. R—QB3, Resigns.

14

Riga, 1919

White | Black
NIMZOWITSCH | C. BEHTING

1. P—K4 **P—K4**
2. Kt—KB3 **P—KB4**
According to C. Behting's view, which I am inclined to share, this move is quite playable. At any rate I do not know a refutation of it.

3. Kt ×P **Q—B3**
4. P—Q4 **P—Q3**
5. Kt—B4 **P ×P**
Theory (the practice of the other Masters) now recommends 6. Kt—QB3, Q—KKt3; 7. P—KB3, but after 7. . . . .P ×P; 8. Q ×P, Kt—KB3; 9. B—Q3, Q—Kt5; 10. Q—K3 ch, B—K2; 11. 0—0, Kt—QB3; 12. P—Q5, Kt—QKt5; 13. R—B4, Q—Q2; 14. Kt—Kt6, P ×Kt; 15. R ×Kt the game is even.

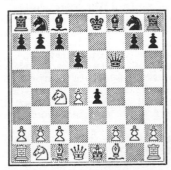

Position after Black's 5th move
Does the blockading move Kt—K3 appear justified?

6. Kt—K3! . . . . . .
Against this move speak (1) tradition which rather demands 6. Kt—QB3; (2) the principle of economic development, i.e., not to let one piece go a-wandering; (3) the apparently small threat effect of the blockader. And yet 6. Kt—K3, taken with the move next following, is in every respect a

master-move. And even if all the
rest of the world play here 6. Kt—
QB3, I yet hold my move Kt—K3
to be more correct, and this for
reasons based on the 'system'.

6. ......   P—QB3
7. B—B4!!   ......
The point. In order to be able
to castle Black must now play
P—Q4, but this move will hold out
another field for the Kt (after
B—Kt3 and P—QB4).

7. ......   P—Q4
8. B—Kt3   B—K3
Or 8. .... P—QKt4; 9. P—QR4,
P—Kt5; 10. P—QB4, etc.

9. P—QB4   Q—B2
10. Q—K2   Kt—KB3
11. 0—0   ......
Not Kt—QB3 because of B—
QKt5. White wants to bring the
maximum pressure to bear on
Black's PQ4. If we look at the
blockading KtK3 more closely, do
we find that he meets the require-
ments asked of a blockader? Yes,
for (1) he establishes a strong
blockade, hindering the approach of
enemy pieces (to, e.g., his KKt4);
(2) exercises threats from where he
is stationed; (3) is very elastic, as
we shall see later. In short, the
KtK3 is an ideal blockader.

11. ......   B—QKt5!
12. B—Q2   B×B
13. QKt×B   0—0
14. P—KB4   ......
Intending P—KB5 in order to
win the QP.

14. ......   P×QBP
15. Kt(Q2)×BP   Q—K2
16. P—B5   B—Q4
Black seeks to maintain the point
Q4.

17. Kt×B   P×Kt
18. Kt—K3   ......
Hardly has the KtK3 disappeared
than a new KtK3 stands in his

place. Against such 'elasticity' not
even Death can prevail!

18. ......   Q—Q2
19. Kt×P!   ......
The threat effect of the blockader
from his post culminates in this
decisive sacrifice.

19. ......   Kt×Kt
20. Q×P   R—Q1
21. P—B6!   ......
The point of the combination and
at the same time a further illustration of the pawn's lust to expand
(the KBP was a 'candidate').

21. ......   P×P
If 21. .... Kt—QB3, then 22.
P—B7 ch, K—R1; 23. B×Kt, Q×
B?; 24. P—B8 =Q ch, followed by
Q×Q. And if 22. .... K—B1, then
23. B×Kt, Q×B; 24. Q×RP,
and wins.

22. R—B5   K—R1
23. R×Kt   R—K1
If 23. .... Q—K1, then 24. B—
B2! wins a whole R.

24. R×Q   R×Q
25. R—Q8 ch   K—Kt2
26. R—Kt8 ch   K—R3
27. R—KB1   Resigns
And now a companion picture to
the above game.

15

Wilna, 1912

White   Black
NIMZOWITSCH   VON FREYMANN

1. P—K4   P—K3
2. P—Q4   P—Q4
3. P—K5   P—QB4
4. Kt—KB3   P×P
4. .... Q—Kt3 seems to be
better.

5. Kt×P   Kt—QB3
6. Kt×Kt   P×Kt

7. B—Q3	Q—B2
8. B—KB4	P—KKt4

Not quite sound but leading to interesting play. The resulting position is discussed under Diagram 166 in II. v, q.v.

9. B—Kt3	B—KKt2
10. Q—K2	Kt—K2
11. 0—0	P—KR4
12. P—KR3	Kt—B4
13. B—R2	......

13. B×Kt, P×B; 14. P—K6, would be obviously bad because of 14. .....P—B5; 15. P×P ch, K× P.

13.	P—Kt5

The pretty point of the attack started by 8. .....P—KKt4.

14. R—K1	......

The answer to 14. P×P, P×P; 15. Q×P, would have been 15. .....R×B; 16. K×R, B×P ch; followed by B×QKtP.

14.	K—B1
15. Kt—QB3	......

This Kt proposes to make his way to KB4 (after the Black KtB4 is exchanged off).

15.	Q—K2
16. B×Kt	P×B
17. Q—K3	R—R3
18. Kt—K2	P—QB4
19. Kt—B4!	......

This Kt is to be regarded as primarily the blockader of Black's PKB4 and its adherent mass of pawns; but in addition he acts as an 'anti-blockader' for his own aspiring PK5.

19.	P—Q5
20. Q—Q3	Q—Q2
21. Q—B4	Q—B3
22. P×P!	......

The necessary prelude to Kt—Q3. If at once 22. Kt—Q3 there would have followed 22. .....P×P; 23. Q×P ch, Q×Q; 24. Kt×Q, R—KKt3; 25. P—KKt3, and White stands badly.

22.	B—QR3
23. Q—Q5!!	Q×Q

Most interesting would have been 23. .....RP×P; the result would have been a triumphant march of the KP to K8. For instance, 23. .....RP×P; 24. P—K6 (with attack on the Q), 24. .....Q×Q; 25. P—K7 ch, K—K1; 26. Kt×Q, followed by check at QB7. (The 'unexpected advance of the unstopped pawn'.)

24. Kt×Q	B—B5

If 24. RP×P, then again P—K6, winning the exchange.

25. Kt—B6	RP×P
26. B—B4	R—Kt3

27. Kt—Q7 ch and won the QBP and after twenty further moves the game.

What interests in the above game is above all the rôle which the KtB4 has played. As a blockader he was strongly posted and excellently supported (by the BKR2). Again he had a crippling effect on Black's BKKt2 and RKR3, etc. Further, his 'threat effect' was considerable, particularly on the points Q5 and K6. (The mobility of White's KP affords a piquant antithesis to the immobility of Black's PKB4.) And lastly, his elasticity was striking, for he could composedly go on his travels, leaving the B to take his place.

The three following games show the connexion between the 'pin' and the 'centre'.

16

San Sebastian, 1911

White	Black
NIMZOWITSCH	P. S. LEONHARDT

1. P—K4	P—K4
2. Kt—KB3	Kt—QB3
3. Kt—QB3	Kt—KB3
4. B—Kt5	B—Kt5
5. 0—0	0—0

6. B × Kt   QP × B
7. P—Q3   ......

White has now a solid position, since the enemy Q ' file 'bites on granite' (the protected PQ3). This solidity, however, also finds expression in the fact that White's KP can never be troubled by an advance of Black's QP; in other words, the centre cannot be opened.

7. ......   B—KKt5
The pin.

8. P—KR3   B—R4
9. B—KKt4   ......
9. P—KKt4 would have been premature, because of 9. ..... Kt × KKtP; 10. P × Kt, B × P; followed by P—KB4.

9. ......   Q—Q3
10. B × Kt   Q × B
11. P—KKt4   ......

The 'question' is here indicated, since the B will be driven into a desert, which, because of the impossibility of P—Q4, can never be transformed into a 'flowering garden'. (See I. vii. §4a.) Observe how the KR and KKt P's slowly develop into storm troops.

11. ......   B—KKt3
12. K—Kt2   QR—Q1
13. Q—K2   B × Kt
else Kt—Q1—K3—B5 would have followed.

14. P × B   P—QB4
15. Kt—Q2   ......

White now intends to bring his Kt to KB5 via QB4 and K3; on the other hand he proposes to prevent the embarrassing move P—QB5 for as long as possible without the aid of P—QB4, since this move would leave the outpost position in the Q file (at his Q4) unguarded.

15. ......   Q—K2
16. Kt—B4   P—QKt3
17. Kt—K3   P—KB3

In order at length to free the B; this move, however, invites P—KKt5 when an opportune moment comes.

18. R—KKt1   Q—Q2
19. K—R2   K—R1
20. R—Kt3   Q—Kt4
21. Q—K1   Q—R5
22. Q—QB1   R—Q2
23. P—KR4   B—B2
24. P—QB4   ......

Black has succeeded in provoking P — QB4; in the meantime, however, White has got the K's wing beautifully arranged to suit himself.

24. ......   B—K3
25. Q—Kt2   P—QR4
26. QR—KKt1   Q—B3
27. R(Kt1)—Kt2!!   ......

White quietly makes his last preparations for a worthy reception of the enemy Q at her Q5, for which point she is striving. Observe how the first player has succeeded in combining the defence of the centre with his plans for a K side attack.

27. ......   Q—Q3
28. Q—QB1   Q—Q5?
29. Kt—Q5!   ......

Wins the Q. This 'trap' was everywhere applauded. That it was subordinate to the strategic ends which I had set myself in this game was taken into consideration by no one. The aim of my strategy was, however, to prevent a break through or any manœuvring in the centre and to make possible the ultimate advance P—KKt5 with the attack. There followed 29. .... R × Kt; 30. P—QB3, Q × QP; 31. KP × R (31. BP × R was more precise), 31. .... Q × PB4; 32. P × B, Q × KP; 33. Q—B2, P—QB5; 34. Q—KB5, Q × Q; 35. P × Q and White won.

The student may see from the laborious and tedious defence which White adopted (see moves 21, 22,

25, 28) that he fully recognized the fact that the disposition of his K sides Ps (PKR3, PKt4) demanded a closed centre.

This game elucidates the problem of the 'Question' in an instructive manner.

17

Played by correspondence in 1913.

White	Black
NIMZOWITSCH	DR. FLUSS
1. P—K4	P—K4
2. Kt—KB3	Kt—QB3
3. Kt—QB3	Kt—KB3
4. B—B4	B—B4
5. P—Q3	P—Q3
6. B—KKt5	P—KR3
7. B—R4	......

Of course 7. B—K3 is also playable.

| 7. ...... | P—KKt4 |

Here B—K3 was probably better. Cf. I. vii. §4(d), p. 89, the game Nimzowitsch—Capablanca.

8. B—KKt3	B—KKt5
9. P—KR4	Kt—KR4
10. P×P	......

As already remarked (I. vii. p. 87) White ought here to have given more attention to the problem of the centre. For instance 10. Kt—Q5, Kt—Q5; 11. P—B3 and White's game for choice.

| 10. ...... | Kt—Q5 |

And here Black by 10. .....Kt× B; 11. P×Kt, Kt—Q5; could utilize the centre which White has neglected. As we have already said (I. vii. §3a under Diagram 89) 12. Kt—Q5 would not be sufficient, since Black has the Queen sacrifice at his disposal (namely 12. .....B× Kt; 13. P×B, Q×P; 14. P— KKt4, P—QB3; 15. R—R5, P×

Kt, etc.), nor would the sacrificial combination 12. B×P ch, K×B; 13. Kt×P ch, P×Kt; 14. Q×B be enough, for after 14. .....Q×P; 15. Q—Q7 ch, K—Kt3; Black would be safe. Hence 10. P×P instead of the central thrust 10. Kt—Q5, which we indicated, would seem to be a decisive mistake, of which Black could take advantage with 10. .....Kt×B, followed by 11. .....Kt—Q5.

| 11. B×KP! | ...... |

A disconcerting evasion. White gives up his B, but leaves Black with a Kt in the air and a K in much the same state.

| 11. ...... | B×Kt |

If immediate P×B then 12. B×P ch, K×B; 13. Kt×P ch, K—Kt1; 14. Q×B, and wins.

| 12. P×B | P×B |
| 13. R×Kt | R—KKt1 |

On the surface White's position is by no means an enviable one, for the KtQ5 exerts pressure and the KKtP seems lost.

| 14. P—KB4 | ...... |

The saving move.

| 14. ...... | P×BP |
| 15. Q—Kt4 | |

The point. White is not afraid of Black's attack (Kt×P ch, etc.) which would be a mere flash in the pan.

15.	Kt×P ch
16. K—Q2	Kt×R
17. B×P ch!	Resigns

for if 17. .....K×B, then 18. Q— B5 ch, K—K1; 19. Q—K6, K— B1; 20. P—Kt6, and wins; or 19. .....Q—K2; 20. Q×R ch, Q— B1; 21. Q—R7, Q—K2; 22. P— Kt6, Q×Q; 23. P×Q, B—Q5; 24. Kt—Kt5; or 22. .....B—Q5; 23. Kt—Kt5, Q—Kt5 ch; 24. K—Q1 and wins.

18

Introduces a whole assortment of pins, poisonous and harmless ones following in quick succession.

Marienbad, 1925

White	Black
RUBINSTEIN	NIMZOWITSCH

1. P—Q4	Kt—KB3
2. Kt—KB3	P—QKt3
3. P—KKt3	P—QB4
4. B—Kt2	B—Kt2
5. P×P	P×P
6. P—QB4	......

The line of play chosen by White is certainly not to be blamed. He holds the Q file with the outpost station belonging to it at Q5, whereas Black's majority in the centre (the QB, Q, and K pawns against the QB and K pawns) gives evidence of but slight mobility.

6.	P—KKt3
7. P—QKt3	B—Kt2
8. B—Kt2	0—0
9. 0—0	......

Each side castles now with a clear conscience, for not even the most hyper-modern pair of masters can produce more than four bishops developed 'askew'!

9.	Kt—QB3

A normal move which, however, has a deeper meaning. The Kt is better placed at QB3 than at QKt3 (Kt—Q2—Kt3), for White is clearly planning the configuration KtQB3, QQB2, PK4. Black therefore relies on the counter configuration KtQB3, PQ3, PQR4, followed by Kt—Q5 and (when opportunity comes) P—QR5, thus sheltering his QP behind the KtQ5.

10. Kt—QB3	P—QR4
11. Q—Q2	P—Q3
12. Kt—K1	......

The start of a tiring journey: Kt — K1 — B2 — K3 — Q5. More natural would seem to be 12. Kt—Q5. For instance, 12. Kt—Q5, Kt× Kt; 13. B×B, K×B; 14. P×Kt.

12.	Q—Q2
13. Kt—B2	Kt—QKt5!
14. Kt—K3	B×B
15. K×B	......

To retake with the Kt would mean straying off the road to the goal of the journey (Q5).

15.	Q—QKt2 ch
16. P—KB3	......

If 16. K—Kt1, then 16...... Kt— K5; 17. Kt×Kt, Q×Kt; and P—QR5 becomes an actual menace.

16.	B—R3

A pin of the harmless order, since obviously this last move implies a serious weakening of his own (Black's) King's wing.

17. QKt—Q1	......

Now the threat is B×Kt, P×B Q×P.

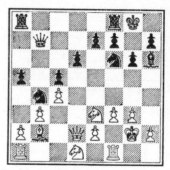

Position after White's 17th move

17.	P—QR5

See the note to 9..... Kt—QB3.

18. P×P	KR—K1!!

This purely defensive move (against the aforesaid threat B×Kt, etc.) is the more surprising, since, after the energetic thrust at move 17, which had been so eagerly looked forward to for so long, anything but a defensive move was to be expected. This amalgamation of attack and defence stamps the combination as a truly original one.

19. B×Kt	P×B
20. K—B2	......

Now White plans to break the pin by P—KB4, after which he would at last be in a position to take possession of the point Q5 for good and all.

20. ......   P—KB4!!
Revealing Black's plan. Against the double threat of 21. .....P—B5; 22. P ×P, B ×P, with an enduring pin on the one hand, and 21. ..... B—Kt2, followed by B—Q5 with an equally chronic pin on the other, White is defenceless.

21. Q ×P   B—Kt2!
22. R—QKt1   B—Q5
Threatening Kt—Q6 ch.

23. K—Kt2   ......
The poor Knights! At the 17th move they had to break their journey, and now they actually both have to die without reaching their journey's end.

In reply to 23. R—Kt3, Black, with 23. .....R—K3; 24. Q—B4, Q—K2 (threatening Kt—B7); 25. K—Kt2, QR—K1, would have pushed forward the siege in the most energetic way.

23. ......   B ×Kt
24. Kt ×B   R ×Kt
25. Q ×QBP   ......
Now it is White's turn to pin.

25. ......   R ×P ch
26. R—B2   R ×R ch
27. Q ×R   ......
Forced, for 27. K ×R, Kt—Q6 ch, followed by Kt ×Q, thus protecting his own Q at QKt2, would lose at once.

27. ......   R ×P!
The 'immediate unpinning' by Q—K2, is avoided, for White can get no profit out of the pin.

28. P—QR3   ......
If 28. Q—QKt2, then 28. .... Q—B1!; for this is the only feasible retreat for the piece behind the pinned one. Q—B2 would be bad

because of 29. R—K1, just as Q—B3 would be because of 29. R—Q1. That 28. .....R ×P?? would be a gross mistake (because of Q ×R, Kt ×Q, R ×Q) is obvious.

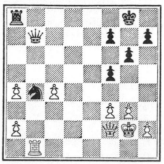

Position after White's 27th move

28. ......   R ×P
29. Q—K2   R—R1
Now he goes back home, tired but happy.

30. P—B5   Q—R3
The unpinning.

31. Q ×Q   Kt ×Q
32. R—QR1   ......
A last pin.

32. ......   Kt—B2
A last unpinning.

33. R ×R ch   Kt ×R
And White resigned on the 38th move.

There follow six games illustrating the Pawn-Chain.

19

Played in 1888

Illustrates the fight against a pawn-chain (siege).

White	Black
Louis Paulsen	Dr. Tarrasch
1. P—K4	P—K3
2. P—Q4	P—Q4

3. P—K5   P—QB4
4. P—QB3   Kt—QB3
5. Kt—KB3   Q—Kt3
6. B—Q3   ......

More natural would have been
B—K2, for the PQ4 is the 'base,'
and as such should be protected as
thoroughly as possible, and B—K2
'protects' more thoroughly than
B—Q3.

6. ......   P×P
7. P×P   B—Q2
8. B—K2   KKt—K2
9. P—QKt3   Kt—B4
10. B—Kt2   B—Kt5 ch
11. K—B1   ......

Forced (see I. ix, §5a, Diagram
110a, p. 107).

11. ......   B—K2

In order to keep up the pressure
on the QP (12. P—KKt4, Kt—R5);
but as shown in loc. cit., Diagram
110b (q.v.) Black should have
played to take direct advantage of
White's spoiled King's wing, by
11. ....0—0!, etc.

12. P—KKt3   P—QR4?

In order to exploit the new 'weakness' White's PQKt3. The only
pity is that this point is no weakness; he should have gone for the
weak King's position.

13. P—QR4   R—QB1
14. B—QKt5   ......

The point QKt5 now becomes a
good pivot for White's pieces.

14. ......   Kt—Kt5
15. B×B ch?   ......

Quite wrong. With 15. Kt—QB3
(see the next game) White could
have overcome all difficulties. For
instance:— 15. Kt—QB3, B×B; 16.
Kt×B, Kt—B7; 17. R—QB1, Kt
—K6 ch; 18. P×Kt, Kt×P ch;
19. K—K2, Kt×Q; 20. R×R ch,
K—Q2, 21. R×R, Kt×B; 22.
R—QB1 and wins.

15. ......   K×B
16. Kt—QB3   Kt—QB3

17. Kt—QKt5   Kt—R2
18. Kt×Kt?   ......

Never in this life ought White to
have relinquished his QKt5; 18.
Q—Q3, Kt×Kt; 19. P×Kt would
have after all sufficed. We can see
what harm Black's PQR4 has done
him.

18. ......   Q×Kt
19. Q—Q3   Q—R3!

Now we shall see how a weakened
'base' becomes a weakness in the
end game.

20. Q×Q   P×Q
21. K—Kt2   R—B7
22. B—B1   R—QKt1
23. R—QKt1   R—B6
24. B—Q2   R(B)×P
25. R×R   R×R
26. B×P   ......

Now White is happily rid of his
weakness at QKt3 (in an open file!),
but his Q4 and QR4 are hard to
defend.

Position after White's 26th move

26. ......   R—Kt7

Not R—R6 because of R—QB1,
but now the answer to R—QB1
would be Kt—K6 ch, followed by
Kt—B5.

27. B—Q2   B—Kt5
28. B—B4   P—KR3

There's no harm in this; Black's
position can stand this little weakening (the PKR3 is now a possible
objective).

29. P—Kt4   Kt—K2
30. R—QR1   Kt—QB3
31. B—B1   R—B7.
32. B—R3   R—B5
B × B would have been simpler.

33. B—Kt2   B—B6
34. B × B   R × B
35. R—QKt1   K—B2
36. P—Kt5   R—B5
At length!

37. P × P   P × P
38. P—R5   R—R5
39. K—Kt3   ......
A last despairing attempt to continue the attack begun by P—Kt5.

39. ......   R × RP
And Black won 40. K—Kt4,
R—R6; 41. R—Q1, R—Kt6; 42.
P—KR4, Kt—K2; 43. Kt—K1,
Kt—B4; 44. Kt—Q3, P—QR4;
45. Kt—B5, R—QB6; 46. R—
QKt1, Kt × QP; 47. Kt—R6 ch,
K—Q1; 48. R—Kt8 ch, R—B1;
49. R—Kt7, K—K1; 50. Kt—
B7 ch, K—B1; 51. Kt—Kt5, Kt ×
Kt; 52. R × Kt, R—QR1, etc.
We recommend the student to study
this well played ending by Dr.
Tarrasch.

20

San Sebastian, 1912

White   Black
NIMZOWITSCH DR. TARRASCH

The first 14 moves (with transposition) are as in Game No. 19.

15. Kt—QB3!   Kt—QR3
For 15.....B × B; 16. Kt × B,
Kt—B7, see note to move 15 in
the last game.

16. K—Kt2   Kt—R2
17. B—K2   B—Kt5
18. Kt—R2   Kt—QR3
19. B—Q3   Kt—K2
20. R—QB1   Kt—B3

21. Kt × B   Kt(R3) × Kt
22. B—Kt1   ......
White has now overcome the difficulties of development, the base (Q4) is thoroughly protected; and so the game can now take another turning. White opens an attack against the Black King's wing which is cramped by the PK5.

22. ......   P—KR3
23. P—KKt4   ......
To make castling appear unhealthy; but R—B3—K3 was also good, perhaps even better.

23. ......   Kt—K2
24. R × R ch   B × R
25. Kt—K1   R—B1
26. Kt—Q3   P—KB3
27. Kt × Kt   Q × Kt
28. P × P   R × P

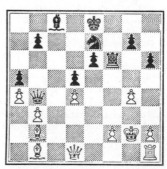

Position after Black's 28th move

29. B—B1   ......
The courage required deliberately to let oneself be kept under pressure for hours, simply for the sake of a remote chance of attack, now has its reward. White gets a direct attack. Note the Bishop which has been roused to activity.

29. ......   Kt—B3
30. P—Kt5   P × P
31. B × P   R—B1
32. B—B3   Q—K2
33. Q—Kt4   Q—B3
34. R—KKt1   R—KR1
35. K—R1   R—R5
36. Q—Kt3   R × QP

Despair! B—Kt5 was threatened
as also Q × P.

37. B × R	Kt × B
38. Q × P	Q—B6 ch
39. Q—Kt2	Q × Q ch
40 R × Q	Kt × P
41. P—KR4	Resigns.

Burn remarks on this game: 'An
excellent game on the part of Herr
Nimzowitsch, well illustrating his
strategic skill. Dr. Tarrasch, himself one of the greatest masters of
strategy, is completely outplayed.'
Flattering as this praise is I must,
nevertheless, remark that it is probably not so very difficult to manœuvre well if one has a complete
system to fall back upon. P—K5,
as I even then knew, seriously
cramps Black's King's wing, and if
White succeed in holding his Q4
without any counter-balancing disadvantage elsewhere, a moment
must sometime come when fortune
will smile on him, in the form, that
is, of an attack with his pieces on
the Black King in his cramped
position, or else a vigorous onslaught on the chain by P—KB4—
B5 × KP, etc. To-day all this rings
plausible; at the time this game was
played it seemed nothing short of
revolutionary.

21

The following game illustrates
my idea of the two theatres of war
in a particularly striking manner.

Breslau, 1925

White	Black
PROF. BECKER	NIMZOWITSCH
1. P—K4	P—K3
2. P—Q4	P—Q4
3. Kt—QB3	Kt—QB3

The 'odds-giving style' to use
Dr. Lasker's expression. Lasker
means by this that one chooses a
variation which one considers in-
ferior, with the idea of setting the

opponent a difficult problem to
solve. Lasker plays by preference
—and with inimitable virtuosity—
this style. It is this that might
make people believe that the heel
of Achilles lay for Lasker in his
treatment of the opening. But
such a judgment rests on an entire
misconception.

The move 3.....Kt—QB3 was
introduced by Alapin. It, however,
obstructs the QBP, and therefore
in the event of P—K5 there is a very
dark side to Alapin's innovation.

4. Kt—KB3	B—QKt5
5. P—K5	B × Kt ch
6. P × B	Kt—R4
7. P—QR4	......

Not very intelligible. Better was
7. Kt—Q2, Kt—K2; 8. Q—Kt4,
Black would then have had laboriously to defend himself by 8.....
Kt—KB4; 9. B—Q3, R—KKt1;
10. Q—R3, P—KR3

| 7. ...... | Kt—K2 |
| 8. B—Q3 | P—QKt3 |

Preparing to attack the White
Base (Q4) by P—QB4.

| 9. Kt—Q2! | P—QB4 |
| 10. Q—Kt4 | ...... |

How is Black to defend his
KKtP?

| 10. ...... | P—B5 |

The answer is not at all, for all
direct defences would here be compromising.

| 11. B—K2 | ...... |

If Q × KtP then R—Kt1 and
P × B.

| 11. ...... | Kt—B4 |

The KKtP is protected, but the
pressure on White's Q4 is removed
and White now again gets a free
hand to make play on the right
wing.

| 12. Kt—B3 | P—KR3 |

In order to be able to maintain
the KtB4 at his good post. The

threat was B—Kt5, Q moves, Kt—R4. Lasker prefers, and rightly, the elastic defence 12. .... Kt—QB3 and if 13. B—Kt5, then 13. ....P—KB3. An interesting possibility would be 12. ....Kt—QB3; 13. P—QR5!?, Kt×RP; 14. B—Kt5, P—KB3; 15. P×P, P×P; 16. B—R4, for now 16. .... Kt×B would fail against 17. Q—Kt7!; on the other hand 16. ..... Q—K2 would seem to consolidate the position sufficiently.

13. Q—R3 ......

Diagram after White's 13th move

How can Black counter the following elegant threat to break through? i.e., the threat 14. P—KKt4, Kt—K2; 15. P—Kt5, P—R4; 16. P—Kt6, Kt×P; 17. Kt—Kt5, followed by R—KKt1.

13. ...... K—Q2
My King likes going for walks.

14. P—KKt4 Kt—K2
15. Kt—Q2 ......
Threatening Q—B3 followed by Q×BP or Kt×P!

15. ...... Q—K1
The Q takes possession of the throne, which the K has vacated! Moreover, she has her eye on the QRP for which she seems to have a fancy.

16. P—KB4
The scene shifts! The old theatre of war vanishes as in a flash, and

new plans of attack appear. White intends to attack the base of the chain by P—KB5.

16. ...... K—B2
The K proceeds on his walk.

17. B—QR3 B—Q2
18. Q—KB3 P—KR4!
White's King's wing provides him with a terrible instrument of attack. To blunt this was the object of Black's last move. 18. ....B—B3, to counter the other threat (Kt×P) would, however, not have sufficed. E.g., 18. ....B—B3; 19. P—B5, followed by P—B6, and the wedge would have been unendurable.

19. Kt×P! ......
If 19. P×P then Kt—B4, and the King's wing, which had been all ready to march to the attack, is crippled. But if 19. P—KR3, then 19. ....P×P; 20. P×P, R×R ch; 21. Q×R, Q—KR1, and White finds all his attention occupied.

19. ...... Kt×Kt
20. B×Kt P×P
Naturally not P×B?? because of B—Q6 ch, and Q×R.

21. Q—Kt2 Kt—B4
22. B—Q3

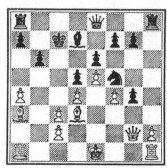

Position after White's 22nd move

22. ...... B×P!!
A lunch under dangerous conditions!

23 B ×Kt   P ×B
24. Q ×QP   . . . . . .
24. P—QB4 would also have been
difficult to parry. The defence
would be found in 24. . . . . Q—B3;
25. Q ×QP (not P ×P because of
Q—B6 ch); 25. . . . . Q ×Q!; 26.
P ×Q, B—Kt4!!; for then the
establishment of the B at Q4 (via
B5) could not have been prevented.

24. . . . . . .   B—B3
Black's King's position is threatened on all sides, but the situation is
not hopeless.

25. Q—Q6 ch   K—B1
Having regard to the planned
combination; but 25. . . . . K—Kt2;
26. P—Q5, B—Kt4 was also possible.

26. P—Q5   R—KR3
27. P—K6   . . . . . .

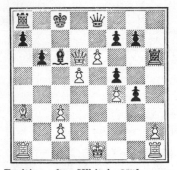

Position after White's 27th move

27. . . . . . .   B ×P!
This was afterwards pronounced
the 'only move.' Black had, however, another one, namely 27. . . . .
R ×P ch; 28. P ×R, B ×R; 29.
0—0—0, B—B6! (not B—K5 because of P—K7 and then Q—K5
and the White Q has now new
squares for decisive operations);
30. P ×P, Q ×P; 31. Q—Q8 ch,
K—Kt2; 32. R—Q7 ch, K—R3,
and Black is safe.

28. Q ×B   Q ×P ch
29. Q ×Q ch   R ×Q ch

White now has a piece for two
pawns, but his own pawns are weak.

30. K—Q2   K—Kt2
31. QR—K1   R—KR1
32. R ×R!   P ×R
33. R—K1!   R ×P ch
34. K—Q3   P—Kt6
Anything but a passive Rook
position (RR3?).

35. R—KKt1   . . . . . .
After 35. R ×P, P—KKt4!; 36.
P ×P, P—Kt7; White's PKKt5
would prove an obstruction.

35. . . . . . .   R—R6
Much better than P—Kt7 for, as
will shortly appear, it is important
to have a clear road to QB7.

36. K—Q4   K—B3
37. R—Kt2   P—QR4
38. P—B4   R—R7!
39. R ×P   R ×P
Cf. the last note.

40. R ×P   R—K7
41. B—B1   R—K5 ch
42. K—Q3   P—Kt4
43. P ×P ch   K ×P
44. B—K3   K—B3
45. R—KB7   P—R5
46. R—B8   P—R6
47. R—QR8   P—K4
48. R—R6 ch   K—Kt4
49. R—Kt6 ch
Prof. Becker is absolutely bent
on winning, and so it comes about
that in the end he loses. The game
continued 49. . . . . K—R4; 50. R—
KB6, P—R7; 51. B—Q2 ch, K—
Kt4; 52. B—B3, R—Q5 ch. After
six hours of hard fighting to get
such a problem check is hardly
pleasurable! 53. K—K2? (Right
was 53. K—B2, R—B5; 54. K—
Kt2, R ×B; 55. R ×P), 53. . . . .
R ×P; 54. R—B8, K—B5; 55.
B—R1, R—K5 ch; 56. K—Q2,
P—B5. Now White may be said
to be lost. 57. R—QB8 ch, K—
Q4; 58. R—Q8 ch, K—K3; 59.
R—K8 ch, K—B4; 60. R—KKt8,
P—B6; 61. Resigns.

The following game shows how an advance on the wrong wing should be punished.

22

Marienbad, 1925

White	Black
OPOCENSKY	NIMZOWITSCH

1.	P—Q4	Kt—KB3
2.	P—QB4	P—K3
3.	Kt—QB3	B—Kt5
4.	Q—B2	P—QKt3
5.	P—K4	B—Kt2

The expansive power of White's centre pawns is less than might at first sight appear.

6.	B—Q3	Kt—QB3
7.	Kt—KB3	B—K2!

By this unexpected retreat, which threatens Kt—QKt5, Black manages to muzzle White's mass of pawns in the centre while still keeping his valuable KB.

8.	P—QR3	P—Q3
9.	0—0	P—K4
10.	P—Q5	......

The muzzling.

10.	......	Kt—QKt1
11.	P—QKt4	QKt—Q2

Position after Black's 11th move

12. B—Kt2   ......
The pawn-chain PK4, PQ5; PK4, PQ3; called for the play P—QB5, of course after due preparation. For of the two theatres of war resulting from P—Q5 (see our remarks in I. ix. §1) only one is available, namely attack on Black's base, the PQ3. The other theoretically possible plan, i.e., an advance with pieces against the wing cramped by P—Q5, must be regarded as nipped in the bud by the presence of an obstruction at QB4.

The only plan of campaign feasible here (P—QB5) could, however, have been prepared for by 12. P—KR3, followed by 13. B—K3. For instance 12. P—KR3, P—KR3! (the best chance); 13. B—K3, P—KKt4; 14. Kt—KR2. Black will try to attack White's King's wing, but White's attack (Kt—QR4, P—QB4) is quickly put in motion, while his castled position is defendable. Hence 12. P—KR3, and 13. B—K3 was the right continuation.

12. ......   0—0
13. Kt—K2   ......
White's pieces desert the Queen's wing in order to demonstrate on the other. By this movement, however, the effect of his own centre is weakened. For with the Kt still at QB3, P—QB3 could be answered by P×P, while this Kt, too, casts a threatening eye on the point Q5 as an outpost station. If, however, the KtQB3 is gone on a journey, the thrust P—QB3 gains in effect. True for the moment this thrust is not a present threat, for on the Queen's wing Black is the weaker; however in the end he will come to it.

The way in which the theatre disdained by White is made a base of operations by his opponent makes the game of fundamental interest to the student.

13. ......   Kt—KR4
14. Q—Q2   ......
The answer to P—KKt4 would have been KKt—B3. Black wants to be attacked on the King's side,

since he regards that theatre as
unavailable. See note to move 12.

14.	P—KKt3
15. P—KKt4	Kt—Kt2
16. Kt—Kt3	P—QB3!

What sense can there be in this
move? If in the end P×QP is
played, then the answer BP×P
would attain nothing other than
the exposure of his own base Q3.
Black then in this case would have
worked for his opponent, for (let
us suppose Black's P still at QB2)
the strategic advance indicated for
White, namely P — QB5 × QP,
would after P×P, lead to exactly
the same pawn configuration, and
that the one which is the object of
White's efforts!

This calculation contains, however, two logical errors. Firstly
White in advancing P—QB5 will
certainly not content himself with
P×QP; this is only one threat.
The insertion of a wedge (in other
words the transference of the attack)
by P—QB6 would be by long odds
the sharper threat. Secondly, White
by B—QKt2, Kt—K2—KKt3, etc.,
has been untrue to his Queen's
wing; the just punishment will lie
in Black's becoming strong there!

17. Q—R6	R—QB1
18. QR—QB1	......

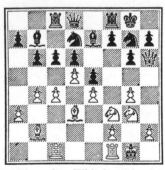

Position after White's 18th move

18.	P—QR3!!

A very difficult move. The
answer to 18.....P×P could be
19. KP×P, and Black, it is true,
would get by 19.....P—KB4; 20.
KtP×P, P×P, two powerful
pawns; but after 21. K—R1, and
22. R—KKt1, Black would stand
badly; the mobility of his KP and
KBP would in fact prove to be
illusory, whereas White's King's
side attack would be a very real
one. Black intends to play P×
QP at a moment when KP×P is not
feasible.

19. KR—Q1	R—B2
20. P—KR4?	P×P
21. BP×P	......

Since P—KR4 has still further
weakened White's position (the
point KKt4), 20.....P×P seems to
be in place. The answer to 21.
KP×P would have been Kt—KB3
as in the game; moreover, the threat
to break through by P—QKt4 would
be in the air.

21.	R×R
22. R×R	Kt—KB3
23. Kt—R2	K—R1

The White Q goes in danger of
her life. For instance 24. P—B4?,
Kt—Kt1; If White had played
23. Kt—Kt5 then 23.....Q—Q2;
24. P—B3, R—QB1, and the B
threatens danger to her at KB1.

24. Q—K3	Kt—Q2
25. Kt—B3	Kt—B3
26. Kt—R2	Kt—Kt1
27. P—KKt5	P—KB3
28. Kt—B3	P×P
29. P×P	B—B1
30. R—B6	......

A clever resource, which is extraordinarily difficult to parry. Observe, too, that in the position now
arrived at it looks for all the world
as if White had all the time exclusively operated on the Queen's
wing (by P—QB4—B5×QP, on
which P×P had followed), whereas
Black had sought salvation by a
counter-attack directed against the
base of the pawn-chain, White's
PK4.

| 30. ...... | B—Q2 |
| 31. B×QRP | ...... |

31. ......R×QKtP would have been answered by 32. R×Kt. The sacrifice of the exchange is very promising.

31.	B×R
32. P×B	Q—B2
33. P—QKt5	......

Position after White's 33rd move

| 33. ...... | P—KR3! |

This pawn sacrifice yields Black freedom to manœuvre; without this sacrifices at Q6 or K5 would have been possible for White. Take for instance, the following variations: 33. ....Kt—K3 (instead of the text move); 34. P—QR4, B—Q1; 35. B—R3, Q—KB2; 36. B×P!, Q×Kt; 37. B×P ch, Kt—Kt2; 38. Q×Q followed by 39. P—B7.

34. P×P	Kt—K3
35. P—QR4	B—Q1
36. B—R3	Q—KB2

For now B×P, Q×Kt, B×P ch would be answered simply by K—R2.

37. Kt×P	P×Kt
38. B×R	Q×B
39. P—R5	Kt×P

Black has also his 33rd move to thank for the possibility of the Kt's intervention.

| 40. P×P | Kt—Kt5 |
| 41. P—B7 | Kt×Q |

| 42. P—B8 =Q | Q—B6 |
| 43. P×Kt | Q×Kt ch |

44. Resigns for Black will take the KP with a check and then the QKtP.

23

Carlsbad, 1911

White	Black
RUBINSTEIN	DURAS
1. P—QB4	P—K4
2. Kt—QB3	Kt—KB3
3. P—KKt3	B—Kt5
4. B—Kt2	0—0
5. Kt—KB3	R—K1
6. 0—0	Kt—QB3

The exchange B×Kt was to be considered.

7. Kt—Q5	B—B1
8. P—Q3	P—KR3
9. P—QKt3	P—Q3
10. B—Kt2	Kt×Kt
11. P×Kt	Kt—K2
12. P—K4	P—QB4

In the long run something must be done for the QBP.

13. P×P e.p.	Kt×P
14. P—Q4	B—KKt5
15. P—Q5	Kt—K2

We have now got our pawn-chain, and the Black base, the PQ3, already seems exposed (from the side), just as if the typical attack had been made on it by P—QB4—B5×QP, BP×P.

| 16. Q—Q3 | Q—Q2 |
| 17. Kt—Q2 | ...... |

The Kt is already being sent forward to the attack of the exposed base.

| 17. ...... | B—R6 |
| 18. P—QR4 | ...... |

To safeguard the Kt position at QB4.

18.	B×B
19. K×B	KR—QKt1
20. Kt—B4	P—QKt4

Q

21. P×P	Q×P
22. R—R3	......

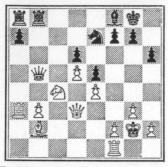

Position after White's 22nd move

In this and similar positions the
question arises, which pawn is the
weaker, White's QKtP or Black's
QRP? In the present case this
problem could be solved by logical
deduction. Since Black's PQ3 is
weaker than White's PQ5, a like
relation must exist throughout
what remains of the Queen's wing.
Were this not the case then White's
P—QR4 must have been wrong,
and that is unlikely. Was he in
fact not justified in supporting his
own important KtQB4? But that
would be absurd. No, Kt—QB4
was indicated, similarly P—QR4;
hence P—QKt4 must have led to a
less favourable position for Black.
And the course of the game proves
the correctness of this judgment.

22.	Kt—Kt3

Kt—QB1 would perhaps have
been better.

23. KR—QR1	P—QR3
24. B—B1	R—Kt2
25. B—K3	P—KB3
26. P—KB3	......

If Black could manage to play
P—KB4, his position would not be
so bad. But this is out of the
question, and Black is besieged.

26.	Kt—K2
27. Q—KB1	......

Threatening Kt×QP

27.	Kt—QB1
28. Kt—Q2	Q—Kt5
29. Q—QB4	Q×Q
30. Kt×Q	R(R)—Kt1
31. Kt—Q2	R—QB2
32. R×P	......

The masterly and varied uses
made of the points Q2 and QB4 will
be noted.

32.	R—B7
33. R(R6)—R2	R×R
34. R×R	......

The rest of the game, which con-
sists of bringing the K to the centre
followed by an advance in close
order of the fighting unit B, Kt and
K is easily intelligible. There
followed 34. .... B—K2; 35. K—
B2, K—B2; 36. K—K2, K—K1;
37. K—Q3, K—Q2; 38. K—B3,
B—Q1; 39. Kt—B4 (QB3 is our
shelter), 39. .... B—B2; 40. P—
KKt4, B—Q1; 41. R—R6, B—
B2; 42. P—KR4, B—Q1; 43.
P—R5, B—B2; 44. P—QKt4, B—
Kt2; 45. R—R8, K—Q1; 46.
K—Kt3, R—Kt1; 47. R×R, B×
R; 48. P—QKt5, Kt—K2; 49.
P—Kt6, P—KB4; (there is nothing
left to hope for) 50. KtP×P,
Kt—Kt1; 51. B—B2, Kt—B3;
52. B—R4 Resigns.

In the following game the transference of the attack from one
point to another is carried out in
classical style.

24

Barmen, 1905

White	Black
Maróczy	Süchting
1. P—Q4	P—Q4
2. P—QB4	P—K3
3. Kt—QB3	Kt—KB3
4. B—KKt5	QKt—Q2
5. P—K3	B—K2
6. Kt—KB3	0—0
7. Q—B2	P—QB3
8. P—QR3	Kt—KR4

Hardly in place; better was R—K1 or P—KR3

9. P—KR4   P—KB4
P—B3 would be answered by B—Q3.

10. B—K2   Kt(Q2)—KB3
11. Kt—K5!   B—Q2
12. Q—Q1   B—K1
13. P—QB5   ......
Weaving the chain.

13. ......   Q—B2
14. P—QKt4   P—QR4
15. P—KKt3!   ......
No one knows better than Maróczy how to prevent freeing moves (here P—B5).

15. ......   P×P
16. P×P   R×R
17. Q×R   Kt—K5
18. P—KKt4!   Kt×Kt
19. Q×Kt   Kt—B3
20. B—KB4!   ......
Threatens Kt—Kt6 and thus gains time for P—KKt5.

20. ......   Q—B1
21. P—KKt5   Kt—Q2
22. Kt—Q3!   ......
To exchange would make it more difficult to break through.

22. ......   B—B2
23. K—Q2   B—Q1
24. R—QR1   ......
Only now does play begin on the real theatre. The idea is naturally attack on the base (PQB3) by P—QKt5.

24. ......   B—QB2
25. R—R7   R—K1
26. B×B   Q×B
27. P—KB4   ......
Stops all attempts to break through by PK4.

27. ......   R—QKt1
28. P—QKt5   ......
At last!

28. ......   Q—B1

Or 28. ....P×P; 29. Kt—Kt4, etc.

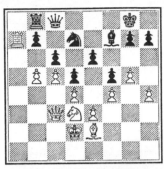

Position after Black's 28th move

29. P—QKt6   ......
With this White transfers the attack to the new base, the PQKt2. Play against the base PQB3 could have been pursued by 29. Kt—Kt4 followed by say Q—R3—R4; but the transference of the attack to Black's QKt2 is still stronger, and above all safer. Süchting is now helpless.

29. ......   B—K1
30. Kt—B1   Kt—B1
31. Kt—Kt3   P—K4!
The only way of saving the QKtP, otherwise there would have come Kt—R5, Kt×KtP; and if R×Kt, B—R6.

32. QP×P   Kt—K3
33. B—Q3!   P—KKt3
34. P—R5   B—B2
35. Kt—R5   Kt—Q1
36. P—K6!   ......
Our sacrificing advance of the unblockaded passed pawn. The pieces to the rear come to life. (See I. iv. §2a.)

36. ......   Q×P
37. P—R6   P—Q5
38. Q×P   Q—R7 ch
and White won 39. K—K1, Kt—K3; 40. Q—K5, R—K1; 41. Kt×KtP, Q—Kt6; 42. B—K2, Q—Kt8 ch; 43. K—B2, Q—KR8;

44. Kt—Q6, Q—R5 ch; 45. K—
Kt2, Kt ×P ch; 46. Q ×Kt, B—
Q4 ch; 47. B—B3, B ×B ch; 48.
K ×B Resigns.

25

Illustrates the idea of collective
mobility, and touches also on the
problem of prophylactic.

Semmering, 1926

White	Black
Nimzowitsch	Dr. Michel

1. Kt—KB3　　P—Q4
2. P—QKt3　　Kt—KB3
3. B—Kt2　　P—QB4
4. P—K3　　P—K3

A new idea. Black avoids developing the Kt at QB3, since it might
be pinned by B—QKt5.

5. Kt—K5　　QKt—Q2
6. B—QKt5　　P—QR3?

B—Q3 was much better here than
the text move, firstly with regard to
his development, and secondly
because White threatens to make
strong use of the diagonal QKt2 to
KKt7, taking advantage of it to
support his outpost at K5. A
prophylactic measure was urgently
needed. For instance 6. . . . B—
Q3!; 7. Kt ×Kt, B ×Kt; 8. B ×
B ch, Q ×B; 9. B ×Kt, P ×B;
and the doubled pawn has both its
dark and its bright side. (See II.
ii.) Further we consider 6. . . . .
B—K2 also better than the text
move (P—QR3).

7. B ×Kt ch　　Kt ×B
8. Kt ×Kt　　B ×Kt
9. 0—0　　P—KB3

An admission of weakness in the
long diagonal. There came under
consideration also 9. . . . B—Q3,
e.g., 9. . . . B—Q3; 10. Q—Kt4,
Q—B2, followed by 0—0—0.

10. P—QB4　　P ×P
The threat was 11. P ×P, P ×P;
12. Q—R5 ch, followed by Q ×QP.

11. P ×P　　B—Q3
12. Q—R5 ch　　P—KKt3
13. Q—R6　　B—KB1
14. Q—R3!!　　......

The best place for the Q and one
difficult to find. P—K4 would now
only surrender the point Q4 to
White. For instance 14. . . . . P—
K4; 15. Q—Kt3 (threatening B ×
P), B—Kt2; 16. P—K4, followed
by P—Q3 and Kt—QB3—Q5 with
advantage in position for White.

14. ......　　B—K2
15. Kt—QB3　　0—0
16. P—QR4!　　......

White plans the configuration
PK4, PKB4, etc., which would leave
his QP backward. As he thus
sacrifices the effective power of his
QP, he must necessarily first paralyse the three Black Q side pawns.
Hence the text move.

16. ......　　B—Q3
17. P—KB4　　Q—K2
18. P—K4　　B—B3
19. P—KKt4　　.. . ...

A 'pawn roller' which can hardly
be rendered innocuous.

19. ......　　P—KB4
If Black does nothing, White has
the choice between a direct attack
on the one hand and play against
the QBP on the other. The latter
could be carried out in some such
way as say 19. . . . . QR—K1; 20.
Q—K3 and then P—R5 and B—R3,
finally driving away the defending
BQ3 by P—K5. After the text
move a mating attack wins the game
straight off.

20. KtP ×P　　KP ×P
Or KtP ×P; 20. K—B2, etc.

21. P—K5　　......
The following variation may be
dedicated to those who love combinative complications. 21. Kt—
Q5 (instead of P—K5), Q ×P; 22.
QR—K1, Q ×QBP; 23. Kt—K7
ch, B ×Kt; 24. R ×B, R—B2; 25.

R×R, Q×R; 26. Q—QB3, K—
B1!; and Black, it would appear,
has a sufficient defence.

21. ......   B—B2
22. Kt—Q5   B×Kt
If on his 21st move Black had
played his B back to QKt1, he
would now have been able to answer
the entry of the Kt by Q—K3; but
this, too, would have availed nothing. For example: 21. . . . . B—Kt1;
22. Kt—Q5, Q—K3; 23. Kt—B6
ch, R×Kt; 24. P×R, Q—K5 (his
one chance); 25. P—B7 ch, and
White wins by 25. . . . . K×P; 26.
Q×RP ch; K—B1; 27. Q—Kt7
ch, K—K1; 28. R—K1, etc.

23. P×B   Q—Q2
24. P—K6!   Resigns.
For if Q×QP, Q—R6 forces
mate, or the loss of a R, and if
24. . . . . Q—K2, the fatal Q shows
herself at her QB3 and there is no
answer.

The following game shows how
easily the early surrender of the
centre can lead to disaster. Nevertheless, this procedure seems to us
to be in itself quite practicable,
provided we bring to bear on the
problem all the tenacity which we
possess, and do not allow ourselves
to be forced down an inclined plane.
If we do this our prospects for
the future are good. As examples
we may point to Rubinstein's games
of this kind which he won at St.
Sebastian in 1911, and further to
Game No. 28 in this book. We
now proceed to

26

Berlin, 1916

White	Black
DR. TARRASCH	J. MIESES

1. P—K4	P—K3
2. P—Q4	P—Q4
3. Kt—QB3	P×P

Gives up the centre, but opens
the Q file and the long diagonal
QKt2 to KR8 for pressure on
White's centre.

4. Kt×P	Kt—Q2
5. Kt—KB3	KKt—KB3
6. B—Q3	Kt×Kt
Better would be P—QKt3, but
the text move is playable.

| 7. B×Kt | Kt—KB3 |
| 8. B—Q3 | ...... |
If 8. B—KKt5, B—K2; 9. B×
Kt, then best 9. . . . . P×Kt.

8.	P—QKt3
9. B—KKt5	B—Kt2
10. 0—0	B—K2
11. Q—K2	0—0
12. QR—Q1	P—KR3?
The tenacity of purpose so necessary to tournament play fails him
here. Why not Q—Q4? If then
13. P—QB4, Q—QR4 followed
presently by QR—Q1; and the
pressure is already sensible. If,
however, 13. P—QB4, Q—QR4;
14. P—Q5, then 14. . . . . QR—K1!,
with strong counter-threats. For
instance 15. P×P?,   B×Kt;
followed by Q×B. Why the mere
contact with the point Q4 must
bring a blessing is evident. This
point in the first place is the outpost station in the Q file, and in the
second the same thing in the
diagonal QKt2 to KR8, while
lastly, Q4 is a blockading point.
The enormous strategical importance to Black of the point Q4
makes it clear that any, the most
passing, contact with it must
work wonders.

| 13. B—KB4 | Q—Q4 |
Now this move is unfavourable,
since the QBP is in the air. The
inclined plane makes its appearance.

| 14. P—QB4 | Q—QR4 |
| 15. B×BP | B×Kt |
15. . . . . QR—QB1 was to be considered here, and after 16. B—K5,
KR—Q1, the advance of White's

pawn majority s very much hindered.

16. P×B!   Q×RP?

Black will not resign himself to the loss of a pawn, runs risks in seeking compensation, and thus loses the Queen.

With 16. . . . . KR—QB1; 17. B—K5, Kt—Q2! (with a view to the threatened K—R1 and R—KKt1), he could still have put up a resistance. For if now 18. B—K4, then 18. . . . . Kt×B; 19. B×R, Kt—Kt3, and Black threatens Kt—B5 with later B—Q3 and Q—KR4.

17. R—QR1   Q—Kt6
18. B—B2   Q—Kt5
19. R—R4   Resigns

The Q is prettily trapped.

27

In a situation very similar to that in the preceding game Tartakower succeeds in making the point Q4, which Mieses so badly neglected, the basis of an undertaking which he carried out with great virtuosity.

Semmering, 1926

White	Black
Grünfeld	Dr. Tartakower

1. P—Q4   P—Q4
2. P—QB4   P×P
3. Kt—KB3   B—Kt5
4. Kt—K5   B—R4
5. Kt×P   . . . . . .

The best answer to 5. Kt—QB3 would be 5. . . . . Kt—Q2, and the proud KtK5 will be forced to declare his intentions.

5. . . . . . .   P—K3
6. Q—Kt3   . . . . . .

Threatening both Q×KtP and QKt5 ch.

6. . . . . . .   Kt—QB3
7. P—K3   R—QKt1!

He does not hesitate at employing the Rook to protect the modest pawn!

8. Kt—QB3   Kt—KB3
9. B—K2   B×B
10. Kt×B   B—Kt5 ch
11. Kt—QB3   0—0

Both sides have now completed their development, and the game is about equal. But White's centre, which is otherwise well protected, betrays a striking measure of immobility. *My System,* however, teaches that every immobile complex tends to become a weakness. The truth of the proposition will here be shortly manifested.

12. 0—0   Kt—Q4!

He feels himself here as if at home, for P—K4 is not possible because of Kt×QP.

13. Kt×Kt   . . . . . .

If 13. Kt—K4, the result would be the mobilization of Black's Q side by 13. . . . . P—QKt4; 14. Kt—K5, Kt×Kt; 15. P×Kt, P—QB4; 16. P—QR3, P—QB5, etc.; or 14. Kt—Q2, P—K4, etc., and White's game is disorganized.

13. . . . . . .   Q×Kt!
14. Q—B2   P—K4

White's centre is already being demolished.

15. Kt×P   Kt×Kt
16. P×Kt   Q×KP
17. B—Q2   B×B
18. Q×B   KR—Q1
19. Q—B2   R—Q4!

He makes use of the point Q4 in excellent fashion.

20. QR—Q1   QR—Q1
21. R×R   R×R
22. R—Q1   P—KKt3
23. R×R   Q×R
24. P—QR3   P—QB4

Black has a decided advantage for the end game. Pawn majority on the Q side, the Q file, and last but not least the central position of his

Q. This advantage is, however, still only a small one.

25. P—KR3   P—QKt4
26. P—KB4   P—B5

Centralization proceeds apace! White's pawn majority is much less easily realizable than Black's (if for instance 26. P—KB3, than 15. ....P—KB4, and White's K4 is in bondage), and this is sufficient to explain the loss of the game.

27. Q—B3   Q—K5
28. K—B2   P—QR4

The whole ending is played by Tartakower with wonderful precision and truly artistic elegance. Tartakower is, in my opinion, without question the third best end game artist of all living masters.

29. P—KKt4   P—KR3
30. P—KR4   Q—KR8!

Only now, and this tardiness is to his credit, does he give up the central position in favour of a diversion.

31. K—Kt3   Q—Kt8 ch
32. K—B3   Q—R7!
33. P—Kt5   P—KR4
34. K—K4   Q×RP
35. Q×RP   Q—R8 ch
36. K—K5   Q—B3!

In order on 37. Q—K1 to put in operation the following manœuvre: 37. ....Q—B4 ch; 38. K—K4, Q—KB4 ch followed by Q—QB7 and wins.

37. Q—R7   P—R5
38. P—B5   ......

White is already at his last gasp.

38. ......   P×P
39. K×P   Q—B6 ch
40. K—K5   P—R6
41. K—Q4   Q—Kt5 ch
42. Resigns.

The following game illustrates the plan of action 'centre file's attack on a flank'.

28

New York Tourney, 1913

White	Black
KLINE	CAPABLANCA

1. P—Q4   Kt—KB3
2. Kt—KB3   P—Q3
3. P—QB3   QKt—Q2
4. B—KB4   P—QB3
5. Q—B2   Q—B2
6. P—K4   P—K4
7. B—Kt3   B—K2

White has now the attacking position in the centre. This is unquestionably an advantage. But here the weakness of his PK4 (we shall quickly see why K4 is weak) will soon force White to surrender this advantage; that is to say he will find himself obliged to equalize with P×KP.

8. B—Q3   0—0
9. QKt—Q2   R—K1!
10. 0—0   Kt—KR4

In order to exchange the B.

11. Kt—QB4   B—B3
12. Kt—K3   Kt—B1
13. P×P   ......

Since the B is needed at Q3 for the protection of the KP, the QP can only be protected against a Kt at K3 by exchanging him. The student should consider carefully the motif here used, aimed at forcing the opponent to declare himself (whether for P×P or for P—Q5).

13. ......   P×P
14. B—R4   Q—K2
15. B×B   Q×B?

With this and the next move a diversion is put *en train* which may be said to run counter to the spirit of the opening. The right line of play consisted in B—K3 and the doubling of the R's in the Q file. By this means advantage could have been taken of the rather uncomfortable position of White's BQ3. Black's simplest course would have been to play B—K3 on his 14th move.

16. Kt—K1	Kt—B5
17. P—KKt3	Kt—R6 ch
18. K—R1	P—KR4
19. Kt(K3)—Kt2	P—KKt4
20. P—KB3	Kt—Kt3
21. Kt—K3!	P—R5

Position after Black's 21st move

22. P—KKt4?? ......

The entry of the Kt at KB5 would, according to my analysis, have decided the game in White's favour. See the Diagram. The retreat of the Black Kt at R6 is cut off. The attempt at a rescue undertaken by means of a reckless advance of the K side pawns gives opportunity, often occurring in such a position, for a decisive counter stroke, by an invasion in the centre, in the present case by Kt—B5.

For instance 22. Kt—B5, P×P; 23. P×P, B×Kt; 24. P×B, Kt—K2; 25. K—Kt2, K—Kt2 (is the P sacrifice 25. .... P—Kt5; 26. P× P, Kt—Kt4 any better?); 26. K× Kt, R—KR1 (or 26. .... Kt— Q4; 27. Q—K2); 27. K—Kt2, Q—R3; 28. K—B2; Q—R7 ch; 29. Kt—Kt2, R—R6; 30. K— K1, R×P; 31. Kt—K3, etc. Moreover, as a superabundance, 26. R—KR1 is also playable, which I showed to be a win for White in an analysis I published in the *Rigaer Rundschau*.

22. ...... Kt(R6)—B5

Now the Kt rejoices in his rediscovered freedom, and Black,

after this doubtful excursion, which could easily have ended fatally for him, takes up the right line, play in the Q file, and pursues it with complete mastery to victory. What remains needs but few remarks. The continuation was: 23. R—B2, Kt × B; 24. Kt × Kt, B—K3; 25. QR— Q1, KR—Q1; 26. P—QKt3, Kt— B5; 27. Kt—KKt2, Kt × Kt(Q3); 28. R × Kt, R × R; 29. Q × R, R— Q1 (why not B × KKtP?); 30. Q— K2, P—R6; 31. Kt—K3, P— QR4; 32. R—B1, P—R5; 33. P—QB4, R—Q5!; 34. Kt—QB2, R—Q2; 35. Kt—K3, Q—Q1; 36. R—Q1, R × R; 37. Kt × R, Q—Q5 (Q file and centralization); 38. Kt— B2, P—QKt4!; 39. BP × P, RP × P; 40. RP × P, B × QKtP (threatening Q—R8 ch); 41. Kt × P, B— Q8; 42. Q—KB1, P × P; 43. K— Kt2, P—Kt5; 44. Q—Kt5, P— Kt6; 45. Q—K8 ch, K—Kt2; 46. Q—K7, P—Kt7; 47. Kt × P, B— Kt6 and wins.

The next game illustrates the plan of action: play in a file against the enemy centre: First restrain, then blockade, and lastly destroy!

29

Carlsbad, 1911

White	Black
RUBINSTEIN	LÖWENFISCH
1. P—K4	P—K3
2. P—Q4	P—Q4
3. Kt—QB3	Kt—KB3
4. B—KKt5	B—K2
5. P—K5	KKt—Q2
6. B × B	Q × B
7. Q—Q2	O—O
8. P—KB4	P—QB4
9. Kt—KB3	P—KB3

It would be more in the spirit of a correct attack on a pawn-chain first to play 9. .... P × P; 10. Kt × P, and not till then P—KB3. But after 10. .... P—KB3; 11. P ×

KBP, Q × P; the position arrived at is after all similar to that of the text.

10. P × KBP	Q × P
11. P—KKt3	Kt—QB3
12. 0—0—0	P—QR3
13. B—KKt2	Kt—Kt3

The diagonal attacking range KKt2 to Q5 is a necessary element in White's plan of operations; for this, after KP × BP, holds up the freeing thrust P—K4 better than any other possible disposition could.

14. KR—K1	Kt—B5
15. Q—KB2	P—QKt4
16. P × P!	

Bravo! The flank attack Kt × KtP has no terrors for him, since a flank attack by itself can never ruin a strongly centralized game. And White's game is centralized, for he holds the centre files and pressure in them is already making itself felt, and further he has the prospect of occupying the central points Q4 and K5. Observe now how Black's wing attack is thrown back by action in the centre.

16.	Kt × KtP
17. K × Kt	P—Kt5
18. Kt—Q4!	P × Kt ch
19. K—R1	......

There will come a Rook presently to gobble up the QBP.

| 19. ...... | Kt × Kt |

If 19.....B—Q2, then 20. Kt × KP, B × Kt; 21. R × B, followed by B × QP.

| 20. Q × Kt | R—QKt1 |
| 21. R—K3 | P—KKt4 |

Now he has a go on the other wing.

22. R × BP	P × P
23. P × P	B—Q2
24. P—B6	Q × Q
25. R × Q	B—K1
26. B—R3	R—KB3
27. P—B7	......

It would have pleased me even better if the decision had been brought about in a Bishop ending instead of through the somewhat 'tacked on' action of the passed PQB7; for instance from such a position as White: K, K5; B, KR3; P's, QR2, QB3, KB4, KR2. Black: K, K2; B, KB2; P's, QR3, Q4, K3, KR2; with the continuation P—KB5, P × P; B × P, and White wins the QP and the game. We should then have the general idea more markedly brought out, namely first to keep the KP and QP under restraint, then to blockade them and only at the end to destroy them. But as played the game was instructive enough! (e.g., Moves 13, 16 and 18).

27.	R—QB1
28. R × QP	R × QBP
29. B × P ch	Resigns

The following game is instructive for the way in which Black turns his majority in the centre to account despite disturbing counter-measures.

30

London, 1927

| White | Black |
| BOGOLJUBOW | NIMZOWITSCH |

1. P—QB4	P—K3
2. Kt—QB3	Kt—KB3
3. P—K4	P—QB4

Since P—K5 did not seem to be dangerous.

| 4. P—KKt3 | ...... |

There was also to be considered 4. Kt—B3, Kt—QB3; 5. P—Q4, P × P; 6. Kt × P, B—Kt5; 7. Q—Q3 (Bogoljubow's suggestion).

4.	P—Q4
5. P—K5	P—Q5
6. P × Kt	P × Kt
7. QP × P	......

An interesting idea. He, so to speak, sacrifices a P, in that he makes his pawn majority on the Q side of no value; but he hopes, by occupying certain central points, to be able to bring counter-pressure to bear. Cf. the next note.

7.	Q × P
8. Kt—KB3	P—KR3
9. B—Kt2	B—Q2!
10. Kt—Q2	......

White's command of the diagonal KKt2 to QKt7 coupled with that of the point K4 is no small embarrassment to Black. If now 10. . . . . . Q—K4 ch?, then 11. Kt—K4 and B—KB4.

10.	B—B3
11. Kt—K4	Q—Kt3
12. Q—K2	......

Not 12. . . . . . .P—KB4 because of the reply 13. B—B3 followed by Kt—Q2 and Black's K4 will remain a weak point.

| 13. 0—0 | 0—0 |

Position after Black's 13th move

| 14. P—KR4 | ...... |

An ingenious move, which, however, brings about a disturbance of the equilibrium which up to now may be said to have existed. Better was 14. P—KB4!, Kt—Q2; 15. B—Q2, K—R1!; 16. QR—K1, Kt—B3; 17. B—QB1. After the text move the balance weighs in Black's favour.

| 14. ...... | P—KB4 |
| 15. Kt—Q2 | B × B |

Not 15. . . . . .B × RP because of 16. Kt—KB3!

| 16. K × B | Kt—QB3 |
| 17. Kt—B3 | P—B5 |

Otherwise B—B4, and the balance is readjusted.

| 18. R—K1 | R—B3 |
| 19. Q—K4 | ...... |

The game is already lost for White, for the occupation of the point K4 which seems to consolidate the position proves to be deceptive. White's KKt3 is in fact sick unto death.

19.	P × P
20. P × P	B—Q3
21. P—KKt4	Q × Q
22. R × Q	QR—KB1
23. R—K3	R—B5
24. P—Kt5	......

24. R × P, R × KtP ch; 25. K—B2, Kt—K4 would lead to a *débâcle*.

| 24. ...... | R—Kt5 ch |
| 25. K—R1 | ...... |

Or 25. K—B2, Kt—K4; 26. K—K2, R—Kt7 ch; 27. K—B1, R—Kt6 winning a piece.

25.	P × P
26. P × P	K—B2
27. Kt—Kt1	......

If 27. P—Kt6 ch then, best, K—B3 (not K—K2 because of 28. Kt—R2, R—KR1; 29. R—K2, R(Kt)—R5??; 30. B—Kt5 ch).

27.	R—KR1 ch
28. Kt—R3	K—K2
29. P—QKt3	B—B5
30. R—B3	Kt—K4
31. Resigns.	

31

In which seven White pawns show greater collective mobility than eight Black ones. Thus does mind (i.e., dynamic effect) triumph over mere matter.

Played in 1924

| White | Black |
| NIMZOWITSCH | ANTON OLSON |

| 1. P—KB4 | P—QB4 |
| 2. P—K4 | Kt—QB3 |

3. P—Q3   P—KKt3
4. P—QB4   B—Kt2
5. Kt—QB3   P—QKt3
6. Kt—KB3   B—Kt2
7. P—KKt4   ......

The collective mobility of White's King's side pawns already makes itself quickly felt.

7. ......   P—K3
8. B—Kt2   KKt—K2
9. Kt—QKt5!

In order to provoke P—QR3, after which the lack of protection under which the QKtP will suffer is to form the basis of a sharp combination.

9. ......   P—Q3
10. 0—0   P—QR3
11. Kt—R3   0—0
12. Q—K2   Q—Q2
13. B—K3   · Kt—QKt5

Else there would follow QR—Q1 and P—Q4 with advantage to White.

14. Kt—B2!   B×P
15. QR—QKt1   B—B6
16. Kt×Kt   B×Kt

or P×Kt; B×QKtP.   Cf. the note to White's 9th move.

17. B—QB1!   ......

White has succeeded in wresting the long diagonal from his opponent.

17. ......   P—KB3
18. B—Kt2   P—K4
19. P—Kt5   ......

The connexion between 'sacrifice' and 'blockade' would have stood out in even sharper relief had the continuation been 19. P—KB5, P—KKt4, 20. P—KR4 with an enduring attack, while Black's pawn plus would have but an illusory value.

19. ......   Kt—B3
or 19.....P×KtP; 20. Kt×KtP (threatening B—KR3), 20.....Kt—B3; 21. P—KB5.

20. P×BP   Q—Kt5
21. P×KP   P×P
22. Q—K3   Q—R4

To protect the KP.

23. Kt—Kt5   B—QB1
24. P—B7 ch   K—Kt2
25. Q—B4   K—R3
Forced.

26. Kt—K6 ch!   P×Q
27. B—Kt7 mate.

In the following game we have an example of a 'mysterious' Rook move, also a striking one of the difference between a true and a false freeing move. As this game in addition illustrates very clearly our conception of prophylactic strategy, it is inserted here.

32

Petrograd, 1914

White   Black
BLACKBURNE   NIMZOWITSCH

1. P—K3   P—Q3
2. P—KB4   P—K4
3. P×P   P×P
4. Kt—QB3   B—Q3

The best move, for the early development of the Kt's advocated by Lasker would not get at the root of the matter here. This root lies rather in the pawn configuration and in the prevention of any freeing pawn moves.

5. P—K4   B—K3
Preventing B—QB4

6. Kt—KB3   P—KB3

Black plays (as will become evident in his 8th move) to prevent the advance of the QP to his fourth which would in a certain sense have a freeing effect; since it would make White's majority in the centre felt. Black, as he plays it, succeeds in completely crippling the enemy majority in the centre. And now the reader may ask, why does Black give White the opportunity of playing P—Q4 on his 7th move?

7. P—Q3   ......

White forgoes the advance, and rightly, for 7. P—Q4 would here be the typical false liberating move, which merely creates new weaknesses. E.g., 7. P—Q4, Kt—Q2!; 8. P—Q5 (otherwise ultimately KP×QP with play against White's isolated KP), 8. . . . B—KB2 followed by the occupation of the point QB4 by B or Kt.

| 7. . . . . . . | Kt—K2 |
| 8. B—K3 | P—QB4! |

With the aid of the resources he has in the Q file Black now succeeds in forcing his opponent to act on the defensive. See Black's 9th and 10th moves.

9. Q—Q2	QKt—QB3
10. B—K2	Kt—Q5
11. 0—0	0—0
12. Kt—Q1	Kt(K)—QB3
13. P—QB3	. . . . . .

The reward which Black's systematic scheme of operations has earned for him. White's PQ3 is now a weakness.

| 13. . . . . . . | Kt×B ch |
| 14. Q×Kt | . . . . . . |

See diagram 139, p. 146.

| 14. . . . . . . | R—K1! |

The 'mysterious' Rook move, which in the event of White playing P—Q4 threatens to make things uncomfortable for him in the K file. In addition to this it makes room for the B at KB1 to which square the latter wishes to go.

| 15. Kt—KR4 | B—KB1 |
| 16. Kt—B5 | K—R1! |

White has made pertinent use of the open KB file, his one advantage. Black's move for all its unpretentiousness has its significance in position play. Black insures the eventual possibility of playing P—KKt3 and P—KB4 without being disturbed by a check at R6.

| 17. P—KKt4 | Q—Q2! |

Renders possible a parry to the ever threatening advance P—KKt5. For example: 18. P—Kt5, P—KKt3; 19. Kt—Kt3, P—KB4!; with an excellent game. Cf. the previous note.

| 18. Kt—KB2 | P—QR4 |

White's QRP is constantly threatened, and if P—QKt3, P—R5 will now be possible. It is evident that White's Q wing is sympathetically affected by the weakness of his centre.

| 19. P—QR3 | P—QKt4 |

B—Kt6 would have been a strong move here, although by it Black would have to forgo this parry he had planned to P—KKt5. Nevertheless, B—Kt6 could have composedly been played (one should not be a slave to one's parries!), e.g., 19. . . . . B—Kt6; 20. P—KKt5, P × P; 21. B ×KtP, P—QB5! (Lasker's suggestion); 22. P ×P, Q—K3; 23. Kt—K3, Q—KKt3; 24. Q—Kt4, B—QB4!, and wins. Or 23. Q—KB3!, B ×BP; 24. KR—Q1, and Black has a slight advantage.

| 20. QR—Q1 | QR—QKt1 |

Some tempi could have been saved by playing P—QKt5 at once.

| 21. R—Q2 | P—QKt5 |
| 22. RP×P | RP×P! |

If BP ×P, then P—Q4!

| 23. P—QB4 | |

Black ought now to play out his trumps.

| 23. . . . . . . | R—QR1? |

Black had brought about a strategically won position, only he should not have delayed any longer playing out his trumps. These consisted of Kt—Q5, which would lead to B × Kt, and of P—KKt3 and B—R3, in order to dominate the diagonal. Thus: 23. . . . . P—KKt3 (instead of R—QR1); 24. Kt—Kt3, Kt—Q5!; 25. B × Kt, BP × B, followed by B—R3. Or 25. Q—Q1 (instead of exchanging), R—QR1, followed by Q—QR5; the exchange of Q's will be forced and Black has a good end-game. He could also play out his trumps in the reverse order; e.g., 23. .... Kt—Q5; 24. B×Kt, BP×B; 25. Q—B3 (best), P—KKt3; 26. Kt—Kt3, Q—K2; 27. Kt—Q1, B—R3; 28. R—KKt2, B—Kt4! followed by R—QR1—R8 etc.

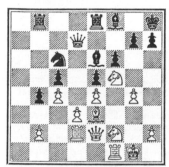

Position after White's 23rd move

24. Q—B3   R—R7?
There was still time for Kt—Q5 etc.

25. P—Kt5   ......
Thanks to a tactical sally (White's 26th move) this thrust which was thought to have been prevented, is now after all possible.

25. ......   P—KKt3
26. Kt—Kt4!
Robs Black of the fruits of his deep plan of campaign.
There followed 26. .... P×Kt; 27. Kt×BP, Kt—Q5; 28. Q—B2 (Q—R5 would have won quicker), Q—QB3; 29. Kt×R, Q×Kt; 30. B×Kt, KP×B; 31. P×P, and won easily.
What we have to learn from this game is the ability to distinguish between true and false freeing moves. The manner in which Black was able to hold in check the thrusts P—Q4 and later (until the moment of aberration) P—KKt5 is worthy of special notice. See II. ii. §3.

The following game illustrates the effect of preventive measures and the idea of collective mobility.

33

Dresden, 1926

White	Black
NIMZOWITSCH	RUBINSTEIN
1. P—QB4	P—QB4
2. Kt—KB3	Kt—KB3
3. Kt—QB3	P—Q4
4. P×P	Kt×P
5. P—K4	......

A novelty which at the price of a backward QP aims at securing other advantages.

5. ......   Kt—Kt5
Preferable was Kt×Kt; 6. KtP×Kt, P—KKt3.

6. B—QB4!   P—K3
It was not possible here to take immediate advantage of White's weakness at Q3. For instance, 6. .... Kt—Q6 ch; 7. K—K2! Kt—B5 ch; 8. K—B1, with the threat P—Q4. Or 6. .... Kt—Q6 ch; 7. K—K2, Kt×B ch; 8. R×Kt, Kt—QB3; 9. B—QKt5, B—Q2; 10. B×Kt, followed by P—Q4 with the superior end-game.

7. 0—0   QKt—QB3
I should prefer P—QR3 here, though it is true that even then White with 8. P—QR3, Kt—QB3; 9. PQ3 and BK3, would have an excellent game. See II. i. 4, p. 124.

8. P—Q3   Kt—Q5
P—QR3 was threatened.

9. Kt×Kt   P×Kt
10. Kt—K2   ......
White now stands very well; any weakness at Q3, which may exist, is covered up, the collective mobility of White's K side (P—KB4!) is considerable, and, most important, the apparently blocked KB plays from the background a

preventive rôle (directed against a
possible P—K4) which goes far to
turn the scale in White's favour.

10. ......   P—QR3
Directed against the threat B—
Kt5 ch, B—Q2; Kt ×P.

11. Kt—Kt3   B—Q3
12. P—KB4   ......
Q—Kt4 would have been very
strong here; e.g., 12. Q—Kt4, 0—0;
13. B—KKt5!, B—K2; 14. B—
KR6, B—B3; 15. B ×KtP, B ×B;
16. Kt—R5; or else 13. . . . . P—K4;
14. Q—R4, with the sacrifice at
Kt7 to follow (Kt—R5 ×KtP).
The best answer to Q—Kt4 would
have been Q—KB3; for instance,
12. Q—Kt4, Q—B3; 13. P—KB4;
but even in this case White's superiority in position would have been
very great. After the less incisive
text move Black can approximately
equalize.

12. ......   0—0
13. Q—KB3   ......
A direct mating attack is no
longer feasible. For example: 13.
P—K5, B—B2!; 14. Q—Kt4, K—
R1; 15. Kt—R5, R—KKt1; 16.
R—B3, P—KB4!; 17. P ×P e.p.,
P ×P; 18. Q—R4, R—Kt3; 19.
R—R3, Q—K2; and Black threat-
ens to consolidate his position by
B—Q2 and QR—KKt1.

13. ......   K—R1
14. B—Q2   P—KB4
15. QR—K1   Kt—B3
Rubinstein has defended himself
skilfully, but White has always a
trump in hand, the K file.

16. R—K2   Q—B2
Not good. In cramped positions one should never give away
the slightest future possibility of a
move. But Q—B2 gives away the
possibility of playing Q—KB3, after
P ×P, P ×P. The right move was
therefore 16. . . . . B—Q2, and if then
17. P ×P (best), P ×P; 18. KR—
KI, then 18. . . . . Q—B3, and Black

stands much better at any rate than
he does in the game.

17. P ×P   P ×P

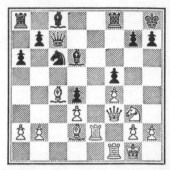

Position after Black's 17th move

18. Kt—R1   ......
The Kt starts on a long journey
with KKt5 as his goal, in order to
support with all the means at his
disposal the KB who now wakes up
and throws off his preventive rôle
for one of direct activity. And
meanwhile White's K file, thrown,
so to speak, on its own resources,
makes a desperate but successful
struggle for existence. This vitality of the K file gives point to the
Kt manœuvre.

18. ......   B—Q2
19. Kt—B2   QR—K1
20. KR—K1   R ×R
21. R ×R .   Kt—Q1
We see now that 21. . . . . R—K1
would be met by 22. Q—Q5.

22. Kt—R3   B—B3
And here 22. . . . . R—K1 would
lead to a combination full of
pleasantries, e.g., 22. . . . . R—K1;
23. Q—R5!. R ×R; 24. Kt—Kt5,
P—KR3; 25. Q—Kt6, P ×Kt; 26.
Q—R5 mate.

23. Q—R5   P—KKt3
24. Q—R4   K—Kt2
25. Q—B2!   ......
Black's castled position was still
too strongly defended, so White

intends first to force a re-grouping of the enemy forces.

25. ......   B—QB4
Or 25. .... Q—Kt3; 26. P—QKt4 and B—B3!

26. P—QKt4   B—Kt3
27. Q—R4   ......
The switch-back theme, such as usually only occurs in problems, 27. Q—K1 would, however, also have been good, e.g., 27. Q—K1, B—K5; 28. Kt—B2, winning a P by Kt ×B etc.

27. ......   R—K1
The answer to R—B3 would have been Kt—Kt5, P—KR3; Kt—R7 winning at once.

28. R—K5!   Kt—B2
If 28. .... P—KR3 there would follow 29. P—KKt4 with a very strong attack. Thus: 29. P—Kt4, P×P; 30. P—B5, Q×R; 31. P—B6 ch, Q×P; 32. Q×P mate. Or 29. P—Kt4, P—Kt4?; 30. P×KtP, threatening mate at R6. After the text move White forces an elegant win.

29. B×Kt   Q×B
If 29. .... R×R; then 30. P×R, Q×B; 31. Kt—Kt5, Q—Kt1; 32. P—K6, B—Q4; 33. Q—B4, with an easy win.

30. Kt—Kt5   Q—Kt1
31. R×R .   B×R
32. Q—K1!   B—B3
If 32. .... K—B1, White wins by 33. Q—K5, B—Q1 (best; the reply to 33. .... Q×P would be 34. Q—B6 ch, K—Kt1; 35. Kt—K6; or 34. .... B—B2; 35. Kt×B and Q×B); 34. Kt—K6 ch, K—K2; 35. Q—QB5 ch!, K—Q2; 36. Kt—B8 ch! Observe how White on his 35th move forgoes the discovered check and how the Black King has got tangled up with his own pieces.

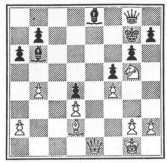

Position after White's 32nd move

A remarkable position: Black is lost. In spite of the scanty material a mating attack is in the air. Some pretty play now follows.

33. Q—K7 ch   K—R1
If K—R3, then obviously Kt—K6.

34. P—QKt5   ......
Pulls the noose taut!

If 34. .... P×P, then 35. Kt—K6, P—KR4!; 36. Q—B6 ch, K—R2; 37. Kt—Kt5 ch, K—R3; 38. B—Kt4 leads to a mate.

34. ......   Q—Kt2
Desperation.

35. Q×Q ch   K×Q
36. P×B and White won.

34

Illustrates the restraint of a double complex in an extraordinarily striking manner.

Baden-Baden, 1925

White	Black
NIMZOWITSCH	MARQUIS S. ROSSELLI DEL TURCO
1. Kt—KB3	P—Q4
2. P—QKt3	P—QB4
3. P—K3	Kt—QB3
4. B—Kt2	B—KKt5

5. P—KR3   B ×Kt
6. Q ×B   P—K4
7. B—QKt5   Q—Q3
8. P—K4   ......

We have here to do with the remarkable situation which we have already had occasion to notice (see II. ii. §2, Diag. 133), namely the one in which we do not at once cause the doubled pawns by B ×Kt, P ×B, but rather bring this about by a roundabout way. As a fact after 8. B ×Kt ch, P ×B we should never be able to force our obstinate opponent to accommodate us by playing P—Q5, e.g., 8. B ×Kt, P ×B; 9. P—K4, Kt—KB3, etc.

8. ......   P—Q5
9. Kt—QR3   ......

Threatening Kt—B4, Q—B2; B × Kt ch, P ×B; and the weakness of the double pawn is evident.

9. ......   P—KB3
10. Kt—B4   Q—Q2
11. Q—R5 ch   ......

The manoeuvre of the Q is intended to help prevent Black's castling on the Q side; not on the K side as one might at first sight think.

11. ......   P—KKt3
12. Q—B3   Q—QB2

Not O—O—O because of Kt—R5 and the covering move KKt—K2 is ruled out because of Q ×BP.

13. Q—Kt4!   ......

Now she rejoices in the observation post she has won for herself. This Q manoeuvre has quite a hypermodern air to it.

13. ......   K—B2

Q—K6 ch, K—Q1 (or B—K2; Kt—R5); B ×Kt, and the unpleasant doubled pawn is a fact.

14. P—KB4   P—KR4
15. Q—B3   P ×P
16. B ×Kt   ......

At the right moment, for the Q dare not retake. For instance, 16.

....Q ×B; 17. Q ×P, R—K1; 18· O—O!!, Q ×P (R ×P; Kt—K5 ch); 19. Q—QB7 ch!! and wins (19. ....Q—K2; 20. Kt—Q6 ch followed by Kt ×R).

16. ......   P ×B

At last White has achieved his end, at the cost it is true of a P, but this here plays but a subordinate rôle.

17. O—O   P—Kt4

For (see the previous note) Black's position can be broken up. (Obviously White must not allow Black to safeguard his position by Kt—K4.) To break up Black's game three pawn moves are necessary, (i) P—QB3, (ii) P—K5, and (iii) P—KR4. If White contented himself with only two of these his work were but half done. In the game all three are brought about.

18. P—QB3   R—Q1

Now this R is happily tethered! (to his PQ5).

19. QR—K1!   Kt—K2
20. P—K5   Kt—B4
21. P ×QP!   Kt ×P

If 21. .....P ×QP; then 22. P ×P, K ×P; 23. Q—K4, and Kt—Kt6 is impracticable on account of B×P ch.

22. Q—K4   B—K2

The reply to P—KB4 would have been Q—QKt1, an attacking move in the best modern spirit. For example, 22. ....P—B4; 23. Q—Kt1, K—K3 (to protect the KBP); 24. Q—Q3! and Kt—Q6! with a decisive attack.

23. P—KR4   ......

Now the undermined Black position tumbles like a house of cards.

23. ......   Q—Q2
24. P ×BP   B ×P
25. P ×P   Resigns

For after 25. ....B—Kt2; 26. Kt—K5 ch, B ×Kt; 27. Q ×B, Black's King is in his helplessness a pathetic figure.

35

Illustrates a position held under complete restraint, and may serve as a pendant to my game (No. 8) against Sämisch.

Dresden, 1926

White	Black
JOHNER	NIMZOWITSCH

1.	P—Q4	Kt—KB3
2.	P—QB4	P—K3
3.	Kt—QB3	B—Kt5
4.	P—K3	0—0

Black intends to bring into existence the double complex only under conditions favourable to himself. Cf. No. 34.

5.	B—Q3	P—QB4
6.	Kt—KB3	Kt—QB3
7.	0—0	B × Kt
8.	P × B	P—Q3

The prognosis for the complex PQB2, PQB3, etc., is in a measure (but not pronouncedly) in favour of Black. Yet after, e.g., 9. P—K4, P—K4; 10. P—Q5, Kt—QR4; Black would not have bought the barricade which he has achieved altogether cheaply, for his QBP would then have been much better placed if it were still at QB2. (See the remarks on the double complex in II. ii. §2 my game against Janowski; Diag. 133, p. 139.)

9. Kt—Q2!   ......

A fine idea. In reply to 9. .... P—K4; 10. P—Q5, Kt—QR4, the intention is by 11. Kt—Kt3 to bring the aggressive Black Kt at R4 to reason.

9. ......   P—QKt3
10. Kt—Kt3?   ......

There was time enough for this. P—KB4 should first have been played. If then 10. .... P—K4, there would follow 11. BP × P, QP × P; 12. P—Q5, Kt—QR4; 13. Kt—Kt3, Kt—Kt2; 14. P—K4, Kt—K1, and the weak point QB4,

which is now attackable also from Black's Q3, will be protected by Q—K2, while White for his part can use the KB file together with P—QR4—R5 as a base of operations. The game would then stand about even.

10.	......	P—K4
11.	P—KB4	......

For the reply to 11. P—Q5 would now be P—K5! Thus: 11. P—Q5, P—K5; 12. B—K2, Kt—K4!; or 12. P × Kt, P × B; with advantage to Black.

11. ......   P—K5
11. .... Q—K2 was also possible, for if say 12. BP × P, QP × P; 13. P—Q5, then 13. .... Kt—Q1; 14. P—K4, Kt—K1; and Black by Kt—Q3 and P—KB3 gets a strong defensive position. (Cf. the note to move 10.)

12. B—K2   Q—Q2
Black sees in White's K side pawns (KB, KKt and KR) a qualitative majority. The text move involves a complicated system of restraint. A simpler one could have been brought about by 12. .... Kt—K1. For example: 12. .... Kt—K1; 13. P—KKt4 (or 13. P—KB5, Q—Kt4), 13. .... P—KB4; 14. QP × P! (observe the 'dead' B at QB1 and consider further how ineffectively posted the White pieces are for an attack to be launched in the KKt file); 14. .... QP × P; 15. Q—Q5 ch, Q × Q; 16. P × Q, Kt—K2; 17. R—Q1, Kt—Q3; and Black has rather the better game.

13. P—KR3   Kt—K2
14. Q—K1   ......
If 14. B—Q2, Black would still get the advantage. For instance: 14. B—Q2 (to threaten B—K1—R4), 14. .... Kt—B4; 15. Q—K1 (best; Black threatened Kt—Kt6 and to exchange the B, when White's QB4 would become very weak), 15. .... P—KKt3; and if now

16. P—KKt4, Kt—Kt2; 17. Q—
R4, then Kt(B)—K1, and the pawn
movement is strangled at birth;
for now would follow at the next
move the powerful P—KB4. So
we get always the same picture.
The awkwardness of White's pieces
as a result of the doubled pawns
renders more difficult by far the
carrying out of any action on the
K side however this is planned.

| 14. ...... | P—KR4! |
| 15. B—Q2 | ...... |

Q—R4 will not do because of 15.
......Kt—B4; 16. Q—Kt5, Kt—
R2; 17. Q×RP, Kt—Kt6.

| 15. ...... | Q—B4! |

The Q is bound for—KR2!
Where she will be excellently placed,
for then the crippling of White's
K side by P—R5 will at once be
threatened. It must be conceded
that the restraint manœuvre Q—
Q2—B4—R2 represents a remarkable conception.

| 16. K—R2 | Q—R2! |
| 17. P—QR4 | Kt—B4 |

Threatening Kt—Kt5 ch; P ×
Kt, P ×P ch; K—Kt1, P—Kt6, etc.

| 18. P—Kt3 | P—QR4! |

In this position the backwardness
of the QKtP is easy to put up with.

19. R—KKt1	Kt—R3
20. B—KB1	B—Q2
21. B—QB1	QR—QB1

Black wishes to force P—Q5 in
order then to operate undisturbed
on the K side.

| 22. P—Q5 | ...... |

Otherwise B—K3 would follow
and P—Q5 would be forced after all.

| 22. ...... | K—R1 |
| 23. Kt—Q2 | R—KKt1 |

And now comes the attack. So
was Q—Q2—B4—R2 actually an
attacking manœuvre? Yes and no.
No, since its whole idea was to
restrain White's K side pawns. Yes,

since every restraining action is the
logical prelude to an attack, and
since every immobile complex tends
to be a weakness and therefore must
sooner or later become an object of
attack.

24. B—KKt2	P—KKt4
25. Kt—B1	R—Kt2
26. R—QR2	Kt—B4
27. B—R1	......

White has very skilfully brought
up all his defensive forces.

| 27. ...... | QR—KKt1 |
| 28. Q—Q1 | P ×P |

Opens the KKt file for himself,
but the K file for his opponent.
This move, therefore, demanded
deep deliberation.

29. KP ×P	B—B1
30. Q—Kt3	B—R3
31. R—K2	......

Seizes his chance. Black's KP
now needs to be defended. If he
has limited himself to purely defensive measures, as say 31. B—Q2
a pretty combination would have
resulted; namely, 31. B—Q2, R—
Kt3!; 32. B—K1, Kt—Kt5 ch; 33.
P ×Kt, P ×P ch; 34. K—Kt2, B ×
P!; 35. Q ×B, and now follows the
quiet move 35......P—K6; and
Q—R6 mate can only be parried
by Kt ×P, which move, however,
would cost White his Q.

| 31. ...... | Kt—R5 |
| 32. R—K3 | ...... |

Here I naturally expected Kt—
Q2 for Black's obligation to defend
the important KP furnished White's
only counter chance, as has already
been observed. But a result of
that move would have been a
delightful Q sacrifice, namely: 32.
Kt—Q2, B—B1; 33. Kt ×P, Q—
B4; 34. Kt—B2, Q ×RP ch; 35.
Kt ×Q, Kt—Kt5 mate. The point,
moreover, lies in the fact that the
moves B—B1 and Q—B4 cannot be
transposed. E.g., 32. Kt—Q2, Q—
B4? (instead of B—B1); 33. Q—
Q1!, B—B1; 34. Q—KB1, and

everything is protected; whereas if
32. .... B—B1,   33. Q—Q1,   the
move B ×RP! would wipe out the
corner stone of White's building.
(34. K ×B, Q—B4 ch, etc.)

32.	B—B1
33. Q—B2	B ×P!
34. B ×P	......

34. K ×B, Q—B4 ch; 35. K—
R2 would have led to mate in
three.

| 34. ...... | B—B4 |

Best, for P—KR5 can no longer
be withstood. After the fall of
White's KRP the defence is hopeless.

35. B ×B	Kt ×B
36. R—K2	P—R5
37. R(Kt)—Kt2	P ×P double
38. K—Kt1	Q—R6 ch
39. Kt—K3	Kt—R5
40. K—B1	R—K1!

A precise finish, for now there is
threatened 41. .... Kt ×R; 42. R ×
Kt, Q—R8 ch; 43. K—K2, Q ×R
ch!; and against this threat White is
defenceless.   If 41. K—K1, then,
41. .... Kt—B6 ch; 42. K—B1 or
Q1, Q—R8 ch would lead to mate.
Therefore White resigns.

One of the best blockading games
that I have ever played.

36

Illustrates the isolated QP.

Petrograd, 1913

White	Black
NIMZOWITSCH	TAUBENHAUS
1. P—Q4	P—Q4
2. Kt—KB3	Kt—KB3
3. P—QB4	P—K3
4. P—K3	P—QB4
5. B—Q3	Kt—QB3
6. 0—0	QP ×P
7. B ×BP	P ×P
8. P ×P	B—K2
9. Kt—QB3	0—0
10. B—K3	......

P—Q5 would be bad because of
Kt—QR4;   P—QKt3, B—QKt5;
nor would 10. B—KKt5 be good,
e.g., 10. .... P—QKt3, etc.

| 10. ...... | P—QKt3 |

P—QR3 and P—QKt4 would un-
necessarily weaken the point QB4.

11. Q—K2	B—Kt2
12. KR—Q1	Kt—QKt5
13. Kt—K5	R—QB1
14. QR—QB1	QKt—Q4
15. Kt—QKt5	......

A strategically noteworthy conception. White says to himself:
in the centre I am strong, therefore
a strategical diversion is justified;
moreover, I have no particular
wish after say 15. B—QR6 or Q3
to be saddled with hanging pawns.
The right move was, nevertheless,
B—QR6. For example: 15. B—
QR6, Kt ×Kt; 16. P ×Kt, Q—B2;
17. B ×B, Q ×B; 18. P—QB4 with
eventually P—QR4—R5.

| 15. ...... | P—QR3 |
| 16. Kt—R7! | R—R1 |

If R—B2, then B ×P.

17. Kt(R)—B6	Q—Q3
18. Kt ×B ch	Q ×Kt
19. B—Q3!	Kt ×B

There was no occasion for this.
There were other lines of play to
be considered, (i) 19. .... P—QR4
and KR—QB1, or (ii) 19. .... KR—
Q1 followed by Kt—Q2—KB1; for
(iii) Kt—K1, see the remarks on
Diag. 150 in II. iii. §4, p. 158.

20. P ×Kt   P—QKt4
Weakens the point QB4. After
20. .... P—QR4 (instead of the text
move) and KR—QB1, there would
not be much wrong with him.

21. R—B5
By occupying this outpost station
White gets play in the QB file.

21.	KR—QB1
22. R(Q1)—QB1	P—KKt3
23. P—QR3	......

What now follows could serve as
a text book example for play in an
open file.   The slowness with which
White step by step gains in terrain
is also of significance from the point
of view of position play.

23. ......   Kt—K1
24. P—QKt4   Kt—Q3
If Q—Kt4, then Kt ×BP!

25. Q—KB2   P—KB4
In order to relieve the KBP and
to make Q—Kt4 possible.

26. Q—B4   Kt—K1
Black can undertake nothing.

27. B—K2!   Kt—Q3
28. B—B3   ......
Breaks down the opposition in
the QB file.

28. ......   R ×R
29. QP ×R   Kt—K1
If 29. .....Kt—K5; then 30. P—
B6!, P—KKt4;   31. P ×B, R—
KB1;   32. R—B8 and wins.

30. R—Q1   Kt—B3
31. P—B6   ......
The QBP, the fruit of the operations on the Q's file, now brings the
decision.

31. ......   B—B1
32. P—B7   R—R2
33. R—Q8 ch   K—Kt2
34. R ×B   R ×P
35. Kt ×P   Resigns.

37

Is dedicated to hanging pawns,
and is characteristic of these though
only in a quite special sense.   It
shows the frightful dangers to which
hanging pawns are exposed at birth.
Infant mortality is very high among
them, and appreciably exceeds the
mortality of grown up hanging
pawns, who if the worst comes to the
worst can seek refuge in 'blockaded
security'.

Petrograd, 1909

White   Black
RUBINSTEIN ZNOSKO-BOROVSKY

1. P—Q4   P—Q4
2. P—QB4   P—K3
3. Kt—QB3   Kt—KB3
4. B—Kt5   B—K2
5. P—K3   QKt—Q2
6. Kt—KB3   0—0
7. Q—B2   P—QKt3
P—QB4 is possible here.   For instance, 7. .....P—QB4; 8. P ×QP,
Kt ×P; 9. B ×B, Q ×B; 10. Kt ×
Kt, P ×Kt; 11. P ×P, Kt ×P; and
the isolani does not look so bad.

8. P ×P   P ×P
9. B—Q3   B—Kt2
10. 0—0—0   Kt—K5
11. P—KR4   P—KB4
12. K—Kt1   P—QB4
The correctness of this move
stands or falls by that of the pawn
sacrifice recommended in the next
note.   Sound and good is, instead of
P—QB4, 12. ....R—QB1 as given
by Dr. Lasker.   For instance, 13.
Q—Kt3, Kt ×Kt ch, followed by
P—QB4.   Not quite so good, yet by
no means bad would seem to be
12. .....P—KR3; 13. B—KB4, B—
Q3;   14. B ×B, P ×B.

13. P ×P   P ×P
13. ....R—QB1 was possible
here.   If then 14. P ×P, Kt ×P,
Black would have attacking
chances; the answer to 14. Kt—
Q4 could be Kt(Q2) ×P.   The outcome of the game would have been
doubtful in either case, whereas now
there is no doubt whatever.   It may
be observed that if 13. .....Kt(Q2) ×
P, then 14. Kt ×QP!, B ×Kt; 15.
B—QB4 wins.

14. Kt ×Kt   BP ×Kt
15. B ×KP   P ×B
16. Q—Kt3 ch   K—R1
17. Q ×B   P ×Kt
18. R ×Kt   Q—K1
19. R ×B   Q—Kt3 ch
20. K—R1   QR—QKt1

The gale has not only blown away the hanging pawns but has also taken a piece along with them. Black's desperation attack is warded off easily.

21. Q—K4   ......
Lasker praises this move, but 21. Q—Q5 seems to do as well. E.g., 21. .....P×P; 22. Q×KtP, Q—QB7; 23. B—B6! True, many roads lead to Rome.

21. ......   Q×Q
22. R×Q   P×P
23. R—KKt1   R×KBP
24. R—KB4   R—QB7
If 24. ....R(Kt1)×P; then R—B8 ch! and wins outright.

25. P—QKt3   P—KR3
There followed 26. B—K7, R—K1; 27. K—Kt1, R—K7; 28. B×P, R—Q1; 29. B—Q4, R—QB1; 30. R—KKt4, Resigns.

38

Took an instructive course. It was played in a simultaneous exhibition in Leipzig in 1926. White: Schurig with, up to the 12th move, K. Laue of Halle.

White	Black
THE ALLIES	NIMZOWITSCH
1. Kt—KB3	P—K3
2. P—KKt3	P—Q4
3. B—KKt2	P—QB3
4. P—QKt3	B—Q3
5. B—QKt2	Kt—KB3
6. P—Q3	QKt—Q2
7. QKt—Q2	Q—B2

7. ....P—K4 was also possible. With the text move an original manœuvre begins. Black plans an attack on the extreme Q's wing; but before launching it wishes to safeguard his centre against the possible threat of P—K4—K5; and accordingly first sees to the over-protection of his K4. Further, from where she stands his Q has at her disposal a reserve square in QKt1 to which she can withdraw if need arise, e.g., should the QB file be opened.

8. 0—0   P—QR4
9. P—QB4   P—QKt4
The question whether a flank attack is admissible or not can only be solved by reference to the actual position in the centre. If this be secure a flank attack cannot be wholly amiss. So, too, here. And what matters it that the K has not yet castled? As it is he is unassailable.

10. P×KtP   P×P
11. R—QB1   Q—Kt1
The withdrawing room.

12. Q—B2   ......
P—K4 seems more to the point.

12. ......   0—0
13. P—K4   B—Kt2
14. Kt—Q4   KR—QB1
15. Q—Kt1   R×R
16. R×R   P—Kt5
17. Kt—B6   ......
A bit premature in my opinion.

17. ......   B×Kt
18. R×B   P—R5
Every free moment is used to the strengthening of the position on the extreme Q's wing.

19. P—Q4   ......
This move must be credited to Black's strategy in over protecting his K4. The valuable diagonal QKt2 to KB6 is now obstructed; but by no other means could the thrust P—K5 have been effected. Those engaged in this over-protection have once more stood the test excellently. Moreover, they have had to put up with no inconveniences, but have made themselves felt in all directions.

One variation should be mentioned, namely 19. P—KB4 in order to keep the QP at Q3. The continuation might have been 19. ....B—B4 ch!, and White has after

all to submit to playing 20. P—
Q4, and after 20. .∖..B—B1; 21.
P—K5 we should have arrived at
the position in the text.

19. ......   B—B1
20. P—K5   Kt—K1
The White bishops have now
small possibilities of action.

21. P—KB4   Q—Kt4
P—R6 at once would have been
more precise.

22. Q—B2   P—R6
23. B—QB1   ......
It was essential to interpolate
here B—KB1.

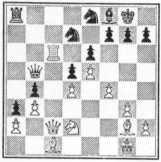

Position after White's 23rd move

Black with the move forces his way
into the enemy game by means of
a sacrifice, and wins the entrenched
QRP. How does he do it?

23. ......   B—B4
This interesting combination
should begin with Kt—B4 (not
B—B4). The difference will soon
be manifest.

24. R ×B   Kt ×R
25. P ×Kt?   ......
The interpolation here of B—KB1
(which would not have been possible
if Black had played 23. ....Kt—
B4) would have yielded him an
extra tempo for the end game.

25. ......   R—QB1
We can see by his face that White's
QRP is marked out for death.

26. Kt—Kt1   Q ×P ch
27. Q ×Q   R ×Q
28. B ×QRP   ......
Or 28. B—Q2, R—B7; 29. B—
KB1, R ×QRP; 30. B ×QKtP, R—
KKt7 ch!, and wins. If White had
had one tempo more (see note to
White's 25th move) this combina-
tion would have been impossible.
There followed: 28. ....P ×B; 29.
Kt ×P, R—R4; 30. Kt—B2, R ×
P; 31. Kt—Q4, R—QKt7; 32.
P—B5, Kt—B2; 33. P ×P, Kt ×
P; 34. Kt—B6, P—Q5, and White
resigned.

39

Illustrates over-protection and
also the problem of the isolated QP.

Played in 1921

White	Black
THREE SWEDISH	
AMATEURS	NIMZOWITSCH

1. P—K4   Kt—QB3
2. P—Q4   P—Q4
3. P—K5   P—KB3
4. B—QKt5   ......
P—KB4 is held to be better.

4. ......   B—KB4
5. Kt—KB3   Q—Q2
6. P—QB4   B ×Kt!
With this exchange, which is anything but obvious, Black plans to
win the square Q4 for his Kt.

7. R ×B   0—0—0
8. P ×QP   ......
If P—B5, then P—KKt4. A
fight would then take place for
possession of the point K4. For
example, 8. P—QB5, P—KKt4; 9.
Q—K2 (to threaten P—K6 shutting
Black in), 9. ....Q—K3; 10. P—
KR3, Kt—R3, followed by Kt—
B2, or else Kt—QKt1. In either
case Black would not stand badly.

8. ......   Q ×P
9. B ×Kt   Q ×B

10.	0—0	P—K3
11.	B—K3	Kt—K2
12.	Q—K2	Kt—Q4

We may with a clear conscience regard White's QP as isolated. His weakness (for the end game!) is evident; further Black has in his Q4 a very strong point. As regards any compensating advantage for what we have called his isolated QP White has the outpost station QB5 which will serve some purpose, on the other hand his K5 is of no use to him, as a station for his Kt, I mean. The game is about equal.

13.	KR—QB1	Q—Q2

It is very questionable whether P × P would not have been better for White than the R move. True his opponent would have had the KKt file and a centrally posted B at Q3, but the K file must not be despised, at any rate as a counter weight. The curious over-protection which is built up in moves 13-18 has been discussed in II. iv. §1, p. 177, under Diagram 167.

14.	R—B4	K—Kt1
15.	Q—Q2	R—QB1
16.	Kt—K1	B—K2
17.	Kt—Q3	KR—Q1
18.	Q—QB2	P—KB4

Having consolidated his position, Black passes to the attack, which indeed is not easy to conduct since for one thing objectives are wanting and for another White himself has some attacking chances.

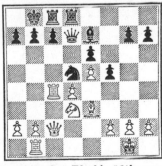

Position after Black's 18th move

19.	R—QB1	......

Without question 19. P—QKt4 should have been played here; with the intention of playing when opportunity offered Kt—B5; B × Kt, KtP × B. The question now arises, is Black's position strong enough to bear weakening? Two moves in particular come under consideration in answer to 19. P—QKt4, namely 19.....P—QKt3, and 19. ....P—QKt4. If 19.....P—QKt3, then 20. Kt—B5! can be played, but after 20.....B × Kt!; 21. KtP × B, P—QB3, Black would stand very well. However, he must emphatically not accept the Kt. sacrifice as the following combination proves. (See Diagram.) 19. P—QKt4!, P—QKt3; 20. Kt—B5!, P × Kt; 21. KtP × P ch, K—R1? (the return sacrifice Kt—Kt3 was essential); 22. P—B6, Q—K1; 23. R—R4 (threatening R × P ch), Kt—Kt3; 24. P—Q5!!, R × P; 25. R × P ch, K × R; 26. Q—R4 ch, K—Kt1; 27. B × Kt, P × B; 28. R × P ch, K—B2; 29. R—Kt7 ch, K—Q1; 30. P—B7 ch!, R × P; 31. R—Kt8 ch, R—B1; 32. R × R ch, and Q × Q ch and wins. A true Morphy Combination.

We may quietly note the fact that his over-protected central position is so strong that Black can here without a qualm leave himself unprotected and yet remain master of the situation as he was before, for he is in a position laughingly to evade any enemy combination, be it ever so diabolical.

We have still to show what would happen if Black played 19..... P—QKt4 in reply to 19. P—QKt4. In this case, too, Black would not fare badly; e.g., 20 R—B6, K—Kt2; 21. Kt—B5 ch, B × Kt; 22. R × B, Kt—Kt3; followed by P—QB3, and Black is strong on the White squares.

19.	......	P—KKt4

20. Kt—B5   B × Kt
21. R × B   R—KKt1
22. Q—K2   P—KR4!
23. B—Q2   ......
23. Q × RP?, P—Kt5 and R—R1.

23. ......   P—R5
24. P—QR4   P—Kt5
25. P—R5   P—QR3!
26. P—QKt4   P—QB3
White has at last spent his fury.

27. R—QKt1   Q—KB2
28. R—Kt3   P—B5
29. Q—K4   P—B6!
For White would not be able to hold out after 30. P × P, P × P ch; 31. K—B1, QR—KB1 (stronger than R—Kt8 ch).

30. R—QB1   P × P
31. K × P   QR—KB1
Note, with what surprising ease the Black Rooks are brought into action, a further proof, to my mind, of the enormous vitality of over-protecting pieces.

32. R—KB1   P—Kt6!
33. RP × P   P × P
34. P—KB4   ......
After R × P, R × R ch the King would be exposed.

34. ......   Kt—K2
35. B—K1   Kt—B4
36. R—KR1   R—Kt5
37. B × P   Q—Kt3
38. Q—K1   Kt × B
Decisive, though so simple and even insipid. It wins the pawns which are so conveniently exposed in the 4th rank.

39. R × Kt   R(B1) × P
40. R(R1)—R3   R × P
41. Q—B2   R × R ch
42. R × R   Q—K5 ch
43. K—R2   Q × P
44. K—Kt2   Q—Q4 ch
45. Resigns.
One of my favourite games.

40

The Hanham defence. Illustrates combined play on both wings. The fearlessness with which Black is able up to a certain point to ignore his own weakness at Q3 is noticeable.

San Sebastian, 1911

White	Black
TEICHMANN	NIMZOWITSCH

1. P—K4   P—K4
2. Kt—KB3   P—Q3
3. P—Q4   Kt—KB3
4. Kt—QB3   QKt—Q2
5. B—QB4   B—K2
6. 0—0   0—0
7. Q—K2   P—QB3
8. B—KKt5   ......
P—QR4 would have been preferable here.

8. ......   P—KR3
9. B—R4   Kt—R4
10. B—KKt3   Kt × B
10. ....B—B3 was also to be considered.

11. RP × Kt   P—QKt4
12. B—Q3   P—QR3!
Black's pawn-mass is now of such a constitution (I mean inner structure), that they must inspire respect. Notice the two-fold possibility of deployment by P—QB4 or, on occasion, P—Q4.

13. P—QR4   ......
He tries to nip the latent strength of Black's pawns in the bud.

13. ......   B—Kt2
14. QR—Q1   Q—B2
15. RP × P   RP × P
16. P—KKt4   KR—K1
17. P—Q5   ......
To get out of the way of his *vis-à-vis*.

17. ......   P—Kt5
18. P × P   B × P
19. Kt—Kt1   Kt—B4
20. Kt(Kt1)—Q2   Q—B1

White's attempt to pick a quarrel, *sit venia verbo*, must be regarded as having failed, for Black's PQ3 is easily defendable while the two Bishops in conjunction with the QR file and the threatening diagonal QB1 to KKt5 exercise no mean influence.

21. B—B4 ......
A witty defence of the KKtP (Q ×P??, B ×P ch).

21. ...... P—KKt3
22. P—KKt3 K—Kt2
23. Kt—R2 B—KKt4!
The weakness at Q3 is here of but slight importance.

24. P—KB3 ......
If 24. P—KB4?, then 24. ....
P×P; 25. P×P, B—B3, winning a P.

24. ...... Q—B2
Threatening Kt—R5, and if R—QKt1 then B ×Kt and B ×KP.

25. KR—K1 R—KR1
26. Kt(Q2)—B1 P—KR4
The moves now following lead to the occupation of the important files and diagonals.

27. P ×P R ×P
28. B—Q5 QR—KR1
29. B ×B Q ×B
30. Q—B4 Q—Kt3!
31. K—Kt2 ......
A weakness has now slowly crystallized out; namely that of White's base. With the Black Kt placed at Q5 the invasion of White's 2nd rank would be decisive.

31. ...... Kt—K3
He has his eye on Q5 but at the same time threatens the K's wing; i.e., by R ×Kt ch; Kt ×R, R × Kt ch; K ×R, Q—B7 ch; K—R3, B—B5! See Diag. 175, p. 187.

32. R—K2 ......
But for the threat just referred to White could perhaps find an adequate defence by 32. Q—Q5, Kt—Q5; 33. P—B4.

32. ...... Kt—Q5
But now this move takes place with the win of a tempo.

33. R(K2)—K1 ......
Or R—KB2?, B—K6.

33. ...... Q—Kt2
R—QB1 can no longer be parried, a good example this of how one can devote one's attention to several weaknesses at the same time.

34. R ×Kt ......
After 34. P—QB3, P ×P; 35. P ×P, Q—Kt7 ch, the weakness of White's 2nd rank would have been shown up.

34. ...... P ×R
35. Kt—Kt4 Q—Kt3
or 35. Q ×QP ch, B—B3; 36. Q × QP, R—Q1.

36. P—KB4 B—K2
37. R—Q1 P—KB4
38. Kt—B2 P ×P
39. Q ×P ch Q ×Q
40. R ×Q P—Q4
41. P—KKt4 B—B4!
42. R—Q1 R—R5
43. R ×P B ×Kt
44. K ×B R ×P
Black in order to maintain his advantage had always to try to combine attack on the K with play in the centre. (Cf. his 40th and 41st moves.)

45. K—K3 R—QB1
And now the Q's wing is brought in too.

46. K ×P R—B5 ch
47. K—Q3 R(QB) ×KBP
Now things go easier. 48. Kt—K3, R—Kt6; 49. R—K5, K—B3; 50. R—K8, K—B2; 51. R—K5, R—B3; 52. P—B4, P—Kt6; 53. K—K4, R—K3; 54. R ×R, K × R; 55. Kt—Q5, P—Kt4 and White resigned.

41

A most complicated game in the strategical sense. Lasker manœuvres on one wing and breaks through on the other. The why and wherefore of this procedure will be found explained in the notes.

Petrograd, 1909

White	Black
Dr. Lasker	Amos Burn

1. P—K4	P—K4
2. Kt—KB3	Kt—QB3
3. B—Kt5	P—QR3
4. B—R4	Kt—KB3
5. 0—0	B—K2
6. R—K1	P—QKt4
7. B—Kt3	P—Q3
8. P—QB3	Kt—QR4
9. B—B2	P—QB4
10. P—Q4	Q—B2
11. QKt—Q2	Kt—B3
12. Kt—B1	0—0?

Black ought to have tried to force White to declare his intentions in the centre; therefore 12. . . . . BP×P; 13. P×P, B—Kt5.

13. Kt—K3	. . . . . .

Intending to invade the centre with Kt—Q5.

13.	B—Kt5
14. Kt×B	. . . . . .

The reply to 14. Kt—Q5 would have been 14. . . . . Q—R2; 15. Kt×B, Kt×Kt! With the text move Lasker plays for the advantage of the two B's.

14.	Kt×Kt
15. P—KR3	Kt—B3
16. B—K3	Kt—Q2
17. Q—K2	B—B3
18. QR—Q1	Kt—K2
19. B—Kt1	Kt—QKt3
20. P—QR3	Kt—KKt3
21. P—KKt3	KR—K1

Black has consistently kept his end in view, that is to prepare for P—Q4; so now Lasker finds himself forced to play P—Q5 thus blocking

his own B. The game now enters a new stage.

22. P—Q5	Kt—Q2
23. K—Kt2	Q—Q1

Instead of this he should have played P—QB5 followed by Kt—B4. The Kt would then have been well posted and, more important, would have a preventive effect, for White was preparing for P—KB4 *inter alia*.

24. P—KR4	B—K2
25. P—R5	Kt(Kt3)—B1
26. R—KR1	P—KR3
27. QR—KKt1	Kt—R2

Black's KKt4 seems now strongly fortified.

28. K—B1	K—R1
29. R—R2	R—KKt1
30. Kt—K1	. . . . . .

If Kt—R4, Black would simply exchange (B×Kt, R×B), and the game would then take on a somewhat rigid aspect. Lasker, therefore, wisely avoids Kt—R4 and seeks to preserve whatever latent dynamic force there is in the position, little though this be.

30.	R—QKt1
31. Kt—B2	P—R4
32. B—Q2	B—B3
33. P—KB3	Kt—QKt3
34. R—KB2	. . . . . .

White intends to play Kt—K3 and wishes to hold the move P—KB4 in readiness should Black play B—Kt4 (Lasker).

34.	Kt—QB1
35. K—Kt2	Q—Q2
36. K—R1	Kt—K2
37. R—R2	R—Kt2
38. R—KB1	R—K1
39. Kt—K3	Kt—Kt1
40. P—KB4	B—Q1
41. Q—B3	. . . . . .

Lasker has succeeded in carrying out P—KB4 under circumstances favourable to himself; but there was no direct advantage to be got by the move. However, Black's pieces which have to keep on the look-out against the threat of an invasion by Kt—B5, are less well posted in case of an attack on the Q's wing. And so we may say that Lasker has laid the K's wing under siege in order to bring the enemy pieces out of contact with their own Q's wing, and will now roll up this (left) wing and thus score a double advantage; definite weaknesses are to be created, and in addition his B's are to get room for manœuvring; for instance, by P—QB4, P—Kt5; B—B2 followed by Q—Q1 and B—QR4.

41.	P—B5
42. P—QR4	B—Kt3
43. P×KtP	Q×P

The decisive error. The right course, as Lasker pointed out in the book of the Congress, was 43. . . . . B×Kt; 44. B×B, Q×KtP followed by P—R5 and R—QR1, and Black's game is tenable.

| 44. Kt—B5 | Q—Q2 |
| 45. Q—Kt4 | P—KB3 |

The KtB5 can no longer be driven away by, say, Kt—K2. Black has now evident weaknesses on both wings and Lasker exploits them without any particular trouble.

46. B—B2	B—B4
47. R—QR1	R(K1)—QKt1
48. B—B1	Q—QB2
49. B—R4	Q—Kt3
50. R—KKt2	R—KB2
51. Q—K2	Q—R3
52. B—B6	......

Threatening P—QKt4.

| 52. ...... | Kt—K2 |

At last he manages to oust the intruder at his KB4, but meanwhile White is grown too strong on the Q's wing.

| 53. Kt×Kt | R×Kt |
| 54. R—R4 | P×P |

Desperation.

There followed: 55. P×P, P—KB4; 56. P—K5, Kt—B3; 57.

R×BP, Kt—Kt5 (if 57. . . . . Kt× RP; 58. K—R2); 58. R×B, Q× Q; 59. R×Q, P×R; 60. P—Q6, R—QR2; 61. P—K6, R—R3; 62. P—K7, Kt—B3; 63. P—Q7, Kt× P; 64. B×Kt, Resigns.

This fine game is instructive as illustrating, *inter alia*, the struggle of united Bishops for open country in which to manœuvre.

The following game won a brilliancy prize in the New York tournament, 1927.

42

New York, 1927

| White | Black |
| NIMZOWITSCH | MARSHALL |

1. P—QB4	Kt—KB3
2. P—Q4	P—K3
3. Kt—KB3	P—QB4
4. P—Q5	P—Q3
5. Kt—QB3	P×P
6. P×P	P—KKt3
7. Kt—Q2	......

To establish himself at QB4.

7.	QKt—Q2
8. Kt—B4	Kt—Kt3
9. P—K4	B—Kt2
10. Kt—K3	......

Planning P—QR4—R5 and to post the Kt anew at QB4. Black would have done better to exchange Kts on his 9th move. White now gets the advantage.

10.	O—O
11. B—Q3	Kt—R4
12. O—O	B—K4
13. P—QR4	Kt—KB5
14. P—R5	Kt—Q2
15. Kt—B4	Kt×B
16. Q×Kt	P—KB4
17. P×P	R×P
18. P—KB4	......

The prelude to a complicated attacking operation which was the more unexpected since Kt—K4 gave a good game without any effort. But for once I wanted to go in for a combination.

18.	B—Q5 ch
19. B—K3	B × Kt
20. Q × B	Kt—B3
21. Q—QKt3	......

White gets compensation for the QP. Note, *inter alia*, that Black's Queen side is difficult to develop.

Position after White's 21st move

21. ......   R × QP
The answer to Kt × QP would have been QR—K1!!, by which B—K3 would have been prevented because of B × QBP. Black would then have been quite helpless, and White could have won by, e.g., B—Q2 followed by the doubling of the R's in the K file.

| 22. P—B5! | P × P |
| 23. B—Kt5 | ...... |

There is a peculiar point in this move.

If, that is to say, 23. . . . . B—K3, and it is with this parry that White has above all things to reckon, then 24. Q × P (threatening B × Kt and the win of a piece), 24. . . . . R—QB1; 25. QR—K1!, and the B must give up the defence of one or other of the R's; on which B × Kt would lead to the win of whichever is left defenceless.

23.	R—Q5
24. Kt—Kt6 ch	P—QB5
25. Q—QB3	P × Kt
26. Q × R	K—Kt2

| 27. QR—K1 | ...... |

The quickest road to the win.

| 27. ...... | P × P |
| 28. R—K8 | ...... |

Violent but intelligible.

28.	Q × R
29. Q × Kt ch	K—Kt1
30. B—R6	Resigns.

43

Semmering, 1926

| White | Black |
| NIMZOWITSCH | ALEKHINE |

1. P—K4	Kt—KB3
2. Kt—QB3	P—Q4
3. P—K5	KKt—Q2
4. P—KB4	P—K3
5. Kt—KB3	P—QB4
6. P—KKt3	Kt—QB3
7. B—Kt2	......

Black's King's wing seems somewhat boxed in, but as compensation his centre is the more mobile.

7.	B—K2
8. 0—0	0—0
9. P—Q3	Kt—QKt3

9. . . . . P—Q5 would have been bad because of Kt—K4 and the Knight is centrally established. On the other hand 9. . . . . P—KB3 was well worth consideration. For instance, P × P, B × P and Black controls the centre.

| 10. Kt—K2 | P—Q5!? |

Black wants to score the Kt move as an error, for now the Kt can no longer get to K4. This is, however, a mistake and therefore it would have been much better to play P—KB3 instead of P—Q5. For example: 10. . . . . P—KB3; 11. P × P, B × P; 12. P—QB3, P—K4; 13. P × P, Kt × P, and Black would not stand badly.

| 11. P—KKt4 | P— KB3 |

This move, which Black has twice passed over, leads now, thanks to the weakness of his K5, to a result which promises little fruit. The 'prophylactic' defence, 11.....R—K1; 12. Kt—Kt3, B—KB1; 13. Kt—K4, Kt—Q4 (putting a stop to P—B5), would therefore have deserved the preference.

12. P×P   P×P
There was also no true joy to be got out of 12.....B×P; 13. Kt—Kt3, P—K4; 14. P—B5.

13. Kt—Kt3   Kt—Q4
Black seeks to defend his threatened wing from the centre, but this plan should not here have been sufficient to save the situation.

14. Q—K2   B—Q3
15. Kt—R4   ......
To threaten B×Kt and Kt—B5.

15. ......   Kt(B)—K2
16. B—Q2   ......
Kt—R5 would have been sharper here. E.g., 16. Kt—R5, Kt—Kt3; 17. B×Kt, P×B; 18. Kt—B5 with a winning attack.

16. ......   Q—B2
17. Q—B2   ......
Kt—R5 was still preferable.

Position after White's 17th move

17. ......   P—QB5!
18. P×P   Kt—K6!
With this ingenious diversion Dr. Alekhine succeeds in bringing his opponent's attack to a standstill for some time. The game up to this point is discussed in II. i. §6, p. 130, in connexion with 'centralization'.

19. B×Kt   P×B
20. Q—B3   Q×P
The position is in a measure cleared up. Black has a passed pawn which it is true is very sick, but very highly insured against death. We mean to say that the Bishop diagonals QB3—KR8 (after B—Q2—B3) and QB4—KKt8 are compensation. Instead of chasing after the dubious win of the pawn it would have been more to the purpose had White gone on with his King side attack; and this by P—Kt5. Neglect of this move throws White back.

21. Kt—K4   B—B2
22. P—QKt3   Q—Q5
23. P—QB3   Q—Kt3
24. K—R1   ......
White has localized the enemy thrust.

24. ......   Kt—Q4
B—Q2 was certainly better.

25. P—B5   ......
He here misses his opportunity to play P—KKt5, which would have won. For instance: 25.....P×P; 26. Kt×P, R×P; 27. Q—R5; or 25.....P—B4; 26. Q—R5, P×Kt, 27. B×P, etc.

25. ......   Kt—B5!
26. KR—Q1   K—R1
Better, according to H. Wolf, would have been 26.....P—K7 27. R—Q2, Q—Kt4 followed by Q—K4.

27. B—B1   P×P
28. P×P   B—K4
29. R—K1   B—Q2
It happens now as was indicated in the note to the 20th move. White wins the P, but Black keeps the pressure by means of his two Bishops.

30. R ×P   B—B3
31. QR—K1   Kt—Q4
With R—KKt1 Black could have increased the pressure.

32. R—Q3   Kt ×P
Pretty but insufficient. True the acceptance of the sacrifice would have been ruinous (33. R ×Kt, B ×R; 34. Q ×B, Q—B7), but White has a truly startling counter-combination at his disposal.

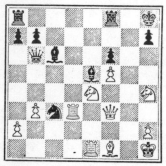

Position after Black's 32nd move

33. Kt—Kt6 ch   P ×Kt
34. Q—Kt4!!   ......
The point. To strike at once would have been bad, e.g., 34. P × P, K—Kt2; 35. Q—R3, R—KR1; 36. R—Q7 ch, B ×R; 37. Q ×B ch, K ×P, and White is threatened with mate.

34. ......   R—B2?
R—KKt1 was imperative. The continuation would have been 35. P ×P, K—Kt2; 36. R—Q7 ch, B ×R; 37. Q ×R ch, K ×P; 38. B—Q3!, K—R3; 39. Q—R3 ch, K—Kt2; 40. R—KKt1 ch, Q × R ch!, and the win is still far away.

35. R—R3 ch   K—Kt2
36. B—B4!   B—Q4
37. P ×P   Kt ×Kt
38. P ×R ch   K—B1
39. R ×Kt   ......
A simpler win would have been 39. Q—Kt8 ch, K—K2; 40. P—B8 =Q ch, R ×Q; 41. R—R7 ch, K—K1; 42. Q ×B.

39. ......   B ×R ch
40. Q ×B   K—K2
41. P—B8 =Q ch   ......
The passed pawn's lust to expand!

41. ......   R ×Q
42. Q—Q5   Q—Q3
42. ....Q—B3 would have led not to the exchange of Queens but to the loss of his Queen, namely 43. R—R7 ch, K—K1; 44. B—Kt5.

43. Q ×P ch   K—Q1
44. R—Q3   B—Q5
45. Q—K4   R—K1
46. R ×B   Resigns.

44

Illustrates in an instructive manner the connexion between play in the centre on the one hand, and diversions undertaken on the wings on the other. The dependence of a flank attack for success on the 'state of health' of the centre is very clearly brought out.

One of four simultaneous consultation games.

Upsala, 1921

White   Black
E. ANDERSSON,
R. ENSTRÖM, AND
O. OEBERG   NIMZOWITSCH

1. P—K4   P—K3
2. P—Q4   P—Q4
3. Kt—QB3   ......
The right move is P—K5

3. ......   B—QKt5
4. B—Q3   Kt—QB3
A new train of thought.

5. KKt—K2   KKt—K2
6. 0—0   0—0
7. P—K5   ......
Looks very good.

7. ......   Kt—B4
8. B—K3   P—KB3

Black has now got over the difficulties of the opening.

9. B×Kt   P×B
10. P—KB4   B—K3

Obedient to the law that a passed pawn must be blockaded.

11. Kt—Kt3   B×Kt!
12. P×B   Kt—R4!

It was only reluctantly and after much deliberation that I determined on this diversion on the extreme flank; which looks risky, since the situation in the centre is by no means secure. For one of my leading principles lays down that a flank attack is only justified if the centre is secure. Yet in the present case White cannot force his opponent to play P×KP, and if he takes the KBP himself, he gets, it is true, the point K5 (after R×P), but Black by bringing up his reserves can mitigate this danger.

13. Q—Q3   Q—Q2
14. R—B3   P—KKt3
15. Kt—K2   R—B2!
16. P—KR4   P—KR4
17. K—R2!   QR—KB1!

The reserves, see the last note.

18. R—Kt3   K—R2
19. Kt—Kt1!   ......

Aiming for KKt5 or K5. It will be seen that the consulting players are thoroughly exercised in the art of manœuvring, and are opponents to be taken seriously.

19. ......   R—KKt2
20. Kt—B3   Q—R5

At last Black proceeds with the attack to which his 11th move was the prelude. This slowness is all to his credit.

21. P×P   R×P
22. Kt—Kt5 ch   K—Kt1
23. B—Kt1   Kt—B5
24. R—K1   B—Q2!!

This simple strategical retreat reveals my plan of defence. As my system lays down, the ideal aimed at by every operation in a file is the entry into the 7th and 8th ranks. However, here the points of invasion, K7 and K8 are safeguarded, and the RKt3 cannot co-operate since he is deprived of the square K3.

25. Kt—B3   B—Kt4
26. Q—Q1   Q×RP
27. Q—K2   ......

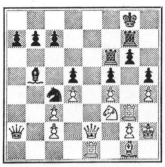

Position after White's 27th move

27. ......   Kt—Q3!!

With this retreat a manœuvre is started which is designed to neutralize the enemy's apparently strong hold on the K file. Less good would have been 27.....Q—R6 with the idea of getting home safely with the booty by means of 28.....Q—Q3, thus: 27.....Q—R6; 28. Kt—K5, Q—Q3; 29. Kt×Kt, B×Kt; 30. Q—KB2, R—K3; 31. R—K5! and White still has drawing chances, whereas the phlegmatic manœuvre in the text wins.

28. Q—K5   Kt—K1!

With this the regrouping R—Q3 and KtKB3 is threatened, whereby the R and Kt will have exchanged stations. If White prevents this by 29. Kt—Kt5 (29.....R—Q3?; 30. Q×Kt ch and mate next move), White will be undoubtedly strong in the K file, yet the distinctive characteristic of the position, namely the spearhead station of White's Q will prevent him from

taking full advantage of the file.
For instance, 29. Kt—Kt5, B—
B3; 30. R(Kt)—K3, Q×P; or
30. R—K2, Q—B5 (Blockade!); 31.
R(Kt)—K3, P—QR4, and wins,
for Kt—K6? is impossible because
of R—K2, and he has no other
effective move in the K file at his
disposal. In the game the continuation was:—

29. Kt—Q2   R—Q3
30. P—QB4   B—Q2
31. R—QB3   Kt—B3

And now this difficult regrouping
manœuvre (under enemy fire) has
been successfully carried out.

32. P×P   ......

A gross mistake, but even after
32. Q—K2, R—K3; 33. Q—Q1,
R(Kt)—K2, White's game would
would have been hopeless.

32. ......   Kt—Kt5 ch
33. Resigns.

In the following game two armies
out of contact with one another
operate in the centre and on a flank.
It is interesting to see how contact
is finally established between them.

45

London, 1927

White	Black
YATES	NIMZOWITSCH

1. P—K4   P—QB4
2. Kt—KB3   Kt—KB3

The innovation introduced by me
in 1911 at San Sebastian.

3. P—K5   Kt—Q4

The relationship between the
Alekhine Defence (1. P—K4, Kt—
KB3) introduced in 1921 and my
treatment of the Sicilian will be
noted. (Cf., too, Bogoljubow's application of the idea in 1. P—Q4,
Kt—QB3.)

4. B—QB4   Kt—Kt3

5. B—K2   Kt—QB3

White has lost a tempo with his
B, on the other hand the Kt at
QKt3 is not particularly well
placed, so that the B manœuvre is
not to be blamed.

6. P—QB3   P—Q4
7. P—Q4   ......

We should have given 7. P×P
e.p. the preference.

7. ......   P×P
8. P×P   B—B4
9. 0—0   P—K3
10. Kt—QB3   B—K2
11. Kt—K1   ......

If the attack planned by this
move, namely P—KB4 with P—
KKt4 and P—B5 should really
prove possible to carry out, this
would be a proof of the incorrectness
of 8. ....B—B4, and that would be
an absurdity. In point of fact the
matter stands thus: No particular
result is achieved by 11. Kt—K1,
and this diversion would better
have been abandoned in favour of a
systematic utilization of the QB file.
For example, 11. B—K3, 0—0;
12. R—QB1, followed by P—QR3,
P—QKt4 and Kt—Q2—Kt3—B5,
when the establishment of an outpost advocated by my system would
have been attained.

11. ......   Kt—Q2!
12. B—Kt4!   ......

Cleverly played. The answer to
12. P—KB4 would have been, of
course, Kt×P; Q×Kt??, B—QB4.
12. B—K3 would also have been
unfavourable because of 12. ....
Kt(Q2)×KP; 13. P×Kt, P—Q5;
14. B—Q2, P×Kt; 15. B×P, Q—
B2, with advantage in position for
Black. By aid of the text move
(12. B—Kt4) Yates is able in a
quite startling manner to make the
advance, P—KB4, at which he was
aiming.

12. ......   B—Kt3
13. P—KB4   Kt×QP
14. Kt×QP!   Kt—QB3

If 14. ....B—QB4, then 15. P—
QKt4 would have been strong.
14. ....P ×Kt would have also been
bad because of B ×Kt ch, followed
by Q ×Kt.

| 15. Kt ×B | Q—Kt3 ch |
| 16. K—R1 | Kt ×Kt |

20. K—Kt1	Kt—QKt3
21. Q—KB3	Kt(Kt3)—Q4
22. P—QKt3	Q—Kt3 ch
23. R—B2	......

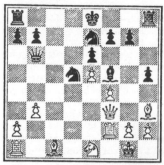

Position after White's 23rd move

Position after Black's 16th move

17. Q—R4 ......
A typical sin of omission!
In the face of Black's obvious
plan to occupy the central points,
White should, by himself centralizing, have disputed them with his
opponent, thus: 17. Q—K2 (intending B—K3), 17. ....Kt—Q4;
18. B—B3, Q—B4; 19. B—Q2,
Kt(Q2)—Kt3; 20. R—QB1, Q—
K2, and White has more of the
centre than Black. And even if
such a 'more' were not attainable,
what matter! Even in this case
White ought to have fought for it.
As it is a just punishment now
overtakes him.

| 17. ...... | P—KR4 |
| 18. B—R3 | ...... |

Forced, for if B—B3, then Kt—
KB4 with a further gain of terrain
in the centre; moreover, there
would then be a mating threat in
the air, namely P—R5 and Kt—
Kt6 ch.

| 18. ...... | B—B4 |
| 19. Q—R3 | Q—Kt4 |

Making room for the Kt at Q2,
which is aiming for Q4 via QKt3.

23. ...... R—QB1
This move in conjunction with the
one next following leads to a de-
centralization of one of his R's, and
so to a defect in his position which
has been so harmoniously constructed. On the other hand the
continuation 23. ....0—0—0! held
out the promise of untroubled
harmony; for after 24. ....K—
QKt1 and 25. ....P—Kt3 nothing
stood in the way of employing the
two R's centrally, e.g., 26. ....R—
Q2; 27. ....R—QB1.

However, 23. ....B—KKt5 seems
to be still better. For instance,
24. B ×B, P ×B; 25. Q ×P, R ×P;
26. Q ×KKtP, 0—0—0; 27. K ×
R, Q ×R; 28. Kt—Q3, Q—K7,
and Black must win. Or, lastly,
it was also possible to combine the
two plans, thus: 23. ....0—0—0;
24. B—R3 and now 24. ....B—
Kt5. If then perhaps 25. R—QB1
ch, K—Kt1; 26. B—QB5, then
26. ....Q ×B; 27. R ×Q, B ×Q;
28. R ×B, R—QB1 with a victor-
ious incursion via the QB file.

24. B—Q2 R—R3
Interesting, for when all is said
and done, Black's position, centralized even to the extent that it is,
can support an adventurous raid;

8

yet 24. .....0—0 with P—KKt3 and
KR—Q1 was certainly more correct.

25. R—Q1	B ×B
26. Q ×B	Kt—KB4
27. Q—Q3	R—Kt3
28. Kt—B3	R—Kt5
29. P—KR3	R—Kt6
30. P—QR4	Kt—R5

Black's structure suffers under an
inner discord. The position of the
cut off R makes a mating attack
seem desirable; but the disposition
of the rest of the army is rather
directed towards the end game, in
which the KtQ4 would have enormous effect, while the white squares
would be in Black's undisputed
possession.

| 31. K—B1 | R—QB3 |

To draw the sting of the threat
Q—R7 and Q—Kt8 ch, the R runs
away betimes. Black has in fact
to manœuvre very cautiously.

| 32. P—R5 | Q—Q1 |
| 33. K—Kt1 | Kt—B4 |

33. ....Kt × Kt ch; 34. R × Kt,
R ×R; 35. Q ×R, P—KKt3, would
not have been good because of 36.
P—B5.

| 34. K—R2 | P—QR3 |
| 35. Q—QKt1 | ...... |

To threaten Kt—Q4.

| 35. ...... | Q—K2 |

He does not mind the threat, has
his eye, moreover, on his QB4
(Q—B4).

| 36. Kt—Q4 | ...... |

Loses; R—QB1 was better.

| 37. ...... | Q—KR5! |

As the detachments which have
been cut off cannot get back to the
army, the latter comes to them.

| 37. B—K1 | ...... |

If 37. Kt ×R, then R ×RP ch
and mate in two moves.

| 37. ...... | Kt ×BP |

Again threatening mate, this time
by R ×KtP ch etc.

| 38. R ×Kt | R ×RP ch |

Simplest.

| 39. P ×R | Q ×R ch |
| 40. K—Kt2 | Kt—K6 ch |

And mate in two moves.
For this game I was awarded the
special prize of £10, 'for the best
played game' in the tournament.

There follow five games of historical interest.

46

A most instructive game from
A to Z, one which I regard as the
first in which my new philosophy
of the centre was exhibited. See I.
ix, §5, p. 105.

Carlsbad, 1911

| White | Black |
| NIMZOWITSCH | SALWE |

1. P—K4	P—K3
2. P—Q4	P—Q4
3. P—K5	P—QB4
4. P—QB3	Kt—QB3
5. Kt—KB3	Q—Kt3
6. B—Q3	......

See note to this move in Game
No. 19.

Position after White's 6th move

| 6. ...... | B—Q2 |

A very plausible move.
Since White still delays P ×P,
Black intends to force his hand with

R—QB1.   The right course was 6.
....P×P;   7. P×P and thus to
pass into quite other channels.
See Games Nos. 19 and 20.

7. P×P!!   B×P
8. 0—0   P—KB3

Black swells in triumph and
throws himself hungrily on the
last remaining member of the once
so proud chain-family, to destroy
him.   His war cry is 'Room for the
KP!' But it happens quite otherwise.

9. P—QKt4   ......
In order to be able to provide
his K5 with an enduring defence.
9. Q—K2 would also have been a
defence, but no enduring one, for
there would follow 9.....P×P;
10. Kt×P, Kt×Kt;   11. Q×Kt,
Kt—B3 and the blockading Q at
K5 will be easily driven away.

9. ......   B—K2
10. B—KB4   P×P
Again we have the exchange
operation which we have so often
discussed; this time, however, it
is not really justified, for the new
blockader, the BK5, proves to be a
stout fellow.

11. Kt×P   Kt×Kt
12. B×Kt   Kt—B3
For the otherwise desirable B—
B3 would fail against 13. Q—R5
ch, P—KKt3;   14. B×P ch, P×
B; 15. Q×P ch, K—K2; 16. B×
B ch, Kt×B;   17. Q—Kt7 ch.

13. Kt—Q2   ......
That the win of a pawn by 13.
Q—B2?, 0—0 etc. is a snare, has
been pointed out under Diagram
107, p. 104.

13. ......   0—0
14. Kt—B3!   ......
The blockading forces are to be
reinforced by the Kt.

14. ......   B—Q3

14. ......B—QKt4 would yield
little profit for 15. B—Q4, Q—R3;
16. B×B,   Q×B;   17. Kt—Kt5,
would win a pawn.

15. Q—K2   ......
That 15. B—Q4 would be pre-
mature has been pointed out under
Diagram 107.

15. ......   QR—QB1
16. B—Q4   Q—B2
17. Kt—K5   ......
The immobility of the KP is now
greater than ever.   White has util-
ized his resources very economically.
The possibility of a successful
occupation of the points Q4, K5,
hung on a hair, on taking minute
advantage of the terrain, i.e., of
the points Q4, K5, QB2, and K2.

17. ......   B—K1
18. QR—K1   B×Kt
19. B×B   Q—B3
20. B—Q4   ......
In order to force Black's QB who
also has his eye on the KR4 to come
to a decision.

20. ......   B—Q2
21. Q—B2   ......
The decisive re-grouping.

21. ......   R—KB2
22. R—K3   P—QKt3
23. R—KKt3   K—R1
24. B×KRP   P—K4
24.....Kt×B loses because of
Q—Kt6.

25. B—Kt6   R—K2
26. R—K1   Q—Q3
27. B—B3   P—Q5
28. B—Kt5   R×P
29. R×R   P×R
30. Q×P and White won.
30. ....K —Kt1;   31. P —QR3,
K—B1;   32. B—R4, B—K1;   33.
B—B5, Q—Q5;   34. Q×Q, P×
Q;   35. R×R, K×R;   36. B—
Q3, K—Q3;   37. B×Kt, P×B;
38. P—KR4, Resigns.

47

Of special interest historically as being the first game in which what has been called the 'Ideal Queen's Gambit' was played, where Black forgoes altogether the occupation of the centre by his pawns. It was played in the all-Russian Tournament in Petrograd, 1913.

White	Black
GREGORY	NIMZOWITSCH
1. P—Q4	Kt—KB3
2. Kt—KB3	P—K3
3. B—KKt5	......

In answer to 3. P—QB4 I had intended P—QKt3. The point Q4 is to remain permanently un-occupied.

3.	P—KR3
4. B × Kt	Q × B
5. P—K4	P—KKt3

Black has the two Bishops, and in what follows is concerned to keep them.

6. Kt—QB3	Q—K2

In order after P—Q3 not to be exposed to the move P—K5, which would open the game.

7. B—B4	B—Kt2
8. 0—0	P—Q3
9. Q—Q3	0—0
10. QR—K1	P—QR3
11. P—QR4	P—QKt3
12. Kt—K2	......

The mobility of White's centre must be rated as very slight, for any thrust would be intercepted without any trouble; e.g., 12. P—K5, P—Q4!; or 12. P—Q5, P—K4!

12.	P—QB4

A strategical device which the Hyper-modernist may care to note, makes its appearance here. I mean the continuity of an attack directed against a pawn-mass. This is to be understood thus: the threatened advance must first have its sting drawn (in this game this was done by Q—K2). It is only when this

has happened that we may regard the mass as semi-mobile, and attack it; for only those objects which have been made immobile should be chosen as a target.

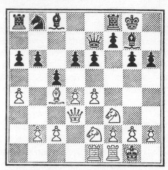

Position after Black's 12th move

The critical position

13. P—QB3	B—Q2
14. P—QKt3	......

14. Kt—Q2 was to be considered. For instance, 14. .... B × RP; 15. P—KB4 with definite chances.

14.	Q—K1
15. Q—B2	P—QKt4
16. P × KtP	P × KtP
17. P—Q3	Q—QB1
18. P × P	P × P
19. P—K5	Kt—B3
20. B × QKtP	......

If 20. Kt—Kt3 then 20. .... P—QKt5 and if 21. P—QB4, B—K1 with the superior game.

20.	Kt × P
21. Kt × Kt	B × B
22. Kt—B3	Q—Kt2
23. Kt—Q2	B—QB3
24. P—KB3	KR—QKt1

Now the Bishops assert their rights.

25. Kt—KKt3	Q—R2
26. R—KB2	B—Q4
27. K—B1	Q—R7
28. Q × Q	R × Q
29. P—QB4	B—Q5
30. R(B2)—K2	B—QB3
31. R—Q1	R—Kt7

32. R—QB1	P—R4
33. K—K1	R—QR1

Threatens complete paralysis by R(R1)—R7, since R—Kt1 is then impossible because of R ×R ch and R—R8.

34. Kt—R1!	R(R1)—R7
35. Kt—B2	R ×Kt
36. R ×R	R ×R
37. K ×R	B ×Kt

The win is still some considerable way off. In what follows Black manœuvres against the QBP, but also keeps before himself the possibility of an incursion of his K at KKt6, as for instance at the 70th move. However, this by itself would not suffice, Black has also still to play out the duel on the K's Wing with his pawn-majority, and in doing so his position will become broken up, and with all this the QBP is not to be joked with.

38. R—QKt1	K—B1
39. P—QKt4	P ×P
40. R ×P	K—K2
41. R—Kt8	B—Q5
42. R—QB8	B—Q2
43. R—QR8	P—K4
44. K—B2	B—B3
45. R—QB8	B—R5 ch
46. K—Q3	B—Q2
47. R—B7	K—Q3
48. R—Kt7	B—KKt8
49. P—R3	P—R5

The point KKt6 now looks ripe for an invasion by Black.

50. R—Kt8	B—K3
51. R—QR8	B—QKt3
52. R—KR8	B—KB7
53. R—QR8	B—B4 ch
54. K—K2	B—QKt3
55. R—KR8	P—Kt4
56. R—KKt8	P—B3
57. R—KB8	K—K2
58. R—QKt8	B—Q5
59. R—Kt5	B—KKt3
60. R—R5	B—KB4
61. R—R6	B—QB1
62. R—QB6	B—Q2
63. R—R6	B—QB4
64. K—Q3	B—B4 ch

65. K—K2	P—K5!

At last the fitting moment has arrived.

66. R—B6	B—Q5
67. R—R6	B—K3
68. R—R4	P—K6!
69. K—Q3	B—QB4

Now the King threatens to journey to his KKt6.

70. R—R6	B ×P ch

71. Resigns.

This game aroused lively interest at the time, and the idea was tried at the same tournament by other masters though with indifferent success. I continued my studies of the opening, and employed it the next year, 1914, in the Great Petrograd Tournament, and against Janowski and Bernstein. The first 18 moves of the former game were given and discussed in II. ii. §2, p. 139. Against Bernstein (White) the game ran: 1. P—Q4, Kt—KB3; 2. Kt—KB3, P—K3; 3. P—QB4, P—QKt3; 4. Kt—QB3, B—Kt2; 5. P—K3, B—QKt5; 6. Q—Kt3, Q—K2; 7. P—QR3, B ×Kt ch; 8. Q ×B, P—Q3; 9. P—QKt4, QKt—Q2; (Black now has an excellent game; the mobility of the White centre is slight, and the diagonal QKt2 to K5 is an important asset). 10. B—Kt2 P—QR4 (good enough, but Kt—K5 and P—KB4 was preferable); 11. B—K2. P ×P; 12. P ×P, R ×R ch; 13. B ×R, 0—0; 14. 0—0, Kt—K5; 15. Q—B2, P—KB4; 16. Kt—Q2, Kt ×Kt (16. . . . .P—QB4 with its hyper-modern savour would seem to be more in keeping here.) 17. Q ×Kt, R—QR1; 18. B—QB3, Q—K1 (with 18. . . . .Kt—KB3 in order to anticipate P—Q5, Black's game would still have been good); 19. P—Q5!, P—K4 (P ×P?, B—KB3); 20. P—KB4, B—B1; and, after a sequence of highly dramatic complications, the game ended in a draw.

In the same tournament Alekhine adopted my innovation—the 'Ideal Queen's Gambit'—and with success.

48

Being the first game in which the thesis of the relative harmlessness of the 'pawn-roller' was stated.

San Sebastian, 1911

White	Black
SPIELMANN	NIMZOWITSCH

1. P—K4   P—QB4
2. Kt—KB3   Kt—KB3

This set Spielmann thinking. After some minutes I raised my eyes from the board and saw that my dear old companion in arms was quite disconcerted. He looked at the Kt, now confidently, now suspiciously, and after much hesitation gave up the possible chase started by P—K5 and played the more circumspect Kt—QB3. Next year I tried 2. . . . . Kt—KB3 on Schlechter, and in the Book of the Congress we find the following note to this move by Tarrasch: 'Not good, since the Kt is at once driven away, but Herr Nimzowitsch goes his own road in the openings, one, however, which cannot be recommended to the public.'

Ridicule can do much, for instance embitter the existence of young talents; but one thing is not given to it, to put a stop permanently to the incursion of new and powerful ideas. The old dogmas, such as the ossified teaching on the centre, the worship of the open game, and in general the whole formalistic conception of the game, who bothers himself to-day about these? The new ideas, however, those supposed by-ways, not to be recommended to the public, these are become to-day highways, on which great and small move freely in the consciousness of absolute security.

My game against Schlechter ran as follows: 1. P—K4, P—QB4; 2. Kt—KB3, Kt—KB3; 3. P—K5, Kt—Q4; 4. P—Q4. Why, asks Dr. Tarrasch, should not P—QB4 be played here? The Black Kt would then certainly be driven on to unfavourable squares. Alas, no; even in the case of 1. P—K4, Kt—KB3 (Alekhine's defence); the effect of driving the Kt by 2. P—K5, Kt—Q4; 3. P—QB4, Kt—Kt3; 4. P—Q4 is merely to compromise White's game.

In my game against Schlechter the continuation was: 4. . . . . P × P; 5. Q × P, P—K3; 6. B—QB4, Kt —QB3; 7. Q—K4, P—Q3!; 8. P × P (or 8. B × Kt, P × B; 9. Q × P, P × P; with two B's and a compact pawn majority), Kt— KB3; 9. Q—KR4, B × P; 10. Kt— QB3. Kt—K4!; and Black obtained a certain freedom for manœuvring in the middle of the board.

To return to my game with Spielmann.

3. Kt—QB3   P—Q4
4. P × P   Kt × P
5. B—B4   P—K3
6. 0—0   B—K2
7. P—Q4   Kt × Kt
8. P × Kt   0—0
9. Kt—K5   Q—B2

What now follows is play against the hanging pawns which will soon come into existence.

10. B—Q3   Kt—QB3
11. B—KB4   B—Q3
12. R—K1   P × P!

This exchange in conjunction with Kt—QKt5 is the point of the proceedings started by 9. . . . . Q—B2.

13. P × P   Kt—Kt5
14. B—KKt3   Kt × B
15. Q × Kt   P—QKt3
16. P—QB4   B—R3

The hanging pawns, which come under heavy fire, prove, however, in the end to have a lot of vigour. The game is about equal.

17. QR—QB1   QR—QB1
18. Q—Kt3!   P—KB3
19. Q—R4?   . . . . . .
19. P—B5, B × Kt; 20. P × B would have led to a draw.

19. . . . . . .   P × Kt
20. P × P   B—R6!
21. Q × KB   B × P

22. R—K4   Q—Q2
23. P—KR3   B—Q4

With his B thus posted Black's advantage is clear.

24. R—K2   Q—Kt2
25. P—B4   Q—KB2
26. R(K2)—QB2   R × R
27. R × R   Q—Kt3
28. Q—QB3   ......

White cannot well give up the QB file; if, however, 28. R—B3 then 28.....P—KR4; 29. P—KR4, R × P.

28. ......   B × RP!
29. B—R4   B—Q4
30. B—K7   R—K1
31. B—Q6   Q—K5
32. Q—B7   P—KR3
33. R—KB2   Q—K8 ch
34. R—B1   Q—K6 ch
35. R—B2   P—QR4
36. B—K7   Q—K8 ch
37. R—B1   Q—K6 ch
38. R—B2   K—R1

Directed against B—B6.

39. B—Q8   Q—K8 ch
40. R—B1   Q—K6 ch
41. R—B2   Q—K8 ch
42. R—B1   Q—KKt6
43. R—B2   R—B1
44. Q × QKtP   R × P
45. B—K7   P—R5

A passed pawn plus a mating attack, a wicked affair.

46. K—B1?

But he was lost whatever he did.

46. ......   Q × P ch
47 Resigns.

49

This being the first game in which my idea of a sacrifice for the sole purpose of establishing a blockade was illustrated.

San Sebastian, 1912

White   Black
NIMZOWITSCH   SPIELMANN

1. P—K4   P—K3
2. P—Q4   P—Q4

3. P—K5   P—QB4
4. Kt—KB3   Kt—QB3
5. P × P   B × P
6. B—Q3   KKt—K2
7. B—KB4!   ......

The over-protection of the strategically important PK5.

7. ......   Q—Kt3
8. 0—0   Q × KtP

This was no ordinary pawn sacrifice for the attack. Its motive was simply and exclusively this, to maintain the point K5, in order to use it as a base for a blockading action. We know this motive in draughts, where a man is sacrificed in order to make it possible to lock up an enemy majority by our minority. To have translated this idea to the field of chess was a revolutionary act.

9. QKt—Q2   Q—Kt3
10. Kt—Kt3   Kt—Kt3
11. B—Kt3   B—K2
12. P—KR4   ......

This, too, is no attacking move in the ordinary sense; its meaning is: 'Get away from the Key Square K5.'

12. ......   Q—Kt5
13. P—QR4   P—QR3
14. P—KR5   Kt—R5
15. Kt × Kt   B × Kt
16. P—QB3   Q—K2
17. B—R2   P—KB4

This move, which throws open all lines of approach to his opponent, he has got to make in order to give himself air; and with it White's attack first appears in evidence.

18. P × P e.p.   P × P
19. Kt—Q4   P—K4
20. B—KB5 with a strong attack and White won on the 44th move.

My game against Leonhardt (Black) in the same tournament took much the same course: 1. P—K4, P—K3; 2. P—Q4, P—Q4; 3. P—K5, P—QB4; 4. Kt—KB3 (later I discovered the still more

revolutionary Q—Kt4), see No. 50.
4. . . . . Q—Kt3;   5. B—Q3, P×P;
6. 0—0, Kt—QB3;   7. P—QR3,
KKt—K2;   8. P—QKt4, Kt—Kt3;
9. R—K1, B—K2;   10. B—Kt2,
P—QR4. Black now has to give
up the pawn again; after 10. . . . .
P—QR3!, we should have had the
state of affairs we have discussed,
namely pawn plus vs. a cramping
policy.

The same strategical device appeared in a particularly plastic
shape in a game played in 1913,
when the position shown in the
diagram was reached.

Brinckmann—Nimzowitsch

The game continued 19. . . . .
P—QKt4!!; Black sacrifices a P in
order to exchange White's KB,
after which the blockade of White's
position by Kt—KB4 will become
effective. There followed, 20. B ×
QKtP, R(QR)—QKt1; 21. B—K2,
Kt—Kt3 (more precise was Kt—
Kt2 at once; for if P—KR5, then
Kt—Kt3, followed by the forced
exchange at B5 [Kt—B5, B×Kt],
and finally by the occupation of his
KB4 by the Kt, with a positional
winning advantage for Black). 22.
K—Q1 (he could have saved himself by 22. B×Kt, Kt—B5; 23.
Q—B2, Kt×RP; 24. Q—Q2); 22.
. . . . Kt—B5; 23. B×Kt, R×B;
24. R—Kt5, Kt—Kt2; 25. P—
KR5, Kt—B4; 26. P×P, BP×P;
and Black won without difficulty.

50

From a match; the first game in
which appears my idea of a pawn
sacrifice in the opening, not to
obtain an attack, but merely, with
gain of a tempo, to overprotect a
strategical point with a view to
cramping the enemy forces.

Kristianstad, 1922

White	Black
NIMZOWITSCH	A. HAAKANSON
1. P—K4	P—K3
2. P—Q4	P—Q4
3. P—K5	P—QB4
4. Q—Kt4	

My innovation.

4.	P×P
5. Kt—KB3	Kt—QB3
6. B—Q3	P—KB4
7. Q—Kt3	KKt—K2
8. 0—0	Kt—Kt3
9. P—KR4	Q—B2
10. R—K1	

Position after White's 10th move

White's plan is now clear. He
has given up a pawn, careless when,
if ever, he recover it provided his
PK5 is maintained as an instrument
to cramp Black's game. There is
no idea of attack in 9. P—KR4, its
object is solely to pave the way to
the removal of some of the pressure
on the PK5. The pawn sacrifice
clearly comes within the category
of sacrifice for the sake of blockade,
cf. game No. 49.

10. ......   B—Q2
B—B4 was essential here so as to
leave the KB square free for the Kt
to retreat to after P—R5.

11. P—QR3   0—0—0
12. P—QKt4   ......
White could, of course, have won
the exchange here by 12. P—R5,
Kt—K2; 13. Kt—Kt5, R—K1; 14.
Kt—B7, R—Kt1; 15. Kt—Q6 ch;
but with his undeveloped Q side
and his unprotected PR5 he would
have had some difficulties to con-
tend with. The text move is the
logical continuation.

12. ......   P—QR3
Rather better was 12. .... K—
Kt1; e.g., 13. P—QB3!, P×P; 14.
Kt×P, Kt×QKtP;   15. P×Kt,
Q×Kt;   16. B—K3, Q×B;   17.
B×P ch, K—B1; 18. KR—QB1
ch, B—B3; 19. P—Kt5!, Q×P;
20. Kt—Q4 with complications,
which, of course, White, had he been
so minded, could have avoided by
simply playing 13. B—QKt2.

13. P—R5   Kt—K2
14. B—Q2   P—KR3
15. P—R4   P—KKt4
16. P—Kt5   P—B5
17. Q—Kt4   ......
The Q is well placed here.

17. ......   Kt—QKt1
18. P—QB3   R—K1
His only move. It will be noted
that the over-protector, the RK1,
now has the QB file opened for him
without any trouble to himself. In
order to avoid loss of material
Black has to submit to a curious
regrouping of his forces.

19. P×P   K—Q1
20. R—QB1   Q—Kt3
21. P—R5   Q—R2
22. P—Kt6   Q—R1
The Q finds herself in a position to
which as a rule she would only be
consigned in a problem.

23. R—B7   Kt—KB4
24. Kt—QB3!   B—K2
25. Kt×QP   Kt×QP
26. Kt×Kt   P×Kt
27. Q×B ch—and mates next
move.